LAW RELATING TO SUBJECTS OF *MANDAMUS*

LAW RELATING TO SUBJECTS OF *MANDAMUS*

DR. RUSHIKESH MEHTA
B.Sc., LL.M.
(Goldmedalist), Ph.D.
Principal, Maneklal Nanavati Law College
Lal Darwaja, Ahmedabad-380 001
dr.rushikeshmehta@gmail.com

DEEP & DEEP PUBLICATIONS PVT. LTD.
F-159, Rajouri Garden, New Delhi-110027

LAW RELATING TO SUBJECTS OF *MANDAMUS*

ISBN 978-81-8450-362-3

Typeset by S.S. COMPOSERS
3190, Mohindra Park, Shakur Basti, Delhi-110034.

Printed in India at MAYUR ENTERPRISES
WZ Plot No. 3, Gujjar Market, Tihar Village, New Delhi-110018.

Published by DEEP & DEEP PUBLICATIONS PVT. LTD.
F-159, Rajouri Garden, New Delhi-110027.
Phones: 25435369, 25440916
E-mail: ddpbooks@yahoo.co.in • ddpubs@gmail.com
Showroom:
2/13, Ansari Road, Daryaganj, New Delhi-110002 • Telefax: 23245122

This Work is a Tribute to

My Dear Father
Late Shri Vipinchandra S. Mehta

....Who always Tried to Show me a Path of
Learning and Thinking,
Always Encouraged me in Studying....

Contents

Preface

Writ of or in the nature of *mandamus* is the most extensive, effective and popular remedy availed by the litigants through a High Court of State or the Supreme Court of India.

The book is pertaining to subjects of *Mandamus* issued by the High Courts and the Supreme Court against various bodies and persons. Here it is briefly discussed against whom writ of *mandamus* can be issued along with the criticism regarding the decided cases of the Supreme Court of India. In order to compare and analyse the law relating to subjects of *mandamus,* decisions of the English Courts viz. Court of King's Bench and Queen's Bench are also included in the research work. The current position prevailing with respect of issuance of writ of *mandamus* by the High Courts and the Supreme Court is discussed taking into consideration the relevant articles of the Constitution of India. The discussion is also pertaining to the fact that after more than sixty years of the commencement of the Constitution of India, how far the law regarding issuance of *mandamus* against various bodies or persons has developed. Along with present position it is also suggested that what possible changes can be made in the subjects of issuance of *mandamus* by High Courts and the Supreme Court.

The introduction of *mandamus* and the meaning of the subject is discussed in Chapter-1. Alongwith above contents, this chapter also contains the origin of *mandamus* and its development in India as well as England. Chapter-2 contains the subjects of *mandamus* in different other countries in their Constitution. At the end of the chapter a short comparison is given relating to the subjects of *mandamus* in India and other countries. Chapter-3 deals with the subjects of *mandamus* in India, against Union of India, State Governments, Local Authorities, and Public Officials. In Chapter-4 it is discussed separately the list of "other authorities" against whom *mandamus* is issued by the Courts. Relevant criticism is also given after having discussed certain cases. Position regarding issuance of *mandamus* against private persons is always a controversial issue. It is discussed in Chapter-5 wherein the views of the Supreme Court and High Courts is discussed. Chapter-6 contains the suggestions for the expansion of scope of issuance of *mandamus* by the High Courts and the Supreme Court of India in the era of globalisation and liberalization. The possible difficulties to implement the suggestions are highlighted and its solutions are also given.

The methodology adopted in this work is doctrinal. It is based upon the study of relevant documents of English Common Law, Halsbury's Laws of England, Writ Jurisprudence, English Books on writs and Journals, U.S. Journals and Indian Law Reports. A comparison is made regarding the trend of courts regarding subjects of *mandamus* before the year 1981 and after the year 1981, up to the year 2002. Also the present view of the Supreme Court for issuance of *mandamus* is discussed by taking into consideration the judgments of the year 2005 alongwith conclusions and suggestions.

In this work a serious attempt is done to define *mandamus*, its origin as well as development in India and other countries. Different subjects of *mandamus* in our country available in pre-independence as well as the post-independence era are discussed with the help of the decided cases of Privy Council, Court of King's Bench, Court of Queen's Bench, Supreme Court of India and selected judgments of different High Courts.

The scope of issuance of writ of *mandamus* in the post-independence era is further categorized by taking into consideration the definition of 'State' under Article 12 of the Constitution of India. The scope of issuance of *mandamus* against 'Other Authorities' is described in detail starting from the case of *University of Madras* v. *Shantha Bai and Rajasthan Electricity Board* case. The author has highlighted about the widening of scope of 'State' by including statutory corporations like LIC, ONGC and FCI within the meaning of 'Other Authorities' in the case of *Sukhdev* v. *Bhagatram* and the inclusion of Government Company within the ambit of 'State' in the case of Som Prakash by the Supreme Court of India. The effects of the guidelines for including any entity within the meaning of 'Other Authorities' given by Justice Bhagawati (in the cases of *R.D. Shetty* v. *International Airport Authority* as well as *Ajay Hasia* v. *Khalid Munib*) are covered in this research work.

An approach of liberal interpretation for inclusion of any entity within the definition of 'State' under Article 12 of the Constitution was dependent upon the six guidelines given in the case of Ajay Hasia for considerable long time. But there was a radical change from the decision of the Supreme Court in the year 2002. A seven Judges' Bench of the Supreme Court of India while deciding the issue as to whether the Council of Scientific and Industrial Research (CSIR) was 'State' or not under Article 12, the earlier guidelines of Ajay Hasia's case were curtailed by giving the reason of the change in the economic policy and approach of the Government and era of liberalization and privatization.

In the above mentioned circumstances undoubtedly the scope of *mandamus* is narrowed down by the Supreme Court. The real academic issue involved in the research is that with the increasing trend of privatization, Government is withdrawing itself from public sectors. Unless the scope of *mandamus* is expanded, the protection of fundamental rights by issuance of writ of *mandamus* will remain on papers only.

I am sure this book will be helpful for LL.M. students, academicians, researchers and practising advocates in tracing the origin, development and comparing the earlier and recent trend of the Supreme Court and High Courts while issuing writ of *mandamus* and to expand the scope of *mandamus* in future.

DR. RUSHIKESH MEHTA
dr.rushikeshmehta@gmail.com

List of Abbreviations

AIR	: All India Reporter
AISSEA	: All India Sainik School Employees Association
All.	: Allahabad (High Court)
All E.R.	: All England Reports
BCCI	: Board of Control of Cricket in India
BDA	: Bangalore Development Authority
BOGSS	: Board of Governors Sainik School Society
Cal.	: Calcutta (High Court)
CIDC	: Central and Industrial Development Corporation
Cr.L.J.	: Criminal Law Journal
CSIR	: Council for Scientific and Industrial Research
DB	: Division Bench
FB	: Full Bench
FCI	: Food Corporation of India
GSFC	: Gujarat State Financial Corporation
Guj.	: Gujarat (High Court)
ICPS	: Institute of Constitutional and Parliamentary Studies
ICRISAT	: International Crops Research Institute
IFC	: Industrial Finance Corporation
ILR	: Indian Law Reports
IOC	: Indian Oil Corporation
JT	: Judgments Today
KB	: King's Bench Decisions
Ker.	: Kerala (High Court)
LIC	: Life Insurance Corporation of India
Mad. L.J.	: Madras Law Journal
NCERT	: National Council of Educational Research and Training
NHRC	: National Human Rights Commission
Pat.	: Patna (High Court)
PC	: Privy Council
QB	: Queen's Bench Decisions
Raj.	: Rajasthan (High Court)

Rang.	: Rangoon (High Court)
RBI	: Reserve Bank of India
SC	: Supreme Court
SCC	: Supreme Court Cases
SCW	: Supreme Court Weekly
UCC	: Union Carbide Corporation

1

Introduction

1.1 COSMOS

1.1.1 Meaning of *Mandamus*

Mandamus is a Greek word and its English equivalent is "command".

The precise and exhaustive definition given by Lord Halsbury explaining the meaning of writ of *mandamus* is as follows: 3rd Edition, Vol. II, Para. 84,

> 'The writ of *mandamus* is a high prerogative writ of a most extensive remedial nature, and is, in form, a command issuing from the High Court of Justice, directed to any person, corporation, or inferior Court, requiring him or them to do some particular thing therein specified which appertains to his or their office and is in the nature of a public duty. Its purpose is to supply defects of the justice; and accordingly it will issue, to the end that justice may be done, in all cases where there is a specific legal right and no specific legal remedy for enforcing such right; and it may issue in cases where, although there is an alternative legal remedy, yet such mode of redress is less convenient, beneficial and effectual.'[1]

Blackstone defines *mandamus* as follows:

> A command issuing in the King's name from the Court of King's Bench, and directed to any person, corporation or inferior Court of judicature within the King's dominions, requiring them to do some

1. Halsbury's Laws of England, 3rd Edition, Vol. II, para 84.

particular thing therein specified, which appertains to their office and duty, and which the Court of King's Bench has previously determined, or at least supposes, to be consonant to right and justice.[2]

Lord Mansfield has in the case of ***R. v. Barker*** given instances where writ of *mandamus* can be issued:

> *'Whenever there is a right to execute an office, perform a service, or exercise a franchise; (more especially, if it be in a matter of public concern, or attended with profit); and a person is kept out of possession, or dispossessed of such right, and has no other specific legal remedy, this Court ought to assist by a mandamus, upon reasons of justice, as the writ expresses, and upon reasons of public policy, to preserve peace, order and good Government.*
> *The interposing this writ where there is no other specific remedy, is greatly for the benefit of the subject and the advancement of justice.*
> *......A mandamus is a prerogative writ; to the aid of which the subject is entitled, upon a proper case previously shown, to the satisfaction of the Court. The original nature of the writ, and the end for which it was framed; direct upon what occasions it should be used. It was introduced to prevent disorder from a failure of justice and defect of police. Therefore, it ought to be used upon all occasions where the law has established no specific remedy, and where in justice and good Government there ought to be one'.*[3]

Markose has defined *Mandamus* as follows:

Mandamus is a judicial remedy which is in the form of an order from a superior court (the Supreme Court or a High Court) to any Government, Court, corporation or public authority to do or to forbear from doing some specific act which that body is obliged under law to do or refrain from doing, as the case may be, and which is in the nature of a public duty and in certain cases of a statutory duty.[4]

The meaning of *Mandamus* given under the Law Lexicon is:

> *"Mandamus is an action or judicial proceeding of a civil nature extraordinary in the sense that it can be maintained only when there is no other adequate remedy, prerogative in its character to the extent that the issue is discretionary, to enforce only clear legal rights, and to compel Courts to take jurisdiction or proceed in the exercise of their jurisdiction, or to compel corporations, public and private, and public boards, commissions, or officers, to exercise their jurisdiction or discretion and to perform ministerial duties, which duties result from an office, trust, or*

---

2. Blackstone's Commentaries, 3rd Vol., p. 110.
3. *R. v. Barker* (1762) 3 Burr 1265 (1266, 1267).
4. Markose: Judicial Control of Administrative Action in India, 1956, p. 364.

station, and are clearly and peremptorily enjoined by law as absolute and official."[5]

Tomlin's Law Dictionary briefly defines *Mandamus* as follows:

"It is a high prerogative writ of a most extensive remedial nature, and may be issued in some cases where the injured party has also another more tedious method of redress, as in the case of admission or restitution to an office; but is issues in all cases where the party hath a right to have anything done, and hath no other specific means of compelling its performance. A Mandamus, therefore, lies to compel the admission or restoration of the party applying, to any office or franchise of a public nature, to academically degrees; to the use of a meeting-house, etc. It lies for the production, inspection, or delivery of public books and papers; for the surrender of the regalia of a Corporation; to oblige Bodies Corporate to affix their common seal; to compel the holding of a Court; and for an infinite number of other purposes, which it is impossible to recite minutely. But on this part of the subject it is to be particularly remarked, that it issues to the Judges of any inferior Court, commanding them to do justice according to the powers of their office, wherever the same is delayed. For it is the peculiar business of the superior Court to superintend all inferior tribunals and therein to enforce the due exercise of those judicial or ministerial powers with which the Crown or Legislature have invested them; and this not only by restraining their excess, but also by quickening their negligence, and obviating their denial of justice. A Mandamus may therefore be had to a subordinate Court to enter up judgment, to a Spiritual Court to grant an administration, to swear a churchwarden and the like."[6]

***Mandamus*: A prerogative writ—Neither writ of right, nor writ of course but writ of discretion:**

Under the English law, some of the writs are 'writs of right' and others are merely discretionary remedies. But the writ of *mandamus* is neither a writ of right nor writ of course but writ of discretion. Accordingly, the court may grant the writ even though the right in respect of which it is applied for appears to be doubtful and, on the other hand, the writ may be refused, not only upon merits, but also by reason of the special circumstances of the case.[7]

Granting of writ of *Mandamus* is entirely within the discretion of the Court and cannot be demanded as of right. But the discretion has to be exercised according to judicial principles. One of the limitations imposed by the Courts on themselves is that they will not interfere unless substantial injustice has ensued or is likely to ensue.

---

5. Law Lexicon by P.K. Ramanatha Iyar.
6. Tomlin's Law Dictionary, 3 Comm. 110.
7. Halsbury's Laws of England, IInd Edition, Vol. 9, para 1270, p. 745.

The nature of a discretionary writ as distinguished from a writ of right, was described by Cockburn, C.J. in *re Forster*, while pointing out the distinction between the right of a party and that of a stranger, in the following words:

> *'I entirely concur in the proposition, that although the Court will listen to a person who is a stranger, and who interferes to point out that some other Court has exceeded its jurisdiction, whereby some wrong or grievance has been sustained, yet that is not ex debito justitiae, but a matter upon which the Court may properly exercise its discretion; as distinguished from the case of a party aggrieved, who is entitled to relief ex debito justitiae if he suffers from the usurpation of jurisdiction by another Court.'*[8]

A writ of *mandamus* being controlled by equitable principles can be issued only in favour of a person who comes to the Court with clean hands and is not guilty of fraud or bad faith in respect of the matters in controversy between the parties.

Mandamus in U.S.A.:

A great reliance is put to the *mandamus* remedy in U.S.A. An effort is made to trace origin of it in U.S.A. as well and it has been observed by the authors about *mandamus*,

> *'In origin the writ was highly prerogative—a mere letter issued from the King to a subordinate functionary, commanding the performance of his duty. The King's prerogative was part of the common law of England. It was the aggregate of the King's special powers and privileges, the personal rights or power of supreme character exercisable without question and without responsibility. The earlier writs were such writs of direction, created and enforced by authority of the royal will. The command was a law in itself, from which there was no appeal. It was not only declaratory of a duty under an existing law, but was a law in itself. It created the law and imposed the duty, the performance of which it commanded. Then it became a legislative power, and finally became judicial and issued in the King's name out of the court of King's Bench to any person, corporation or inferior court, thus supplanting the personal of the sovereign. By the end of the reign of Edward I this form of mandamus was in common use in aid of the police power, and such was settled in England long prior to the time when the common law passed to this country (America).'*[9]

The Courts of U.S.A. defined *mandamus* as follows:

'Mandamus is an extraordinary legal remedy which equity has nothing to

8. Cockburn, C.J. in re Forster.
9. The law of Extraordinary Legal Remedies, p. 219 by Ferries and Ferries.

do, and in consideration of which no equitable rights or principles can be taken into consideration except solely for the purpose of determining whether, in the exercise of legal discretion, the writ should issue.'[10]

It has been further observed by the U.S. Courts while appreciating the remedy of *mandamus*,

'Mandamus has been denominated a hard and fast writ, an unreasonable writ, a cast-iron writ, the right arm of the court, the exponent of judicial power; an inflexible peremptory command to do a particular thing therein specified without condition, limitation or terms of any kind; one of the highest writs known to the law.'[11]

Justice S.B. Sinha, in the case of **Union of India v. S.B. Vora**, defined *mandamus* while dealing with the issue involved in the above case in Para. 12 and 13 of the judgment as under:

'12. Mandamus literally means a command. The essence of mandamus in England was that it was a royal command issued by the King's Bench (now Queen's Bench) directing performance of a public legal duty.

13. A writ of mandamus is issued in favour of a person who establishes a legal right in himself. A writ of mandamus is issued against a person who has a legal duty to perform but has failed and/or neglected to do so. Such a legal duty emanates from either in discharge of a public duty or by operation of law. The writ of mandamus is the most extensive remedial nature. The object of mandamus is to prevent disorder from a failure of justice and is required to be granted in all cases where law has established no specific remedy and whether justice despite demanded has not been granted.'[12]

1.1.2 Meaning of Subject

From the title of the work, it is clear that the purpose of the work is in the direction of the issuance of writ of *mandamus*. During the entire research work, an attempt is made to draw attention upon the persons/ authorities against whom writ of *mandamus* can be issued under the Constitution of India along with criticism. Articles 32 as well as 226 of the Constitution give power to the Supreme Court and High Courts respectively to issue writ of *mandamus* in certain circumstances and against certain persons. The Supreme Court of India can, under Article 32 issue writ of *mandamus* only against those bodies or persons, who are covered within the meaning of "state"as defined in Article 12 of the Constitution of India. High

10. Goldwyn Pictures Corp. *v.* Howells Sales Co. 287 Fed. 100.
11. State ex rel Kansas City *v.* Kansas City Gas Co. 254 Mo. 515.
12. AIR 2004 SC 1402.

Courts of States have wide powers under Article 226 to issue writs as compared to the Supreme Court. In the present work, there is a detailed discussion with regard to the powers of a High Court and the Supreme Court for issuance of writ of *mandamus* against all bodies, entities and persons.

After the conclusion of the entire research work, the required changes in the Constitution are suggested. In the present research work an attempt is made to describe advantages, possible difficulties/hurdles as well as its solutions of expansion of the existing scope of *mandamus* under the Constitution of India.

Hence the title .of the present research work is chosen as **"Law Relating to the Subjects of *Mandamus*".**

1.2 ORIGINS AND DEVELOPMENT

1.2.1 Origin of Prerogative Writs

Origin of writs lies in England. It was a prerogative power of the King to issue writs in appropriate cases. The writs *viz. habeas corpus, mandamus, certiorari, quo warranto* and *prohibition* narrated under Articles 32 and 226 of the Constitution of India are known as prerogative writs under the English Law.

The origin of writs lies in ***"Magna Carta"* (1215)**, which was an agreement of compromise between the King and Earls (a particular upper class of people). The direction in *"Magna Carta"* that the Crown was bound neither to deny justice to anybody nor to deny anybody obtaining justice, is a recognition of the prerogative of the sovereign to issue to writ.

Wharton defines prerogative writs as follows:

"Processes issued upon extraordinary occasions on proper cause shown."[13]

In the words of **Dicey,**

"Prerogative writs are the bulwark of English Liberty. For thereby individual rights are safeguarded even without the declaration that they are fundamental."

The following passage from **Halsbury's Laws of England** is important to know the origin and exact meaning of prerogative writs under the English Law:

'The common law regards the King as the source or fountain of justice, and certain ancient remedial processes of an extraordinary nature which are known as prerogative writs have from the earliest times issued from the Court of King's Bench in which the Sovereign was always present in

---

13. Wharton's Law Lexicon, 14th Edition (1939), p. 1392.

contemplation of law. The prerogative writs were issued only upon cause shown, as distinguished from the original or judicial writs which commence suits between party and party and which issue as of course. The Court of King's Bench retained all the jurisdictions of the Curia Regis in so far as it was not distributed among the Courts, and this jurisdiction, including the granting of the prerogative remedies, is now, under the Supreme Court of Judicature (Consolidation) Act, 1925, S. 18 vested in the High Court of Justice.'[14]

1.2.2 Origin of Mandamus

The first reported case of writ of *mandamus* is traced to the year 1573 in Middleton's case (3 Dyer 332-b), wherein writ of *mandamus* was issued by considering ratio laid down in an unreported case of similar nature.

While tracing history of the writ of *mandamus* Justice C.C. Ghosh of Calcutta High Court, in *re* **Jatindra Mohan Sen Gupta** described the principles of *mandamus* as follows:

> *'The writ is of very ancient origin, dating back, at any rate, to the time of Edward II. In Bacon's Abridgment, it is said to be founded on Magna Charta, by which the Crown was bound neither to deny justice to anybody nor to delay anybody in obtaining justice. It seems originally, according to Mr. High, (in his book Extraordinary Legal Remedies), to have been one of that large class of writs or mandates, by which the Sovereign of England directed the performance of any desired act by his subjects, the word "mandamus" in such writs, letters or missives having given rise to the present time of the writ. These letters, missives or mandates to which the generic term, "mandamus" was applied, were in no sense judicial writs being merely a command issuing directly from the Sovereign to the subjects, without the intervention of the Courts, and they have long become entirely obsolete.*
>
> *The term "mandamus" seems gradually to have been confined in its application to the judicial writ issued by the King's Bench, which has by steady growth developed into the writ of mandamus. It is a high prerogative writ and is granted to implicate justice and to preserve a right where there is no specific legal remedy. And it has been said that the Court, in the exercise of this authority to grant the writ of mandamus, will render it as far as it can be the supplementary means of substantial justice in every case where there is no other specific legal remedy for a legal right, and will provide as effectively as it can that others exercise their duty wherever the subject-matter is properly within its control.'*[15]

1.2.3 Development of Mandamus in England

The first reported case of writ of *mandamus* is ***Rex* v. *Warran***

14. Halsbury's Law of England, 3rd Edition, Vol. II.
15. AIR 1925 Cal 48 (51, 52).

Hastings[16] in the year 1775. In this case, writ of *mandamus* was sought against the Supreme Council of the Governor-General, which was not granted.

In the case of ***R.* v. *Powell*,** Lord Denman, C.J., while deciding the writ of *mandamus* filed against the Crown, observed at page 361,

> *'As it has been already discussed above, the jurisdiction to issue the 'prerogative writs' belonging to the Sovereign as the fountain of justice came to be exercised by the King's Bench. The Supreme Court of Judicature (Consolidation Act, 1925) vested the jurisdiction in the High Court of Justice but the jurisdiction to issue writs of mandamus, prohibition and certiorari belonging to the Queen's Bench Division of the High Court as before.*
>
> *Under Sec. 7(2) of the Administration of Justice Act, 1938, in any case where the High Court could have, before this Act, issued a prerogative 'writ' of mandamus, the Court may now make "an 'order' requiring the act to be done". But this Act has not affected the principles according to which an 'order' of mandamus is to be issued. The principles governing the prerogative 'writ' of mandamus are, therefore, still in force, so that there has been no change in substance.'*[17]

In England, besides the prerogative writ or order of *mandamus*, there are two other analogous remedies, namely,

(a) a statutory interlocutory order for *mandamus* or mandatory injunction, under Sec. 45 of the Judicature Act, 1925; and

(b) an action for *mandamus*, introduced by the Common Law Procedure Act, 1854.

1.2.4 Development of Writ of *Mandamus* in India

The East India Company in 1765 obtained the grant of the dewani from the person whom it recognized as the rightful claimant to the throne at Delhi of the Mughal Emperors. This grant was expressed to cover Bengal, Bihar and Orissa (as the comprised but which now has long been part of Bengal). Sovereignty and the right of administering civil and criminal justice were vested in the Mughal Emperor whose government of the provinces of Bengal consisted of two parts: The Dewani or collection of the revenues and the administration of the principal branches of the department of civil justice, and Nizamut or the military branch of the Government with the superintendence of the criminal department of judicature: and of these the Dewani was subordinate to the Nizamut.[18]

---

16. (1775) 1 ID (OS) 1005.
17. (1841) 1 QB 352.
18. Cowell, "History and Constitution of the Courts and Legislative Authorities in India", 6th Edition, p. 19.

The company did not undertake the administration of the dewani-revenue and civil justice by its own servants until 1776, but when in that year it "stood forth as dewan", a system of civil courts was set-up. These courts were not courts of His Majesty the King of England, nor did they administer the law of England. They were manned by European servants of the company, who were not skilled in any system of law but had the assistance of "law officers"—kazis, muftis, maulvis, or pandits—to inform them as to the Mohammedan and Hindu laws. Strictly speaking, criminal jurisdiction was part of the nizamat and not the dewani; and the company, at least after 1775 did not profess to administer this at its own hand until 1790 but left it, nominally at least and subject to some interference or supervision in the hands of the Naib Nazim, whose Chief Court (Nizamat Adalat) sat at Murshidabad. From 1790, however, the Company took criminal jurisdiction into its own hands and continued the Mohammedan Criminal Law as the public law of the land, applying it with modification made from time to time to Hindus as well as to Muslims. Appeals from civil courts went to the Sadar Dewani Adalat and appeals from the criminal courts to the Sadar Nizamat Adalat—courts which consisted until 1801 of the Governor General, and Member of the Council. The Company's Courts—Civil or Criminal—had no jurisdiction over British Subjects.[19]

The Regulating Act

In 1773 by the Regulating Act (13 Geo. III, Cap. 63), Parliament intervened for the first time to control the company's administration. Perhaps, the most remarkable clauses of the Regulating Act were those which provided for the creation of the Supreme Court, *[which had since 1726 existed as an English Court applying English Law to the town and settlement]* by means of a Royal Charter. The Act specified the lines on which the Charter of the Supreme Court was to be issued.

The Supreme Court was to enjoy a very wide jurisdiction. It was authorized to decide civil cases, and to administer justice in criminal cases in the character of the Court of Oyer and Terminer and Gaol Delivery for Calcutta, the factory of the Fort William England. Grand Jury and Petty Jury consisting of British subjects resident in the town of Calcutta were to be used for the trial of criminal cases. The Court was further empowered to exercise Admiralty and Ecclesiastical jurisdiction.

The Court was to be a Court of Record. The jurisdiction of the Court was, however, to be limited and was to extend to: (a) All British subjects residing in Bengal, Bihar and Orissa; (b) All of His Majesty's subjects residing in Bengal, Bihar and Orissa; and (c) All persons employed by or directly in the service of, the company or any of His Majesty's subjects.

Besides, the Court was authorized to hear and determine any suit of action by any of His Majesty's subjects against any inhabitant of India residing within the provinces of Bengal, Bihar and Orissa, if—(i) there was

19. Ryots of Garabandho *v.* Zamindar of Parlakemidi, A.I.R. 1943 P.C. 164.

a contract or agreement in writing between the said inhabitant and His Majesty's subject, (ii) in the agreement, the said inhabitant agreed that in case of a dispute, the matter would be heard and determined in the Supreme Court, and (iii) the cause of action exceeded five hundred rupees.

Such an action or suit could be brought in the Supreme Court of Judicature either in the first instance, or by way of appeal from the sentence or order of any of the Courts established by the Company in the Dewani area.[20]

The Act also directed that the Charter to be issued by the King, establishing the Supreme Court, was to contain provisions allowing appeals to the King in Council from the decisions, judgments or determination of the Supreme Court under such conditions and circumstances as were thought reasonable and proper by the Crown and laid down in the Charter.

The Charter of the Supreme Court (1774)

To give effect to the express provisions of the Regulating Act, King George III, issued a Royal Charter on March 26, 1774, establishing the Supreme Court of Judicature at Fort William in Bengal, and making it a Court of record. The Supreme Court, in the first place, was to have power and jurisdiction to hear, try and determine all civil causes, actions and suits, arising against—(a) the Mayor and Aldermen of Calcutta; (b) any of his Majesty's subjects residing within the provinces of Bengal, Bihar and Orissa; (c) any person, who was employed by, or was directly or indirectly in the service of (i) the Company; (ii) the Corporation of Calcutta, or (iii) any of His Majesty's subjects; (d) the Company; and (e) any inhabitant of Bengal, Bihar and Orissa, if—(i) he entered into any contract or agreement in writing; (ii) the other party to such a contract was His Majesty's subject; (iii) the cause of action exceeded five hundred rupees; and (iv) the Indian inhabitant in this contract agreed that in case of dispute, the matter would be determined in the Supreme Court of Judicature at Fort William.

Clause 21 of that *Charter*, can be said to be the first instrument of power conferring the right of issuance of prerogative writs by a Court in India. It stated:

> *'The Court of Requests and Court of Quarter Sessions established at Fort William and the Justices, Sheriffs and Magistrates appointed for the said districts were made subject to the order and control of the Supreme Court in such manner and form as the inferior Courts and Magistrates in England were by law, subject to the order and control of the Court of King's Bench and to that end the Supreme Court was empowered to issue writs of Mandamus, Certiorari Precedendo, and Error, to be directed to such courts or Magistrates.'*

20. M.P. Jain, "Outlines of Indian Legal History", pp. 74-75.

Clause (4) of the same charter is as follows:

'And it is our further Will and pleasure that the Chief Justice have such jurisdiction and authority as our Justices of our Court of Kings Bench have and may lawfully exercise within that part of Great Britain called England ......'

It may be stated that clause (4) was significantly wider than clause (21). A writ, which was not specified in the latter clause could be easily covered by the general scope of the former clause.

The Charter laid down that under the circumstances detailed above, the matter could be heard and determined in the Supreme Court of Judicature, either in the first instance, or by way of appeal from the decision of a Court of Justice established in the country by the Company.

The Supreme Court, in the second place, was to be a Court of Equity and as such was to have full power and authority to administer justice as nearly as may be, according to the rules and proceedings of the High Court of Chancery in Great Britain.

The Charter vested the Supreme Court, in the third place, with criminal jurisdiction. The Supreme Court was to be a Court of Oyer and Terminer and Gaol Delivery, in and for the town of Calcutta, the factory of Fort William, and the factories subordinate thereto. On this capacity, it was to have the same powers and authority, as the Justices of Oyer and Terminer and Galo Delivery had or exercised in England.

The Supreme Court, in the fourth place, was empowered to exercise Ecclesiastical jurisdiction throughout the province of Bengal, Bihar and Orissa, on the British subjects residing there. As such, the Court could grant probate of wills and testaments of the British subjects dying within the three provinces of Bengal, Bihar and Orissa. It could issue letters of administration for the effects of the British subject dying intestate or dying without appointing an executor to his will. The Supreme Court was further constituted into a Court of Admiralty for the province of Bengal, Bihar and Orissa.

The judges of the Supreme Court were to have the same jurisdiction and authority, as the justices of the Court of King's Bench in England under the Common Law. The authority of the judges of the Supreme Court was thus assimilated to that of the judges of the King's Bench.

The Charter also empowered the Supreme Court, as a superior Court to superintend and control the Court of Requests and the justices of the peace in such manner and form as the inferior Courts and magistrates of England were, by law subject to the order and control of the Court of King's Bench. To achieve this subject, the Supreme Court was authorized to issue various Prerogative Writs like the *Mandamus, Certiorari.*

The Act of Settlement, 1781

For seven years following the inauguration of the Supreme Court there arose a host of difficulties in Bengal, Bihar and Orissa. The relations between the Court and the Council practically reached the braking point. Claiming to be authorized by its Charter, the Court proceeded to entertain proceeds (*inter alia*) against the officers of the Company's Court in respect of their official acts and the consequence of its proceedings in the "Patna" and "*Cossijurrah*" Cases was that the Company's Government, the Council, took steps to employ military force to prevent the orders of the court for being carried out, and petitioned the authorities in England against the actions of the Court as attempts to extend the authority of the English law to the inhabitants of Bengal and Bihar. The Court also claimed to exercise jurisdiction over the English and the Indian officers of the Company employed in the collection of revenues and to punish them for corrupt or oppressive acts done by them, in their official capacity in the collection of revenue.

The result was the stature of 1781 (21 Geo. III, Cap. 70), the preamble recited (*inter alia*) that it was expedient that the lawful government of the provinces should be supported and that the inhabitants should be maintained and protected in the enjoyment of all their ancient laws, usages, rights and privileges. The Act fundamentally altered the scope and conditions of the Supreme Court's jurisdiction, superseding to a great extent, but without formally amending the Charter of 1774. It exempted the Governor General and Council from the Court's jurisdiction in respect of their official acts: it deprived the Court of jurisdiction in matters of revenue; it provided that no one was to be liable to its jurisdiction by reason of being a landholder or farmer of land or land rent; that no one should be amenable to the court's jurisdiction by reason of being employed by the Company or by a British subject in any matter of inheritance or contract, but only in respect of action for wrongs and trespasses or in other civil cases by agreement in writing to submit thereto. It provided for the maintenance of a register of the names of Indians so employed. It gave the Supreme Court jurisdiction to try actions and suits against all inhabitants of Calcutta providing that the Hindu and Mohammedan laws respectively should be applied to their affairs; or the law of the defendant in cases where only one of the parties was Hindu or Mohammedan. It preserved the right of fathers of families. It confirmed the Court of Sudder Dewani Adalat as a Court of Civil appeal from the country courts, and made it a court of record, and its judgments final and conclusive save for appeal to His Majesty in Council. It gave to the Sadar Court exclusive jurisdiction over offences and extortions in the collection of the revenue. It made the judicial officers of the country courts, whether they were British or Indian, immune from actions in respect of any order made by them and gave protection likewise to others for any acts done by their order.

It conferred on the Governor General and Council the power to make regulations 'for the Provincial Courts and Councils'—a very limited power which strengthened by an Act of 1797, 37 Geo. III, Cap. 142, s. 8—has produced the extensive system of laws known as he Bengal Regulations[21] mentioned in case of *Ryots of Garabandho* v. *Zamindar of Parlakimedi.*

The result of the two Acts—the Regulating Act and the Act of Parliament—in effect was to establish and perpetuate two judicial systems, the Presidency Towns System and the Mofussil or Provincial System. The two judicial systems continued to exist for long side by side, distinctly and independently of each other, each working in its own demarcated sphere. It was only in 1861 that steps were taken in the direction of removing the exclusiveness between the two judicial systems and bringing them nearer to each other. This was sought to be effected by establishing a High Court at Calcutta in which the Supreme Court of Judicature and the Sadar Dewani Adalat of the Company were merged together.

Supreme Courts at Bombay and Madras

In the presidency towns of Bombay and Madras, the judicial system, inaugurated by the Charter of George III in 1753 continued in operation till in 1797 the British Parliament passed an Act (37 Geo. III, Cap. 142) authorizing the Crown to supersede the judicial arrangements of 1753 and establish the Recorders' Courts instead. The Recorder's Court was to be a court of record. It was to have full power and authority to exercise and perform all Civil, Criminal, Ecclesiastical and Admiralty jurisdiction. The jurisdiction, powers and authority to be conferred on the Recorder's Court by the Royal Charter to be issued by the Crown in pursuance of the Act of 1797, were to be on the lines similar to those of the Supreme Court of Judicature at Calcutta. All the restrictions imposed on the Supreme Court of judicature at Fort William by means of the Act of Settlement of 1781, were also extended to the Recorder's Court. In pursuance of the Act of 1797, King George III issued on February 1, 1798, Charters establishing Recorder's Courts at Bombay and Madras presidency towns.

In 1800, the British Parliament passed an Act authorizing the Crown to abolish the Recorder's Court and erect a Supreme Court of judicature in its stead by a Royal Charter. The letters patent granting the Charter of Justice to the Supreme Court at Madras were issued by the King on the 26th December, 1801. The Supreme Court was to enjoy Civil, Criminal, Admiralty and Ecclesiastical jurisdiction on the same basis as the Supreme Court of Judicature at Calcutta. An Act passed in 1823 authorized the English Crown to abolish the Recorder's Court at Bombay and establish a Supreme Court of Judicature in its place. The letters Patent granting a Charter of justice to the Supreme Court of Bombay were issued by the Crown on 8th December, 1823. The powers of the Supreme Court at Madras and Bombay were placed on an equal footing with those of the Supreme Court at Calcutta, in an explicit manner by the 17th section of the Act of 1823, which declared that it should be lawful for the Supreme Court of judicature at Madras and the Supreme Court of Judicature at Bombay, within their

21. A.I.R. 1943 P.C. 164.

respective territorial jurisdiction, to do, execute, perform and fulfil all such acts, authority, duties, matters and things whatsoever, as the Supreme Court of Judicature at Fort William was or might be authorized, empowered, or directed to do, execute, perform and fulfil within the factory of Fort William in Bengal or places subject to or dependent upon the Government thereof.[22]

The High Courts—The Indian High Courts Act, 1861

The year 1861 is a conspicuous land mark in the process of development of the legal institutions in India. Hitherto, there existed two parallel judicial systems in the provinces of Bengal, Bombay and Madras. One set of courts, being the Crown's Courts, consisted of the Supreme Courts of Judicature which functioned in the presidency towns. The other set of courts, being the company's courts and having Sadar courts at the apex, functioned in the provinces beyond the Presidency towns.

In course of time, the existence of two parallel systems was found to be inconvenient. It was considered to be eminently desirable that a greater unity and harmony should be established in respect of the judicial administration. In the context of changed circumstances after 1858, the distinction between the Crown's Court and the Company's Courts had lost all its validity. The year 1861, therefore, witnessed the merger of two sets of courts and the consequent emergence of three High Courts, in three provinces. The process of establishing High Courts, initiated in 1861, continued, as a result of which more and more High Courts were created in India during the years to follow.[23]

Power of High Courts to Issue Writs

Before the commencement of the present Constitution of India, the position regarding the writ issuing power of the High Court in India was as follows:

> As already noticed, the three High Courts of Calcutta, Madras and Bombay were the inheritors of, and the successors to the jurisdiction of the Supreme Courts at Calcutta, Madras and Bombay respectively. Certain provisions in the Charters of the Supreme Courts gave them such jurisdiction and authority as the Justices of the Court of King Bench had by common law in England. The Court of King's Bench could issue the prerogative writs and so the Supreme Courts in India could also issue the prerogative writs. Naturally, the three High Courts of Calcutta, Madras and Bombay secured these powers and became entitled to issue the prerogative writs within the same ambit as the Supreme Courts could have done.

22. M.P. Jain, Outlines of Indian Legal History, pp. 121-26.
23. M.P. Jain, Outlines of Indian Legal History, pp. 121-26, p. 330.

The other High Courts did not possess any authority to issue any prerogative writ except an order in the nature of writ of *habeas corpus* under the provisions of Section 491 of the Criminal Procedure Code of 1898.

Even the ambit of writ issuing power of the High Courts of Calcutta, Madras and Bombay was obscure and vague. The most important question that often arose was whether these High Courts could issue any prerogative writ outside the limits of their ordinary original civil jurisdiction. The territorial extent of the ordinary original civil jurisdiction of the Presidency High Courts was limited to the boundaries of the presidency towns as their predecessors, the Supreme Courts, enjoyed jurisdiction only within those limits. These High Courts could therefore without any difficulty issue the prerogative writs within the ambit of their ordinary civil jurisdiction. The disputed point was whether these High Courts were competent to issue the writs beyond those limits. In the beginning some opinions were expressed that the High Courts could issue the writs even outside the limits of their civil jurisdiction. But in course of time, it came to be held by the High Courts as well as by the Privy Council that their inherent power in this respect did not entitle them to issue the writs beyond the limits of the presidency towns. The basis for this view was simple. The High Courts derived their authority from the Supreme Courts. The Supreme Courts' jurisdiction was limited territorially to presidency towns. They could not issue a writ beyond those limits except in special cases when the party to whom the writ was being issued happened to be a British subject or a Company's servant who was personally liable to the court's jurisdiction. The High Courts, therefore, could not issue a writ when the Supreme Courts themselves could not have done so.

In the well-known case of **Ryots of Garabandho v. Zamindar of Parlakimedi,**[24] the Judicial Committee of the privy Council held that the High Court of Madras had no power to issue a writ of certiorari on any one outside the presidency town of Madras unless he was a British subject though the High Courts of Calcutta, Madras and Bombay had power to issue certiorari in the exercise of their local jurisdiction, and that the power of superintendence given by S. 15, Indian High Courts Act of 1861, and afterwards by S. 107, Government of India Act, 1915, did not include a right to issue a writ of *certiorari* to individuals or official bodies exercising judicial functions in the mofussil.

Similarly, in **Hamid Hasan v. Banwarilal Roy**[25] it was held that the Original Civil Jurisdiction which the Supreme Court of Calcutta possessed over certain classes of persons outside the territorial limits of that jurisdiction had not been inherited by the High Court, that the power to grant an information in the nature of *quo warranto* arose in the exercise of the Ordinary Original Civil Jurisdiction of the Court, that such jurisdiction was confined to the town of Calcutta, and that therefore the High Court had

24. A.I.R. 1943 PC 164.
25. A.I.R. 1947 PC 90.

no jurisdiction to grant such information where the person who was called upon to show cause why the information should not be exhibited against him, did not reside and the office which he was alleged to have usurped was not situate, within those limits.

In Madras, the Supreme Court of Judicature took up the place of the Recorder's Court in 1800 and clause 47 of the Madras Charter of 1800 reproduced the phraseology of clause 21 of the Calcutta Charter. Similarly, in Bombay Clause 13 of Bombay Charter of 1823 empowered the Supreme Court of Bombay to issue prerogative writs.

The Supreme Courts in Bombay, Madras and Calcutta were later superseded by the High Courts in those three Presidency Towns by the *Charter Act of 1861 (Sec. 9)*. But the power to issue the prerogative writs were restricted to the original jurisdiction of those three High Courts. Section 9 of the High Courts Act of 1861 was reproduced with some modifications in section 106 of the Government of India Act of 1915 and later in section 223 of the Government of India Act, 1935. The power to issue writs was restricted to only the above three High Courts. The other High Courts in India viz. High Court of Allahabad, Patna, Lahore and Nagpur were created by the Crown under Section 16 of the High Courts Act, 1861 and they had no such power.[26]

Writ of Mandamus and Specific Relief Act, 1877

It is necessary to mention that under Sec. 45 of the Specific Relief Act, 1877, even the High Courts of Madras, Calcutta and Bombay could not issue the writs of prohibition and *certiorari* or an order outside the local limits of their original civil jurisdiction. Vide Ryots of *Garabandho* v. *Parlakimedi*.[27]

The Supreme Courts in India had authority to issue writ of *mandamus*. Section 50 of the Specific Relief Act, 1877, abolished this prerogative writ of *mandamus* by enacting that neither the High Court nor any Judge thereof shall hereafter issue any writ of *mandamus*.'

As observed in the case of **Surajmall v. Commissioner of Income Tax**, Section 45 of the Act, however, confers on the High Courts of Calcutta, Madras and Bombay to make orders which secure the same result as the writ of *mandamus* issued by the King's Division Bench, and the conditions which are set forth in that section are substantially the same as those under which the writ of *mandamus* is issued in England.[28]

Regarding the powers of the High Court in issuing writ of *mandamus* under Sec. 45 of the Specific Relief Act, 1877, it is observed by Calcutta High Court in the case of **P.K. Banerjee v. L.J. Simonds**[29] as follows:

---

26. M.P. Jain, Outlines of Indian Legal History, p. 354.
27. A.I.R 1943 PC 164.
28. A.I.R. 1930 Pat. 538.
29. A.I.R. 1947 Cal. 307.

'Section 45 of the Specific Relief Act can be invoked against a person holding a public office only when the doing or forbearing of an act is clearly incumbent upon him in his public character. There must be a duty or an obligation, in his public character, on the part of the person against whom an order is sought, to do or to forbear from doing an act in favour of the applicant. The remedy under this section is in substitution for the high prerogative writ of mandamus, which by Sec. 50 of the Act, is no longer available; but the provisions of Sec. 45 in substance, give statutory effect to the principles governing mandamus. The decisions of the Courts in England relating to mandamus are applicable to Sec. 45.'

Section 50 of the Specific Relief Act, as now substituted by the Adaptation of Laws Order, 1950 reads as follows: "Nothing in this Chapter shall affect the power conferred on a High Court by clause (1) of Article 226 of the Constitution."

In **Nathmal v. Commissioner, Civil Supplies**[30], it was observed that the power under Art. 226 is unfettered by the restrictions given in Section 45 of the Specific Relief Act.

As pointed out in the case of **Mathen v. District Magistrate of Trivandrum**[31], the Legislature had taken away through the High Courts Act, 1861 and the Code of Criminal Procedure (Old), the power of the High Court to issue the writ of *Habeas Corpus* in matters covered by Section 491, Cr.P.C. The later section was limited to the appellate jurisdiction of the High Court.

The power to issue the Common Law writ of *mandamus* was taken away by the Specific Relief Act, 1877 which had in Section 45 of that Act a provision for the issue of an order in the 'nature of *mandamus*', however restricted to requiring anything to be done or forborne within the local limits of the ordinary jurisdiction of the High Courts. The High Courts had also no jurisdiction to issue the writ of *certiorari* to any Mofussil Court or quasi-judicial bodies exercising jurisdiction outside the Original Jurisdiction of the High Court.

Specifically Article 226 of the Constitution did not repeal the Calcutta High Court, soon after the commencement of the Constitution, i.e. in the year 1952 clarified that Sec. 45 of the Specific Relief Act, 1898. But the said Article has expanded the scope of the High Court regarding issuance of writ of *mandamus*. It is observed by the Calcutta High Court, while explaining the position of *mandamus* under the constitution of India in the case of **Union of India v. Elbridge Watson**[32] as under:

'.. Before the Constitution, the High Court could not issue any writ of mandamus after the Specific Relief of 1877 came into force. But the High

---

30. A.I.R. 1952 Raj. 74, p. 79.
31. A.I.R. 1939 PC 213.
32. AIR 1952 SC 601.

Courts of Calcutta, Madras, Bombay and Rangoon could make orders under Sec. 45 of that Act for the enforcement of public duties. But in dealing with an application under Sec. 45 of the Act, the principles applicable to a writ of mandamus were generally followed. Sec. 45, Specific Relief Act, has not been repealed by Art. 226 of the Constitution. That Article has enlarged the jurisdiction of these courts for the issue of the writs mentioned in that Article. Our Courts for the issue of the writs mentioned in that Article. Our Constitution has adopted the nomenclature of the English Writs and the English law relating to these writs must govern the issue of the writs herein so far as they are not opposed to our Constitution.'

As discussed above, originally, the High Courts in the three Presidency Towns of Madras, Bombay and Calcutta had, by virtue of their jurisdiction inherited from the old Supreme Courts, power to issue within the limits of the Presidency Town the writ of *Mandamus*. But after the enactment of the Specific Relief Act, 1877, this power was expressly taken away by Sec. 50 of the Act, which provided that

> *"neither the High Court nor any Judge thereof shall hereafter issue any writ of mandamus"*[33]

But in the place of the original power of issuing a writ of *mandamus*, a new power was conferred on the above three High Courts under Sec. 45 of the Specific Relief Act, viz. the power to make an order requiring any specific act to be done or forborne. The jurisdiction of the High Courts in this respect was confined to the limits of the Presidency Towns. But, though the power of issuing a writ of *mandamus* was taken away and was replaced by the power of issuing an order u/s. 45 according to the conditions and limitations prescribed u/s. 46, such conditions and limitations were, as already stated, substantially the same as those which governed an application for a writ of *mandamus* or order or *mandamus* under the English Law. In dealing with an application u/s. 45, Specific Relief Act, 1877, the principles applicable to a writ of *mandamus* were generally followed subject to the provisions of the Indian Act.

33. Specific Relief Act, 1877—by Pollock and Mulla.

2

Subjects of *Mandamus* in Other Countries

2.1 SUBJECTS OF *MANDAMUS* IN AUSTRALIA

Australian Constitution itself provides remedy of writ of *mandamus* to the individual. Section 75(v) of the Constitution of Australia[1] deals with the writ of *mandamus,* to be issued by the High Courts of Australia. This power does not go into any further details than barely conferring the power upon the High Court to issue the writ in its original jurisdiction.

Sec. 75: In all matters

(i) ....
(ii) ....
(iii) ....
(iv) ....
(v) in which a writ of mandamus or prohibition or an injunction is sought against an officer of the Commonwealth, the High Court shall have original jurisdiction.

The above power is obviously limited inasmuch as it is not available against State Officers.

As to who is a 'Commonwealth Officer', it has been held that he must be a person appointed and removable, paid by and responsible to the Commonwealth. It would thus be available against Commonwealth judges and quasi-judicial tribunals; Members of Commonwealth Boards and of Court-martial; the Commissioner of Taxation.

---

1. M.V. Pylee's Constitutions of the World (Australia), p. 60.

2.2 SUBJECTS OF *MANDAMUS* IN BANGLADESH

The provisions for issuance of writs (in the form of directions or orders) are described under the Constitution of Bangladesh itself. The High Court Division has power to issue writs for the violation of fundamental rights. Thus, the writ jurisdiction of the High Court in Bangladesh is similar to that of India. However, the specific word 'writ' is not used in the Constitution of Bangladesh but from the language of Article 102 it becomes clear that the said article deals with various kinds of writs. Article 102 of the Constitution of Bangladesh[2] is reproduced here below:

Article 102. Power of High Court Division to issue certain orders and directions, etc.

(1) The High Court Division on the application of any person aggrieved, may give such directions or orders to any person or authority, including any person performing any function in connection with the affairs of the Republic, as may be appropriate for the enforcement of any of the fundamental rights conferred by Part III of this Constitution.

(2) The High Court Division may, if satisfied that no other equally efficacious remedy is provided by law—

(a) On the application of any person aggrieved, make an order—

(i) directing a person performing any functions in connection with the affairs of the Republic or of a local authority to refrain from doing that which he is not permitted by law to do or to do that which he is required by law to do; or

(ii) declaring that any act done or proceeding taken a person performing functions in connection with the affairs of the Republic or of a local authority has been done or taken without lawful authority and is of no legal effect; or

(b) on an application of any person, make an order—

(i) directing that a person in custody be brought before it so that it may satisfy itself that he has not being held in custody without lawful authority or in an unlawful manner; or

(ii) requiring a person holding or purporting to hold a public office to show under what authority he claims to hold that office.

(3) ....

(4) ....

(5) In this article, unless the context otherwise requires, "person" includes a statutory public authority and any court or tribunal, other than a court or tribunal established under a law relating to the defence service of Bangladesh or any disciplined force or a tribunal to which Article 117 applies.

---

2. M.V. Pylee's Constitutions of the World (Bangladesh), pp. 104-05.

From the above mentioned article it becomes very clear that Article 102 deals with the writ jurisdiction. Though not specifically categorized, by reading sub-clause (i) of clause (a) of Article 102(2) we can presume that the aforesaid sub-clause deals with the powers to issue writ of *mandamus*. In the same manner, Article 102 (2)(a)(ii) is of writ of *certiorari*, Article 102(2)(b) (i) and (ii) describes powers of writ of *Habeas Corpus* and of writ of *Quo Warranto* respectively.

Moreover, sub-clause (5) to above article makes it clear that the term "person" includes statutory public authority, any Court or tribunal. This term is somewhat in resemblance with the term "state" defined in Article 12 of the Constitution of India. But here the limitation in the Constitution of Bangladesh is that the term "person" does not include Government itself nor the legislature. The powers to issue writ, order or direction are issued only to the High Court by the Constitution of Bangladesh.

2.3 SUBJECTS OF *MANDAMUS* IN BRAZIL

Article 5 of the Constitution of Brazil[3] is a specific chapter of fundamental rights, which says as follows:

Article 5

LXIX: A writ of mandamus shall be issued to protect a clear legal right which is not protected by habeas corpus or habeas data, when the part responsible for the illegal act or abuse of power is a public authority or an agent of a legal entity performing government duties;

LXX: a collective writ of mandamus may be filed by:

(a) a political party, represented in Congress;
(b) a trade union, professional entity, or association legally organized and in operation for at least one year, to defend the interest of its members or associates.

LXXI: an injunction shall be issued whenever the absence of regulations makes it unfeasible to exercise the constitutional rights and liberties and the prerogatives inherent to nationality, sovereignty, and citizenship.

From the above article it is clear that in Brazil, scope of writ of *mandamus* is wider, as even a political party or a trade union or a professional entity, like a company or an association, can file it. Thus, writ of *mandamus* is not restricted only to an individual, whose fundamental or legal right is violated.

Further Article 102-I as well as II narrates the power of Federal Supreme Court to adjudicate writ of *mandamus* at the original and appellate stage respectively. The relevant contents of Article 102-I and II is described here below[4]:

---

3. M.V. Pylee's Constitutions of the World (Brazil), p. 199.
4. M.V. Pylee's Constitutions of the World (Brazil), pp. 250-51.

Article 102. Functions, Constitutional Court

(0) The Federal Supreme Court is responsible, mainly, for safeguarding the Constitution and it is incumbent upon it:

I. to process and adjudicate, originally;

(a) ... .

(b) ... .

(c) ... ...

(d) habeas corpus when the petitioner is any one of the persons referred to in the proceeding subsections; writs of mandamus and habeas data against acts of the President of the Republic, of the Presiding Boards of the House of Representatives and of the Federal Senate, of the Audit Tribunal of the Union, of the Attorney General of the Republic, and of the Federal Supreme Court itself;

II. to adjudicate, at ordinary appeal level:

(a) habeas corpus, writs of mandamus, habeas data and writs of injunction decided in a sole instance by the Superior Courts, in the event of denial;

(b) ....

Article 105 gives power to the Superior Courts to issue writs of *mandamus* in the event of violation of individual's right by Ministers or the Court. Aforesaid article is reproduced here below[5]:

105. Functions of the Court

(0) It is incumbent upon the Superior Court of Justice:

I. To process and adjudicate, originally:

....

(b) writs of mandamus and habeas data against an act of Minister of State or of the Court itself.

The same powers to issue writ of *mandamus* are assigned to the Federal Regional Courts in Brazil under Article 108.[6] Moreover, the power to issue writ of *mandamus* is specifically given to the Federal Judge through Article 109[7] of the Constitution of Brazil. Relevant lines of both of these articles are reproduced here:

Article 108. Functions of Federal Regional Courts

It is incumbent upon the Federal Courts to:

5. M.V. Pylee's Constitutions of the World (Brazil), p. 252
6. M.V. Pylee's Constitutions of the World (Brazil), p. 254
7. M.V. Pylee's Constitutions of the World (Brazil), p. 255

1. process and adjudicate, originally:

(a)..............

(b)..............

(c) writs of mandamus and habeas data against an act of the Court itself or of a federal judge;

....

....

Article 109. Federal Judges' Functions:

(0) It is incumbent upon the Federal Judges to process and adjudicate:

....

....

....

....

VIII. Writs of mandamus and habeas data against an act of a Federal Authority, except for those cases coming under the jurisdiction of the Higher Federal courts;

....

....

The Constitution of Brazil empowers different courts to issue writ of *mandamus*. As compared to that the Constitution of India gives only the Supreme Court and High Court of a State to issue writ of *mandamus*.

2.4 SUBJECTS OF *MANDAMUS* IN NEPAL

Article 88 of the Constitution of Nepal gives power to the Supreme Court of Nepal to issue writ of *mandamus* for the enforcement of the fundamental rights given under the Constitution or for the enforcement of any other legal right for which no remedy is made available and for several other instances. The relevant text of Article 88 is narrated below[8]:

Article 88. Jurisdiction of the Supreme Court

(1)..............

(2) The Supreme Court shall, for the enforcement of the fundamental rights conferred by this Constitution, for the enforcement of any other legal right for which no remedy has been provided or for which the remedy even though provided appears to be inadequate or ineffective, or for the settlement of any constitutional or legal question involved in any dispute of public interest or concern, have the extraordinary power to issue necessary and appropriate orders to enforce such rights or to settle the dispute. For these purposes the Supreme Court may, with a view to imparting full justice and providing the appropriate remedy, issue appropriate orders and writs including habeas corpus, mandamus, certiorari, prohibition and quo warranto:

8. M.V. Pylee's Constitutions of the World (Nepal), p. 972

....

....

The Constitution of Nepal gives power to issue writs only to the Supreme Court of Nepal. No such other Courts are given writ jurisdiction by its Constitution.

2.5 SUBJECTS OF *MANDAMUS* IN PAKISTAN

The Constitution of Pakistan gives powers to the High Court and Supreme Court to issue writ of *mandamus* in the same manner as of Indian Constitution, which is described as follows:

Extraordinary Jurisdiction

Under the 1956 Constitution, the Supreme Court and the High Courts had the power to issue the prerogative writs of *mandamus, habeas corpus, certiorari,* prohibition and *quo warranto;* the Supreme Court could issue these writs only to protect a fundamental right, whereas the High Courts could also issue them "for any other purpose". The position under the 1962 Constitution was however changed. The basic content of each form of writ has been set out at length in the Constitution itself, probably in order to define with certainty the limits within which the courts could act.

The Constitution of 1973 followed the scheme of the Constitution of 1962 which gave Extraordinary Jurisdiction to the High Courts as follows under Article 199 of its Constitution, which is mentioned hereunder[9]:

Article 199: Jurisdiction of High Court

Subject to this Constitution, a High Court may, if it is satisfied that no other adequate remedy is provided by law—

(a) *on the application of an aggrieved party, make an order—*

(i) *directing a person performing within the territorial jurisdiction of the Court functions in connection with the affairs of the Federation, a Province or a Local authority to refrain from doing anything he is not permitted by law to do, or to do anything he is required by law to do; or*

(ii) *declaring that any act done or proceeding taken within the territorial jurisdiction of the Court by a person performing functions in connection with the affairs of the Federation, a Province or a Local Authority has been done or taken without lawful authority, and is of no legal effect; or*

(b) *on the application of any person, make an order—*

(i) *directing that a person in custody within the territorial jurisdiction of the Court be brought before it so that the court may satisfy itself that he is not being held in custody without lawful authority or in an unlawful manner; or*

9. M.V. Pylee's Constitutions of the World (Pakistan), pp. 1096-97.

(ii) *requiring a person within the territorial jurisdiction of the Court holding or purporting to hold a public office to show under what authority of law he claims to hold that office, or*

(c) *on the application of any aggrieved person, make an order giving such directions to any person or authority, including any Government, exercising any power or performing any function in, or in relation to, any territory within the jurisdiction of that court as may be appropriate for the enforcement of any of the Fundamental Rights conferred by Chapter 1 of Part-II.*

(2) Subject to the Constitution, the right to move a High Court for the enforcement of any of the Fundamental Rights conferred by Chapter 1 of Part-II shall not be abridged.

2.6 SUBJECTS OF *MANDAMUS* IN SRI LANKA

Under Article 168 of the Constitution of Sri Lanka,[10] the Supreme Court has sole and exclusive jurisdiction to issue writ of *mandamus* in the event of violation of fundamental or the language rights of an individual. *Article 168. Jurisdiction regarding Fundamental and Language rights:*

(1) *The Supreme Court shall have sole and exclusive jurisdiction to hear and determine any question relating to the infringement or imminent infringement by State action including executive or administrative action, of any fundamental right or language right declared and recognized by Chapter III or Chapter IV or by judicial action by courts exercising original criminal jurisdiction, of a fundamental right declared and recognized under Article 10.*

(2) *Where any person alleges that any such fundamental right or language right relating to such person has been infringed or is about to be infringed by State action including executive or administrative action, or by judicial action he may himself or by an attorney-at-law or a person or a body of persons in terms of Article 26, on his behalf, within three months thereof, in accordance with such rules of court as may be in force, apply to the Supreme Court by way of petition in writing addressed to such Court praying for relief or redress in respect of such infringement. Such application may be proceeded with only with leave to proceed first had an obtained from the Supreme Court, which leave may be granted or refused as the case may be by not less than two Judges of such Court.*

(3) *Where in the course of hearing in any court, of an application for orders in the nature of a writ of habeas corpus, certiorari, prohibition, mandamus or quo warranto, it appears to such court that there is prima facie evidence of an infringement or imminent infringement of*

10. M.V. Pylee's Constitutions of the World (Sri Lanka), p. 1572.

the provisions of Chapter III or Chapter IV by a party to such application, such court shall forthwith refer such matter for determination by the Supreme Court.

In the Constitution of Sri Lanka the power to issue writs of or in the nature of *mandamus* is given to the Supreme Court. But as per clause (3) of Article 168, during the course of argument before any court, if that court feels that there is a violation or infringement of any of the Fundamental rights of a person by a party to litigation, it has power to refer the same forthwith to the Supreme Court for the determination of the case.

2.7 SUBJECTS OF *MANDAMUS* IN U.S.A.

The State Courts have the power to issue the common law writ of *mandamus* in their original jurisdiction as a heritage of the English Common law which the colonial court brought with them.

The federal courts possess the power to grant an order of *mandamus* only in aid of their appellate jurisdiction, except in Columbia. It is not yet settled whether Sec. 10(b) of the Federal Administrative Procedure Act, 1946 authorises the Federal Courts to issue a mandatory injunction in lieu of an order of *mandamus*, in their original jurisdiction, and free from the technicalities of the Common law writ of *mandamus*.

Analysis and Inferences

In a comparison the powers of the Courts to issue *mandamus* in different countries alongwith India, the fascinating thing is that in India High Courts as well as the Supreme Court can issue *mandamus* at original stage. Except Brazil, the powers given to the Courts in different countries are very narrow as compared to India. Though there is a divergence of practice in the different States in issuance of *mandamus*, there is a common agreement in following the broad principles governing the English Common law of writ of *mandamus*. From the above summary it can be seen that number of democratic countries has included a remedy of *mandamus* in their Constitution itself or in their legal system by enacting legislations. This shows effectiveness, popularity and importance of *mandamus* all over the world.

3

Subjects of *Mandamus* in India

Looking to the importance and effective as well as speedy remedy giving justice through writ of *mandamus*, the framers of the Constitution have rightly inserted this remedy in the Constitution of India under Articles 32 and 226. The power to issue writ of *mandamus* was given to the Supreme Court under Article 32 and almost same power was given to High Courts under Article 226 of the Constitution of India.

Under Article 32 of the Constitution the Supreme Court has power to issue writ, order or direction in the nature of *mandamus* for the infringement of fundamental rights enshrined in Part III of the Constitution; whereas the High Courts have power to issue writ of or in the nature of *mandamus* or order or direction for the infringement of fundamental right or otherwise.

With the help of these two articles the judiciary is helping a common man whenever his fundamental or legal right is infringed or taken away by the state. Still, however, there is a restriction upon the High Courts and the Supreme Court that writ of *mandamus* cannot be issued upon any private person in certain circumstances.

Writ of *Mandamus* as effective remedy and reasons for its inclusion in the Constitution of India

The idea of providing in the Constitution effective remedies for the enforcement of the fundamental rights was from the very beginning present in the minds of its framers. When the Sub-Committee on Fundamental Rights assembled for the first time, on February 27, 1947, Alladi Krishnaswami Ayyar pointed out that the citizens' rights to be embodied in the Constitution should consist of guarantees enforceable in courts of law and that it was no use laying down precepts which remained unenforceable or ineffective. Shri K.M. Munshi was emphatically of the view that the Constitution should provide for writs to be issued by the courts. Dr. Ambedkar supported this suggestion.[1]

1. B. Shiva Rao, The Framing of India's Constitution, pp. 301-02.

In his note on fundamental rights Munshi pointed out that fundamental rights in the United States and civil liberties in Britain had been preserved by reason of two factors: (a) an independent judiciary and (b) the prerogative writs of *habeas corpus, mandamus, prohibition, certiorari* and *quo warranto*. He further said that in India, only the High Courts of Madras, Bombay and Calcutta were vested with the power to issue writs and this power extended only to the respective city areas where these courts exercised original jurisdiction, with the result that except in these three cities the machinery for enforcing civil rights was tardy remedy of a suit and the public conscience was not therefore keenly alive to the assertion of rights against the executive (pre-Constitutional era). Within the area under their jurisdiction these High Courts, inheriting the independence of the King's Bench in the United Kingdom, had built-up a strong tradition of prerogative writs. If writs were not provided for in the new Constitution, people would have to subject themselves to the loss of valuable rights before the constitutionality of an act of a Government was tested in a suit which might take years to be finally decided. In his draft provisions on fundamental rights Shri Munshi strongly favoured four out of five writs (except *quo warranto*) to be issued by the courts within the union. Talking about *mandamus* he said that it is a writ of enforcement to secure the performance of any specific act by a unit, an officer or a corporation in discharge of a definite public duty, obligation or requirement with which it was specifically charged by the Constitution or by any law.

Shri Munshi's views were generally shared by other members of the sub-committee. The corresponding provision in Ambedkar's draft only differed from the proposals of Shri Munshi in that it vested the authority to issue prerogative writs exclusively in the Supreme Court and included writ of *quo warranto*.

Alladi Krishnaswami Ayyar pointed out that the power to issue writ of *habeas corpus* to the Supreme Court under the Constitution and the rest of the writs including writ of *mandamus* should be regulated by the Union law. But nobody supported him.

Thereafter, the clause was taken up for consideration in the Constituent Assembly on May 2, 1947. Shri K. Santhanam opined that all original jurisdictions should be vested in the High Courts so that they might become the lynchpin for the enforcement of fundamental rights. Shri Vallabhbhai Patel accepted this amendment of Shri K. Santhanam. The Draft Committee also accepted the entire clause as settled by it as Article 25 of the Draft Constitution (At present Article 32 of the Constitution of India).[2]

At the time of framing the Constitution, reference has already been made to the recommendations made by the Patel Committee, in its report for remedial provision being made specifically in the Constitution itself.

2. Constituent Assembly Debates Vol. III pp. 520-22.

Following it up, the Drafting Committee inserted in its report clause 25, which read as follows:

(1) 'The right to move the Supreme Court by appropriate proceedings for the enforcement of the rights conferred by this part is guaranteed.
(2) The Supreme Court shall have power to issue directions or orders in the nature of writs of *habeas corpus, mandamus, prohibition, quo warranto,* and *certiorari,* whichever may be appropriate for the enforcement of any of the rights conferred by this Part.
(3) Parliament may by law empower any other court to exercise within the local limits of its jurisdiction all or any of the powers exercisable by the Supreme Court under clause (2) of this Article.
(4) The rights guaranteed by this article shall not be suspended except otherwise provided for by this Constitution.'[3]

The draft provision was fully discussed in the Constituent Assembly. Explaining the importance and significance of the provision, **Dr. Ambedkar** observed,

'If I was asked to name any particular Article in the Constitution as the most important—I could not refer to any other Article except this one (Article 32). It is the very heart of it and I am glad that the House has realized its importance. I prefer the British method of dealing with rights. The British method is a peculiar method, a very real and a very sound method. British jurisprudence insists that there can be no right unless the Constitution provides a remedy for it. It is the remedy that makes a right real. If there is no remedy, there is no right at all, and I am therefore not prepared to burden the Constitution with a number of pious declarations which may sound as glittering generalities but for which the Constitution makes no provision by way of a remedy. It is much better to make them real by enunciating remedies rather than to have a lot of pious wishes embodied in the Constitution.'[4]

While explaining the various prerogative writs in the Constituent Assembly, Dr. Ambedkar said that these remedies were not new as *habeas corpus* existed in the Code of Criminal Procedure and *mandamus* found a place in the Specific Relief Act, 1877. After having discussed in detail in the Constituent Assembly, about the writ remedies, Dr. Ambedkar and Naziruddin Ahmed moved the above clause for voting with certain amendments and it was adopted and renumbered as Article 32 of the Constitution.

3. Shiva Rao, Framing of India's Constitution, Vol. I–B.
4. Constituent Assembly Debates, Vol. VII, p. 952.

Therefore, the enumeration of specific rights in Part III of the Constitution does not necessarily mean that there are no "rights" recognized outside the list. The only effect of the actual provisions made is that the Supreme Court cannot be moved by independent proceedings, under Article 32, for the enforcement of any unenumerated rights. An aggrieved party, can, however, move the High Court concerned, under Article 226, for the enforcement of such rights. Article 226 is wider in its scope and gives power to a High Court to issue writs, directions or orders for the enforcement of any of the rights conferred by Part III and for any other purpose.

The only change made by the Constituent Assembly in the draft provision is to improve the language of clause (2) of Article 32, which says "directions, orders or writs, including writs in the nature of *habeas corpus, mandamus, prohibition, quo warranto and certiorari* ..." To a proposal that clause (4) of the Article should be deleted, **Dr. Ambedkar** gave a firm refusal and said:

> *"I know of no Constitution which gave fundamental rights but which gives them in such a manner as to deprive the State in times of emergency to protect itself by curtailing the rights of the individual".*

In certain cases where, for instance, the State's very life is in jeopardy, those rights must be subject to a certain amount of limitation.

"Normal peaceful times are quite different from times of emergency".

Hence, the special provisions made for emergency suspension of "rights" in Article 358 and 359. The first Article remains power to the State in an emergency to suspend only the rights of freedom conferred by Article 19, but no other "rights". The second Article gives power to the President in an emergency to make an order suspending the extraordinary legal remedies provided in respect of fundamental rights.

About Writ Jurisdiction of High Courts

Talking about the powers of issuance of prerogative writs by the High Courts, Alladi Krishnaswami Ayyar and Shri K.M. Munshi said that under the law as it stood, only the High Courts of Bombay, Madras and Bengal had the right to issue prerogative writs within the limits of their ordinary original jurisdiction. Other High Courts did not have this power, nor did the power of the three courts extend beyond the towns of Mumbai, Madras or Calcutta, where they exercised original jurisdiction. The new Constitution for a free India would be a king of charter, containing the fundamental rights of citizens, and the intention of the first proposal of Alladi Krishnaswami Ayyar was that all the High Courts should for this purpose have within their jurisdiction powers to issue writs. This proposal, alongwith other two proposals was accepted by Shri Vallabhbhai Patel, the Chairman of the Provincial Constitution Committee and adopted by the Assembly. This is how Article 226 came into existence.[5]

5. B. Shiva Rao, Framing of India's Constitution, Vol. I, pp. 307-09.

Dr. Ambedkar's further views on prerogative writ remedy:

Explaining the nature and scope of the remedies specified in Article 32 and Article 226, Dr. Ambedkar stated that the object was to give general power to the Supreme Court and the High Court as well as to specify particular remedies. He added:

> *'While the power of the Supreme Court to issue orders and directions are there, the draft Constitution has thought it desirable to mention these particular writs. Now, the necessity for mentioning and making reference to these particular writs is quite obvious. These writs have been in existence in Great Britain for a number of years. Their nature and the remedies that they provided are known to every lawyer and consequently we thought that as it is impossible even for a man who has the most fertile imagination to invent something new, it was hardly possible to improve upon the writs which have been in existence for probably thousands of years and which gave complete satisfaction to every Englishman with regard to the protection of his freedom. We therefore thought that a situation such as the one which existed in the English jurisprudence which contained these writs and which, if I may say so, have been found to be knave-proof and fool-proof, ought to be mentioned by their name in the Constitution without prejudice to the right of the Supreme Court to do justice in some other way if it felt it was desirable to do so....'*[6]

While explaining the nature of writs as provided under the Constitution of India, **Dr. Ambedkar** observed:

> *'Anyone who knows anything about the English Law will realize and understand that the writs which are referred to in the Article fall into two categories. They are called in one sense prerogative writs, in the other case they are called writs in action. A writ of mandamus, a writ of prohibition, a writ of certiorari can be used or applied for both: it can be used as a prerogative writ or it may be applied for by a litigant in the course of a suit or proceeding. The importance of these writs which are given by this article lies in the fact that they are prerogative writs; they can be sought for by an aggrieved party without bringing any proceeding or suit. Ordinarily you must first file a suit before you can get any kind of order from the court whether the order is of the nature of mandamus, prohibition or certiorari or anything of the kind. But here, so far as this article is concerned without filing any proceeding you can straightaway go to the court and apply for the writ. The object of the writ is really to grant what I may call interim relief. For instance, if a man is arrested, without filing a suit or proceeding against the officer who arrests him, he can file petition to the court for setting him at liberty. It is not for him to first file a suit or a proceeding against the officer. In a proceeding of this kind were the*

6. Constituent Assembly Debates, 1948, Vol. III, p. 952.

> *application is for a prerogative writ all that the court can do is to ascertain whether the arrest is in accordance with law. The court at that stage will not enter into the question whether the law under which a person is arrested is a good law or a bad law, whether it conflicts with any of the provisions of the Constitution or whether it does not conflict. All that the court can require in a habeas corpus proceeding is whether the arrest is lawful and will not enter into the question—at least that is the practice of the court—of the merits of the law. When a person is actually arrested and his trial has commenced it is in the course of those proceedings that the court would be entitled to go into the facts and come to a decision whether a particular law under which a person is arrested is a good law or a bad law. Then the court will go into the question whether it conflicts with the provisions of the Constitution. Consequently, the amendment moved by my friend Shri V.S. Sarwate, if I may say so, is quite out of place. It is not here that such a provision should be made. If he refers to Article 115 (now 139) he will find that provision for similar writs has been made there. But those writs which could be issued in connection with questions of fact and law. They would certainly be investigated by the courts.'*[7]

Importance of Article 12 in writ remedy before the Supreme Court

Alongwith Articles 32 of the Constitution of India, Article 12 plays significant role so far as the issuance of writ of *mandamus* for the enforcement of or protection of fundamental rights are concerned. As per Article 12, the extra-ordinary remedy of writ of *mandamus* is available only against certain persons/authorities *viz.* Union and State Governments, Public Officials, Parliament and State Legislatures, Local Authorities and Other Authorities. Except the term "other authorities" law regarding issuance of writ of *mandamus* is very certain. The view of the Supreme Court regarding the interpretation of the term "other authorities" has changed consistently since Rajasthan Electricity Board case to Ajay Hasia's case. Still, there is further scope of expansion of the scope of issuance of writ of *mandamus* only in the direction of the term 'other authorities'. Therefore, an effort can be made so as to widen the scope of issuance of writ of *mandamus* in this direction only.

But, it is pertinent to note here that every time it is not necessary while issuing writ under Article 226 by High Court to see as to whether the respondent falls within the definition of "State" as defined under Article 12 or not. Under Article 226 of the Constitution of India, every High Court of State is given powers to issue writ, order or direction including writ of or in the nature of *Habeas Corpus, Mandamus, Certiorari, Prohibition* or *Quo Warranto* in the event or violation of fundamental rights or otherwise. The term "otherwise" makes it specifically clear that the High Court has power to issue writs in the event of violation of fundamental rights or even in case of violation of constitutional rights, statutory rights

7. Constituent Assembly Debates, 1948 Vol. III, p. 952.

or common law rights. When the duty discharged by the respondent is of public nature, the writ of *mandamus* can be issued by a High Court, though the respondent may not fall under the definition of "state" under Article 12 of the Constitution. Therefore, we can say that the definition of "state" under Article 12 is mandatory to be followed by the Supreme Court only, whereas the High Court can issue writ of *mandamus* even in case where the respondent is not covered under the definition of "State".

3.1 *MANDAMUS* AGAINST UNION OF INDIA

Under the English law *mandamus* could not issue against the *Crown* or the servants of the *Crown* acting as such. So also, *mandamus* could not issue under the English law against the Government in the absence of statutory power in that behalf. (The relevant cases are discussed in the chapter 3.2: *Mandamus* against State Governments).

No *Mandamus* against the President of India and a Governor of a State

In our Constitution such kind of immunity is given to the President of India or Governor of State. No writ of *mandamus* can be issued against the President of India or Governor of State as per Article 361 of the Constitution of India. Whatever acts done by the President in exercise and performance of the powers and duties of his office are not amenable to the writ jurisdiction.

But, under Article 32 and Article 226 of the Constitution of India, it is expressly provided that the writs mentioned therein can be issued against any authority including in appropriate cases any Government, i.e. Central or State Government. As per our Constitution, it is the responsibility of the Government to see that the people in the country can effectively enjoy fundamental rights. Hence, maximum numbers of writs of *mandamus* in our country are against the Government, i.e. Union of India or State Governments. The law is well established from the contents of Articles 32 and 226 that writ of *mandamus* is maintainable against the Union. Our law of writs has developed more than the English law, which does not permit the issuance of writ of *mandamus* against the *Crown* nor against government itself. It happens in our country that the most of the fundamental rights are violated by the Government or its servants and by taking into consideration this aspect the framers of the Constitution made it clear that the writs including *mandamus* shall be maintainable against the Government as well. Several examples are given in order to demonstrate that the *mandamus* can be issued against Union.

The study of the cases of issuance of *mandamus* against the Union of India would be after the commencement of the Constitution, i.e. after 1950 as there was nothing like Government of India prior to independence. The writ was issued against different States by the Chartered High Courts at Bombay, Madras and Calcutta. The law regarding issuing of *mandamus* against Union has become very well established and undisputed in our country.

From the following cases of issuance of *mandamus* against Union of India, the position under the Constitutional Law of India becomes crystal clear:

Chiranjit Lal Chaudhari v. Union of India[8]

This was perhaps the first important case dealt with by the Supreme Court on the subject of equality of law under Article 14 of the Constitution. It was arisen out of an application presented by the petitioner, a shareholder for a writ of *mandamus* and certain other reliefs were demanded under Article 32 of the Constitution. The facts of the case are narrated here below.

The Sholapur Spinning and Weaving Company Limited was a company incorporated under the Indian Companies Act, with its registered office within the State of Bombay. On 27th July 1949, the Directors of the Company gave a notice to the workers that the mills would be closed and pursuant to that notice, the mills were in fact closed on the 31st August following. On the 9th January, 1950 the Governor-General of India promulgated an Ordinance which purported to make special provisions for the proper management and administration of the Company. It was stated in the preamble to the Ordinance:

> *'On account of mismanagement and neglect, a situation has arisen in the affairs of the Sholapur Spinning and Weaving Company Limited which has prejudicially affected the production of an essential commodity and has caused serious unemployment amongst certain section of the community.'*

Section 3 of the Ordinance empowered the Central Government to appoint by notified order as many persons as it thinks fit, to be Directors of the Company for the purpose of taking over its management and administration and to appoint one of such Directors to be the Chairman. Section 4 of the Ordinance provided that on the issue of a notified order under Section 3 all the Directors of the Company holding office as such immediately before the issue of the order shall be deemed to have vacated their offices, and any existing agent thereof shall be deemed to have terminated. The powers and the duties of the Directors were specified in section 5 and this section *inter alia* empowered the Directors to vary or cancel, with the previous sanction of the Central Government, any contract or agreement entered into between the Company and any other person if they were satisfied that such contract or agreement was detrimental to the interests of the Company. Section 10 laid down that no compensation for premature termination of any contract could be claimed by the managing agents or any other contracting party. Section 12 provided that so long as the management of the statutory Directors continued, the shareholders would be precluded from nominating or appointing any person to be a

8. AIR 1951 SC 41.

Director of the Company and any resolution passed by them would not be effective unless it was approved of by the Central Government. It was laid down further that during that period, no proceeding for winding up of the Company, or for appointment of receiver in respect thereof could be instituted in any Court unless it was sanctioned by the Central Government, and the Central Government would competent to impose any restrictions or limitations as regards application of the provisions of the Indian Companies Act to the affairs of the company. Under Section 16, the Central Government could, by notified order, direct that all or any of the powers exercisable by it under that Ordinance could be exercised by the Government of Bombay. The Central Government in accordance with the said provision did delegate all its powers exercisable under the Ordinance to the Government of Bombay.

On 7th April, 1950, the Ordinance was repealed and an Act was passed by the Parliament of India, known as the Sholapur Spinning and Weaving Company (Emergency Provisions) Act, which re-enacted almost in identical terms all the provisions of the Ordinance and provided further that all actions taken and orders made under the Ordinance would be deemed to have been taken or made under the corresponding provisions of the Act. The preamble to the Ordinance was not, however, reproduced in the Act. The constitutional validity of both the Ordinance and the Act was challenged amongst others, on the ground that the enactment denied to the Company and its share-holders equality before law, and equal protection of laws and thus offended against the provisions of Article 14 of the Constitution. The contention of the petitioner was that the Act was a piece of legislation directed against his company alone, was palpably discriminatory and hostile in character, and unreasonably arbitrary. A majority of three Judges of the Court held that a legislation relating to one individual or corporation would not per se violate the equality right, that it was for the petitioner to prove to their satisfaction that the selection for such treatment of a particular body corporate, to the exclusion of others, was unreasonable and arbitrary, and that, inasmuch as the petitioner failed so to prove, the Court could not hold that Article 14 of the Constitution had been violated. By making such observation the Supreme Court, by majority of 3:2 denied to issue writ of *mandamus*.

The important question involved was that who should seek redress by way of filing petition for writ of *mandamus* under Article 32 in such circumstances, a majority of three Judges expressed the view that, in so far as the petitioner's rights as a shareholder were curtailed he was entitled to apply for relief in his own right on the ground that the Act denied him the equal protection of laws and therefore contravened Article 14, even though the other share-holders did not join him in the application.

Sohan Lal v. Union of India[9]

It was held in the above case by the Supreme Court that *mandamus*

9. AIR 1957 SC 532.

may be issued against the Union of India if a displaced person has been evicted from his property in contravention of the Public Premises (Eviction) Act, by the Union of India and the property is in the possession of the latter. But no remedy by way of a writ under Article 226 is available against the Government, if the property is in the possession of another displaced person, who entered into possession without its knowledge that the eviction was illegal and without any collusion with the Union of India.

Supreme Court Advocates-on-Records Association v. Union of India[10]

In a writ petition filed by the petitioner Association the allegations were made regarding the non-performance of its public duty by public authority. Further the petitioner tried to show that the public authority had failed to perform its constitutional or statutory duty. A question was put in the aforesaid writ petition as to why such public authority should not be directed by writ of *mandamus* to perform its duties. It was held that in order for a *mandamus* to issue to compel performance of duty, it must clearly appear from the language of the statute that a duty was imposed, the matter of mere discretion. But even in cases where the duty is discretionary, as distinct from a statutory obligation, a limited *mandamus* could issue directing the public authority to exercise its discretion within a reasonable time on sound legal principles and not merely on whim. While giving an example the Supreme Court said that if the executive which is charged with a duty under the Constitution to undertake a periodical review of the Judge-strength, fails in the performance of that duty, an order of *mandamus* can lie to compel performance within a reasonable time.

From the commencement of the Constitution, till today, there is no change regarding the position in law so far as issuance of writs against the Central Government, i.e. Union of India is concerned. Under Article 226 as well as under Article 32, the High Court and the Supreme Court of India respectively are having power to issue *mandamus* against the Union of India.

Saurabh Chaudhari v. Union of India[11]

(*mandamus* not issued)

In a writ petition filed by the petitioner before the Supreme Court under Article 32 of the Constitution a relief was sought against the Central Government for making a law by issuance of *mandamus*. Three Judges' bench of the Supreme Court in while delivering judgment expressed the opinion that the courts are normally reluctant to issue any direction to the Central Government for making law. Therefore, instead of issuing any direction in that regard it is hoped and trusted that the Central Government would expeditiously consider making of a legislation or taking such steps

10. (1993) 4 SCC 441.
11. (2003) 11 SCC 146.

as are necessary in that behalf keeping in view the requirement of coordination in higher education in terms of Entry 66 List I of the Seventh Schedule.

Thus, the Supreme Court did not issue *mandamus* to the Central Government directing it to enact a legislation, it expected from the Central Government to do needful.

Union of India v. Naveen Jindal[12]

An appeal was preferred by the Union of India against the judgment of the High Court in a writ petition filed under Article 26 by the present respondent. The question for consideration was whether the right to fly the National Flag by Indian citizen is a fundamental right within the meaning of Article 19(1)(a) of the Constitution of India or not. The respondent herein, Naveen Jindal was a Joint Managing Director of a public limited company incorporated under the Companies Act. He being in charge of the said company situated at Raigarh in Madhya Pradesh was flying National Flag at the office premises of his factory. He was not allowed to do so by the Government officials on the ground that the same was impermissible under the Flag Code of India. Against this restriction, the respondent filed writ petition before the High Court on the ground that no law could prohibit flying of National Flag by Indian citizens. Flying of National Flag with respect and dignity being fundamental right, the Flag Code which contains only executive instructions of the Government of India and, thus, being not a law, cannot be considered to have imposed reasonable restrictions in respect thereof within the meaning of clause 2 of Article 19 of the Constitution of India. The High Court accepted the arguments of the respondent and held that—

- The question as to whether the provisions of the Emblems and Names (Prevention of Improper Use) Act, 1950 have been violated or not is a matter which would fall for determination of the Court of law and not by the executive.
- The restrictions imposed by the Flag Code on flying the National Flag being not law within the meaning of Article 19(2) of the Constitution of India, the same cannot be construed to be a penal provision.
- However, if contravention of any of those instructions and guidelines had been issued under the aforesaid 1950 Act or under the Prevention of Insults to National Honour Act, 1971, the same would constitute a penal offence.
- Referring to the debates held in the Constituent Assembly as also a passage from the book titled "Our National Flag" by K.V. Singh, the High Court observed that the citizens were required to be educated by issue of Flag Code and the National Flag must

12. AIR 2004 SC 1559.

be flown in a respectful manner and so long as a citizen of India does so, no restriction can be imposed on the basis of instructions contained in the Flag Code.

The Union of India preferred appeal before the Supreme Court against the decision of the High Court. By critically examining the facts of the cases and various judgments pertaining to the fundamental right of freedom of speech and expressions along with reasonable restrictions imposed upon it, the Supreme Court (Per V.N. Khare, C.J.) came to the conclusion that right to fly a National Flag with respect and dignity is a fundamental right under Article 19(1)(a) of the Constitution of India and the Central Government or its officers had no right to put any restriction upon it. Thus, indirectly it was held that the Madhya Pradesh High Court was right in issuing writ of *mandamus* against the Union of India.

Union of India v. S.B. Vohra[13]

In an appeal filed by the Union of India against the judgment of the High Court in a writ petition under Article 226 of the Constitution of India involving a question that how far and to what extent a writ of or in the nature of *mandamus* should issue directing the Union of India to pay salary to the officers of the High Court in a particular scale of pay. The respondents were the Assistant Registrars of the Delhi High Court. The recommendations for revision of the scales of the respondents were made by the Chief Justice of the Delhi High Court vide his letter based upon the report of a committee constituted by the Chief Justice. But the said recommendation was not implemented hence the writ petition was filed.

In a writ petition filed by the respondents before the Delhi High Court, the present appellants herein contended that the Assistant Registrars should not have been placed in a higher scale of pay of Rs. 3000-4500 as the Fourth Pay Commission. Further it recommended the scale of pay of Superintendent, Court Master and Private Secretary as also the Assistant Registrar at Rs. 2000-3500 and thus it must have given a go-bye to the old relativities and treated both categories of the post as equal or merged. The Delhi High Court refused to accept the contention of the appellants.

An appeal was filed by the appellants being aggrieved by the Judgment of the Delhi High Court. It was held by the Supreme Court that no standard can be laid down exhaustively as to in what situation a writ of *mandamus* would be issue and in what situation it would not. It added that the High Court should not, ordinarily issue a writ of or in the nature of *mandamus* and ought to refer the matter relating to fixation/revision of pay of its officers back to the Central/State Government with suitable directions pointing out the irrelevant factors which are required to be excluded in taking the decision and the relevant factors which are required to be considered therefore. The Supreme Court, lastly added that the High

13. AIR 2004 SC 1402.

Court should in an exceptional circumstances, interfere in its judicial side with care and caution.

The Supreme Court also said that the Chief Justice of the High Court was not bound to accept plea of Central Government that the posts of Assistant Registrar and Court Masters should be merged. The question as regard to merger of the two posts was within the exclusive domain of the Chief Justice. Whether the post of Assistant Registrar should be a promotional post or not, thus, could not fall for the decision of the Central Government. The Supreme Court with these observations dismissed the appeal.

Union of India v. C. Krishna Reddy[14]

An appeal was filed by special leave by the Union of India against the judgment and order of the Division Bench of Madras High Court in a writ petition whereby the order passed by a learned Single Judge directing the appellant herein to pay Rs. 25 lakhs in addition to the sum of Rs. 10 lakhs already paid by way of reward for giving information to custom authorities.

As per the facts of the case, the Supreme Court observed that the scheme or the policy of the Government of India regarding grant of reward to informer and Government servants assisting the Government in seizure of contraband goods and detection of evasion of duty made it clear that the authority was competent to grant the reward. The scheme specifically mentioned that the reward was an *ex-gratia* payment and subject to the guidelines and might be granted on the absolute discretion of the authority competent and further that no one could claim the reward as a matter of right.

The Supreme Court was of the opinion that the High Court in writ jurisdiction could not examine or weigh the various factors which had to be taken into consideration while deciding a claim regarding grant of reward. These are matters exclusively within the domain of the authorities of the department as they alone could weigh and examine the usefulness or otherwise of the information given by the informer. In the writ petition filed by the respondent-claimant no details had been given on the relevant issues. The reward could not be claimed as a matter of right. Thus, no writ of *Mandamus* could be issued by the High Court, commanding the Government to give a particular amount by way of reward.

The Supreme Court said that the issuance of writ of *mandamus* in such cases by the learned single Judge of a High Court directing the Union of India to pay Rs. 25 lakhs in addition to Rs. 10 lakhs, the amount of reward already paid was not proper. In appeal the Division Bench of the High Court modified the order and directed the present appellant to pay Rs. 5 lakhs within three weeks from the date of the passing of order, with the remark that the failure to comply with the order passed by the Division

14. AIR 2004 SC 1194.

Bench within stipulated time, the department would be liable to pay the amount as directed by the single judge. In this situation, the Supreme Court observed that passing of such peremptory orders would be illegal. Thus, the Supreme Court set aside both the orders passed by the learned single Judge and the Division Bench of the High Court by allowing the appeal filed by the Union of India.

Analysis and Inferences

From the above mentioned discussion it is obvious that *mandamus* can be issued against Union, i.e. Central Government. In this area, we have traveled ahead from British system in a sense that in England writ could not be issued against the *Crown* or his servants; whereas in India writ is maintainable against the Union Government and its servants. There is no dispute regarding this point and it is well-established law that writ of *mandamus* is maintainable against Union of India. Only the exception is that *mandamus* cannot be issued upon the Union of India directing it to enact a legislation.

3.2 *MANDAMUS* AGAINST STATE GOVERNMENTS

As per the English law *mandamus* will not issue if the claim of the applicant is against the government, and he wants to obtain a *mandamus* against the officer representing the government or the government directly. Issuance of writ of *mandamus* against *Crown* in England is specifically barred under the *Halsbury's Laws of England*. It is observed,

> *'As no Court can compel the Sovereign to perform any duty, no writ of mandamus will lie to the Crown. Where it is sought to establish a right against the Crown the appropriate procedure is by way of petition of right. Nor will the writ lie against a Secretary of State in his capacity as an agent for the Crown; for in that capacity he is responsible to the Crown alone, and is under no legal duty towards a subject. He is acting in such a capacity when carrying out the provisions of a royal warrant.'*[15]

Justice Coleridge observed in the case of Baron de Bode regarding issuance of *mandamus* against the Government as follows:

> *'But, against the servants of the Crown, as such, and merely to enforce the satisfaction of claims upon the Crown, it is an established rule that mandamus will not lie. I call this an established rule. I believe it has never been broken in upon.'*[16]

15. Halsbury's Laws of England Hailsham's Edition, Vol. 9, para. 1293.
16. (1838) 6 DR 776, quoted in AIR 1936 PC 269.

The Queen v. Lords Commissioners of Treasury[17]

In the above case Rule was issued calling upon the Lords of Treasury to show cause why a writ of *mandamus* should not issue commanding them to issue a Treasury minute or authority to the pay master of civil contingencies or other proper officer, directing and authorizing him to pay or caused to be paid to the treasurer of the County palatine of Lancaster certain sum specified in a schedule annexed.

It was held that a *mandamus* would not lie, in as much as the Lords of Treasury received the money, which was granted to *Her Majesty,* as Servants of the *Crown,* and no duty was imposed upon them as between them and the persons to whom money was payable.

While refusing to entertain writ of *mandamus* against the Lords of Treasury, being a Servant of the *Crown,* **Cockburn, C.J.** observed,

> '*... Although the Lords of Treasury have made a very great mistake, and although the present state of things is of the most anomalous and most unsatisfactory character, I regret to say, according to the true principle upon which this prerogative jurisdiction ever has been and ought to be exercised, I do not see that this Court has authority to issue this writ of mandamus ....*'

Millor, J. in this case also expressed the same opinion and the following quotation from his views are important:

> "*.... And therefore I am clearly of the opinion that we cannot issue this mandamus commanding the servants of the Crown, who hold the money and whose duty it is to distribute it pursuant to the obligations which they owe to the Crown, to pay this money, or to take the steps which this rule calls upon them to perform.*"

The Queen v. The Commissioners of Inland Revenue (In re NATHAN)[18]

Statute provided for the return by the Commissioners of Stamps and Taxes of probate duty on proof by oath and proper vouchers to their satisfaction of the payment of debts of the deceased, whereby the amount of probate duty payable on the estate is reduced below the amount which has been paid. By a subsequent Act the Commissioners of Inland Revenue are substituted for the Commissioners of Stamps and Taxes. On an application by an administrator for a *mandamus* to the commissioners to pay to the applicant the amount of duty overpaid by him, on the ground that he had supplied evidence of overpayment and had no other legal remedy.

It was held that the *mandamus* ought not to issue, for the statute created no duty between the commissioners and the applicant, whose remedy, if the decision of the commissioners could be reviewed, was by

17. 1872 Q.B. 387.
18. (1884) Vol. 12, Q.B. 461.

petition of right. Thus, *mandamus* was refused on the ground of alternative remedy, i.e. petition of right. Otherwise this case was distinguished from the ratio laid down in earlier case of *R. v. Lords Commissioners of the Treasury*.

In this case while expressing his opinion **Day, J.** said,

> '...*We are not, therefore, directing a mandamus to issue to the commissioners qua servants of the Crown, but to them as under a statutable duty to the applicant which they have not discharged. It is said that we are not at liberty to direct the issue of writ of mandamus, even if we have authority to do so, because, by recognized practice, such a writ never issues when there is another specific legal remedy.* ....'

The following ratio has been reiterated by **Charles, J.** in the case of ***R. v. Secretary of State for War***[19] showing strong objecting against issuance of writ of *mandamus* in his words,

> '*That there can be no mandamus to the Sovereign, there can be no doubt, both because there would be an incongruity in the Queen commanding herself to do an act, and also because disobedience to the writ of mandamus is to be enforced by attachment.*
>
> *There are, no doubt cases where servants of the Crown have been constituted by Statute agents to do particular acts, and in those cases a mandamus would lie against them as individuals designated to do those acts. But mandamus cannot be directed to the Crown* ....'

Position under the Specific Relief Act, 1877

The provision regarding issuance of writ of *mandamus* was given under the Specific Relief Act, 1877 prior to the commencement of the Constitution of India, wherein the High Court had power to issue order of *mandamus*. The texts of Sec. 45 and Sec. 46 are reproduced herewith[20]:

Sec. 45: Power to order public servants and others to do certain specific acts.

> '*Any of the High Courts of judicature at Calcutta, Madras and Bombay may make and order requiring any specific act to be done or forborne, within the local limits of its ordinary original civil jurisdiction, by any person holding a public office, whether of a permanent or a temporary nature, or by any corporation or inferior Court of Judicature:*
>
> provided—
>
> *(a) that an application for such order be made by some person whose property, franchise or personal right would be injured by the forbearing or doing (as the case may be) of the said specific act;*

19. (1891) 2 QB 326.
20. Specific Relief Act, 1877 by Mulla and Pollock.

(b) *that such doing or forbearing is, under any law for the time being in force, clearly incumbent on such person or Court in his or its public character, or on such corporation in its corporate character;*

(c) *that in the opinion of the High Court such doing or forbearing is consonant to right and justice;*

(d) *that the applicant has no other specific and adequate legal remedy; and*

(e) *that the remedy given by the order applied for will be complete.*

Exceptions from such powers:

Nothing in this section shall be deemed to authorize any High Court—

(f) *to make any order binding the Central Government or any State Government;*

(g) *to make any order on any servant of the Government, as such, merely to enforce the satisfaction of a claim upon the Government; or*

(h) *to make any order which is otherwise expressly excluded by any law for the time being in force.'*

Sec. 46. Application how made:

'Every application under Section 45 must be founded on an affidavit of the person injured, stating his right in the matter in question, his demand of justice and the denial thereof; and the High Court may, in its discretion, make the order applied for absolute in the first instance, or refuse it, or grant a rule to show cause why the order applied for should not be made.'

Procedure thereon:

'If in the last case, the person, Court or corporation complained of shows no sufficient Order in alternative, cause, the High Court may first make an order in the alternative, either to do or forbear the act mentioned in the order, or to signify some reason to the contrary and make an answer thereto by such day as the High Court fixes in this behalf.'[21]

The above mentioned provisions have been omitted in the new Specific Relief Act, 1963 upon the recommendations given in the Ninth Report of the Law Commission. As per the report of the Law Commission, Sections 45-51 of the Specific Relief Act, 1877 became inapplicable and practically useless after the commencement of the Constitution of India. On the other hand, these sections found to be

21. Specific Relief Act, 1877 by Mulla and Pollock.

inconsistent with the powers of writ given to the High Court under Article 226 of the Constitution of India.

Therefore, the Law Commission constrained to recommend to omit the aforesaid provisions. The comments regarding the texts of Secs. 45 and 46 of the Specific Relief Act, 1877 is as under:

> *'Chapter VIII (Sections 45-51) provides for an order in the nature of mandamus. In view of Art. 226 of the Constitution, there would appear to be no need for retaining this Chapter. The scope of section 45 of the Act is narrower than that of Art. 226. In fact, clauses (f) and (g) of the proviso to section 45 are inconsistent with Art. 226 and section 50 which was substituted by the Adaptation order, 1950, practically renders these clauses nugatory.*
>
> *It was urged that while evidence can be taken in a proceeding under section 45, the High Courts while exercising jurisdiction under Art. 226 are generally averse to investigating disputed facts by taking evidence. But there is nothing in Art. 226 to prevent their doing so. In fact, we find that just as the Rules framed under section 45 confer discretionary power upon the High Court to take evidence, so the Rules framed under Art. 226 by a number of High Courts, such as those of Orissa, Mysore, Madhya Pradesh, Allahabad, Rajasthan, Bombay and Assam confer similar discretionary power on the Court to take evidence, oral or documentary. For instance, Rule 7 of the Rules framed by Orissa High Court says—*
>
> *'All questions arising for determination under this Chapter shall ordinarily be decided upon affidavits but the Court may direct that such questions as it may consider necessary be decided on such other evidence as it may deem fit. Where the Court orders that certain matters in controversy between the parties shall be decided on such evidence, the procedure prescribed in the Code of Civil Procedure, 1908, for the trial of suits shall, so far as applicable, be followed.*
>
> *We recommend that Sections 45-51 be omitted, and questions such as that of taking evidence be left to the rule-making power of the High Courts, and that Rules similar to the aforesaid Rule of the Orissa High Court may be framed by those High Courts which have not made similar rules.'*

The effect of clause (f) of Sec. 45 of the Specific Relief Act, 1877 (Pre-constitution era) an order under Sec. 45 could not be issued against the government, Central or provincial or against the Secretary of State, or the *Crown* Representative. Even, under the clause as adapted after the Constitution, an order under the section could not be issued against the Central Government or the Government of any State. The above provisions, like the other provisions, of Sec. 45, are based upon the principles of English law relating to *mandamus*.

Under the English law *mandamus* could not be issued against the *Crown* or the servants of the *Crown*. In the case of *R. v. Treasury Lords*

Commissioners,[22] while deciding the case against *Crown*, it was observed,

> *"As no Court can compel the Sovereign to perform any duty, no writ of mandamus will lie to the Crown. There would be incongruity in Queen commanding herself."*

So also, *mandamus* could not issue under the English law against the Government in the absence of statutory power in that behalf.

Position after the commencement of Constitution of India

Under Article 32 of the Constitution of India, *mandamus* can be issued against the State Government in the event of violation of fundamental rights. Also, under Article 226, it is expressly provided that the writs mentioned therein can be issued against any Authority including in appropriate case any Government. Thus, a writ of *mandamus* can issue under the Constitution of India against the State Government. The following cases would make is clear that writ of *mandamus* can be issued against the State Government.

Chintaman Rao v. State of M.P.[23]

This is a case wherein the petitioners have filed under Article 32 of the Supreme Court for the enforcement of their fundamental rights under Article 19(1)(g) of the Constitution of India. The petitioners were proprietor and an employee respectively of a bidi manufacturing concern of District Sagar of Madhya Pradesh State. It was contended that the law in force in the State authorizing it to prohibit the manufacture of bidies in certain villages including the ones wherein the petitioners reside was inconsistent with the provisions of Part III of the Constitution of India.

The Central Provinces and Berar Regulation of Manufacture of Bidis (Agricultural Purposes) Act, 1948 was the law in force in the State at the time of commencement of the Constitution. Sections 3 and 4 thereof were prohibiting the manufacture of bidis in agricultural seasons in certain villages. The Deputy Commissioner was given power by the aforesaid law to fix the period of agricultural seasons by Notification. During the notified agricultural seasons no person residing in the specified area was permitted to manufacture bidis nor anyone could employ the persons to manufacture bidis.

The petitioners have challenged this notification and the provisions of the said Act alleging that they had nothing to do with agriculture and they were not connected with the agricultural produce. Still, however, they were deprived from manufacturing bidis. This restriction therefore, violates Article 19(1)(g) of the Constitution and it did not fall within the reasonable restrictions defined in clause (6) of Article 19(2). A bench comprising of five

22. (1872) LR 7 Q.B.
23. AIR 1951 SC 118.

judges accepted the arguments of the petitioners and in its judgment (Per Mahajan, J.) observed in paragraph 8,

> *'....There seems no reason for prohibiting them from carrying on this occupation. The statute as it stands, not only compels those who can be engaged in agricultural work from not taking to other avocations, but it also prohibits persons who have no connection or relation to agricultural operations from engaging in the business of bidi making and thus earning their livelihood. These provisions of the statute, in our opinion, cannot be said to amount to reasonable restrictions on the right of the applicants and that being so, the statute is not in conformity with the provisions of Part III of the Constitution....'*

After having made aforesaid observations, the Supreme Court declared the order issued by the Deputy Commissioner prohibiting the manufacture of bidis as void, inoperative and ineffective. Further the Supreme Court also gave direction to the respondents not to enforce the provisions contained in section 4 of the said Act against the petitioners.

State of Punjab v. Ajaib Singh[24]

Initially, a writ petition was filed before the Bombay High Court alleging the violation of Article 19 of the Constitution of India by the original petitioner Ajaib Singh. In Bombay High Court it was held by Khosla and Harnam Singh, JJ. that a citizen of India who is detained in a camp under section 4 of the Abducted Persons (Recovery and Restoration) Act, 1949, cannot be said to have been deprived of the rights guaranteed by Article 19. Bhandari, J., however, agreed that the impugned Act did not contravene sub-clauses (d), (e) and (f) of Article 19(1). His argument was that it is a fundamental right of a citizen of India to stay within the territory of India, for clause (g) of Article 19(1) declares in express terms that he has a right to practice any profession or to carry on any occupation, trade or business. This right would be meaningless if it does not include a right to stay in the country for a live. If the constitution has stated expressly or by necessary implication that a citizen shall not be expelled from India it would not be open to Parliament to frame a statute so as entirely to defeat the object of the constitution by directing that he shall be expelled under escort of the police. Nor is it open to Government to state that the taking away of a citizen from India to Pakistan is no worse than taking a prisoner from one prison to another. It is a well-known legal maxim that whatever is prohibited by law to be done directly cannot legally be effected by an indirect and circuitous contrivance. For all practical purposes, a person who is "conveyed out" of India under the provisions of Section 7 is deprived of the rights guaranteed under Article 19(1)(g) of the Constitution.

24. AIR 1953 SC 10.

In the appeal filed by the State Government, the Supreme Court negatived the view of Justice Bhandari and held that the provisions of the impugned Act were *intra vires* and the same were not inconsistent with the freedoms given under Article 19 of the Constitution.

Ramprasad v. State of Bihar[25]

In this case the provisions of the Bihar Sathi Lands (Restoration) Act were challenged and the same declared invalid by the Supreme Court. Writ of *mandamus* issued by the Supreme Court directing State Government not to take any steps in pursuance of the Act or to interfere with the appellant's possession.

K.N. Guruswamy v. State of Mysore[26]

A writ petition under Article 32 of the Constitution was filed by the petitioner against the improper cancellation of bid to obtain licence to sell liquor for the year 1953-54. A liquor contract was knocked down in an auction by the Deputy Commissioner in favour of 'A', who was the highest bidder. B who was present at the auction but did not bid, saw the Excise Commissioner and offered Rs. 5000 in excess of A's bid. B's offer was accepted and A's bid was cancelled. Subsequently, the Deputy Commissioner informed A of the cancellation and accepted B's bid under Excise Commissioner's orders.

The Appeal was filed against the order of cancellation. It was held in appeal that the cancellation, though irregular was proper and as A obtained no right to licence by the mere fact that the contract had been knocked down in his favour the acceptance being subject to sanction, the first relief asked by A for *mandamus* to confirm his right to the licence for the year 1953-54 could not be granted.

It was also held that the auction of Deputy Commissioner in giving contract to B was wrong as it ran counter to the policy of the legislature which is that matters of such consequence to the State revenue cannot be dealt with arbitrarily and in the secrecy of an office. The Supreme Court further observed that in ordinary course A would have been given the writ of *mandamus* as he sought, but as it would be ineffective due to the expiry of the contract year, and as it was not the practice of the Supreme Court to issue meaningless writs, no writ was issued and the appeal was accordingly dismissed.

E.A. Co-op. Housing Society v. State of Maharashtra[27]

Where the Government had denied to itself a jurisdiction which it undoubtedly possessed under S. 154, Maharashtra Co-operative Societies Act by considering that the finality of the order under S. 23(3) of that Act

25. AIR 1953 SC 215, p. 220.
26. AIR 1954 SC 592.
27. AIR 1966 SC 1449.

precluded action under S. 154, a *mandamus* should be issued to Government to deal with the application before it within its jurisdiction under Section 154.

State of Mysore v. Syed Mahmood[28]

The dispute in this case was under Mysore State Civil Services General Recruitment Rules, 1957. As per Rule 4(3)(b) promotion to higher post was given on seniority-*cum*-merit basis. Here the officer cannot claim promotion as a matter of right by virtue of seniority alone. Promotion to posts of senior statistical assistants from cadre of junior statistical assistants was on the basis of seniority list prepared in the year 1958. State Government, in the year 1959, without considering case of petitioners on merits promoted junior statistical assistants ranking below petitioners in seniority list to posts of Senior Statistical Assistants. In a writ petition filed before the High Court it was held that the writ could be issued to the State Government compelling it to perform its duty and to consider whether having regard to their seniority and fitness they should have been promoted on relevant dates when officers junior to them were promoted. The High court issued writ of *mandamus* directing the State Government to promote them with retrospective effect. In an appeal it was held by the Supreme Court, that the High Court was wrong in issuing such writ without giving State Government opportunity in the first instance to consider their fitness for promotion.

Though the appeal filed by the State of Mysore against the issuance of writ of *mandamus* by the High Court, the judicial ratio remains that the *mandamus* can be issued against the State Government.

In the Ninth Report of the Law Commission, the recommendations in it made it clear by observing that clauses (f) and (g) of Sec. 45 of the Specific Relief Act were inconsistent with Article 226 of the Constitution of India and the provisions have now been omitted in the Specific Relief Act of 1963 (new).

It must also be stated here that, although the provisions of Sec. 45 of the Specific Relief Act, 1877 contained general principles and as such are applicable to the issue of a writ of *mandamus* under Article 226 or Article 32, yet they cannot override the express provisions of the two Articles, so as to limit the range of their applicability. This reasoning, it may be pointed out, is a proper approach to the question and has its analogue in the view laid down in the decisions on Sec. 45 of the Specific Relief Act, 1877 that although the principles of English law would apply to the issue of an order under Sec. 45, Courts must be careful to see that they are not led outside the words of the Indian Statute.

As per the Calcutta High Court (AIR 1956 Cal. 437), where the State claims to be owner of certain land in possession of the petitioner and gives

28. AIR 1968 SC 1113.

him notice to quit, the ordinary law applies and no *mandamus* can issue against the State.

Bramo Samaj Education Society v. State of West Bengal[29]

A writ petition under Article 32 was filed by the petitioner on the ground of undue interference of the State of West Bengal in its right to carry on trade, occupation or business enshrined under Article 19(1)(g) of the Constitution of India. As per the West Bengal College Service Commission Act, 1978, the College Service Commission was vested with the duty to select persons for appointment to the post of teachers of a college; by virtue of which, the power of appointment of a teacher in a college or institution affiliated to a university in West Bengal became vested in the government appointed College Service Commission.

The contention taken by the petitioner was that merely because the petitioners are receiving aid, their autonomy of administration could not be totally restricted and institutions could not be treated as a government-owned one. Of course, the State could impose such conditions as were necessary for the proper maintenance of standards of education and to check maladministration. But that control could not extend to the day-to-day administration. The State could regulate the method of selection and appointment of teachers after prescribing requisite qualification for the same. The arguments were made by the petitioner relying upon the decision of *T.M.A. Pai Foundation* v. *State of Karnataka case*[30] that the state could regulate the method of selection and appointment of teachers after prescribing requisite qualification for the same. Independence for the selection of teachers among the qualified candidates was fundamental to the maintenance of the academic and administrative autonomy of an aided institution. Under the University Grants Commissions Act, 1956, the University Grants Commission (UGC) had laid down qualifications to a teaching post in a university by passing Regulations. As per these Regulations, UGC conducts National Eligibility Test (NET) for determining teaching eligibility of candidates. UGC has also authorised accredited States to conduct State-Level Eligibility Test (SLET). Only a person who has qualified NET or SLET will be eligible for appointment as a teacher in an aided institution.

Argument on behalf of the state that the appointment through the College Service Commission was to maintain the equal standard of education all throughout the State of West Bengal was not found impressive by the Supreme Court. The equal standard of teachers, as per the Supreme Court is already maintained by NET/SLET. Similarly, receiving aid from State could not be considered as a justification for imposition of any restrictions that could not be imposed otherwise. The Supreme Court directed the State Government to look into the guidelines given in the case

29. (2004) 6 SCC 224.
30. (2002) 8 SCC 481.

of T.M.A. Pai Foundation case and asked to implement the same. With this observation the appeal was allowed by it.

National Human Rights Commission v. State of Gujarat and others[31]

The National Human Rights Commission, by way of filing writ petition directly before the Supreme Court under Article 32 of the Constitution praying to set-up a committee for overlooking a Special Investigation Team to be set-up by the Government of Gujarat to enquire into those cases of communal violence in which final reports had been filed by the local police station closing the cases. The State of Gujarat appeared as a respondent and pointed out to the Supreme Court that the similar kind of writ petition was pending before the High Court of Gujarat and the petitioner could raise its contentions before the High Court having the jurisdiction to consider each of the grievances raised by the NHRC. The Supreme Court made it clear to the respondent State of Gujarat that it was not going to proceed on the basis that the entire machinery in the State had failed; but at the same time, there should be further/more investigation in-depth into about 2000 cases in which "A" Summary Reports had been filed resulting in closure of cases at the threshold and also directed the State to consider about further extended investigations through its own high-ranking officers.

Om Prakash v. State of U.P.[32]

The appellant, alongwith others filed a writ petition in the High Court challenging the Gazette Notifications prohibiting the sale of "eggs" within the municipal limits of Rishikesh on the ground that the notifications issued imposed unreasonable restrictions affecting their rights under Article 19(1)(g) of the Constitution as they prohibited the sale of "eggs" within the municipal limits. The fact as noticed by the High Court was that District Rishikesh is by and large a place where many temples exist. By perusal of the affidavit it was revealed by the High Court that several citizens, societies and organizations made representations to the Municipal Board, Rishikesh requesting it to impose restrictions on the sale of "eggs" also in public places. In order to put restrictions, the Municipal Board amended the bye-law. The High Court opined that the amended bye-law prohibiting sale of "eggs" was just and proper and said notification did not violate the fundamental right contained in Article 19(1)(a) of the petitioners and hence no writ of *mandamus* could be issued.

Being aggrieved by the judgment of the High Court the appellants preferred appeal before the Supreme Court. The Supreme Court also confirmed the decision of the High Court and held that the High Court was justified in rejecting the writ of *mandamus*. Moreover, the Supreme Court, rejected the contention taken by the appellants regarding the power of the

31. (2004) 8 SCC 610.
32. AIR 2004 SC 1896.

Board to frame bye-laws on the ground that the appellant could not take this point for the first time at the appellate stage. The appeal was dismissed with these observations refusing to issue *mandamus*.

Jamshed N. Guzdar v. State of Maharashtra[33]

A question arose in above appeal before the Supreme Court regarding amendment made by the State Legislature in the Bombay City Civil Court Act, 1987 by which the jurisdiction of civil Court, particularly pecuniary jurisdiction of the City Civil Court was enlarged. Whether writ of *mandamus* could be issued against enforcement or non-enforcement of the Act was the precise question before the Supreme Court. The Notification as to implementation deferred as requisite infrastructure such as Court-room, Judges, etc. were not provided. State Government granted was granted liberty to apply to the Supreme Court seeking permission for implementation of the said Notification placing on record necessary material to show that there is adequacy of infrastructure and requirements as to number of Judges and Court-rooms, etc. But it was held that on the sole ground no writ of *mandamus* could be issued against the State Government.

Kapila Hingorani v. State of Bihar[34]

In this case a writ petition was filed by the employees of Public Sector undertaking Bihar Hill Area Lift Irrigation Corporation (BHALCO) under Article 32 of the Constitution of India. The prayer was regarding the issuance of writ of or in the nature of *mandamus* directing the respondents to pay the due salary of large number of employees for years. So many employees were starving and many had already died. The contention taken by the State Government was that liquidation proceedings of said bodies—Bihar Hill Area Lift Irrigation Corporation (BHALCO) and its successor Jharkhand Hill Area Lift Irrigation Corporation Limited (JHALCO) were pending. State having statutory power and control over function of the said bodies was not exercising the said powers.

The Supreme Court held that the plea of the respondent that the State had no effective control over functions of said public sector undertaking was not proper or acceptable. Further, the stand taken by the State of Bihar was criticized by the Supreme Court by saying that it was not open for the State to raise questions which were expressly rejected earlier. Earlier also the State was directed to deposit sum of Rs. 50 crores for payment of arrears of salaries was not sufficient. Hence, further directions were issued by the Supreme Court to deposit additional amount. It was also clarified lastly the above directions to deposit the additional amount were not issued on the premise that State is bound to pay salaries of employees of Public Sector Undertakings but on ground that employees have human right and

33. AIR 2005 SC 862.
34. AIR 2005 SC 980.

fundamental right under Article 21 of the Constitution, which States are bound to protect.

Analysis and Inferences

Prior to independence, the Chartered High Courts of Mumbai, Madras and Calcutta could issue writ of or order of *Mandamus* under the Specific Relief Act, 1877 (Sections 45 and 46) against different states/ provinces. After the independence, the specific remedy to issue writ of *mandamus* was given to High Courts under Article 226 and also to the Supreme Court under Article 32. Hence, from the beginning, there is no controversy so far as issuance of *mandamus* against State Government is concerned. In majority of the writs filed seeking relief in the nature of *mandamus* the respondent is State Government.

3.3 *MANDAMUS* AGAINST PUBLIC OFFICIALS

As per English Law

*No mandamus **against the servants of the Crown***

So far as the issuance of writ of *mandamus* was concerned, the English Law did not make much difference between the *Crown* and the Servants of *Crown*. It has been observed in the Halsbury's Laws of England in a single paragraph that writ of *mandamus* is not maintainable against the *Crown* and its servants. The relevant extract of the same paragraph is reproduced herebelow:

> '1293 ....*In like manner all other persons acting as servants of the Crown are exempt from the prerogative jurisdiction of the Court, and no writ of mandamus can accordingly issue against them to do any act within the scope of the duties discharged by them on behalf of the Crown.*'[35]

By observing the above principle **Littledale, J.**, in the case of *R. v. Customs Commissioners*[36] expressed his limitation to issue writ of *mandamus* where it was sought to obtain a *mandamus* commanding the delivery up of certain tobacco and observed,

> '*... the goods are in the hands of the officers of the Crown: a mandamus to them in this case would be like a mandamus to the Crown, which we cannot grant.*'

But in the Halsbury's Laws of England in the same paragraph. it has been lastly observed that if the government officials are legally duty bound towards the common man, writ of *mandamus* would definitely lie against them. It is observed,

35. Halsbury's Laws of England Hailsham's Edition, Vol. 9, para. 1293.
36. (1836), 5 Ad. & El. 380, p. 382.

'Where, however, Government officials have been constituted agents for carrying out particular duties in relation to subjects, whether by royal charter, statute, or common law, so that they are under a legal obligation towards such subjects, a writ of mandamus will lie for the enforcement of such duties.'[37]

Observations of Prof. Wade regarding issuance of *Mandamus* against Public Officials

'The distinction turns upon the rule that no third party (the complainant) can compel an agent (of the department) to perform a duty which is owed not to him, but solely to the principal (the Crown). Against other bodies or persons mandamus will only be granted where the applicant has a right to the performance of a legal duty and has no other specific or equally appropriate and convenient means of compelling its performance. He must have demanded its performance and been refused. The duty must be an imperative and not a discretionary one, but there may be an exercise of such discretion is enforceable by mandamus.'[38]

But, at the same time it is specifically narrated in para. 1281 of the Halsbury's Laws of England that a writ of *mandamus* is maintainable against public officials and bodies if they fail to discharge their duties and as a resultant effect any legal right of the petitioner is violated. The contents of paragraph 1281 are reproduced below:

'1281. If public officials or a public body fail to perform any public duty with which they have been charged, a writ of mandamus lie to compel them to carry out, even though the time prescribed by statute for the performance of the duty may have passed in accordance with this principle a mandamus will issue to Government officials in their capacity as public officers exercising executive duties which affect the rights of private persons.'[39]

The following are the examples of the cases decided by English Courts regarding issuance of *mandamus* against public officials. Only short summary and ratio is written below.

Queen v. Price[40]

The Parliamentary Election was held wherein, the Election Commissioner had power to refuse to grant certificate to witness under section 7 of Corrupt Practices Prevention Act. The witness was wrongly refused to grant certificate stating that he had not answered the questions

37. Halsbury's Laws of England Hailsham's Edition, Vol. 9, para. 1293.
38. Constitutional Law by Prof. Wade, 4th Edition, p. 298.
39. Halsbury's Laws of England, Hailsham's Edition, Vol. 9, para 1281.
40. (1871) Q.B. 411.

and if any proceeding be at any time pending against such witness for corrupt practices, such proceedings on production of such certificates shall be stayed.

It was held that if a witness has in point of fact answered all such questions, he is entitled to a certificate; and that if the Election Commissioners refuse to grant a certificate to the witness on the ground that they are of opinion that he has not answered questions, their decision is not final and conclusive, and may be reviewed by *mandamus*.

Here the observations of ***Cockburn, C.J.***, while allowing the writ of *mandamus* are very important. He said,

> *'.... I think that in the present case there is sufficient reason for urging that the witness is entitled to ask this Court for a mandamus, and prima facie case is made out which requires further consideration; and we ought not to hesitate to make the rule absolute for a mandamus upon the return to which the law upon the subject may be more fully considered....'*[41]

R. v. Income Tax Special Purpose Commissioner[42]

In the case of *R. v. Income Tax Special Purpose Commissioner*, by making above mentioned position clear, it was laid down by the Court of Queen's Bench that the writ of *mandamus* will lie to compel a public official or body to perform his public duty whether imposed by statute or otherwise. It was further observed therein by **Lord Esher M.R.** that:

> *'I am of the opinion that the case falls within the class of cases where officials (have) a public duty to perform, and (have) refused to perform, it, mandamus will lie on the application of a person interested to compel them to do so.'*

The Queen v. Thomas[43]

The Queen v. Thomas was a case wherein *mandamus* was granted by the Court of Queen's Bench. In this case, *Rule nisi* was granted for a *mandamus* to the licensing justices of Bristol directing them to hear and determine the application of Eliza Jane Kelland for the renewal of the licence of a beerhouse.

The beerhouse, known as the Crabbs Well, in the city of Bristol, was licensed for the sale of retail of beer to be consumed on or off the premises prior to, and had been continuously so licensed from, the 1st day of May, 1869, until October 10, 1891. At the annual licensing meeting, on August 26, 1891, the application for the renewal of the licence of Mary Ann Osborne was refused upon the grounds among others, that the premises were of a disorderly character and frequented by persons of bad character.

41. (1871) Q.B. 411.
42. (1888) 21 Q.B. 313 (317).
43. (1892) 1 Q.B. 426.

Notices of appeal were duly given against such refusal; but the appeal was adjourned.

At the adjourned annual licensing meeting, held on September 23, Elisa Jane Kelland applied for the renewal of the license to her, alleging that she had entered into an agreement with the owner of the house to take the house from him as his tenant, in succession to Mary Ann Osborne. But the licence to reopen the house was not given and reason given that if the house were reopened it would be a nuisance to the neighbourhood. In an application it was held that a *mandamus* will be granted commanding the licencing justices to hear and determine the application.

It was observed by ***Hawkins, J.***, in the last paragraph of his judgment expressing his opinion,

> *'...It has been argued that this matter is only the subject of an appeal to quarter sessions. It is quite possible that there might have been good grounds for an appeal if the grounds of the decision had been announced to the applicant, and in that case a mandamus would not be granted, for there would be an adequate remedy by appeal. That rule, however, as to the grant of mandamus is not inflexible, or applicable in cases of this kind, where a person does not know the grounds of the decision against him and how to shape his appeal. Here there were four grounds upon which the licence might have been refused, and the applicant would properly want to know upon which of those grounds the refusal was based. All that was said, in fact, was, "Licence refused." The applicant was entitled to know the grounds of that refusal. We think that the circumstances of this case make it very different from the case of* ***Reg. v. Smith,***[44] *because here the justices determined in their own minds of grounds of their refusal, and did not announce them to the applicant. This matter must go back to be heard and determined according to law upon the consideration of the whole case.'*

Justice Wills was not in favour to grant writ of *mandamus* in this case but he was ready to remand the matter for the purpose of rehearing as the licence was refused by giving different grounds. Hence, the matter was remanded for rehearing and irrespective of the order passed earlier rejecting the grant of licence.

Rex v. Hanley Revising Barrister

Rex v. Stake-on-Trent Town Clerk[45]

In the case of ***Rex v. Hanley Revising Barrister, Rex v. Stake-on-Trent Town Clerk,*** a revising barrister for a parliamentary borough owing to an accident to his right hand, availed himself of clerical assistance to mark upon the lists of voters the results of his decisions as pronounced orally in

44. 8 Q.B. 146.
45. (1912) 3 K.B. 518.

Court. By some inadvertence the clerk omitted to strike off the lists the names of some persons who had been successfully objected to and whose names were ordered by the revising barrister to be expunged. The lists with those names remaining on were delivered by the revising barrister to the town clerk, and the names were accordingly printed in the register of electors for the borough. The mistake was not discovered until the expiration of some months after the register had come into operation. The original lists of voters which had been before the revising barrister were either lost or destroyed.

It was held that the Court had jurisdiction to grant writs of *mandamus* to the revising barrister and to the town clerk to have the mistake corrected; that in the circumstances there need not be a previous demand and refusal to do the act sought to be enforced; and that the proper course was for the revising barrister to expunge the names on a copy of the register and to deliver the same to the town clerk, and for the town clerk to make the necessary correction in the register.

Rex. v. Hudson[46] [_Mandamus_ against the Commissioner]

The case arisen due to filing of appeal against the order of the Divisional Court calling upon Alfred Arthus Hudson, Esquire, K.C. (hereinafter referred to as 'Commissioner') to show cause why a writ of *mandamus* should not issue directed to him commanding him to hear and determine pursuant to the status in that behalf the matter of a certain inquiry with regard to a draft extension Order of the Board of Trade made under provisions of Sec. 103 of the National Insurance Act, 1911, on the ground that he had not heard and determined the inquiry according to law.

The Commissioner was of the opinion that the question whether it was or was not within the power of the Board to make the Order was one which he was entitled to decide. The Divisional Court (Lord. Reading C.J., Lord Coleridge and Rowlatt, JJ.) made the rule for a *mandamus* absolute upon the grounds that the Commissioner had no jurisdiction to decide whether the Order was *ultra vires* the Board of Trade, his only function being to ascertain whether it was desirable; (2) that the order was not *ultra vires* inasmuch as the trade of saw milling it dealt with was, within the meaning of Sec. 103 and the Sixth Schedule, a different trade from the saw milling included as an insured trade in clause 7 of the schedule.

In appeal filed by the Commissioner before the Court of King's Bench, it was held that a *mandamus* must issue to the Commissioner to hear and determine the matter of the inquiry according to law. Hence, the decision of issuance of writ of *mandamus* by the Divisional Court was affirmed.

***Rex v. Commissioners for Special Purposes of Income Tax*[47]**

The Court of King's Bench issued writ of *mandamus* in the case of ***Rex***

46. (1915) 1 K.B. 838.
47. (1920) 1 K.B. 26.

v. ***Commissioners*** for Special Purposes of Income Tax against the Commissioners for Special Purposes of Income Tax directing to perform their duties.

A question had arisen with regard to the testator's will which led to litigation, but in March 1916, a compromise was arrived at under which the charitable institution became entitled to two-thirds of the testator's residuary estate.

Between September, 1916, and December 4, 1916, certain payments were made by the executors relating to their costs in the litigation, and thereupon a sum was left in their hands which was distributed by them on December 4, 1916.

It was held that the assent of the executors which had clearly taken place by December 4, 1916, related back to the date of the testator's death, and as it was not the intention of the Legislature to allow exemption to depend upon delays caused by administration or litigation, but to allow exemption where funds were to be used for charitable purposes only, the income of the securities was entitled to exemption as from the date of the testator's death, and that the amount which had been deducted for income tax must be returned to the charitable institution.

If the Court issues a *mandamus* commanding the Special Commissioners to perform their statutory duties, the Court has power to order the Commissioners also to pay costs: the common law rule that the *Crown* neither pays nor receives costs does not apply to that case, since the Commissioners do not merely act as servants of the *Crown* but in the performance of their statutory duty.

The view taken by **Earl of Reading C.J.** while imposing costs after having made rule absolute for a writ of *mandamus* against the Commissioners is discussed here below:

> *'....The argument on behalf of the Commissioners may be stated quite briefly in the following proposition: That the Commissioners for the Special Purposes of the Income Tax Acts are to be regarded for these purposes as the Crown, and at common law the rule is that the King and any person suing to his use neither pays nor receives costs. To quote from 3 Blackstone's Commentaries at page 400: "As it is his prerogative not to pay them to a subject, so it is beneath his dignity to receive them." The common law rule still prevails; costs are not payable by the subject in an unsuccessful litigation with the Crown, nor by the Crown in an unsuccessful litigation with a subject. If this case fell within that proposition then I should accede at once to the Attorney General's contention that no costs could be ordered against him. But there is another proposition of law which has been invoked in this case by the successful applicants. The proposition is stated by Lord Esher M.R. in Reg. V. Commissioners for Special Purposes of the Income Tax*[48]*. It is to be observed that the question in that case was*

48. 21 Q.B. D. 317.

whether a mandamus would lie to the Commissioners for Special Purposes of the Income Tax Acts, that is, to the same officials who have been ordered by this Court to do certain acts. In that case the Commissioners had refused to issue certain orders for repayment, and the Court ordered a writ of mandamus to issue. Lord Esher says this: "With regard to the question whether mandamus will lie, I am of opinion that the case falls within the class of cases, where officials having a public duty to perform, and having refused to perform it, mandamus will lie on the application of a person interested to compel them to do so." To my mind that is a far-reaching and most salutary provision of the common law. It is true that we, sitting here in the King's Court, and issuing orders commanding persons to carry out duties in the name of the Crown, cannot order the Crown to carry out a duty, yet we can order persons who are charged with statutory obligations to carry out those obligations if they fail to do so, provided they come within the terms of the proposition laid down by Lord Esher. It has been said by this Court on more than one occasion that the Court cannot issue a mandamus directed to the Crown or to a person simply acting in his capacity of servant of the Crown.'

Further **Earl of Reading C.J.** observed at page 40 regarding payment of costs.

'...It seems to me to follow as a matter of curse that wherever the Court can order a mandamus to issue to an officer charged with the performance of a statutory duty it can order that officer to receive or pay costs, for the reason that the mandamus is not an order directed to the Crown, which this Court can never issue, but is an order directed to an officer who is bound to perform a certain duty imposed upon him by statute.'[49]

Lastly, he observed in his judgment at page 42,

'On the whole, therefore, I have come to the conclusion that this is a case in which we have jurisdiction to issue a mandamus to the Commissioners, and as we stated yesterday, we exercise that jurisdiction in favour of the successful applicants and say that the Commissioners must pay the costs.'[50]

Justice Darling and Justice Bray expressed the same opinion and allowed writ of *mandamus* and imposed costs upon the Commissioners.

***Mandamus* against Public Officials in U.S.A.**

As it is already discussed earlier in Chapter 2 the powers of issuance of writ of *mandamus* has been given to Judiciary in the U.S.A. by accepting the British Common Law. The Supreme Court of the U.S.A. has power to issue *mandamus* in appropriate cases. The famous case of *Marbury* v.

49. (1920) 1 K.B. 26, p. 40.
50. (1920) 1 K.B. 26, p. 42.

Madison is discussed to appreciate the powers of issuance of *mandamus* by the Supreme Court of U.S.A.

Marbury v. Madison **(Supreme Court of the United States)**[51]

At the end of Eighteenth Century, there were two major political parties in the United States viz. older Federalist party leaded by the then President John Adams and Republican party under the leadership of Thomas Jefferson. The results of the presidential election of the year 1800 were announced on 17th February 1801, wherein there was defeat of President Adams and Republican Party came in power.

Forty nine days prior to the announcement of the election results, President Adams with the concurrence of the Senate named John Marshall, an advocate and the Secretary of State appointed 42 persons as justices of the peace in the District of Columbia. These commissions were signed and sealed by midnight of 3rd March 1801, when the term of office of President Adams expired, but Mr. John Marshall still continued to hold the office of the Acting Secretary of State post.

After the inauguration, President Thomas Jefferson ordered his newly appointed Secretary of State, James Madison, to deliver 25 of these commissions but to withhold the remainder. Admon, the seventeen who did not receive their commissions were William Marbury, Dennis Ramsay, Robert Townsend Hooe, and William Harper, who in due course of time applied to the United Status Supreme Court for a writ of *mandamus* to compel Secretary of State, Mr. Madison to deliver their commissions. Provisions of the Judiciary Act of 1789 were relied upon by the petitioners in support of their position that the Supreme Court had Jurisdiction to issue the writ in this case.

The Supreme Court granted a rule in this case, requiring the Secretary of the State to show cause why *mandamus* should not issue, directing him to deliver to William Marbury his commission as a justice of the peace for the county of Washington in the District of Columbia. The Supreme Court took into consideration the following questions for the decision:

1. Has the applicant a right to the commissions he demands?
2. If he has a right, and that right has been violated, do the laws of his country afford him a remedy?
3. If they do afford him a remedy, is it a *mandamus* issuing from this Court?

Here, unfortunately for the applicant, though the Supreme Court decided first two questions in the favour of the applicant, it did not issue *mandamus* against the respondent on very technical and procedural ground. It initially decided that Marbury had a right to the commission and the laws did afford him a remedy. On the third question the Supreme Court

51. 1803, Cranch 137, 2 L.Ed. 60.

first decided that the *mandamus* was the proper remedy and then proceeded to examine the question whether it could issue the writ.

The Supreme Court observed that the act to establish the judicial courts of the United States authorises the Supreme Court "to issue writs of *mandamus* in cases warranted by the principles and usages of law, to any courts appointed, or persons holding office, under the authority of the United Status."

After having made both of the above observations that the applicant Marbury had a fit case for *mandamus* as well as the Supreme Court of the U.S.A. had power to issue writ of *mandamus,* the Supreme Court said that it could not issue writ of *mandamus* in this case as it has power to issue *mandamus* only in exercise of its appellate jurisdiction. The case in question pertained to original jurisdiction in which writ of *mandamus* could not be issue.

While discussing in detail it was observed that in the distribution of powers it is declared that the Supreme Court shall have original jurisdiction in all cases affecting ambassadors, other public ministers and consuls, and those in which a state shall be a party. In all other cases, the Supreme Court shall have appellate jurisdiction. It was clear from the above proposition that to enable the Supreme Court to issue a *mandamus,* it must be shown to be an exercise of appellate jurisdiction, or to be necessary to enable them to exercise appellate jurisdiction. It was stated at the bar that the appellate jurisdiction might be exercised in a variety of forms and that if it be the will of the legislature that a *mandamus* should be used for that purpose that will must be obeyed. This is true, yet the jurisdiction must be appellate, not original.

It is the essential criterion of the appellate jurisdiction, as observed by the Supreme Court that it revises and corrects the proceedings in a cause already instituted, and does not created that cause. Although, therefore, a *mandamus* may be directed to courts, yet to issue such a writ to the officer for the delivery of a paper, is in effect the same as to sustain an original action for that paper, and therefore, seems not to belong to appellate jurisdiction. Neither is it necessary in such a case as this, to enable the court to exercise its appellate jurisdiction.

The Supreme Court, though not issued writ of *mandamus* in this case, it laid down a principle that a writ of *mandamus* can be issued against the public officers. While appreciating the principles of *mandamus,* the observations made in this case are referred not only in U.S.A., but also in other countries including India.

Position in India under the Specific Relief Act, 1877

The Specific Relief Act, 1877 specifically prohibited the High Courts from covering within its ambit public officials while issuing order of *mandamus*. Since Sec. 45 as well as 46 are narrated herein above, entire section is not reproduced here but only sub-clause (g) of Section 45 of Specific Relief Act is written herebelow:

Sec. 45

(a)

..

..

(d)

Nothing in this section shall be deemed to authorise any High Court—

(e)

(f) ....

(g) *to make any order on any servant of the Government, as such, merely to enforce the satisfaction of a claim upon the Government.*

From the provisions of Section 45 of the Specific Relief Act, 1877, it is very much clear that it gave the same powers of issuance of writ of *mandamus,* (alongwith limitations) to the High Courts in India, which powers were possessed by the British Courts. The effect if clause (g) of Sec. 45 is that a writ of *mandamus* cannot be issued against an officer of the Government to enforce an obligation resting on the Government unless there is incumbent upon the officer a special duty under the law in respect of the matter involved. But as already discussed in the above point that under the Constitution of India, it is specifically mentioned that writ of *mandamus* under Articles 32 and 226 is maintainable before the Supreme Court and High Courts respectively against the Government Servants, i.e. Public Officials. Moreover, the Law Commission in their recommendations in the Ninth Report on the Specific Relief Act, 1877 have observed that clauses (f) and (g) of Section 45 were inconsistent with Article 226 of the Constitution and the provisions are now been omitted in the new Specific Relief Act, 1963.

Commissioner of Income-Tax, Bombay v. Bombay Trust Corporation[52]

In the above case, Income-Tax authorities assessed certain H company for profits and gains received by that H company through its alleged agent B company. On reference to the High Court under Sec. 66, it was ordered that the assessment was illegal. When the reference came back to the Commissioner of Income-tax, he sent the case to the Assistant Commissioner and directed further inquiry into the assessment. The Assistant Commissioner made an assessment under Sec. 23(4) and withheld from refunding the previously imposed tax until this newly assessed tax was paid up or until security was given for its payment. It was contended that the order of the Commissioner asking for further inquiry after the High Court's order and asking of security were illegal. The B company applied by motion to the High Court under Sec. 45, Specific Relief Act. High Court

52. AIR 1936 PC 269.

ordered that further inquiry was unwarranted, that order demanding security was illegal and asked the Income-tax authorities to refund the tax previously paid up.

On appeal to the Privy Council, it was held that orders made under the Specific Relief Act, 1877, should specify with exactitude and clarity the specific act, which the person holding a public office is being commanded to do. The Commissioner was not obliged to discontinue proceedings against the B company as agent of H company in respect of the year of assessment. It was within the jurisdiction of the Commissioner to direct further inquiry if he thought such inquiry to be reasonable and to be profitable in the public interest. Under Section 33(2) he had a general power to make inquiry or to cause an inquiry to be made. The Commissioner was within his rights in directing further inquiry, and however disappointing this course might have been to the assessee, it was matter which a Court of law must leave in the discretion of the Commissioner. But the order asking for some one else in cases of refund in order to enable the realisation of new assessment was certainly wrong and it should suffice now to observe that the income—tax authorities have been with-holding from B company over three lakhs of rupees extracted from them by an illegal assessment order, and that there was no pretence of justice or law in the notion that the money could be withheld, in case, on some further date, a valid assessment might come in to existence. It was further held that the Court cannot claim even in cast upon the principal, the Court cannot enforce against the servant merely as such. Before *mandamus* can issue to a public servant, it must, therefore be shown that a duty towards the applicant has been imposed upon the public servant by statute so that he can be charged thereon, and independently of any duty with as servant he may owe to the *Crown*, his principal.

In the judgment delivered by **Sir G. Rankin, J.** the following observations are made regarding issuance of writ of *mandamus* against the Commissioner of Income Tax:

> *'The action taken by the High Court under the Specific Relief Act was, however, incorrect. In the first place the decision of the Court upon the particular question referred to it in this case was given in its special jurisdiction under S. 66 of the Act and was "advisory", ...But in any case clause (g) in S. 45, Specific Relief Act, does not mean that orders can be made to enforce the satisfaction of a claim upon the Crown provided that the Court acts with some additional motive or has some further intention. The words of the clause have been taken verbatim from a well-known judgment on mandamus, the judgment of Coleridge, J., in Baron De Bode's Case*[53]*:*

53. (1838) 6 DR 776.

But, against the servants of the Crown, as such, and merely to enforce the satisfaction of claims upon the Crown, it is an established rule that a mandamus will not lie. I call this an establish rule. I believe it has never been broken in upon.

The doctrine is well illustrated by that decision and by the cases therein mentioned, but is even more fully expounded in Regina v. Lords Commissioners of Treasury,[54] *{already discussed in detail} The principle is that the Court cannot claim even in appearance to command the Crown, and where an obligation is cast upon the principal the Court cannot enforce it against the servant merely as such. Before mandamus can issue to a public servant it must therefore be shown that a duty towards the applicant has been imposed upon the public servant by statute so that he can be charged thereon, and independently of any duty which as servant he may owe to the Crown, his principal. ...'*

Sree Nivasulu Naidu v. Commissioner of I.T., Madras[55]

In the Case of *Sree Nivasulu Naidu* v. *Commissioner of I.T., Madras,* it was observed: An Act may be self-contained: it may provide in a comprehensive manner the rights and the remedies of the parties. If a party is aggrieved by an order under any provisions of the Act, he will have to resort to the remedy provided there under. But if a party takes the remedy provided by the Act in strict conformity thereof, but the tribunal constituted under the Act refers to discharge its duties provided by the same Act, it is not open to the tribunal or the authority to say that he cannot be compelled to discharge his statutory functions. Section 45 of the Specific Relief Act is intended only to govern such cases and compel officers to discharge their statutory duties. Thus, where the Commissioner illegally refuses to discharge his duties under S. 33-A, Income Tax Act, the aggrieved party can take resort to S. 45 of the Specific Relief Act to compel him to perform his statutory duties.

Commissioner of Police v. Gordhandas[56]

In this case the respondent herein, wanted to build a cinema house in a part of Greater Bombay. He obtained the necessary permission from the commissioner of Police, in exercise of the discretion vested in him to grant a licence under section 22 of the City of Bombay Police Act, 1902. Later the permission was suspended by the Commissioner and the respondent was told to await the orders of the Government. Shortly after the Commissioner sent the respondent the following communication:

"I am directed by the Government to inform you that the permission to erect a cinema granted to you is hereby cancelled."

---

54. (1872)7 Q.B. 387.
55. (1948) 2 Mad. L.J. 386.
56. AIR 1952 SC 16.

The respondent applied for an order in the nature of a *mandamus* under section 45 of the Specific Relief Act against the Commissioner of Police. It was held: Under the Rules framed under section 22, City of Bombay Police Act, the only person vested with authority to grant or refuse a license for the erection of a building to be sued for purposes of public amusement was the Commissioner of Police. It was also clear that under Rule 250 he has been vested with the absolute discretion at any time to cancel or suspend any license which had been granted under the rules. But the power to do so was vested in him and not in the State Government and could only be exercised by him at his discretion. Rule 250 authorised the cancellation of a license already issued.

The Supreme Court set aside the order or cancellation of licence by observing that the Commissioner acted merely as the agent of the Government. Accordingly, the Commissioner should be directed to consider the requests made for cancellation of the license and after bringing to bear his unfettered judgment on the subject, himself to issue a definite order canceling or refusing to cancel the license.

Gurbachan Singh v. State of Bombay[57]

The petitioner was served with an order purporting to have been made by the Commissioner of Police, Bombay, under Sec. 27(1) of the City of Bombay Police Act, 1902, directing him to remove himself from Greater Bombay and to go to his native place at Amritsar in East Punjab. It was mentioned in the order that the petitioner was to comply with its directions within two days from the date it was made, and he was to proceed to Amritsar by rail. On July 25, 1951, the petitioner made an application to the Commissioner of Police and prayed for extension of the time within which he was to remove himself from Greater Bombay, and on this application the Commissioner of Police gave him time till the 30th July next. On 30th July, 1951, the petitioner himself wrote a letter to the Commissioner of Police stating that he did not desire to go to Amritsar and prayed that he might be allowed to stay at Kalyan which is outside Greater Bombay but within the State of Bombay. This he was allowed. The applications for writ were dismissed by the Bombay High Court.

The petitioner then appealed to the Supreme Court under Article 32 on the allegation that his fundamental rights under clauses (d) and (e) of Article 19(1) have been infringed by the externment order. Section 27(1) of the City of Bombay Police Act, 1902 provided as follows:

'Whenever it shall appear to the Commissioner of police,

(a) that the movements or acts of any person in the Greater Bombay are causing or calculated to cause alarm, danger or harm to person or property or that there are reasonable grounds for believing that such person is engaged or is about to be engaged

57. AIR 1952 SC 221.

in the commission of an offence punishable under Chapter XII, XVI or XVII of the Indian Penal Code, or in the abetment of any such offence, and when in the opinion of the Commissioner witnesses are not willing to come forward to give evidence in public against such person by reason of apprehension on their art as regards the safety of their person or property;

(b) the Commissioner of Police may, by an order in writing duly served on him ..... direct such person ....to remove himself outside the State or to such place within the State or to such place within the State and by such route and within such time as the State and by such route and within such time as the Commissioner or Police prescribe and not to enter the State or as the case may be the Greater Bombay.'

It was held that the restrictions imposed by Section 27(1) of the impugned Act upon fundamental rights of the free movement are reasonable. While confirming the judgment of the Bombay High Court, **Mukherjee, J.** who delivered the judgment of the Court observed:

'The second point urged by the learned counsel raises the question as to whether section 27(1) of the City of Bombay Police Act has imposed restriction upon the fundamental right of a citizen which is guaranteed under Article 19(1)(d) of the Constitution and being in conflict with this fundamental right is void and imperative under Article 13(1) of the Constitution. There can be no doubt that the provision of Section 27(1) of the Bombay Act was made in the interest of the general Public and protect them against dangerous and bad characters, whose presence in a particular locality may jeopardize the peace and safety of the citizens. The question, therefore, is whether the restrictions that this law imposes upon the rights of free movement of a citizen, come within the purview of clause 5 of Article 19 of the Constitution; or in other words, whether the restrictions are reasonable? It is perfectly true that the determination of the question as to whether the restrictions imposed by a legislative enactment upon the fundamental rights of a citizen enunciated in Article 19(1)(d) of the Constitution are reasonable or not within the meaning of clause 5 of the Article would depend as much upon the procedural part of the law as upon its substantive part; and the Court has got to look in each case to the circumstances under which and the manner in which the restrictions have been imposed. The maximum duration of the externment order made under Sec. 27(1) of the Bombay Act is a period of two years and the Commissioner of Police can always permit the externee to enter the prohibited area even before the expiration of that period. Having regard to the class of cases to which this sub-section, applies and the menace which an externment order passed under it is intended to avert, it is difficult to say that the provision is unreasonable. The Commissioner of Police can in a proper case cancel the externment order any moment he likes, if in his opinion the return of the

externee to the area from which he was removed ceases to be attended with any danger to the community.'

The Supreme Court, in the above case refused to issue *mandamus* by taking into consideration the fact that the case falls within the reasonable restrictions given under Article 19(5) of the Constitution of India and therefore against that writ cannot be issued.

S.N. Sharma v. Bipin Kumar[58]

This is a case of issuance of *mandamus* where there was misuse of power by the police officers. The power of the police to investigate any cognizable offence is uncontrolled by the Magistrate, and it is only in cases where the police decide not to investigate the case that the Magistrate can intervene and either direct an investigation, or, in the alternative, himself proceed or depute a Magistrate subordinate to him to proceed to enquire into the case.

The use of the expression "as he thinks fit" in Section 159 is primarily meant to give to the Magistrate the power of directing an investigation in cases where the police decide not to investigate the case under the proviso to Section 157(1) of the Criminal Procedure Code and it is in those cases that, if he thinks fit, he can choose the second alternative of proceeding himself or deputing any Magistrate subordinate to him to proceed to hold a preliminary enquiry as the circumstances of the case may require.

Though the Code gives to the police unfettered power to investigate all cases where they suspect that a cognizable offence has been committed, in appropriate cases an aggrieved person can always seek a remedy by invoking the power of the High Court under Article 226 of the Constitution under which, if the power of investigation has been exercised by a police officer *mala fide*, the High Court can always issue a writ of *mandamus* restraining the police officer from misusing his legal powers. The fact that provision giving power to a Magistrate to stop investigation by the police can not be a ground for holding that such power must be read in Section 159 of the Cr.P.C.

Gayatri de v. Mousumi Co-operative Housing Society Ltd.[59]

The appellant herein filed a writ petition before the High Court of Calcutta praying *inter alia* for cancellation of the letter issued by the Special Officer of the Society, for declaration that the possession of the Flat being No. A-2 on 5th floor should be given to the legal heirs of the deceased member. During the course of arguments the question regarding maintainability of writ petition was arose. The factual position clarified by the Special Officer was that he had, by exercising his statutory function

58. AIR 1970 SC 786.
59. AIR 2004 SC 2271.

under the Act issued a letter to the father of the appellant herein that since no claim for transfer of the interest of allottee member of the Society has been made in time by the legal heirs, the flat in question has already been re-allotted and since no claim for payment of the value of the share or interest has been made by any person entitled in law to receive the payment lying in the deceased-member's account after deduction of the amount, if any payable to the Society, the Society will make payment in accordance with law. The appellant was one of the legal representative of the deceased-member, therefore, filed writ petition in the nature of *mandamus* commanding the Co-operative Society therein not to give effect to the letter issued by the Special Officer of the Society and to forbear from acting on the basis thereof and pursuant thereto. Thus, it is seen that the subject matter of the writ petition is the order passed by the Special Officer in discharging of his statutory functions.

It was held by the Supreme Court that the writ petition was maintainable for this reason. The Special Officer is appointed under the provisions of the Act and as such he is a statutory officer and therefore, he should be regarded as a public authority. Apart from that Article 226 of the Constitution is not confined to issue of writ only to a public authority, the bar extends also to issue directions to any person. In a case where the Co-operative Society is under the control of a Special Officer, a writ would lie. The Special Officer was appointed by the High Court to discharge the functions of the Society, therefore, he should be regarded as a public authority and hence the writ petition is maintainable.

Analysis and Inferences

In England the general rule was that no writ could be issued against the servants of the *Crown*. This rule had certain exceptions such as if the function discharged by such servant was pertaining to discharging of public duty, *mandamus* could be issued against him. In India, the law relating to subject of *mandamus* qua public officials remains same in the pre-Constitutional era and post-Constitutional era. The action of the public servant violates fundamental rights or legal rights (for High Courts only), the writ of *mandamus* is maintainable against the public officials. The simple reason for holding public officials liable is that the act done by the public officials in their capacity as public servants is done on behalf of the government. If the government is made answerable for its actions affecting the rights of subjects, then why not the public officials? With this reasons writ of *mandamus* is issued against public officials. There is no change as well as no dispute in this point in their capacity of Public officials.

3.4 *MANDAMUS* AGAINST LEGISLATURE

No writ of *mandamus* can be issued by the Supreme Court under Article 32 against the legislature unless the order passed by or action taken by the speaker of the house violates fundamental right of any individual.

Article 226 empowers a High Court to issue the writs, order or direction mentioned therein to any Authority. But this does not mean that the Supreme Court or a High Court can issue writ to the Legislature of a State or to the Parliament to prevent it from enacting a law which is said to be in violation of or in contravention of the Fundamental Rights.

Here the law is very well settled and therefore, the decisions of the High Courts are accepted by the litigants and they were not challenged before the Supreme Court. Thus, the ratio laid down in majority of the judgments of the High Courts on this point is discussed herebelow.

J.M. Sen Gupta's case[60]

In the case of J.M. Sen Gupta, an application for *mandamus* was made for an order under Section 45 of the Specific Relief Act, 1877 against the President of Bengal Legislative Council to prevent him from putting to the vote a Bill for the payment of salaries to the Ministers. The application was refused on the ground that the applicant, who was a member of the Legislative Council, had no personal grievance and that his personal right was not injured.

Chhotelal v. State of Utter Pradesh[61]

It was conceded in this case that the protection from legal proceedings conferred under Article 361 on the President, Governors and Rajpramukhs in respect of their public duties and powers, did not extend to a Legislature. But it was held that the limitation on the power of the Court arose from Articles 105 and 194 and from the inherent powers of the Legislature to prevent any outside interference with the exercise of its functions. In such a case, *mandamus* will not also lie against Government of the State, because it is not the Government which passed the law, but it is the Legislature.

Reference case under Article 143 of the Constitution: Powers, Privileges and Immunities of State Legislatures[62]

In the above reference case, the Supreme Court (per **Gajendragadkar, C.J**, speaking for majority) has observed regarding powers of a High Court and the Supreme Court to issue writ of *mandamus* against the Legislature as follows:

> *'This (Art. 226) Article confers very wide powers on every High Court...... It is hardly necessary to emphasize that the language used by Article 226 is conferring power on the High Court is very wide. Article 12 defines the "State" as including the Legislature of such State and so, prima facie, the power conferred on the High Court under Article 226(1) read by itself, does*

60. AIR 1925 Cal. 48, p. 54.
61. AIR 1951 All. 228, Para. 27.
62. AIR 1965 SC 745.

not seem to permit such a plea to be raised. Article 32 which deals with the power of this Court, puts the matter on a still higher pedestal; the right to move this Court by appropriate proceedings for the enforcement of Fundamental rights is itself a guaranteed fundamental right, and so, what we have said about Article 226(1) is still more true about Article 32(1).'

Syed Abdul Mansur Habibullah v. the Speaker, W.B. Legislative Assembly[63]

Following the above judgment of the Supreme Court in the reference application, the Calcutta High Court in this case observed that where the proceedings inside the Legislative Chamber have become illegal or unconstitutional the High Court can issue a writ of *mandamus* upon the Legislature.

So far as the issuance of *mandamus* against the legislature is concerned, it appears that the Courts are reluctant to issue the writs against legislature. One of the reasons for it may be the strict observance of the doctrine of separation of powers, which says that in a healthy democratic system as far as possible, three wings of democracy viz. executive, legislature and judiciary should not interfere with the work of one another. It is a function of the legislature to legislate the statutes. Therefore, to guide or direct the legislature to draft certain bills or refrain from doing so by a High Court or the Supreme Court by way of *mandamus* would be direct breach of the doctrine of separation of power.

State of J. & K. v. A.R. Zakki[64]

A jurisdiction of the High Court or the Supreme Court to issue writ of *mandamus* can be extended to the legislature or not. The question arose in the above case before the High Court of J. & K. As it is evident from the established legal position that the writ of *mandamus* cannot be issued to the legislature to enact a particular legislation. Section 110 of the J. and K. Constitution, which is on the same lines as Article 234 of the Constitution of India, vests in the Governor, the power to make rules for appointments of persons other than the District Judges to the Judicial Service of the State of J. and K. and for framing such rules, the Governor is required to consult the Commission and the High Court. This power to frame rules is legislative in nature. A writ of *mandamus* cannot, therefore, be issued directing the State Government to make the rules in accordance with the proposal made by the High Court. In the present case the purport of the direction given by the High Court was that the amendments that have been recommended by the High Court should be incorporated in the rules. It was found in appeal before the Supreme Court against the judgment of the High Court that such a direction was impermissible and cannot be upheld.

63. AIR 1966 Cal. 363, p. 367.
64. AIR 1992 SC 457.

From the above mentioned cases we can without hesitation come to the definite conclusion that no writ of *mandamus* either under Article 226 or under Article 32 is maintainable against the legislature directing it to enact certain legislation.

Maharshi Avadesh v. Union of India[65]

In a writ petition filed by the petitioner under Article 32 of the Constitution of India before the Supreme Court, a relief was sought for issuing writ of *mandamus* to respondents for considering enactment of a common Civil Code for all citizens of India, for declaring Muslim Women (Protection of Rights on Divorce) Act, 1986 as void being violative of Articles 14, 15, 44, 38, 39 and 39-A and for directing Respondents to enact Shariat Act in respect of those affecting dignity and rights of Muslim women and against their protection.

In the above case while declining to give relief of *mandamus*, the Supreme Court said that the same was not maintainable as the relief demanded pertained to legislative sphere, where the Supreme Court could not enter under Article 32 of the Constitution.

Analysis and Inferences

From the above discussion it is clear that judiciary cannot direct the legislature to enact any law which is pending as a bill in the house. (e.g. Common Civil Procedure Code Bill). The Courts, while considering a question as to whether *mandamus* be issued against the legislature or not, highly rely upon the doctrine or Separation of Power, which says that there are three wings of the democracy *viz.* executive, legislature and judiciary. In order to have healthy democratic system, as far as possible, one wing should not interfere with the work of another. But, in the recent years there are many instances wherein the judiciary is constrained to interfere with the work of the executive in order to give justice to the subject. Now it is proper time that the courts should think of issuing *mandamus* against legislature at least in certain cases.

3.5 *MANDAMUS* AGAINST LOCAL AUTHORITIES

Meaning

"Local authorities" as defined in Section 3(31) of the General Clauses Act refers to authorities like Municipalities, District Boards, Panchayats, Improvement Trust and Mining Settlement Boards. The units of the local self-Government like village panchayat, municipal committee or Development authority are also included within the definition of "local authorities".

Justice S. Saghir Ahmad has given various definitions of the term

65. (1994) Supp. 1 SCC 713.

"Local Authority" while coming to a conclusion that Haryana Housing Board is not covered under the term "Local Authority" in the case of *Housing Board, Haryana* v. *Haryana Housing Board Employees Union.*[66]

As per section 2(J) of the Haryana Housing Board Act, 1971 the "Local Authority" means:

> *'2(J) "Local authority" means a municipality constituted under the Punjab Municipal Act, 1911 (Punjab Act 3 of 1911), or a Gram Panchayat constituted under the Punjab Gram Panchayat Act, 1952 (Punjab Act 4 of 1953), or a Panchayat Samity or a Zilla Parishad Act, 1961 (Punjab Act 3 of 1961), or an Improvement Trust constituted under the Punjab Town Improvement Act, 1922 (Punjab Act 4 of 1922)'.*

In the above judgment the concept of "Local Authority" is discussed as per Entry 5, List II of the Seventh Schedule of the Constitution of India which is reproduced below:

> *'5. Local Government, that is to say, the constitution and powers of municipal corporations, improvement trusts, district boards, mining settlement authorities and other local authorities for the purpose of local self-Government or village administration.'*

Further explanation regarding the term 'Local Authority' is given in para. 6 of the aforesaid judgment, which says:

> *'6. The Entry empowers the State Legislature to make law with respect to any subject relating to Local Government including the constitution of "Local Authorities". The State Legislature can also confer such powers as it itself possesses upon a "Local Authority", including the power of taxation (within the limits of List II) for the purpose of Local Self-Government. The "Local Authority", undoubtedly, is a representative body but notwithstanding its representative character, it remains a subordinate Authority created by a statute and therefore, it cannot claim the power of taxation which belongs to the State Legislature except to the extent it is conferred upon it by the statute which creates it.'*

3.5.1 Mandamus against Village Panchayat

Ajit Singh v. State of Punjab[67]

In the case of *Ajit Singh* v. *State of Punjab* the petitioner approached the Supreme Court for obtaining necessary directions and restraining the consolidation of village Ropalon under the East Punjab Holdings (Consolidation and Prevention of Fragmentation) Act, 1948.

66. AIR 1996 SC 434.
67. AIR 1967 SC 856.

While rejecting the petition filed by the petitioner against the acquisition process, the Supreme Court held that the Gram Panchayat is a local authority within the meaning of Article 31-A of the Constitution of India. It was observed by the Supreme Court in para. 28,

> '...... *The Gram Panchayat is a local authority and by virtue of the definition of "State" in Article 12 stands included in that term. Therefore, a law providing for the transfer of ownership or right to possession to the Gram Panchayat is for the purpose of Article 31-A (1) and (2), a law providing for the compulsory acquisition or requisitioning of the property.*'

From the above observation of the Supreme Court it becomes very much clear that Village Panchayats are covered under the term "local authorities" under Article 12 for the purpose of Part III of the Constitution of India.

3.5.2 Mandamus against Town Area Committee

Mohammad Yasin v. The Town Area Committee, Jalalabad and another[68]

Writ of *mandamus* was entertained against local authority, i.e. Town Area Committee in the year 1952 by the Supreme Court in the case of *Mohammad Yasin* v. *The Town Area Committee, Jalalabad and another*. Five Judges Constitutional Bench, without hesitation issued writ of *mandamus* under Article 32 of the Constitution against the Town Area Committee for the protection of the fundamental right of the petitioner enshrined under Article 19(1)(g). The Supreme Court (Per **S.R. Das, J.**) observed as follows:

As per the facts of the case the bye-laws made by a Town Area Committee provided by clause (1) that no person shall sell or purchase any vegetable or fruit within the prescribed limits of the Town Areas Committee, by wholesale or auction, without paying the fee fixed under these bye-laws to the licensee appointed by the Town Magistrate. Bye-law (4)(b) expressly provided that any person can sell in wholesale at any place in the Town Areas provided he pays the prescribed fees to the licensee. On a contention that the effect of the bye-laws was to bring about a total prohibition of the business of wholesale dealers in vegetables and fruits and thereby infringe their fundamental right under Article 19(1) (g) of the Constitution and further that the levy is an unauthorized impost constituting an illegal restraint on their fundamental rights under Article 19(1)(g).

The byc-laws do not, in terms, prohibit anybody from dealing in vegetables and fruits as contended. But the contention that though in form there is no prohibition, in effect, the bye-laws have brought about a total prohibition of the business of the wholesale dealers in a commercial sense

68. AIR 1952 SC 162.

and from a practical point of view, cannot be said to be unsound or untenable.

The bye-laws do not purport to fix a fee for the use or occupation of an immovable property vested in or entrusted to the management of the Town Area Committee including any public street or place of which it allows the use or occupation. Sections 293(i) and 298(j) and (d) of the U.P. Municipalities Act as amended at the time they were extended to the town areas in the Uttar Pradesh do not empower the Town Areas Committee to make any bye-law authorizing it to charge any fee otherwise than for the use or occupation of any property vested in or entrusted to the management of the Town Areas Committee including any public street. Therefore, the bye-laws which impose a charge on the whole-sale dealer in the shape of a prescribed fee, irrespective of any use or occupation by him of immovable property vested in or entrusted, to the management of the Town Areas Committee including any public street are obviously *ultra vires* the powers of the Committee and therefore the bye-laws cannot be said to constitute a valid law which alone may under Article 19(b) of the Constitution impose a restriction on the right conferred by Article 19(1)(g). Such illegal imposition must undoubtedly operate as an illegal restraint and must infringe the unfettered right of the wholesale dealer to carry on his occupation, trade or business which is guaranteed to him by Article 19(1)(g).

Thus, the Supreme Court allowed the petition against the Town Areas Committee on facts, as there was direct infringement of Article 19(1)(g) of the Constitution of India. But at no stage of litigation it was contended that the writ against the respondent was not maintainable. In other words, it can be said that the concept of issuance of writ of *mandamus* against Town Areas Committee, which is a local authority, was very much clear and hence the respondent did not think it proper to challenge the writ petition on technical ground that it was not covered under the definition of "local authority".

3.5.3 *Mandamus* against District Board/Panchayat

Tahir Hussain v. District Board[69]

The petitioner challenged the bye-laws made under the provisions of 174 of the U.P. District Boards Act, 1922 by way of filing writ petition under Article 32 of the Constitution. In the aforesaid petition the petitioner alleged that the provisions of the aforesaid Act prohibits him from establishing, maintaining or running any cattle market in the District within the jurisdiction of the Board.

The District Board, by virtue of the powers given under Section 174 of the U.P. District Boards Act framed bye-laws. Bye-law No. 2 is

---

69. AIR 1954 SC 630.

reproduced herebelow which apparently violated the fundamental right of the petitioner to carry on trade, occupation or business:

> *"No person shall establish or maintain or run any cattle market in the District within the jurisdiction of the Board."*

The petitioner alleged that the restriction put by the aforesaid bye-law did not fall within the reasonable restrictions under Article 19(6) of the Constitution and therefore the same was illegal, void and liable to be struck down. The Supreme Court, relying upon the judgment of *Rashid Ahmed* v. *Municipal Board, Kairana* (discussed earlier)[70] observed that the prohibition imposed by the bye-law No.2 made by virtue of the powers given under Section 174 of the said Act was void and gave further directions.

3.5.4 *Mandamus* against Municipalities (Municipal Corporation)

The Queen v. The Mayor and Assessor of Monmouth
The Queen v. The Mayor and Assessor of Bolton[71]

A writ of *mandamus* was issued upon the Mayor and Assessors of the Borough of Monmouth to show cause why a writ of *mandamus* should not issue commanding them to hold a court and hear the objections of Henry Evans to certain persons as not being entitled to have their names retained on the burgess list of the borough and proceed to revise such lists accordingly. The inferior tribunal also refused to hear the case and hence the writ petition was sought in both of the above mentioned cases.

The following observations made by **Blackburn, J.** agreeing with the opinion of **Cockburn, C.J.** by saying,

> *'..... If persons exercising an inferior jurisdiction, on a mistaken view of the law, refuse to hear a case, they erroneously decline to exercise their jurisdiction; and this Court will compel them by mandamus to hear and decide it. I think, therefore, that the mandamus ought to issue ...'*

Agreeing with **Justice Blackburn**, the same view was taken by **Mellor, J.** and observed,

> *'...Upon the first point, I think the mayor and assessors have declined jurisdiction; and on the decision taken in Reg. V. Freeman of Leicester,*[72] *the rule for the mandamus ought to be made absolute, in as much as, by a mistaken view of the law, an inferior tribunal has refused to hear the case....'*

---

70. AIR 1950 SC 163.
71. 1870 Q.B. 251.
72. 15 Q.B. 671.

Thus, the Court of the Queen's Bench allowed a writ of *mandamus* against the Municipal Corporation.

Queen v. The Mayor and Corporation of the Borough of Bangor[73]

This was a case arisen out of Election dispute wherein the Court of Queen's Bench issued a *mandamus* against the Mayor and Municipal Corporation. As per the facts of the case, in an election for the office of a councilor of one of the wards of a borough, R. and P. were the only candidates. At the close of the poll P. objected that R. was disqualified for election by reason of his being an alderman of the borough whose term of office had not expired and P. claimed himself to be elected whatever might be the result of the poll. But when the returning officer counted the poll, R. was in a majority.

It was held in a *mandamus* preferred by R. that R. was not by reason of his being an alderman disqualified for election to the office of Councilor and that by accepting the later office he vacated the former.

That the returning officer had no power to decide whether R. was disqualified or not.

That by stating at the close of the poll, the number of votes given to each candidate the returning officer had made sufficient declaration that R. was elected and that the effect of that declaration was not altered by reason of public notice.

That the office of Councilor was not *de facto* filled by P., so as to entitle him to hold it until dispossessed by an election petition or by *quo warranto*.

For the following reasons a rule was issued for a *mandamus* commanding to the mayor and Corporation of the borough of Bangor commanding them to receive and count the vote of one John Pritchard at the corporate meeting of the council.

Reg. v. Glamorgan County Council[74]

The dispute in the above case was regarding the payment of the expenses of food and lodging incurred for the troops brought into a county. That the troops were called upon into a county, on an application of the county magistrates, for the purpose of suppressing riots, and preserving peace and order in the county. By agreement with the magistrates certain tradesmen supplied the troops with food and lodging while quartered in the county. The accounts were certified by the magistrates, and were sent in to the county council, but, a dispute having arisen as to the amount, the county council refused to pay anything whereupon an order nisi for a *mandamus* was moved for and obtained. The Divisional Court discharged the order nisi. The prosecutors viz. Miller and others appealed. In appeal the judgment of the Divisional Court was affirmed without interfering with the appeal and no *mandamus* was issued. The reason given by it was only

---

73. (1886) Q.B. 349.
74. (1899) 2 Q.B. 536.

that no duty was imposed by law on those who administered the county funds to pay the expenses of the maintenance of troops. The agreement to supply food and lodging was entered into between tradesmen and magistrates. But nowhere Glamorgan County Council was a party.

Hence, it was held that the prosecutors could avail other remedy but a *mandamus* could not be granted.

The Queen v. Lonson and North Western Railway Company[75]

The owners of certain mines, which lay under a railway, having given notice of their intention to work them, the railway company required a certain amount of support to be left. Arbitrators were appointed to settle the amount of compensation to be paid by the railway company in respect of the minerals required to be left unworked, and in respect of the continuous working of the mines being interrupted, and in respect of their being worked under restrictions so as not to affect the railway.

It was held that the claim of the mine-owners was made under Section 78 of the Railways Clauses Act, and therefore that the provisions of the Lands Clauses Act as to the assessment of compensation applied. In this case it was held by Justice White that the Court will not refuse to grant a prerogative writ of *mandamus* in every case in which an action of *mandamus* would lie.

Rex v. Board of Education[76]

The Court of King's Bench in this case confirmed the ratio laid down by the Divisional Court that a local educational authority had no power under the Education Act, 1902 to differentiate, in the matter of teachers equally qualified and teaching the same subjects, between the salaries paid in provided and non-provided schools as such.

As per the facts of the case, on coming into force of the Education Act, 1902, the local education authority of Swansea continued to pay salaries to the teachers in the schools in the district at the rates previously in existence, the salaries paid to teachers in provided schools being at a higher rate than those paid to teachers of similar qualifications in non-provided schools. Subsequently an increase was made in the salaries paid to teachers in the provided schools only, and the managers of a non-provided schools in the district complained to the Board of Education that the local education authority, by refusing to pay salaries in the non-provided school at the same rate as in the provided schools, had failed to maintain and keep efficient the non-provided school, as provided by Sec. 7 of the Education Act, 1902.

The Board appointed a barrister to hold an inquiry, and after having evidence on behalf of the managers, he reported that the school had regularly earned the grant, but only through the deficiency in salaries

75. (1894) 2 Q.B. 512.
76. (1910) 2 K.B. 165.

having been made good by the managers, and that the local education authority had failed to maintain and keep efficient the school. The Board of Education decided that there had been no such failure by the local education authority, on the grounds that there was no statutory right on the part of the managers of any particular school to receive any particular scale of salaries, and that it had not been shown that the money provided by the local education authority was inadequate for the purpose of maintaining and keeping efficient the school in question.

The managers thereupon applied for a writ of certiorari to quash the decision and for a *mandamus* to get appropriate directions. The Divisional Court held that the local education authority had no power to discriminate between provided and non-provided schools as such in the matter of the salaries paid to the teachers, and they made absolute the rules for *certiorari* and *mandamus* upon the ground that the Board had not decided the true question submitted to them.

The Board of Education filed appeal against this decision before the Court of King's Bench. It was held by the Court of King's Bench that the decision of the Board of Education must be quashed on the ground that it did not answer the question submitted to them and that a *mandamus* must be issued directing the Board to determine the question according to law. Hence, the Court of King's Bench rejected the appeal of the Board of Education and confirmed the decision of the Divisional Court.

Rex v. Poplar Borough Council[77]

In this case appeals were filed from two orders of the Divisional Court making absolute two rules for peremptory writs of *mandamus,* the first commanding the Council of the metropolitan borough of Poplar to pay to the London Country Council the sum of 33,944 l. 10s. 6d., the first instalment due under a precept of the said London County Council dated May 10, 1921, and that if necessary to make the levy a rate for the purpose; the second commanding the same borough council to pay to the Managers of the Metropolitan Asylum District two sums of 7035 l. each due from them under and by virtue of precept of Poplar dated April 9, 1921, and if necessary to make and levy a rate for the purpose of that payment. The Divisional Court made rule absolute in both the cases.

In an appeal the Court of King's Bench held that as regards the precept of the London County Council, that the London Government Act, 1899, did not provide any remedy for breach of duty imposed upon the borough council by that Act, and that therefore the Court could grant a *mandamus;* and as regards the precepts both of the London County Council and of the Managers of the Metropolitan Asylum District, that the remedy by distress was wholly inadequate, and that *mandamus* was the only effective means of securing the performance of the public duty.

77. (1922) 1 K.B. 72.

Rex v. Stepney Borough Council[78]

This case was arisen out of denial of the local authority to place the four hereditaments in the new Special List by the Council. W. & Co. claimed that four hereditaments of which they were occupiers in the metropolitan borough of Stepney should be included in the valuation list as industrial hereditaments in accordance with Sec. 1 sub-sec.1 of the Rating and Valuation (Apportionment) Act, 1928. The Assessment Committee allowed the claim and put the four hereditaments into the special list of industrial hereditament. The revenue officer appealed from that decision, and on December 11, 1929, Quarter sessions allowed the appeal and ordered the four hereditaments to be deleted from the special list. W. & Co. appealed against that decision and the Divisional Court allowed the appeal, holding that the hereditaments were industrial hereditaments and ordered that they should be inserted in the special list. In the meantime the new quinquennial list was prepared in which all the four hereditaments were put into part I, the non-industrial list. The new quinquennial list was finally approved by the Assessment Committee. After the decision of the Divisional Court, W. & Co. requested the local authority to transfer the four hereditaments into the special list of the new quinquennial list, but the same was refused. W. & Co. applied for rule *nisi* for *mandamus* to compel the local authority to alter the quinquennial list and to transfer the hereditaments into the industrial special list in accordance with the decision of the Divisional Court. The Divisional Court discharged the rule by not entertaining *mandamus*.

On appeal, it was held that notwithstanding W. & Co. might have objected under Sec. 11 of the Valuation (Metropolis) Act, 1869, to the incorrectness of the valuation list, yet in the circumstances that was not a sufficient, convenient and appropriate remedy. If W. & Co. had made the objection it would have been useless, as the decision that time must have been given against them, and therefore the rule for a *mandamus* must be made absolute.

Rex v. Bedwellty Urban District Council[79]

A writ of *mandamus* was issued against the Urban District Council of Bedwellty calling upon it to permit a ratepayer to see the accounts. As per the facts of the case, a ratepayer in an urban district, who was also the secretary of the local ratepayers' association, appointed an accountant, who was not a ratepayer in the district, to inspect with him the books and accounts of the local authority. The officers of the Council permitted the accountant to inspect all the books and accounts to which Sec. 60 of the Rating and Valuation Act, 1925 (which expressly authorizes inspection by an agent of the ratepayer), applied, but they declined to permit him to inspect the general books and accounts of the Council, on the ground that

78. (1933)2 K.B. 273.
79. (1934)1 K.B. 333.

he was not himself a "person interested," and that Sec. 247 of the Act did not authorize a person interested to inspect by an agent. The books and accounts were produced to the ratepayers themselves. In this case Avory, J. observed that it was a fit case in which a writ of *mandamus* should be issued and rule should be made absolute. It was held that a person interested was entitled under Sec. 247, sub-sec. 4, of the Public Health Act, 1875, to inspect by an agent, and that a rule for *mandamus* commanding the Council to permit the accountant to inspect the books must be made absolute.

Under the Specific Relief Act, 1877

Maila Singh v. Bourne[80]

It has been held in the above case that Rule 27 under Sec. 8 of Burma Municipal Act, 1898, clearly contemplates disqualification for nomination as well as election and consequently an objection as to the validity of nomination upon the ground of disqualification if not brought under Rule 27, it is not open to bring it under Rule 53, High Court can in a suitable case forbear from doing so.

Govind Laxaman v. Minicipal Corporation for the City of Bombay[81]

The Municipality of Bombay in this case decided to improve and increase the water supply of the city of Bombay and with that view it decided to launch a new project. That project involved the building of a new pipe line. Tenders were invited for the work and the Commissioner recommended to the Standing Committee that the tender of the Hindustan Construction Co. Ltd. should be accepted. The Standing Committee accepted that recommendation and authorised the Commissioner to execute the contract with the Company. The petitioner filed a petition in the Bombay High Court under Sec. 45 of the Specific Relief Act, 1877 praying that the Municipal Commissioner and the Corporation be ordered to forbear from concluding and executing the contract with the company, and also they may be ordered to invite fresh and proper tenders. The petition came on before Bhagwati, J., who made the order prayed for by allowing the petition. He observed in his judgment,

> *'In considering whether a petitioner seeking the intervention of the Court under Sec. 45, Specific Relief Act, has demanded justice and has been refused it before he sought intervention of the Court, it is not necessary that there should be an actual denial of justice after demand. It may be that there was not sufficient time for the respondent to consider the matter and grant or refuse the demand, but the Court is entitled to take into consideration the facts and events as they transpired after the demand for justice was made.*

80. AIR 1931 Rang. 326.
81. 4 DLR (Bom.) 22.

When the respondent opposes the petitioner's petition, the Court is entitled to presume that the respondent would and did in fact refuse to comply with the demand of the petitioner. If a petitioner has other adequate legal remedy open, namely that of filing a regular suit for declaration, he cannot maintain a petition under Sec. 45 of the Act. But even if it would be competent to file a suit, where the suit would be delayed, e.g. by reason of a notice of suit, giving one month's time, being a condition precedent to the institution of the suit, and where before that is done, there is a likelihood of the act complained of being carried and, thus rendering the suit ineffective and abortive, it cannot be said that the remedy by suit would be equally convenient, speedy or beneficial or effective, and hence a petition under Sec. 45 would not be barred.'

Being aggrieved by the order of the Bombay High Court the Municipal Corporation and Municipal Commissioner preferred appeal wherein following propositions were laid down:

(1) It is clear that under Sec. 45 of the Specific Relief Act, in order to satisfy the first proviso, a party must have some interest in property, franchise or personal right, the injury to which alone would entitle him to maintain a petition under the section. No particular quantum of interest appears to be necessary under the section in order to entitle a person to come under it. There does not also seem to be any difference in principle between the title which would entitle a person to sue for an injury done to his property and the title which would be equally necessary to make a petition under Sec. 45 maintainable. It may be that in a particular case the petitioner will fail to get an order under Sec. 45, but yet may succeed in invoking the aid of the Court in a suit filed by him. But that does not mean that the cause of action is in any way different from that in a suit. The title which the petitioner or the plaintiff, as the case may be has to establish, the interest which he has, is identical in both cases. He must show that there is an invasion to his property, franchise or personal right, and there can only be an invasion provided he has a legal specific right in property, franchise or has some personal right.

(2) It is also clear that a rate-payer who has contributed to the sales is injured in his property within the meaning of Sec. 45, Specific Relief Act, if the rates are misapplied or utilized contrary to the law.

It is not necessary that the petitioner in a petition under Sec. 45, Specific Relief Act, must show some right which he enjoys other than the rights enjoyed by the community at large before he can maintain the petition; nor can it be said that a mere public wrong is not sufficient to entitle a person to maintain a petition under Sec. 45 and that he must show that some private wrong has been caused to him and he has been damnified by that wrong. If a corporation consisting of members all of whom are equally interested in the carrying out of its activities according to its charter, acts illegally or contrary to its charter or misapplies its funds, then every member of the Corporation has the right to file a suit to prevent the corporation from so acting. The same principle applies to a rate-payer. Every rate-payer has the right to prevent the public body (Municipality) to come to Court in support of his right and in order to prevent the Corporation or public body from acting contrary to law or their own charter whether relief would be granted to him under Sec. 45 is another matter; it is a summary procedure, and the order to be made is entirely discretionary with the Court, and before the Court would exercise the discretion, the various conditions laid down in Sec. 45 which are all cumulative must be satisfied. The principles of English law dealing with the writ of *mandamus* must be imported in considering the provisions of Sec. 45; the procedure under the section corresponds to the issuing of a high prerogative writ under the English procedure.

Every rate-payer has an interest in the proper application of the municipal fund to which he contributes by paying rates and the mere payment of rates is sufficient to qualify him to challenge the illegal and *ultra-vires* act of a public authority. The fact that the right is shared by him with the community at large or with a large number of persons would not make the right lose its validity or make it less important. A right may be enjoyed in common with every subject or the *Crown*, but when it is infringed in the case of an individual subject, there at once arises in that individual a further right to seek the protection of the Court to enforce such right. The question in every case is whether a right has been infringed qua the petitioner, and the mere fact that he shares it with other persons cannot debar him from obtaining the necessary relief under the law. There is no difference in principle between a person aggrieved within the meaning of the English Statute and a person injured within the meaning of Sec. 45.

(3) Section 45 deals with a procedure which in England corresponds to issuing of a high prerogative writ, and the principles of English law dealing with the writ of *mandamus* must be imported in considering the provisions of Sec. 45.

(4) No special injury has got to be established by the petitioner before he can come under Sec. 45. If he shows any injury and he also shows a title to his property which is likely to be injured that is sufficient to satisfy the first proviso to Sec. 45.

The Bombay High Court, while dealing with the above case in appeal categorically dealt with the rights of the a person under Sec. 45 of the Specific Relief Act, 1877 and laid down the ratio that the above rights are similar to the rights available to a person preferring writ of *mandamus* under the English system.

Hirendra Nath v. Calcutta Corporation[82]

In the above case the buildings committee acted illegally in sanctioning the plans which clearly infringed Rs. 30 and 32 of Sch. 17 of the Calcutta Municipal Act, it was held that the aggrieved party can make an application under Sec. 45 of the Specific Relief Act, 1877, for a mandatory order on the Corporation of Calcutta requiring the Corporation to receive the illegal sanction, and that sections 17 and 19 of the Calcutta Municipal Act would not provide the petitioner with an adequate remedy.

Lakshmimoni Dassi[83]

In re Lakshmimoni Dassi it was held that the right given to Government to interfere under Sec. 18 of the Calcutta Municipal Act and the implied right of the public or the individual to move the Government in some way or another, is not such an alternative remedy as will deprive the individual of the right to apply for *mandamus*. Where the provision is primarily in favour of the general public, (Schedule 17, R. 32, Calcutta Municipal Act) but in the nature of things the breach of it must injure the specific individual to quite a different degree, such a right can be assumed in the specified individual. Hence, where building plans are passed and permission to build is given contrary to building restrictions contained in the bye-laws whereby the premises of adjacent owner is injured as to light, air, health and amenities the corporation owes such a duty to the adjacent owner, and there is in the adjacent owner such a legal right, as to found an application for *mandamus*.

A.C. Mahomed v. Corporation of Calcutta[84]

In the case of *A.C. Mahomed* v. *Corporation of Calcutta*, the Calcutta High Court held that where the amenities and sanitation of a person's property will be substantially prejudiced if a building plan which violates the regulations is sanctioned, such person has a right to call upon the Municipal Corporation to see that the provision of the statute are observed. He can apply for *mandamus* under Sec. 45 of the Specific Relief Act, 1877, as the Calcutta Municipal Corporation Act furnishes no specific and adequate legal remedy to persons in his position.

82. AIR 1941 Cal. 386.
83. AIR 1941 Cal. 391.
84. 45 C.W.N. 408.

Under the Constitution of India

New Manek Chowk Spinning and Weaving Mills v. Municipal Corporation of the City of Ahmedabad[85]

The petitioner textile Mills challenged the validity of the assessment book of the year 1966-67 relating to Special Property section prepared and published by the Municipal Corporation of Ahmedabad City, by way of filing a writ petition under Article 32 of the Constitution of India seeking therein the relief of/or in the nature of *mandamus*. The case of the petitioner was that by the said book the Municipal Corporation imposed property tax on the petitioner on the basis of a flat rate per 100 sq. ft. of the floor area of the petitioner's property as also of all other textile mills, factories, university buildings, etc., under rule 9 of the Taxation Rules under Bombay Provincial Municipal Corporations Act, 1949.

The contention of the petitioner Mills was that the flat rate method adopted for determining the rental value was against the provisions of the Bombay Provincial Municipal Corporations Act and was also in violation of all recognized concepts and principles of valuation for the purpose of rating and was violative of Article 14 of the Constitution.

Further it was held that the Rule 7(2) and (3) of the Chapter VIII of the Schedule of the Bombay Provincial Municipal Corporations Act, 1949 were beyond competence of the legislature. As per Entry 49 of List II of the 7th Schedule of the Constitution of India, the State Legislature has power to levy a tax only on land and buildings. The same could not be levied upon the machinery contained in or situated on the building even though the machinery was there for the use of the building for a particular purpose. Hence, the Supreme Court declared Rule 7(2) as beyond legislative competence of the State and also declared Rule 7(3) as invalid on account of excessive delegation of power as the Municipal Commissioner was the only person who could examine the question of fixing the ratable value upon the building.

By taking into consideration aforesaid aspects a writ of *mandamus* was issued directing the Municipality to treat the relevant entries in the assessment book as invalid and cancelled and to prepare fresh assessment list.

Municipal Corporation of Delhi v. Birla Cotton Spinning and Weaving Mills, Delhi[86]

After having considered Municipal Corporation of Delhi as 'Local Authority' **Justice Hidayatullah** (as he then was) observed (at page 1254 of the A.I.R.):

'Local bodies are subordinate branches of governmental activity. They are

85. AIR 1967 SC 1801.
86. AIR 1968 SC 1232.

democratic institutions managed by the representatives of the people. They function for public purposes and take away a part of the government affairs in local areas. They are political sub-divisions and agencies which exercise a part of State functions. As they are intended to carry on local self-Government the power of taxation is a necessary adjunct to their other powers. They function under the supervision of the government.'

Municipal Corporation of Delhi v. Kishan Das[87]

This case arose out of the judgment and order by the Chief Justice of the Delhi High Court in a writ petition under Article 226 of the Constitution seeking the relief of/or in the nature of *mandamus* to approve the plans submitted by the respondents. The relief was granted by the Delhi High Court. The order of the single judge passed in the writ petition was subsequently confirmed in a Letters Patent Appeal by the Delhi High Court. Being aggrieved by the order of the single Judge, confirmed by the Division Bench of the Delhi High Court, approving the building plans of repairing, addition as well as alteration of the existing building the Corporation preferred appeal challenging the orders of the Delhi High Court.

The respondents were the owners and were in possession of the building within the municipal limits of Delhi. As the building was an old construction and required urgent and extensive repairs, the respondents submitted to the appellant plans for its sanction for execution of work, consisting of repairs, addition and alteration to the said building having Nos. 3766 to 3776. The Commissioner of the Delhi Corporation vide his letter dated 4-2-1966 informed the respondents that their application for execution of construction work in respect of the aforesaid houses had been refused on the grounds "that the proposal was under acquisition and also the land was residential against proposal of commercial".

By taking into consideration the arguments on both the sides the learned Chief Justice of the Delhi High Court allowed the writ petition of the respondent and issued a *mandamus* to the appellant Corporation to approve the plans and grant the sanction asked for. The learned Chief Justice also expressed the view that the Commissioner could decline the sanction only if there was a contravention of Sec. 336(2) or Sec. 340 of the Corporation Act. He further expressed his view that the refusal of the sanction of the Commissioner was wholly irrelevant and not germane to the sanction asked for.

The Corporation preferred Special Leave to Appeal before the Supreme Court challenging the order of the High Court confirming the judgment of the learned Single Judge. The Supreme Court held that in order to sustain the validity of the order of rejection passed by the Commissioner the corporation has to establish that the proposed building or the use of the site for the building, by the petitioner would contravene the provisions of any other law.

87. AIR 1969 SC 386.

It was further observed by the Supreme Court that if a Zonal Development Plane provides for a particular use of any land or building in that Zone, it cannot be put to a different use. Where, therefore, there is no indication in the Master Plan in any manner that the lands of the petitioner are being taken up by any part of the proposed road, mentioned in the Master Plan, there is no violation of any of the provisions of the Development Act. Lastly, the Supreme Court, by confirming the order passed by the High Court observed that the High Court was perfectly right in issuing writ of *mandamus* against the Delhi Municipality.

K. Ramdas Shenoy v. Udipi Municipality[88]

This case is a good example of interference of the apex court where the Municipality acts in excess of the powers conferred by the Act or abuses those powers then in those cases it is not exercising its jurisdiction irregularly or wrongly but it is usurping powers which it does not possess. The right to build on his own land is a right incidental to the ownership of that land. Within the Municipality the exercise of that right has been regulated in the interest of the community residing within the limits of the Municipal Committee. If sanction is given to build by contravening a bye-law the jurisdiction of the Courts will be invoked on the ground that the approval by the authority of building plans which contravene the bye-laws made by that authority is illegal and inoperative.

As per the short facts of the case, the Municipality passed four impeached resolutions facilitating to construct a theatre and to give facilities thereto. The appellant challenged all the four resolutions by way of filing writ petitions before the High Court. The High Court quashed three out of four resolutions and said that the fourth impeached resolution which approved the plan for conversion of Kalyan Mantap-*cum*-Lecture Hall into a cinema theatre was to remain undisturbed. Being aggrieved by the last portion of the judgment of the High Court by not quashing the fourth resolution, the appellant filed appeal before the Supreme Court.

The following were the arguments of the appellant before the Supreme Court:

The Municipality has illegally sanctioned the plan for conversion into a cinema. The appellant as the resident in the area has the right to compel the Municipality to perform duty imposed by the statute. The appellant has a right to insist on such performance of duty because he has an individual interest in the performance of the duty imposed by the Act that the scheme is not violated. The appellant resides in the area where the plan for conversion of the Kalyana Mantap-*cum*-Lecture Hall into a cinema has been granted. This is a residential area. The Municipality cannot act in disregard of the scheme. The Municipality is not the authority to vary or modify the Scheme. The Municipality on 29th April, 1970 refused to sanction a plan for construction of cinema theatre building. The

88. AIR 1974 SC 2177.

construction of the building had been earlier permitted as a Kalyana Mantap-*cum*-Lecture Hall and not for cinema theatre. That was the reason given by the Municipality for refusal to sanction a plan for construction of the cinema theatre building. The resolution of 11 June, 1970 on appeal against the order dated 18 April, 1970 granting the licence for cinema under the Madras Places of Public Resorts Act has been quashed by the High Court. Therefore, there is no licence to exhibit films. Municipality has no power to convert the lecture hall into a cinema theature.

The Supreme Court observed that an illegal construction of a cinema building materially affects the right to or enjoyment of the property by persons residing in the residential area. The Muicipal Authorities owe a duty and obligation under the statute to see that the residential is not spoilt by unauthorized construction. The rights of the residents in the area are invaded by an illegal construction of a cinema building. It has to be remembered that a scheme in a residential area means planned orderliness in accordance with the requirements of the residents. If the scheme is nullified by arbitrary acts in excess and derogation of the powers of the Municipality the courts will quash the orders passed by Municipalities in such cases.

While allowing the appeal the Supreme Court said that the Corporation ought to perform statutory duties and made the following observations in paragraph 29:

> *'29. The Court enforces the performance of statutory duty by public bodies as obligation to rate-payers who have a legal right to demand compliance by a local authority with its duty to observe statutory rights alone. The scheme here is for the benefit of the public. There is special interest in the performance of the duty. All the residents in the area have their personal interest in the performance of the duty. The special and substantial interest of the residents in the area is injured by the illegal construction.'*

The Supreme Court, by making the aforesaid observation allowed the appeal and quashed the resolution permitting to construct cinema theature.

Maneka Gandhi v. Union of India[89]

One of the very interesting and important cases arose on filing of a writ petition under Article 32 of the Constitution of India by Ms. Maneka Gandhi in the event of impounding of her passport "in public interest" by an order dated July 2, 1977. The Government of India declined in the interest of the general public to furnish the reasons for its decision. Thereupon, she challenged the order by way of writ petition under Article 32 of the Constitution. The matter was placed before the seven Judges' Constitutional bench.

89. AIR 1978 SC 597.

The order was challenged on the following grounds:

1. To the extent to which Sec. 10(3)(c) of the Passports Act, 1967, authorises the passport authority to impound a passport "in the interests of the general public", it is violative of Article 14 of the Constitution since it confers vague and undefined power on the passport authority;
2. Sec. 10(3)(c) is void as conferring an arbitrary power since it does not provide for a hearing of the holder of the passport before the passport is impounded.
3. Sec. 10(3)(c) is violative of Article 21 of the Constitution since it does not prescribe "procedure" within the meaning of that article and if it is held that procedure has been prescribed, it is arbitrary and unreasonable.
4. Sec. 10(3)(c) offends against Article 19(1)(a) and (g), since it permits restrictions to be imposed on the rights guaranteed by those provisions even though the restrictions are such as cannot be imposed under Article 19(2) or (6).

It was held by the Supreme Court that it could not be said that a good enough reason had been shown to exit for impounding the passport of the petitioner. Furthermore, the petitioner had had no opportunity of showing that the grounds for impounding it, finally given in the Supreme Court, either did not exist or had no bearing on public interest. But, Section 10(3)(c) of the Passports Act according to the Supreme Court did not offend Articles 14, 19(1)(a) or (g) or Article 21 of the Constitution. The view of the Supreme Court was that the right to go abroad in the circumstances of this case was not a fundamental right.

On the basis of the statement filed by the Attorney General on behalf of the union of India, it was said that the petitioner could make a representation in respect of impounding of passport and that the representation would be dealt with expeditiously and that, even if the impounding of the passport was confirmed, it would not exceed a period of six months from the date of the decision that might be given on the petitioner's representation.

In view of the statement made by the Attorney General, it was held by the majority of the Supreme Court that it was not necessary to formally interfere with the impugned order.

In this case minority view appears to be sound and bold one. Justice Beg, C.J., however, took the view that, as the order actually passed against the petitioner was neither fair nor proper according to the procedure, he would quash the order and direct the impounded passport to be returned to the petitioner.

Here instead of disposing of the petition merely on the statement of the Attorney General, the Supreme Court ought to have accepted minority view and ought to have declared that the Union of India had no authority to impound the passport of the petitioner on the illusory ground *viz.* "in the interest of general public" and a direction should have been given to the Passport Authority to return the passport to the petitioner alongwith the payment of appropriate cost.

British India Corporation Ltd. v. Market Committee, Dhariwal[90]

It was held in the above case that the writ of *mandamus* can be issued against the Market Committee if it is collecting or trying to collect *ultra vires* tax from the people. By issuance of *mandamus* the Market Committee can be directed not to collect tax illegally or without jurisdiction.

Olga Tellis v. Bombay Municipal Corporation[91]

This is a case wherein, for the first time the Supreme Court of India recognized right to livelihood as included in right to life. Justice Chandrachud delivered very considerate judgment. Several writ petitions under Article 32 of the Constitution were preferred by the pavements carrying their business on the footpaths and streets of the Bombay Municipality. The respondent Corporation took steps to demolish the huts and pavements from the streets.

The petitioners filed writ petitions before the Supreme Court and reliefs were asked to the effect that the Corporation should be directed by the issuance of writ of *mandamus* to withdraw the decision to demolish the pavement dwellings and slum hutments. Further to restore possession of the sites to the former occupiers.

During the course of arguments the petitioners contented that they could not be evicted from their squalid shelters without being offered alternative accommodation. They rely for their rights on Article 21 of the Constitution which guarantees that no person shall be deprived of his life except according to procedure established by law. They do not contend that they have a right to live on the pavements. Their contention was that they had a right to live, a right which could not be exercised without means of livelihood. They had no option but to flock to big cities like Bombay, which provide the means of subsistence. The petitioner forcefully argued that the right to life is illusory without a right to protection of the means by which alone life can be lived. And, the right of life can only be taken away or abridged by a procedure established by law, which has to be fair and reasonable, not fanciful or arbitrary such as is prescribed by the Bombay Municipal Corporation Act or the Bombay Police Act. Moreover, reliance was put by the petitioner upon their right to reside and settle in any part of the country given under Article 19(1)(e).

The Supreme Court took into consideration the following aspects before disposing the petitions:

90. AIR 1983 SC 162.
91. AIR 1986 SC 180.

1. The eviction of a person from a pavement or slum will inevitably lead to the deprivation of his means of livelihood, is a proposition which does not have to be established in each individual case.
2. It would unrealistic on the part of the Supreme Court to reject the petitions on the ground that the petitioners have not adduced evidence to show that they will rendered jobless if they are evicted from the slums and pavements.
3. In terms of the constitutional phraseology is that the eviction of the petitioners will lead to deprivation of their livelihood and consequently to the deprivation of life.
4. Section 314 of the Bombay Municipal Corporation Act for removal of encroachments on the footpaths or pavements over which the public has right of passage or access, cannot be regarded as unreasonable, unfair or unjust.
5. It was also observed by the Supreme Court that no one has a right to make use of a public property for a private purpose without the requisite authorization and therefore it is erroneous to contend that the pavement dwellers have right to encroach upon pavements by constructing dwellings on the public street.
6. Section 314 of the Bombay Municipal Corporation Act though, provides that the Commissioner may cause the removal of an encroachment without issuing previous notice. This does not command that the Commissioner shall, without notice, cause an encroachment to be removed. This should be done in exceptional circumstances, but should not be done as a rule. As far as possible there should not be departure from the rule of 'Audi alteram partem'.
7. By way of interim relief, the Supreme Court said that the petitioners should not be evicted from the pavements, footpaths or accessory roads until one month after the conclusion of monsoon season.

After making following observations against the Bombay Municipal Corporation the petition was disposed by the Supreme Court. Here, not only a writ was issued against a local authority by the Supreme Court, but a new principle has emerged out of it *viz.* right to livelihood is a right to life.

3.5.5 Mandamus against Development Authority

Premji Bhai v. Delhi Development Authority[92]

A writ petition was filed under Article 32 of the Constitution of India before the Supreme Court by the petitioner taking the contention that the Delhi Development Authority was not entitled to give discriminatory

92. AIR 1980 SC 738.

treatment by collecting surcharge as component of price in sale of flats constructed under MIG Scheme. While determining price of flats the authority acts purely in executive capacity. It was also argued that the Authority having the trapping of a "State" might be covered by the expression "other authority" in Article 12 and would certainly be precluded from according discriminatory treatment to persons offering to purchase flats in the same scheme. Those who opt to take flats in a particular income-wise and area-wise scheme in which all flats came up together as one project may attract Article 14.

The Supreme Court agreed upon the contention that the Authority might fall within the definition of "State" under Article 12 but according to it what was forbidden by Article 14 was discrimination amongst persons of the same class and for the purposes of allotment of flats scheme-wise, allottees of flats in the same scheme, not different schemes in the same income bracket, will have to be treated as a class and unless in each such class there is unequal treatment or unreasonable or arbitrary treatment, the complaint that Article 14 is violated cannot be entertained. Thus the petition was rejected disbelieving several other contentions as well.

Union of India v. R.C. Jain[93]

In this case, a question for consideration before the Supreme Court was whether the Delhi Development Authority created under the Delhi Development Act, 1957 was a "Local authority" within the meaning of Section 32(iv) of the Payment of Bonus Act or not. On a consideration of all the attributes of the Delhi Development Authority, it was held by the Supreme Court to be a "Local Authority". The Supreme Court, speaking through **Justice O. Chinnappa Reddy** observed:

> *'What then are the distinctive attributes and characteristics, all or many of which a Municipal Committee, District Board or Board of Port Commissioners share with any other local authority? First, the authorities must have separate legal existence as corporate bodies. They must not be mere governmental agencies but must be legally independent entities. Next, they must function in a defined area and must ordinarily, wholly or partly, directly or indirectly, be elected by the inhabitants of the area. Next, they must enjoy a certain degree of autonomy, with freedom to decide for themselves questions of policy affecting the area administered by them. The autonomy may not be complete and the degree of the dependents may vary considerably but, an appreciable measure of autonomy there must be. Next, they must be entrusted by statute with such governmental functions and duties as are usually entrusted to municipal bodies, such as those connected with providing amenities to the inhabitants of the locality, like health and education services, water and sewerage, town planning and development, roads, markets, transportation, social welfare services, etc. Broadly we may*

93. AIR 1981 SC 951.

> *say that they may be entrusted with the performance of civic duties and functions which would otherwise be governmental duties and functions. Finally, they must have the power to raise funds for the furtherance of their activities and the fulfilment of their projects by levying taxes, rates charges, or fees. This may be in addition to monies provided by government or obtained by borrowing or otherwise. What is essential is that control or management of the fund must vest in the authority.'*

It is pertinent to note here that in the year 1980, the Supreme Court did not pay much attention as to whether Delhi Development Authority falls within the definition of 'other authority' or it is a "Local Authority". This might have happened because nowhere in the arguments it was specifically taken as a point and secondly, as the petition was rejected on merits as there was no violation of Article 14, this issue became irrelevant.

But in the year 1981, the same Supreme Court declared that Delhi Development Authority falls within the definition of "State" as it falls in the group of "Local Authority". This time, the Supreme Court came to the right conclusion by applying correct analogy.

Bangalore Medical Trust v. B.S. Muddappa[94]
(Bangalore Development Authority)

This matter came up before the Supreme Court by way of appeal against the judgment and order of the High Court in a public interest litigation filed pursuant to the decision of the State Government and Bangalore Development Authority to convert the Public Park into a private nursing home. The High Court allowed the petition. Being aggrieved by the decision of the High Court a private medical trust, to whom the permission to construct nursing home was given preferred appeal before the Supreme Court.

The Supreme Court confirmed the judgment of the High Court by saying that the purpose of the Authority taking a decision of converting the site is their knowledge of local conditions and what was better for them. That is why participatory exercise is contemplated. If there is any alteration in Scheme, it is to be done by the Chairman and the Chief Minister then Sub-sec. (4) of Section 19 is rendered otiose. There is no provision in the Act for alteration in a scheme by converting one site to another, except, of course, if it appeared to be improvement. But even that power vested in the Authority not the Government. In the instant case every order, namely, converting the site from public park to private nursing home and even allotment to Medical Trust for nursing home was passed by the State Government and the BDA Development Authority acting like a true subservient body obeyed faithfully by adopting and confirming the directions. It was complete abdication of power by the BDA. The Legislature entrusted the responsibility to alter and approve the Scheme to the BDA but

94. AIR 1991 SC 1902.

the BDA in complete breach of faith reposed in it, preferred to take directions issued on command of the Chief Executive of the State. This resulted not only in error of law but much beyond it. The State Government could be concerned or involved with an altered scheme either because of financial considerations or when additional land was to be acquired, an exercise which could not be undertaken by the BDA. A development scheme, therefore, sanctioned and published in the Gazette could not be altered by the Government. The entire proceedings before the State Government suffered from absence of jurisdiction. Even the exercise of power was vitiated and *ultra vires*. Therefore, the orders of the Government to convert the site reserved for public park to civic amenity and to allot it for private nursing home to Bangalore Medical Trust and the resolution of the Bangalore Development Authority in compliance of it were null, void and without jurisdiction.

3.5.6 Mandamus against Municipal Board

Rashid Ahmed v. The Municipal Board, Kairana[95]

In this case the petitioner was a commissioned agent, carrying on wholesale business in vegetables and fruits at Kairana in the Uttar Pradesh. Certain new bye-laws were made by the Municipal Board on and from 1st January, 1950. In anticipation of the new regulations, the Board, on 1st May, 1949, auctioned, the contract for the whole sale of vegetables as a monopoly right. The petitioner had applied for a licence to carry on his business at his shop, but his application was rejected; the rejection was communicated to the petitioner on 9th February, 1950. The rejection of the petitioner's application was on the ground that there was no bye-law authorizing the issue of any licence to him. One of the bye-laws laid down:

> *'No person shall establish any new market or place for wholesale transaction without obtaining the previous permission of the Board and no person shall sell or expose for sale any vegetable, fruit, etc., at any place other than that fixed by the Board for the purpose.'*

The second part of this bye-law merely contemplated that everybody would be entitled to do business at the place fixed by the Board; but as a result of the monopoly already created in favour of another contractor, nobody else could do business at that place.

Therefore, a writ petition under Article 32 was filed by the petitioner, wherein he contended that Article 19(1)(g) of the Constitution was violated.

The Supreme Court accepted the contention and pointed out that the proper order in such circumstances would be to direct the respondent Board not to prohibit the petitioner from carrying on the trade of wholesale dealer and commission agent of vegetables and fruits within the limits of

95. AIR 1950 SC 163.

the Municipal Board of Kairana, except in accordance with the bye-laws as and when framed in favour according to law. Further, it directed the Board to withdraw the prosecution which was pending against the petitioner. Delivering judgment of the Court, **Das, J.** observed as follows:

> *'The Constitution by Article 19(1) guarantees to the Indian Citizen the right to carry on trade or business subject to such reasonable restrictions as are mentioned in clause (6) of that Article. The position, however, under bye-law 2 is that while it provided that no person shall establish a market for wholesale transactions in vegetables except with the permission of the Board, there is no bye-law authorizing the respondent Board to issue the licence. The net result is that the prohibition of this bye-law, in the absence of any provision for issuing licence, becomes absolute. Further bye-law 4 contemplates the grant of a monopoly to a contractor to deal in wholesale transactions at the place fixed as a market. Acting upon that provision, the respondent Board has granted monopoly to Habib Ahmad and has put it out of its power to grant a licence to the petitioner to carry on wholesale business in vegetables either at the fixed market place or at any other place within the municipal limits of Kairana. This certainly is much more than reasonable restrictions on the petitioner as are contemplated by clause (6) of Article 19. This being the position, the bye-laws would be void under Article 14(1) of the Constitution. On the other hand, if there is no bye-law requiring the petitioner to take out a licence, then there can be no justification for the respondent Board to stop the petitioner's business or to prosecute him. Learned Counsel for the respondent Board faintly contended that the bye-laws having come in force on 1st January 1950, i.e., before the Constitution came into force, the petitioner no longer had any right to continue the business and, therefore, his case is not governed by Article 19(1)(g). There is no substance in the argument for, if it were sound, Article 19(1)(g) would only protect persons who were carrying on business before the Constitution came into force.'*

It was argued on behalf of the respondent that the petition under Article 32 should be rejected on the ground that there was an alternative remedy available, i.e. an appeal under section 318 of the U.P. Municipalities Act. The Supreme Court refused to accept this argument by observing that merely an existence of alternative remedy a writ petition made for the enforcement of fundamental rights under Article 32. **Justice Patanjali Sastri** observes it in paragraph 6 of the judgment,

> *'....There can be no question that the existence of an adequate legal remedy is a thing to be taken into consideration in the matter of granting writs, but the powers given to this Court under Article 32 are much wider and are not confined to issuing prerogative writs only. The respondent Board having admittedly put it out of its power to grant licence and having regard to the fact that there is no specific bye-law authorizing the issue of*

licence, we do not consider that the appeal under Sec. 318 to the local Government which sanctioned the bye-laws is in the circumstances of this case, an adequate legal remedy.'

With this observation the Supreme Court allowed the writ of *mandamus* against the respondent under Article 32 of the Constitution.

3.5.7 Mandamus against Housing Boards

Haryana Housing Board v. Haryana Housing Board's Employees' Union[96] (not found to be "Local Authority")

In the case of *Haryana Housing Board* v. *Haryana Housing Board's Employees' Union*, a question before the Supreme Court came for into consideration was whether Haryana Housing Board covered within the definition of 'Local authority' under Article 12 of the Constitution of India or not. While dismissing the appeals the apex court held that Haryana Housing Board does not fall within the definition of "Local Authority" as defined under Article 12 of the Constitution. The Supreme Court disbelieved the arguments of the advocate for the petitioners that the Haryana Housing Board was instrumentality of the Government or, in any case, being a statutory body is an "Authority" within the meaning of Article 12 of the Constitution and since Local authorities had also been referred to in Article 12, the Board should also be treated as Local Authority. An argument was also made for the application of the doctrine of *ejusdem generis* so as to bring the Board within the ambit of Article 12. But the same was not permitted by the Supreme Court by saying that the doctrine of *ejusdem generis* was not made applicable by the Supreme Court itself in earlier cases while interpreting Article 12.

The Supreme Court observed that the functions as are indicated in a Housing Scheme are essentially performed by Municipal Boards or Municipal Council which, undoubtedly, are "Local Authorities" but on that analogy the Haryana Housing Board cannot be treated to be a "Local Authorities" as the extent of control of the State Government under which the Board has to function is so prominently pervasive that it is almost destructive of its independence which will also be apparent from the fact that in the matter of settlement of its Annual Programmes, Budget and Establishment Schedule, the Board has to obtain the sanction of the State Government under Section 24 of the Act. The Supplementary budget and programme, if any, has also to be sanctioned by the State Government. Haryana Housing Board does not have even the semblance of independence, which are normally possessed by local self-Government, like Municipal Boards, District Boards, etc. The Board also does not even partially consist of elected representative of the people.

96. AIR 1996 SC 434..

It was further expressed by the Supreme Court in support of its conclusion that the Board, no doubt, has the power to levy and realize Betterment Charges and various amount of money due from persons in possession of the properties of the Board by way of rent, etc. are recoverable as arrears of land revenue but that by itself is not sufficient to clothe the Board with the status of a "local authority".

Lastly, by taking into consideration the concept of Article 12 of the Constitution of India the Supreme Court said that the definition of "State" which is an inclusive definition and includes Government and Parliament of India. Government and the Legislature of each of the States as also all local or other Authorities. Article 12 does not define "Local Authority" but defines "State. The attempt of the Board to invoke the rule of *ejusdem generis,* which cannot be permitted. While interpreting the definition of "Local Authority" contained in the two Acts, namely, the General Clauses Act and the Haryana Housing Board Act, 1971 (Explained above), the rule of *ejusdem generis* can be invoked but this rule cannot be applied to Article 12 as the definition of "State" in this Article includes several bodies which are heterogeneous in character and, there is no genus in the definition. The appeal was dismissed with this observation and the Haryana Housing Board was not declared as "Local Authority".

Analysis and Inferences

From the above judgments inferences can be drawn that it is undisputed facts that *mandamus* can be issued against "Local Authorities" as described in Article 12 of the Constitution.

4

Mandamus against "Other Authorities"

The plain meaning of the word authority is "a person or body exercising power to command."

In context of Article 12 of the Constitution of India, authority means the power to make laws, orders, regulations, by-laws, notifications, etc. and power to enforce those laws.

Interpretation of the word "Other authorities"

Madras High Court look very restricted view of the term "Other authorities" in the case of **University of Madras v. Shantha Bai**[1]. Importance of this judgment was because of its peculiarity. The point of consideration before Madras High Court was that whether University of Madras could be included in the definition of "Other authorities" or not in other words, can a Writ of *Mandamus* be issued against University of Madras or not.

Here main point under consideration was whether the University of Madras can be held to be local or other authority as defined in Article 12. These wards "Local or other authority" must be construed *"ejusdem generis"* with Government or Legislature and so construed can only mean authorities exercising Governmental functions. They would not include persons, natural or juristic, who can not be regarded as instrumentalities of the Government. The University of Madras is a body corporate created by Madras Act, VII of 1923. It is not charged with the execution of any Government function and its purpose is purely to promote education. Though section 44 of the Act provides for financial contribution, by the local Government, the University is authorised to raise its own funds of income from fees, endowments and the like. It is a state-aided institution but not state-maintained institution.

1. AIR 1954 Mad. 67.

Unfortunately the Division Bench of Madras High Court, by reversing the judgment of learned single judge in appeal held that University of Madras was not "State" as defined in Article 12 of the Constitution and that its regulations are not subject to the prohibition enacted in Article 15(1); that admission to colleges is regulated by Article 29(12) and the regulation of the University requiring that colleges should provide certain facilities for women before they could be admitted are not discriminatory on the ground of sex.

Soon thereafter, i.e., in the year 1956, in the case of **Nambooripad v. Cochin Devaswom Board**,[2] Full Bench of Travancore-Cochin High Court had an opportunity to decide as to whether Cochin Devaswom Board constituted under the Travancore Cochin Hindu Religions Institutions Act, 1950 is covered in the definition of other authorities under Article 12 or not.

Here, without taking the consideration the ratio laid down by Madras High Court in Shanthabai's case, Justice Menon applied his discretion and observed that as per entry 5 of list II of VII the schedule of the cast. Cochin Devaswom Board does not fall under the definition of Local Authorities. But at the same time it may come within the ambit of other authorities under Article 12. The further said that the word "authority" in the context of Article 12, means the power to issue rules, by laws or regulations having the force of law.

By taking into consideration the powers conferred to Cochin Devaswom Board under Section 122 of the Travancore Cochin Hindu Religious Institutions Act, 1950, it was held that aforesaid Board is state under Article 12 of the Constitution (Other authorities).

Scope of Article 12 is effectively discussed by the Supreme Court before 7 Judges' Bench in the case of **Ujjam Bai v. State of U.P.**,[3] wherein assessment order under taxing statute was challenged by the petitioner. The Supreme Court in this case held that "tribunal" falls within the definition of "other authority" under Article 12 of the Constitution, though not expressly mentioned in Art. 12. But, the Apex Court did not out rightly reject the principle of *ejusdem generis qua* Article 12.

The definition of "other authority" was expanded by the judgment of **Electricity Board, Rajasthan V/s. Mohan Lal**[4]. The application of the principle of *ejusdem generis* was completely rejected by the Supreme Court. In the case of Ujjam Bai, through Justice Ayyanger categorically observed that the principle of *ejusdem generis* was not applicable while interpreting Article 12. Justice Subba Rao relied upon the said principle and held that Rajasthan Electricity Board is "State" within the meaning of Article 12.

Yet, the journey so far as the interpretation of the word "other authorities" under Article 12 had to travel a lot. In the year 1975, in the

2. AIR 1956 Trav-Co. 19.
3. AIR 1962 SC 1621.
4. AIR 1967 SC 1857.

case of **Sukhdev Singh v. Bhagatram**[5], five Judges' Bench of the Supreme Court had an occasion to decide as to whether public corporations viz. Oil and Natural Gas Commission (ONGC), Life Insurance Corporation of India (LIC) and Industrial Finance Corporation (IFC) are covered within the definition of "other authorities" under Article 12 of the Constitution of India or not. And consequently, the protection of fundamental rights is available to the employees of the aforesaid corporation or not. By majority decision, the Supreme Court declared all the above mentioned corporations as "State" and observed that they fall within the definition of "other authorities" and hence "State" under Article 12 of the Constitution of India.

In the year 1979, the Supreme Court had an opportunity to decide in the case of **R.D. Shetty v. International Airport Authority of India**[6] as to whether International Airport Authority falls within the definition of "other authorities" under Article 12 of the Constitution or not. While declaring the aforesaid authority as "State", Justice Bhagwati tried to expand the scope of Article 12 so far as the term "other authorities" is concerned. By relying upon the minority, confirming opinion of Justice Methew in the case of **Sukhdev v. Bhagatram,** Justice Bhagwati said that instrumentality or agency of the Government should be included within the definition of "State" under Article 12.

The Supreme Court of India, in the year 1981 was required to decide as to whether a regional Engineering College run by a registered society was a "State" under Article 12 of the Constitution of India or not in the case of **Ajay Hasia v. Khalid Mujib**.[7] While declaring an Engineering College run by a registered society as "State" the Supreme Court gave certain guidelines.

These guidelines are used for ascertaining the fact whether an authority is "State" or not. They are:

1. If the entire share capital of the corporation is held by the government, it would go a long way towards indicating that the corporation is an instrumentality or authority of the government.
2. Where the financial assistance of the State is so much as to meet almost entire expenditure of the corporation it would afford some indication of the corporation being impregnated with government character.
3. Whether the corporation enjoys monopoly status which is State conferred or State protected.
4. Existence of deep and pervasive State control may afford an indication that the corporation is a state agency or instrumentality.

5. AIR 1975 SC 1331.
6. AIR 1979 SC 1628.
7. AIR 1981 SC 487.

5. If the function of the corporation are of public importance and closely related to government functions, it would be a relevant factor in classifying a corporation as an instrumentality or agency of government.
6. If a department of government is transferred to corporation, it would be a strong factor supporting this inference of the corporation being an instrumentality or agency of government.

The Supreme Court while deciding the cases uses these guidelines even today. The important question to be put in this situation of interpretation of the term "other authorities" is whether this interpretation is required to be expanded or not and how it is possible. But first of all it is necessary to have a brief idea regarding the institutions/authorities which are included within the definition of "other authorities". The following bodies are included by the Supreme Court within the definition of "State":

- Statutory Corporations
- Statutory Boards
- Government Companies
- Societies registered under the Societies Registration Act and controlled by the State
- Universities and Educational Institutions
- Judiciary
- Quasi-judicial authorities
- Banks: Reserve Bank of India
Nationalized Banks
Co-operative Banks
Regional Rural Banks
- Improvement Trusts
- Commissions of Inquiry
- Election Commission
- Stock Exchange

The status of all the above mentioned bodies are discussed herein taking into consideration the relevant cases of the Supreme Court of India and courts of U.K.

4.1 *MANDAMUS* AGAINST STATUTORY CORPORATIONS

1. Position in England

Mandamus can be issued in England against the Public or Statutory Corporation. It is well established law. Public Corporation is considered as the third arm of the Government. If the Government is doing its various activities through such corporations then they must be amenable to the writ jurisdiction. British Broadcasting Corporation is one of the examples of statutory corporations. It makes no difference so far as issuance of *mandamus* is concerned whether such corporation came into existence either by a statute or under a statute.

2. Position in India

1. Life Insurance Corporation of India
2. Oil and Natural Gas Commission
3. State Financial Corporation

Sukhdev v. Bhagatram[8]

All the above mentioned corporations are declared as "other authorities" under Article 12 of the Constitution of India by a common judgment in the case of **Sukhdev v. Bhagatram**. The arguments and decision of the Supreme Court is collectively summarized as under:

In the year 1975, in the case of **Sukhdev Singh v. Bhagatram**, five Judges' Bench of the Supreme Court had an occasion to decide as to whether public corporations viz. Oil and Natural Gas Commission (ONGC), Life Insurance Corporation of India (LIC) and Industrial Finance Corporation (IFC) are covered within the definition of "State" under Article 12 of the Constitution of India or not. And consequently, the protections of fundamental rights are available to the employees of the aforesaid corporations or not.

The observations of three judges among majority viz. Justice A.N. Ray, C.J., Justice Y.V. Chandrachud and Justice A.C. Gupta are very interesting. They studied all the three acts under which the aforesaid corporations were created and found out common features. On the basis of the powers to make rules and regulations under the acts and by considering binding effect of the rules as well as regulations to the corporations and their employees, the aforesaid judges came to the conclusion that all the three corporations are covered under the definition of "other authorities" under Article 12 of the Constitution. The observations were as under:

ONGC

It is constituted under the Oil and Natural Gas Commission Act, 1959 as a body corporate having perpetual succession and a common seal.

The commission has power to appoint employees under Sec. 12 of the Act.

Under section 31 of the Act, the Commission has power to make rules regarding:

- Term of office
- Manner of filling casual vacancies, among the members
- Conditions of service
- Disqualification of members, etc.

---

8. AIR 1975 SC 1331.

The power to make regulations conferred upon the ONGC under section 32 should not be inconsistent with the Act and also with the approval of the Central Government. It can make regulation in the following matters:

- Terms and conditions of appointment and service
- Scales of pay of employees
- Time and place of meeting of the commission
- Transaction of business at the meeting
- Maintenance of minutes of the meeting
- Transmission of copies of minutes to the Central Government
- Custody of money and maintenance of Accounts
- Persons by whom and the manner in which the payments, deposits and investments be made.

LIC

It is established under section 3 of the Life Insurance Corporation of India Act, 1956 Under Section 11 of the Act existing employees of an insurer whose controlled business was transferred and vested in the Corporation and who were employed by the insurer wholly or mainly in connection with his controlled business immediately before the appointed day became on and from the appointed day employees of the Corporation.

Section 48 empowers the Central Government to make rules by notification to be published in Official Gazette for the term of office and the conditions of service of its members.

Section 49 of the Act says that the Corporation may, with the previous approval of the Central Government, by notification in official gazette in India, make regulations, not inconsistent with the Act in the following matters:

- powers and functions of the Corporation which may be delegated to Zonal managers.
- Method of recruitment of employees and agents.
- Terms and conditions of services of employees and agents.
- Terms and conditions of service of persons who have become employees of the Corporation u/s 11 of the act.
- Number, term of office and conditions of service of members of boards constituted u/s 22 of the Act.
- Manner in which the fund of the corporation shall be maintained.
- Form and manner in which policies may be issued and contract binding on the corporation may be executed.

IFC

IFC is constituted under section 3 of the Industrial Finance Corporation Act, 1948, Central Government, under section 42 empowers the corporation to make rules in consultation with the Industrial Development Bank, not inconsistent with the provisions of the Act.

Under Sec. 43, the Board of Directors may, with the previous approval of the Industrial Development Bank make regulations, not inconsistent with the provisions of the Act upon the following matters:

- For holding and conduct of the election and final decision of any disputes or doubts regarding the validity of election.
- Manner in which and the conditions subject to which the shares of the Corporation may be held and transferred.
- Manner in which general meeting shall be convened and the procedure to be followed thereat.
- Duties and conduct, salaries, allowances and conditions of service of officers and other employees and of advisers and agents of the Corporation.

Thus, the question for consideration before the court was whether regulations framed under these statutes have the force of law. In other words, whether these statutory corporations were authorities within the meaning of Article 12. All the three corporations, in their regulations mentioned the conditions of services of the employees.

Following contentions were raised on behalf of the Corporations:

- Regulations are framed under powers given by the statute affecting internal management.
- Regulations do not have a statutory binding character.
- Terms and conditions of employment as laid down in the regulations are not a matter of statutory obligations.
- Regulations are binding not as law but as contract. Therefore, employment of each person is contractual.
- Regulations have no force of law.

But the contentions raised on behalf of the employees affected were:

- Regulations are made under the statute.
- Origin and source of power to make regulations is statutory.
- Regulations are self-binding in character.
- Regulations have the force of law in as much as the statutory authorities have no right to make any departure from the regulations.

It was also contended on behalf of the state that the Corporations cannot be declared as "other authority" contemplated in Article 12 as one of the attributes of a state is making laws. The State exercises governmental functions and the executive power of the State is co-extensive with the legislative power of the State. Also, authority as defined under Article 12 means a body of persons established by statute who are entitled as such body to command obedience and enforce directions issued by them on pain of penalty for violation. These corporations cannot make laws like a state and cannot enforce directions.

During the course of arguments learned judges noted that all the three statutory bodies have no free hand in framing the conditions and terms of service of their employees. These statutory bodies are bound to apply the terms and conditions as laid down in the regulations. The statutory bodies are not free to make such terms as they think fit and proper. Regulations prescribe the terms of appointment, conditions of service and procedure for dismissing employees. These regulations in the statutes are described as "statute fetters on freedom of contract".

The Additional Solicitor General **Mr. F.S. Nariman** appearing on behalf of the respondent corporation submitted that the regulations could not have the force of law because these regulations are similar to regulations framed by a company incorporated under the Companies Act. The fallacy lies in equating rules and regulations of a company with rules and regulations framed by a statutory body.

Justice A.N. Ray (C.J.) while giving decision for himself and other two Hon'ble Judges tried to explain the importance of the rules and regulations in any public corporation. The majority also observed that there is no substantial difference between a rule and a regulation in as much as both are subordinate legislation under the powers conferred by the statute. A regulation framed under a statute applies uniform treatment to every one or to all members of same group or class. The Oil and Natural Gas Commission, the Life Insurance Corporation and Industrial Finance Corporation are all required by the statute to frame regulation *inter alia* for the purpose of the duties and conduct and conditions of service of officers and other employees. These regulations impose obligation on the statutory authorities. The statutory authorities cannot deviate from the conditions of service. Any deviation will be enforced by legal sanction of declaration by courts to invalidate actions in violation of rules and regulations. The existence of rules and regulations under statute is to ensure regular conduct with a distinctive attitude to that conduct as a standard. The statutory regulations in the cases under consideration give the employees a statutory status and impose restriction on the employer and the employee with no option to vary the conditions. An ordinary individual in a case of master and servant contractual relationship enforces breach of contractual terms. The remedy in such contractual relationship of master and servant is damages because personal service is not capable of enforcement. In cases of statutory bodies there is no personal element whatsoever because of the impersonal character of statutory bodies. In the case of statutory bodies it has been said that the element of public employment or service and support of statute require observance of rules and regulations. Failure to observe requirements by statutory bodies is enforced by courts by declaring dismissal in violation of rules and regulations to be void. The Supreme

Court has repeatedly observed that whenever a man's rights are affected by decision taken under statutory powers, the Court would presume the existence of a duty to observe the rules of natural justice and compliance with rules and regulations imposed by statute.

In the above mentioned case, **Justice Mathew** gave a separate, but confirming opinion with the majority. According to him there was a time when the Supreme Court itself in case of Rajasthan Electricity Board said that the expression "other authorities" included all constitutional and statutory authorities on whom powers are conferred by law. (Per majority Bhargava, J.) In the same case Justice Shah delivered a separate judgment agreeing with the conclusion reached by the majority preferred to adopt a slightly different meaning to the wards "other authorities". He said that authorities, constitutional or statutory, would fall within the expression "State" as defined in Article 12 only if they are invested with sovereign power of the State, namely, the power to make rules or regulations which have the force of law. Justice Methew further said that there was no controversy for inclusion of the ONGC within the meaning of "other authorities" by applying the test given by the majority. Moreover, it is very clear from the provisions of the ONGC Act itself that the commission is authorised to issue binding directions to third parties not to prevent the employees of the commission from entering into their land and as disobedience of such directions is punishable under the relevant provisions of the Indian Penal Code since those employees are deemed to be "public servants" under section 21 of the Indian Penal Code by virtue of section 27 of the Act. But, the other two Corporations can give no such binding directions, disobedience of which would entail penal consequences. Justice Methew said that the Public Corporations should also be included within the definition of "other authorities" with the passage of time. The concept of state has undergone drastic changes in recent years. Today, state cannot be conceived of simply as coercive machinery wielding the thunderbolt of authority. It has to be viewed mainly as a service corporation. The public corporation has now become third arm of the government.

Justice Methew observed that the Supreme Court of United States in **McCullough v. Maryland**[9] held that the Congress has power to charter corporations as incidental to or in aid of governmental functions. So far as federal corporations are concerned, they are, by hypothesis, agencies of government.

In France, an enterprise publique is an enterprise the whole or the majority of whose capital belongs to the State or other public agencies. By reason of its industrial or commercial activities it is basically subject to private law, but, because of its public nature, it finds itself subjected to a certain degree of dependence on and control by public authority.

The Constitution was framed on the theory that limitation should exist on the exercise of power by the state. The assumption was that the

9. (1819)4 Wheat 316.

State alone was competent to wield power. The emerging principle appears to be that a public corporation being a creation of the State is subject to the constitutional limitation as the State itself. The preconditions of this are two; viz. the corporation is created by State, and the existence of power in the corporation to invade the constitutional right of individual.

At last in conclusion **Justice Methew** said that it is clear from the provisions of the Life Insurance Corporation of India Act and Industrial Finance Corporation Act that the Central Government has contributed the original capital of the Corporations, that part of the profit of these corporations go to that Government that the Central Government exercises control over the policy of the Corporations, both the Corporations carry on business having great public importance and that they enjoy a monopoly in the business. In the above mentioned circumstances these corporations are agencies or instrumentalities of the State and are therefore, "State" within the meaning of Article 12. The fact that these corporations have independent personalities in the eyes of law does not mean that they are not subject to the control of government or that they are not instrumentalities of the government. These corporations are instrumentalities or agencies of the state for carrying on business which otherwise would have been run by the state departmentally. If the state had chosen to carry on these businesses through the medium of government departments, there would have been no question that actions of these departments would be "state actions". In order to be clear and precise as to whether such a corporation is instrumentality or agency of the government or not, a simple question is, for whose benefit was the corporation carrying on the business? When it is seen from the provisions from the Act that on liquidation of the Corporation, its assets should be divided among the shareholders viz. the Central and State Governments and others, if any, the implication is clear that the benefit of the accumulated income would go to the Central and State Governments. Nobody will deny that an agent has a legal personality different from that of the principal. The fact that the agent is subject to the direction of the principal does not mean that he has no legal personality of his own. Likewise, merely because a corporation has legal personality of its own, it does not follow that the corporation cannot be an agent or instrumentality of the state, if it is subject to control of government in all important matters of policy.

Justice Methew fully supported the opinion of the majority and added that even assuming that the regulations framed under the act have no force of law, since the employment under these corporations is public employment, an employee would get a status which would enable him to obtain declaration for continuance in service if he was dismissed or discharged contrary to the regulations. He categorically said that the regulations framed by these corporations were intended to be binding upon them and were the bases on which the employments were made. As the employments were under corporations created by statutes for carrying on businesses of public importance, they were public employment. And even if the regulations have not got the force of law, Justice Methew put reliance on the principle laid down by **Justice Frankfurter** in ***Vitarelli v. Seaton***[10] said,

> ***'An executive agency must be rigorously held to the standards by which it professes its action to be judged .... Accordingly, if dismissal from employment is based on a defined procedure, even though generous beyond the requirements that bind such agency, that procedure must judicially pulously observed... This judicially evolved rule of administrative law is now firmly established and, it I may add, rightly so, He that takes the procedural sword shall perish with that sword.'***

While declaring the above mentioned three corporations as "State" under Article 12 of the Constitution, majority opinion gave following guidelines for considering an entity as instrumentality or agency of state:

1. Financial resources of the state being the chief funding source.
2. Functional character being governmental in essence.
3. Plenary control residing in government.
4. Prior history of the same activity having been carried on by the Government and made over to the new body.
5. Some elements of authority or command.

Dissenting (Minority) opinion of Alagiriswami, J.

Justice Alagiriswami was not ready to include all the above mentioned corporations, viz. ONGC, LIC and IFC within the definition of "other authorities". He raised serious doubts for including such corporation within the ambit of "State" and warned about the consequences thereof. He said that by declaring these corporations as "State", the Supreme Court was at one stroke opening flood gate of thousands of writ petitions a year as the employees of all such similarly situated corporations would be entitled to file writ petitions before High Court or Supreme Court for arbitrariness or non-observance of principles of Natural Justice by their employer. Justice Alagiriswami put reliance upon the definition of the words "rule" and "regulation". He observed that all the three corporations are framed under the different Acts. These Acts confer the corporation regulation making powers. The main argument on behalf of the organizations was that the regulations relate to internal management, that the terms and conditions of service of employees as laid down in the regulations are not law but merely rules for the purpose of internal management. In so far as the appointments of the various employees of these three organizations are concerned they are appointed by contract and these regulations merely form part of those

10. (1959) 359 US 535, pp. 546-547.

contracts. On behalf of the employees the contention was that the source of the power to make regulations is the statute and hence the regulations are themselves law.

Justice Alagiriswami observed that the definitions of "rule" and "regulation" as per the General Clauses Act, 1897 were relevant for the correct conclusion. Under Clause (51) of Section 3 of the General Clauses Act, 1897 "rule" means a rule made in exercise of a power conferred by any enactment and shall include a regulation made as a rule under any enactment.

Section 20 of the same Act gives definition of "regulation" as under:

> '20. *Where, by any central Act, or Regulation, a power to issue any notification, order, scheme, rule, form or bye-law is conferred, then expressions used in the notification, order, scheme, rule, form or bye-law, if it is made after the commencement of this Act, shall, unless there is anything repugnant in the subject or context, have the same respective meanings as in the Act or Regulation conferring the power.*'

The Committee on Ministers' Powers suggested that regulations should be used for substantive law and rules for procedural law, while orders should be reserved to describe the exercise of executive power or the taking of a judicial or quasi-judicial decision. It would be noticed that this scheme is completely different from the Indian legislative practice. There are number of statute books in India where the word "regulation" is used to refer to the regulations made by bodies other than the State.

Regulations framed under the regulation making power conferred by the three Acts in question are not the regulations as mentioned in the General Clauses Act. In interpreting Indian Statutes it is unnecessary and might sometimes be misleading to refer to the provisions of English Law in connection with subordinate legislation. In the context of Indian Legislative practice, though "rule" is defined as including a regulation made as a rule, it cannot be said that regulation making powers conferred on the three organizations in question is a rule-making power. Under the legislative practice in India, the rule-making power is conferred on the State and the power to make regulations is conferred on bodies or organizations created by the statute. By quoting number of Acts and their regulations Justice Alagiriswami tried to point out that under the Indian Legislative practice rules are what the Central Government or the State Governments make and the regulations are made by any institution or organization established by a statute and where it is intended that the regulation should have effect as law the statute itself says so. It is therefore unnecessary and rather misleading to refer to the English practice in interpreting the word "regulation". He further added that merely because the regulations are made in respect of the conditions of service of the employees of a certain institution or organization does not mean that those conditions are statutory. No doubt these are the conditions of service applying to their employees. But if there is a breach of those conditions, it can not be said that there is a breach of any statutory provision. With regard to the regulations of terms and conditions of service in all above organization Justice Alagiriswami said that when regulations standardize the conditions of service of the employees or purport to formulate them, their character is further diluted by the nature of the subject-matter. For, service or employment is basically a contract which is deeply rooted in private law. A mere standardization or enumeration of the terms of a service contract is not, therefore, ordinarily sufficient to convert it into a statutory status. For the statute itself is silent and does not confer any security of tenure on the employee. The Corporation has a complete discretion in framing the regulations and giving such protection thereunder to its employees as it thinks fit. The amount of the protection thus depends on its own discretion. It is not given by amendatory statutory obligation imposed on the corporation from above. For the Corporation can vary the terms of the regulations at any time thus depriving its employees of the security of tenure of service. The matter is thus one between the employee and the employer which is precisely the case of a service contract. A breach of such conditions is therefore a breach of the service contract remediable by damages rather than an *ultra vires* action to be set aside by a declaration or *mandamus*. But it is not correct to say that these statutory bodies have no free hand in framing the conditions and terms of service of their employees. Justice Alagiriswami firmly believed that such statutory bodies are free to frame terms and conditions as they think proper. They are the authorities to make any regulations regarding the conditions and terms of service of their employees and also change them as they please.

He was convinced with the argument of Additional Solicitor General Mr. F.A. Nariman that the regulations could not have the force of law because these regulations are similar to regulations framed by a company incorporated under the Companies Act. He tried to compare these organizations alongwith a company incorporated under the Companies Act. A company makes rules and regulations in accordance with the provisions of the Companies Act. A statutory body makes regulations under the powers conferred by the statute creating that body. Both stand on the same footing as both derive their authority one from the Companies Act and the other from the Act which creates that body, for instance in the case of Life Insurance Corporation from the Life Insurance Corporation Act, 1956. The fact that corporation like LIC is created by the statute itself and a company comes into existence in accordance with the provisions of the Companies Act does not make any difference to this situation. Merely because a body happens to be a statutory body it does not become any less entitled to frame regulations which would be of the same kind as the regulations made by a company. Whether a corporation or a company is created by a statute or under a statute does not make any difference to this principle. If the above three organizations are to be covered under the definition of "other authorities", there is no reason why a different analogy is to be applied to a company.

Majority view of this judgment considering all the three corporations as "State" under Article 12 of the Constitution was firmly opposed by Justice Alagiriswami in minority view. He said that the decision of his learned brothers was unsupportable in principle against the weight of authority and fought with serious consequences. Suddenly overnight by the fiat of this Court all those bodies which till previous day were not considered to be a state or other authority would be considered to be other authority and their employees entitled to provisions of Part III of the Constitution. By this judgment the Supreme Court would be opening a veritable Pandora's Box. The protections given to Government servants in India have no parallels anywhere in the world. They were getting on well enough till the Government of India Act, 1935. Till then there was no statutory protection given to them. He feared that by deciding that all the three organizations in present cases are "other authority" and the regulations they make is law the Supreme Court would at once at one stroke be creating a large mass of neo-Government servants and Articles 14 and 16 would provide ample opportunities for endless litigation. One would readily agree that labour whether employed by private industry or industry run by the Government should be treated equally. But that one class of labour, that is labour employed in industry run by the Government, should be more equal than others is a proposition which no reasonable minded person can agree to. The employees of the public sector industries would get even more advantages than even the Government servants to whom Articles 309, 310 and 311 apply. In the name of industrial action life will be paralysed. They are not subject to same rules and regulations or discipline to which the Government servants are subject. They would be different from the days when they were treated like employees of private firms and were subject to the ordinary law of master and servant and become entitled to be treated even better than the Government employees. Misplaced sympathy is sometimes responsible for our attitude to labour. These days labour is not the weak and helpless force. Labours in both the cases, in public service corporation and private sectors should be treated alike. Unfortunately, this judgment distinguishes the employees under Government and public service corporations on one hand and employees on private companies on the other hand without any justification.

The majority ratio of the Supreme Court declaring all the three statutory Corporations as "State" under Article 12 in the above case was upheld consistently in number of subsequent judgments as the guidelines given are very clear and unambiguous covering number of institutions under the definition of state under Article 12. This judgment is followed in the *R.D. Shetty* v. *International Airport Authority* in the year 1979, *Som Prakash* v. *Union of India* in the year 1981 as well as in the case of *Ajay Hasia* v. *Khalid Mujib* in the year 1981. At the same time in view of the recent trend of the Supreme Court after the judgment of Pradeep Kumar Biswas case (year 2002), it can be said that there was substance in the arguments of minority view of Justice Alagiriswami.

The view taken by the Supreme Court in the Sukhdev's case was further reiterated by the apex court by declaring LIC as "State" under Article 12 of the Constitution of India in other cases. They are shortly summarized as follows:

LIC v. Manubhai Shah[11]

In this case the question arose was pertaining to the violation of fundamental right under 19(1)(a), i.e. freedom of speech and expression. The respondent Shri Manubhai Shah was the executive trustee of the Consumer Education and Research Centre (CERC), Ahmedabad. The respondent, after undertaking research into the working of the Life Insurance Corporation published a study paper titled "A Fraud on Policy Holders—A Shocking Story". This study paper portrayed the discriminatory practice adopted by LIC by pointing that unduly high premiums are charged by the LIC from those taking out life insurance policies thereby denying access to insurance coverage to a vast majority of people who cannot afford to pay the high premiums. The study paper is a research document containing statistical information to support the conclusions reached by the respondent. It was widely circulated.

In reply to the aforesaid study paper, a member of the LIC wrote a counter article "LIC and its Policy Holders" and published the same as an article in the Hindu, a daily circulating newspaper, challenging the conclusions reached by the respondent in his study paper. The respondent prepared a rejoinder to his study paper, which was published in the same newspaper. The member of LIC then published his own counter article in LIC's house magazine called Yogakshema. The respondent thereupon requested the LIC to also publish his rejoinder to the said article in the said magazine but his request was turned down.

The respondent, thereupon filed a writ petition before the High Court contending that the refusal to publish his rejoinder in the magazine violated his fundamental right under Articles 14 and 19(1)(a). The LIC denied this right on the ground that their magazine was an in-house magazine circulated amongst subscribers who were policy-holders, officers, employees and agents of the Corporation. The High Court rejected this contention on two grounds in the main, viz., (i) it is available to anyone on payment of subscription and (ii) members of the public are invited to contribute articles for publication. Even on the assumption that it is an in-house magazine the High Court observed "under the pretext and guise of publishing a house magazine, the Corporation cannot violate the fundamental rights of the petitioner if he has any". According to the High Court a house magazine cannot claim any privilege against the fundamental rights of a citizen.

Being aggrieved by the judgment of the High Court, the LIC preferred appeal before the Supreme Court. But the Supreme Court declined to

11. (1992)3 SCC 637.

interfere with the decision of the High Court by observing that the LIC being covered under the definition of "State" under Article 12 should act reasonably and fairly.

The following observations were made by the Supreme Court:

No serious exception can be taken to this approach which commended itself to the High Court. The LIC is a "State" within the meaning of Art. 12. The statute viz. the L.I.C. Act, 1956 requires it to function in the best interest of the community. The community is, therefore, entitled to know whether or not this requirement of the statute is being satisfied in the functioning of the LIC. The respondent's effort in preparing the study paper was to bring to the notice of the community that the LIC had stayed from its path by pointing out that its premium rates were unduly high when they could be low if the LIC avoided wasteful indulgences. The endeavour was to enlighten the community of the drawbacks and shortcoming of the Corporation and to pin-point the areas where improvement was needed and was possible. By denying information contained in the rejoinder prepared by the respondent to the consumers as well as other subscribers the LIC cannot be said to be acting in the best of interest of the community. It is not the case of the LIC that the rejoinder fall within any of the restrictive clauses of Article 19(2) or that it is in any manner prejudicial to the members of the community or that it is based on imaginary or concocted material. That being so on the fairness doctrine the LIC was under an obligation to publish the rejoinder since it had published counter to the study paper. The respondent's fundamental right of speech and expression clearly entitled him to insist that his view on the subject should reach those who read the magazine so that they have a complete picture before them and not a one-sided or distorted one.

The attitude on the part of LIC refusing to publish the rejoinder in their magazine financed from public funds can be described as both unfair and unreasonable; unfair because fairness demanded that both view-points were placed before the readers, however limited their number, to enable them to draw their own conclusions and unreasonable because there was no logic or proper justification for refusing publication. A monopolistic State instrumentality, which survives on public funds, can not act in an arbitrary manner on the specious plea that the magazine is an in-house one and it is a matter of its exclusive privilege to print or refuse to print the rejoinder.

However, the above view has been taken in the particular facts of the case and it should not be understood as laying down an absolute proposition that merely because the LIC is a state and is running a magazine with public funds it is under an obligation to print any matter that any informed citizen may forward for publication. It appears in the present case that the Supreme Court was not concerned about the violation of fundamental right contained in Article 19(1)(a) only but also violation of Article 14 of the Constitution. As per the observations made by the apex court, the freedom of speech and expression should be without unreasonable restrictions. More particularly, LIC covered within the meaning of "State" cannot violate the fundamental right of citizen.

LIC of India v. Consumer Education and Research Centre[12]

While deciding the case on merits, the Supreme Court, by confirming the ratio laid down in earlier cases, more particularly in the case of *LIC of India* v. *Consumer Education and Research Centre* held that the Life Insurance Corporation is "State" under Article 12 of the Constitution and also conceded that it was its duty to act fairly and reasonably.

Harshad J. Shah v. L.I.C. of India[13]

In this appeal filed by the appellant before the Supreme Court by way of special leave to appeal against the respondent LIC of India the question involved was whether payment of premium in respect of a life insurance policy by the insured to the general agent of the Life Insurance Corporation of India can be regarded as payment to the insurer so as to constitute a discharge of liability of the insured. As per Rule 8 of the Life Insurance Corporation (Agents) Rules, 1981 the agents have been prohibited from collecting moneys on behalf of LIC. In view of such express prohibition in the Rules itself, the agent obtaining bearer cheque of premium amount from the insured can make the LIC of India answerable for not depositing amount of cheque by the agent.

Ram Gopal Sharma v. Sukhdev Raj Rudra[14]

In the above case, the Supreme Court has reiterated the same ratio that the Life Insurance Corporation of India is "State" under Article 12 of the Constitution of India.

3. Oil and Natural Gas Commission

ONGC v. Association of NGC Industries of Gujarat[15]

Based upon the settled principle that ONGC is instrumentality or agency of the government and hence "State" within the meaning of Article 12 of the Constitution, in the case of *Oil and Natural Gas Commission* v. *Association of NGC Industries of Gujarat*, the respondents took the contention that the ONGC, being the "State" must supply fuel to them even after the term of contract is over and without having entered into an agreement on a price for such supply.

Looking into detailed facts of the case, the ONGC had entered into contracts with some industrial undertakings for supply of natural gas against fixed price. The contracts were prior to 30-1-87, i.e. prior to the date when jurisdiction to fix prices came to be vested in the Central Government.

12. (1995) 5 SCC 482.
13. AIR 1997 SC 2459.
14. (2001)9 SCC 201.
15. AIR 1990 SC 1851.

These were ordinary commercial contracts entered into by private treaty between the ONGC and some parties to sell and buy certain goods produced by the ONGC at the prices stipulated in the contract. Looked at purely from the contractual angle, the ONGC was perfectly at liberty to stop the supply on the expiry of relevant contract and refuse to supply further unless a fresh contract could be entered into agreeing upon a price for such supply.

The petitioners filed a writ petition before the High Court as the ONGC refused to supply the natural gas after expiry of the contract. The High Court directed the ONGC to supply the natural gas and observed that the ONGC being "State" within meaning of Article 12 should act reasonably and fairly and in consonance with Directive Principles of the State Policy also.

Being aggrieved by the judgment and order of the High Court, the ONGC, challenged the said decision by way of filing appeal. At the outset the council appearing for the ONGC, clarified that it was undisputed fact that the ONGC is "State" within the meaning of Article 12 of the Constitution and it is bound to act fairly and reasonably so as not to infringe the provisions of Articles 14 and 10 and also in consonance with the directive principles of State policy set in Articles 38 and 39(b). The main point for challenge was the finding of the High Court that the ONGC is "public utility undertaking" which was bound to supply gas to the request of any member of the public at large and to its direction that it should continue to supply gas to the respondent at an uncertain price till the price is fixed in accordance with the procedure outlined by it. The Supreme Court, on merits allowed the contention of the ONGC and quashed the order of the High Court. But here for our purpose of research the important point of consideration is that the Supreme Court reiterated the earlier precedent that ONGC falls within the definition of "State" under Article 12 of the Constitution.

4. U.P. Warehousing Corporation

U.P. Warehousing Corporation v. Vijay Narayan[16]

In the case of *U.P. Warehousing Corporation* v. *Vijay Narayan* a question arose was as to whether U.P. Warehousing Corporation is an instrumentality or agency of the "State" under Article 12 of the Constitution of India or not.

The respondent herein was an employee of the Uttar Pradesh State Warehousing Corporation and was working as a Warehouseman with the Corporation. Upon the complaints of theft, misappropriation of stocks and various other irregularities, he was terminated from the services upon issuance of charge-sheet and a preliminary inquiry. Thereafter, the employee was dismissed from the service and was asked to remit a sum of Rs. 549.61 due to the Corporation.

16. AIR 1980 SC 840.

The respondent filed writ petition challenging the order of dismissal before the High Court under Article 226 of the Constitution of India. The learned single Judge after having heard the petition dismissed it holding that the U.P. Warehousing Corporation was not required to act in a quasi-judicial manner and that the provisions of Article 311 of the Constitution was not applicable to this case.

In an appeal filed by the employee before a Division Bench of the High Court, which reversed the judgment of the learned single Judge, and held that the Corporation was required to act in a quasi-judicial manner.

The Division Bench thereafter, remanded the matter for a decision on merits. After the remand the learned single Judge, by his judgment allowed the writ petition holding that the principles of the natural justices had been violated and he quashed and set aside the order of the dismissal but refused to grant an injunction restraining the appellant from releasing Rs. 549.61 from the respondent.

Against the said judgment of the learned single Judge, the Corporation preferred appeal before Division Bench of the High Court, wherein the Division Bench made no interference. Therefore, against the judgment of the Division Bench, the Corporation preferred appeal before the Supreme Court.

In appeal the Supreme Court observed that the appellant was a Corporation constituted under the Madhya Pradesh State Warehousing Corporation Act, 1956. It was a statutory body wholly controlled and managed by the Government. Its Status was analogous to that of the Corporations which were under consideration in the case of *Sukhdev* v. *Bhagatram*. The ratio of Sukhdev Singh's case, therefore, squarely applied to the case in question. The Corporation was therefore, found to be "State" within the meaning of Article 12 of the Constitution.

Even at the time of the dismissal, the statutory regulations had not been framed or had not come into force, then also, the employment of the respondent was public employment and statutory body, the employer could not terminate the services of its employee without due enquiry in accordance with the statutory Regulations or in absence thereof, with the rules of natural justice. It appeared in this case to the Supreme Court that the rules of natural justice were not followed.

While making arguments, Mr. A.K. Sen, in support of his case, highlighted words of **Justice Wilberforce** from the case of House of Lords in **Malloch v. Aberdeen Corporation,**[17]

> *"...in cases in which there is an element of public employment or service, or support by statute or something in the nature of an officer or a status, which is capable of protection then irrespective of the terminology used, and even though in some inter-parties aspects of the relationship may be called that of master and servant, there may be essential procedure on grounds of natural justice..."*

17. (1971) 1 WLR 1578.

Mr. A.K. Sen also relied upon the judgment of International Airport Authority case. Justice Sarkaria observed on facts and by taking into consideration the settled legal position that the judgment of the High Court with regard to the quashing of the order of dismissal required no interference at all except the direction of payment of full back wages to the respondent.

Justice Chinnappa Reddy was also of the same opinion. But he, in addition to the judgment of Sakaria, J. pointed out that breach of the principles of natural justice was sufficient ground available for the employee to approach the High Court by way of filing writ petition under Article 226 of the Constitution of India. While replying the question as to whether a writ was maintainable against the corporation or not he exhaustively answered in paragraph 22 of his judgment as follows:

> '22. *I find it very hard indeed to discover any distinction on principle, between a person directly under the employment of an agency or instrumentality of the Government or a Corporation, set-up under a statute or incorporated but wholly owned by the Government. It is self-evident and trite to say that the function of the State has long since ceased to be confined to the preservation of the public peace, the ex-action of taxes and the defence of its frontiers. It is now the function of the State to secure 'social, economic and political justice', to preserve 'liberty of thought, expression, belief, faith and worship', and to ensure 'equality of status and of opportunity'. That is the proclamation of the people in the preamble to the Constitution....'*

He further added in the same paragraph,

> '*...... There is no good reason why, if Government is bound to observe the equality clauses of the Constitution in the matter of employment and in its dealing with the employees, the Corporations set-up or owned by the Government should not be equally bound and why, instead, such Corporations could become citadels of patronage and arbitrary action. In a country like ours which teems with population, where the State, its agencies, its instrumentalities and its Corporations are the biggest employers and where millions seek employment and security, to confine the applicability of the equality clauses of the Constitution, in relation to matters of employment, strictly to direct employment under the Government is perhaps to mock at the Constitution and the people. Some elements of public employment is all that is necessary to take the employee beyond the reach of the rule which denies him access to a Court to enforce a contract of employment and denies him the protection of Articles 14 and 16 of the Constitution....*'[18]

18. AIR 1980 SC 840.

With the above observations Chinnappa Reddy, J. agreed with Sarkaria, J. and observed that the U.P. Warehousing Corporation was "State" under Article 12 of the Constitution and hence amenable to the writ jurisdiction.

5. *Mandamus* against International Airport Authority

Ramana D. Shetty v. International Airport Authority of India[19]

Soon after the landmarking judgment of *Sukhdev* v. *Bhagatram*, declaring LIC, ONGC and IFC as inclusive within the definition of "State", in the above case, in the year 1979, an issue of law arose before the Supreme Court was as to whether an International Airport Authority was "State" under Article 12 of the Constitution of India or not.

An appeal was filed before the Supreme Court against the judgment of the High Court having dispute with the respondent regarding refusal of Tender submitted by the appellant and allotted to the respondent No. 4 to run a canteen. The appellant made the allegations against the respondent No. 1 that the respondent No. 4, whose tender was accepted was not having requisite qualification (five years' experience to run a Registered IInd class Hotel). The appellant preferred writ before the High Court. The same was not entertained. The appellant thereupon approached before the Supreme Court taking the contention that the respondent No. 1, being "State" within the meaning of Article 12, can not act in contravention of the rights given under Article 14. They could not be allowed to act in arbitrary manner. The appellant challenged the allotment of canteen contracts by accepting tender of the respondent No. 4, who apparently did not fulfil the terms of the tender issued by the respondent No. 1.

Justice Bhagwati pointed out following aspects while going through the constitution, powers and functions of the respondent No. 1:

1. The International Airport Authority constituted under the provisions of Section 3(1) of the International Airport Authority Act, 1971 as a mandatory requirement of the Central Government.
2. As per sub-section 2 of section 3 it is said that the respondent authority shall be a body corporate having perpetual succession.
3. The chairman of the Airport Authority shall be appointed by the Central Government.
4. As per Section 5(1) of the Act, the Central Government shall fix the term of office and the powers to terminate any of the employees were also given to it.
5. Section 16 of the act provided the functions of the Authority.
6. The Central Government had powers to appoint the Chairman and members of the Airport Authority and also the power to terminate the appointments were vested in the Central Government.

19. AIR 1979 SC 1628.

7. The Central Government had also power to take management of the Authority and entrust it to another.
8. The Central Government had power to give directions in writing from time to time and the same were binding upon the Airport Authority.
9. The Airport Authority had no share capital but the capital needed by it for carrying out its functions. The Central Government was having direct administrative control over the activities of the Airport Authority.
10. The Airport Authority was given power to frame the regulations and any contravention of certain specified regulations shall entail penal consequences.

Justice Bhagwati went into detail while answering a question how to determine whether a corporation was acting as instrumentality or agency of the Government. The answer is given in paragraph 14 of his judgment which is reproduced here below:

> *'14. A corporation may be created in one of two ways. It may be either established by statute or incorporated under a law such as the Companies Act, 1956 or the Societies Registration Act, 1860. Where a Corporation is wholly controlled by Government not only in its policy-making but also in carrying out the functions entrusted to it by the law establishing it or by the Charter of its incorporation, there can be no doubt that it would be an instrumentality or agency of Government. But ordinarily where a corporation is established by statute, it is autonomous in its working, subject only to a provision, often times made, that it shall be bound by any directions that may be issued from time to time by Government in respect of policy matters. So also a corporation incorporated under law is managed by a board of directors or committee of management in accordance with the provisions of the statute under which it is incorporated. When does such a corporation become an instrumentality or agency of the Government? Is the holding of the entire share capital of the corporation by Government enough or is it necessary that in addition, there should be a certain amount of direct control exercised by Government and, if so, what should be the nature of such control? Should the functions which the corporation is charged to carry out possess any particular characteristic or feature, or is the nature of the functions immaterial?.....'*[20]

By putting such question to itself Justice Bhagwati gave the following guidelines/tests gathered by him in this decision:

- One thing is clear that if the Government holds the entire share capital of the corporation it would go a long way towards

20. AIR 1979 SC 1628, pp. 1638-39.

indicating that the corporation is an instrumentality or agency of Government.

- Where the financial assistance of the State is so much as to meet almost entire expenditure of the corporation, it would afford some indication of the corporation being impregnated with governmental character.
- It may also be a relevant factor whether the orporation enjoys monopoly status which is the State conferred or State protected.
- Existence of deep and pervasive State control may afford an indication that the Corporation is a State agency or instrumentality.
- If the functions of the corporation of public importance and closely related to governmental functions, it would be a relevant factor in classifying the corporation as an instrumentality or agency of Government.
- Specifically, if a department of Government is transferred to a corporation it would be a strong factor supportive of this inference of the Corporation being an instrumentality or agency of Government.

The above discussion clearly shows that every test discussed above was satisfied in the case of the Airport Authority and they leave no doubt that the authority was an instrumentality or agency of the Central Government and falls within the definition of "State" under Article 12 of the Constitution.

The observation, highlighting the concept of instrumentality or agency, the cases cited and detailed discussion regarding the concept of "State", are quoted in the judgments of Ajay Hasia and Som Prakash and the tests given in this case are used in the guidelines of Ajay Hasia's case.

6. Air India Statutory Corporation

Air India v. B.R. Age[21]

The issue involved in this case was regarding the directions of the Central Government to the Air India for providing reservation for Scheduled Caste and Scheduled Tribes in the services under the Air India Corporation. This was an appeal arisen against the Judgment of the Bombay High Court. The Supreme Court gave certain direction regarding the appointment of the employees out of Scheduled Caste and Scheduled Tribes in the Corporation.

But it did not decide the issue taken by the counsel for the appellant-Corporation as to whether the Air India Corporation is a "State" under Article 12 of the Constitution or not. The Supreme Court simply said that it would not like to express any opinion on the point of "State" qua the Air India Corporation.

---

21. AIR 1996 SC 276.

Air India Statutory Corporation v. United Labour Union[22]

In the above case the question involved was regarding the definition of "appropriate government" in Sec. 2(1)(a) of the Contract Labour (Regulation and Abolition) Act. The dispute was regarding the abolition of contract labour system but the principles laid down in this case are very important for the present study as they are regarding the instrumentality or agency of the state. These principles are described as follows:

1. The constitution of the corporation or instrumentality or agency or corporation aggregate or corporation sole is not of sole material relevance to decide whether it is by or under the control of the appropriate Government under the Act.
2. If it is a statutory corporation, it is an instrumentality or agency of the State. If it is a company owned wholly or partially by a share capital, floated from public exchequer, it gives indicia that it is controlled by or under the authority of the appropriate government.
3. In commercial activities carried on by a corporation established by or under the control of the appropriate Government having protection under Articles 14 and 19(2), it is an instrumentality or agency of the State.
4. The State is a service corporation. It acts through its instrumentalities, agencies or persons—natural or juridical.
5. The governing power, wherever located, must be subject to the fundamental constitutional limitations and abide by the principles laid in the Directive Principles.
6. The framework of service regulations made in the appropriate rules or regulations should be consistent with and subject to the same public law, principles and limitations.
7. Though the instrumentality, agency or person conducts commercial activities according to business principles and are separately accountable under their appropriate bye-laws or Memorandum of Association, they become the arm of the Government.
8. The existence of deep and pervasive State control depends upon the facts and circumstances in a given situation and in the altered situation it is not the sole criterion to decide whether the agency or instrumentality or persons is by or under the control of the appropriate Government.
9. Functions of an instrumentality, agency or person are of public importance following public interest element.
10. The instrumentality, agency or person must have an element of authority or ability to effect the relations with its employees or public by virtue of power vested in it by law, Memorandum of Association or bye-laws or Articles of Association.

22. AIR 1997 SC 645.

11. The instrumentality, agency or person renders an element of public service and is accountable to health and strength of the workers, men and women, adequate means of livelihood, the security for payment of living wages, reasonable conditions of work, decent standard of life and opportunity to enjoy full leisure and social and cultural activities to the workmen.
12. Every action of the public authority, agency or instrumentality or the person acting in public interest or any act that gives rise to public element should be guided by public interest in exercise of public power or action hedged with public element and is open to challenge. It must meet the test of reasonableness, fairness and justness.
13. If the exercise of the power is arbitrary, unjust and unfair, the public authority, instrumentality, agency or the person acting in public interest, though in the field of private law, is not free to prescribe any unconstitutional conditions or limitations in their actions.

In this case, the Supreme Court has, while deciding the issue of contract labour indirectly held that the Air India Statutory Corporation falls within the definition of "Other Authorities" and hence "State" as defined in Article 12 of the Constitution of India.

7. Food Corporation of India

Workmen, Food Corporation of India v. M/s. Food Corporation of India[23]

The Supreme Court had an opportunity to decide in the case of *Workmen, Food Corporation of India* v. *M/s. Food Corporation of India* that the Food Corporation of India is "State" or not. Supreme Court had to consider and determine the status of 464 workmen of the Corporation in that case.

The corporation was set-up under the Food Corporations Act, 1964. From the perusal of the scheme of the Act the Supreme Court had no hesitation to come to the conclusion that the Food Corporation of India is an instrumentality of the State comprehended in the expression "Other authorities" in Article 12 of the Constitution. Here the Supreme Court had just to follow the ratio laid down in the earlier cases. The decisions of *Sukhdev* v. *Bhagatram*, International Airport Authority case, guidelines of Ajay Hasia and Som Prakash's case made the clear picture as to which authority should be included within the ambit of Article 12. In short it can be said that this judgment is in addition of the earlier decided judgments confirming the ratio that the statutory corporations are covered within the definition of "State".

23. AIR 1985 SC 671.

8. State Financial Corporation

Gujarat State Financial Corporation v. Lotus Hotels (P) Ltd.[24]

In this case the Supreme Court, by relying upon the judgment of *Ramana Dayaram Shetty* v. *International Airport Authority of India* (already discussed) held that the GSFC was an instrumentality of the state and observed in paragraphs 9 and 11 of its judgment that the instrumentality of the State which would be "other authority" under Article 12 cannot commit breach of a solemn undertaking to the prejudice of the other party which acted on that undertaking or promise and put itself in a disadvantageous position. The appellant Corporation, created under the State Financial Corporation Act, fell within the expression of "other authority" in Article 12 and if it backs out from such a promise, it cannot be said that the only remedy for the aggrieved party would be suing for damages for breach and that it could not compel the Corporation for specific performance of the contract under Article 226.

Mahesh Chandra v. Regional Manager, U.P. Financial Corporation[25]

The Supreme Court in its verdict made it clear through this judgment that the public enterprises are accountable to the people. In these circumstances, the authority has to must justify its action as being just, reasonable and fair. Further, the balance between accountability and autonomy should be maintained. With this observation the Supreme Court declared U.P. Financial Corporation as "State" under Article 12.

9. Delhi Transport Corporation:

Delhi Transport Corporation v. D.T.C. Mazdoor Congress[26]

In the above case, validity of Regulation 9(b) of the Delhi Road Transport Authority (Conditions of Appointment and Service) Regulations, 1952 was challenged before a bench of five judges. Regulation 9(b) conferred powers on the authority to terminate the services of a permanent and confirmed employee by issuing a notice without assigning any reasons in the order and without giving any opportunity of hearing to the employees before passing the impugned order. By virtue of the aforesaid regulation the service of permanent employees were terminated. The union, the respondent No. 1 herein, DTC Mazdoor Congress filed writ petition in Delhi High Court challenging the constitutional validity of Regulation 9(b) of the Delhi Road Transport Authority (Conditions of Appointment and Service) Regulations, 1952. The Division Bench of the Delhi High Court allowed the said writ petition and struck down the Regulation 9(b). Being aggrieved by the judgment and order of the Delhi High Court, the Delhi Transport Corporation preferred special leave to appeal before the Supreme Court.

---

24. (1983) 3 SCC 379.
25. AIR 1993 SC 935.
26. AIR 1991 SC 101.

The Supreme Court, by majority of 4:1 declared the impugned order of termination wholly arbitrary, uncanalised and unrestricted violating principles of natural justice as well as Article 14 of the Constitution of India. Government Company or Public Corporation being State instrumentalities are "State" within the meaning of Article 12 of the Constitution and as such they are subject to the observance of fundamental rights embodied in Part III as well as to conform to the directive principles in Part IV of the Constitution.

The aforesaid Regulation 9 is reproduced here below:

'9. Termination of service: (a) Except as otherwise specified in the appointment orders, the services of an employee of the authority may be terminated without any notice or pay in lieu of notice:

(i) During the period of probation and without assigning any reason thereof.

(ii) For misconduct.

(iii) On the completion of specific period of appointment.

(iv) In the case of employees engaged on contract for a specific period, on the expiration of such period in accordance with the terms of appointment.

(b) Where the termination is made due to reduction of establishment or in circumstances other than those mentioned at (a) above, one month notice or pay in lieu thereof will be given to all categories of employees.

(c) Where a regular/temporary employee wishes to resign from his post under the authority he shall give three/one month's notice in writing or pay in lieu thereof to the Authority provided that in special cases, the General Manager may relax, at his discretion, the conditions regarding the period notice of resignation or pay in lieu thereof.'

By careful study of the aforesaid regulation with the touchstone of Article 14, the Supreme Court came to the conclusion that the procedure prescribed by their Regulation must be reasonable, fair and just and not arbitrary, fanciful and unjust. Regulation 9(b) found to have conferred unbridled, uncanalised and arbitrary power on the authority to terminate the services of the permanent employee without recording any reasons and without conforming to the principles of natural justice. Considering from all aspects Regulation 9(b) was declared illegal and void as it was arbitrary, discriminatory and without any guidelines for exercise of power.

The observations made by **Justice B.C. Ray** while expressing his views regarding the role of public corporations as defined in Article 12 are very important. The relevant parts of his view are narrated hereunder:

Justice B.C. Ray (para. 199):

'....... It has also been held consistently by this Court that the Government carries on various trades and business activity through the instrumentality

of the State such as Government Company or Public Corporations. Such Government Company or Public Corporation being State instrumentalities are State within the meaning of Article 12 of the Constitution and as such they are subject to the observance of fundamental rights embodied in Part III ....'

Thus it was held by majority of 4:1 that the Delhi Transport Corporation, being instrumentality or agency of the government and hence "State" within the meaning of Article 12 of the Constitution should act in a just, fair and reasonable manner and not in an unreasonable, capricious or arbitrary manner leaving room for discrimination.

10. State Road Transport Corporation

Andhra Pradesh State Road Transport Corporation:

District Manager, APSRTC, Vijaywada v. K. Sivaji and others[27]

In the case of *District Manager, APSRTC, Vijaywada* v. *K. Sivaji and others,* a point of consideration before the Supreme Court was little different. After having established by the State Government, even if the State Road Transport is separated from the State Government, it is still under the control of the Government and is covered under the definition of "State". This issue was decided by the Supreme Court. (per S. Rajendra Babu and S.N. Variava, JJ.)

The Andhra Pradesh High Court held that the appellant was not under the control of the Central or the State Government and that therefore the provisions of Sec. 11(1)(c) of the A.P. Factories and Establishment (National Festival and other Holidays) Act was applicable. The High Court further held that even though an institution may be treated as "State" within the meaning of Article 12 of the Constitution of India, it did not necessarily mean that it was under the control of the State Government or the Central Government as the case may be.

As per the view of the Supreme Court, the words used in Section 11(1)(c) of the said Act are "any factory or establishment under the control of the Central or any State Government." In Article 12 of the Constitution of India the words used are "under the control of the Government of India." Thus, under both of them what is essential is control of the Government. The Supreme Court failed to see as to how an establishment, deemed to be "State" within the meaning of Article 12 of the Constitution of India, would not be under the Control of the Government for the purpose of Section 11(1)(c) of the said Act.

Thus, the Supreme Court in this case, while dealing with other issue upheld the ratio that the Andhra Pradesh State Road Transport Corporation, established under Section 3 of the Road Transport Corporation Act, 1950 is "State" under Article 12 of the Constitution of India.

27. AIR 2001 SC 383.

11. Port Trusts Constituted under the Major Port Trusts Act
Mumbai Port Trust

M/s. Dwarkadas Marfatia and Sons v. Board of Trustees of the Port of Bombay[28]

An appeal was filed by the appellant against the judgment of the single judge of the High Court of Bombay in a dispute pertaining to Bombay Rents, Hotel and Lodging House Rates Control Act. The Dispute was pertaining to the exemption given to the Bombay Port Trust from the applicability of the aforesaid Act as provided in section 4 thereof to the public bodies. A writ petition before the Bombay High Court was filed by the appellants which was rejected taking the contention that the Bombay Rents, Hotel and Lodging House Rates Control Act were not applicable to the respondent Port Trust.

The Supreme Court also in appeal observed that the Board of Trustees of the Port of Bombay was a statutory authority. Being a statutory authority, the respondent has been exempted from the operation of the relevant Rent Act. The Supreme Court opined that the respondent was a statutory corporation constituted under the Major Port Trust (Amendment) Act, 1974. (Paragraph 3 of the judgment.) The Supreme Court, with this observation dismissed the appeal of the appellants on merits.

Jamshed Hormusji Wadia v. Board of Trustees, Port of Mumbai[29]

It has been held by the Supreme Court, in Special Leave Application against the decision of the division bench of the High Court that in the field of contracts the State and its instrumentalities ought to so design their activities as would ensure fair competition and non-discrimination.

While answering the question as to what was the status of the Bombay Port Trust as a landlord, the Supreme Court held that the Bombay Port Trust was "instrumentality" and hence "State" under Article 12 of the Constitution of India and amenable to the writ jurisdiction. The Supreme Court also reminded the case of *M/s. Dwarkadas Marfatia and Sons* v. *Board of Trustees* of the Port of Bombay (discussed above). The Supreme Court also said that the Bombay Port Trust cannot afford to act with arbitrariness or capriciousness as being an instrumentality of the State. Moreover, it was commented that the Trust must act within the four corners of the statute, which has created and governs it and all its action must be for public good.

4.2 *MANDAMUS* AGAINST STATUTORY BOARDS

4.2.1 *Mandamus* against School Examination Board

Bihar School Examination Board v. Subhas Chandra[30]

In the case of *Bihar School Examination Board* v. *Subhas Chandra*, in the Secondary School Examinations vast majority of examinees at particular

28. (1989)3 SCC 293 = (AIR 1989 SC 1642).
29. AIR 2004 SC 1815.
30. AIR 1970 SC 1269.

center adopted unfair means. School Examination Board cancelled the examination as a whole at that center. In a writ of *mandamus* filed against the Board, the Supreme Court held that it was not necessary to give opportunity to all the candidates to represent their cases. By observing that there was nothing wrong with the order of the High Court, the Supreme Court rejected the writ against the Bihar School Examination Board. The matter was rejected on facts. But this case establishes the view that the writ of *mandamus* is maintainable against the School Examination Board.

4.2.2 *Mandamus* against Shrine Board

Chain Singh v. Mata Vaishno Devi Shrine Board[31]

While deciding the issue as to whether Mata Vaishno Devi Shrine Board is "State" under Article 12 of the Constitution of India or not, the High Court, relying on the judgment of Bhuri Nath's case[32] in a writ petition answered the question in negative. In appeal, the Supreme Court held that the High Court decided issue without taking into consideration the ratio laid down by a seven Judges Bench in Pradeep Kumar Biswas case.

The entire case was therefore remanded to the High Court for afresh decision by taking into consideration the ratio laid down in the case of Pradeep Kumar Biswas by the Supreme Court. It appears from the view of the Supreme Court in remanding the case to the High Court, it is of the opinion that *mandamus* against the shrine board is maintainable and Shrine Board might fall within the meaning of "Other Authorities" under Article 12 of the Constitution.

4.2.3 *Mandamus* against Mining Settlement Board

Mining Settlement Board is a statutory board and therefore it is included within the definition of "other authorities" and hence "State" under Article 12 of the Constitution of India. It appears from the existing legal position and judgments of the Supreme Court that there is no dispute ever regarding the status of Mining Settlement Board. Due to this reason, probably there is no judgment giving clarification as to whether Mining Settlement Board is "State" under Article 12.

4.2.4 *Mandamus* against Railway Board

Railway Board v. M/s. Observer Publications (P) Ltd.[33]

In the above case, the Respondent (Original petitioner in writ petition under Article 226) was the owner and publisher of a weekly newspaper known as "The Indian Observer". Till March 1965 the aforesaid news

31. (2004) 12 SCC 634.
32. (1997) 2 SCC 745.
33. AIR 1972 SC 1792.

weekly was being sold at all the railway stations which were managed and were under the administrative control of the Railway Board. It was alleged that the policy of the news weekly was to publish a constructive criticism and fair comment in public interest on the working of different departments of the Government and suggest remedial measures. In some of the copies of the news weekly, certain matters regarding mal-administration of the Railway had been published. Allegations were made about the black-marketing in deluxe train tickets and corrupt practice of railway staff. After having printed such news, the Northern Railway Administration banned the sale of "The Indian Observer" on the Railway Book Stalls.

The Observer Publication thereupon preferred a writ petition under Article 226 of the Constitution of India for unlawful restriction on the sale of "The Indian Observer" news weekly. The explanation given by the respondent Railway Board that the ban was imposed due to publication of sexy and obscene literature was not believed by the High Court. Therefore, the Punjab High Court set aside the directions of the General Manager of the railway board putting ban on the sale of above named news weekly.

Upon the certificate of the High Court, the appellant Railway Board preferred appeal under Article 133 of the Constitution before the Supreme Court. The Supreme Court rejected the appeal upholding the judgment of the High Court and it observed in paragraph 14 regarding the function of the Railway Board as "State" as follows:

> *'14. The question that has next to be resolved is whether Article 14 could be invoked by the respondent in the present case. It has not been and indeed cannot be disputed that the Railway Board will fall within the definition of "State" as given in Article 12 of the Constitution....'*

With this observation while dismissing the appeal, the Supreme Court observed that the Railway Board, being covered within the definition of "State" under Article 12 could not act discriminatory and hence the Punjab High Court was right in setting aside the direction prohibiting sale of the news weekly "The Indian Observer" on Railway Book Stalls as the same was violative of Article 14 of the Constitution.

Chairman, Railway Board v. Chandrima Das[34]

This is a land marking pronouncement given by the Supreme Court in the case where two employees of Railway committed rape in Railway Rest room on a woman, resident of Bangladesh. A writ petition filed under Article 226 before the High Court and subsequently under Article 32 of the Constitution before the Supreme Court by a practicing advocate of the Supreme Court on behalf of a foreigner woman by reading an article in the newspaper seeking relief directing the respondent Railway Board to pay compensation to the victim.

34. AIR 2000 SC 988.

The Supreme Court observed that since the incident took place in the railway premises by the employees of the Railway, the Railway Board is liable for the Compensation. Article 21 ensures right to life and liberty. It is available even to foreigners. Railway Board is vicariously liable for the act done by its employees. A direction was given to pay amount of compensation to the High Commissioner for Bangladesh in India for payment to the victim as she already left India.

4.2.5 *Mandamus* against Electricity Boards

1. Rajasthan Electricity Board
Electricity Board, Rajasthan v. Mohan Lal[35]

The definition of "Other Authorities"' was expanded by the judgment of *Electricity Board, Rajasthan* v. *Mohan Lal*. The application of the principle of *ejusdem generis* was completely rejected by the Supreme Court. In the case of Ujjam Bai, through Justice Ayyanger categorically said that the principle of *ejusdem generis* was not applicable while interpreting Article 12, Justice Subba Rao relied upon the said principle.

By replying upon plain dictionary meaning of the word "authority" Supreme Court said that meaning of authority is a public administrative agency or corporation having quasi–governmental powers and authorised to administer revenue producing public authorities. Thus, the expression of the term "other authority" is wide enough to.

As per the facts of the case, an employed of Rajasthan Government was occupying the post of foreman at the Electrical and Mechanical Department of Rajasthan Government as a permanent employee. On Constitution of Rajsthan Electricity Board, services of all the employees of the said department were provisionally placed at the disposal of the Board by the notification issued by the Government. In this notification direction was given to the Board to frame new grades and service conditions. But, Board did not frame the rules, nor service conditions. After having worked for about 2 years, the respondent 1, the concerned employee was deputed to the public works department by the state Government. The Government by its order in the year 1960 directed the Board to treat respondent 1 and other co-employees (Respondent Nos. 4 to 14) as on deputation in the year 1962, the Public Works Department reverted the respondent No. 1, back to his parent Department. But actually he was reverted to the Board on 11-7-1963.

Board issued orders posting respondent No. 1 as a foreman. But while respondent No. 1, was deputed in public works department, his co-workers, respondent numbers the Board promoted 4 to 14 as Assistant Engineers, while respondent number 1 was promoted to work as assistant engineer on public works department. On his reversion the respondent No. 1 claimed that he was entitled to the post of Assistant Engineer under the

35. AIR 1967 SC 1857.

Board. Neither Board nor the Government heard his claim. Hence, the respondent preferred writ under Articles 226 and 227 of the Constitution before the High Court of Rajasthan on the ground of violation of Articles 14 and 16 of the Constitution.

Board opposed the petition on two grounds, viz. (1) as the respondent No. 1 was never a permanent employee of the board and hence not entitled to be promoted. (2) Rajasthan Electricity Board could not be held to be "state" as defined in Article 12 of the constitution.

High Court rejected both these ground issued direction to the Board to consider promotions afresh after talking into consideration the claim of the respondent No. 1. Being aggrieved by the judgment of Rajasthan High Court, Board preferred appeal before the Supreme Court.

While deciding the first point the Supreme Court held that the respondent No. 1 was a permanent employee of the Rajasthan Electricity Board. The Board, in its own conduct accepted the fact that the respondent was servant of the board and not an employee of the State Government.

On the second point, i.e. whether Rajasthan Electricity Board is a "State" or not, an argument made to by the Board was that authorities named under Article 12 were Government and Parliament of India and State Government legislature of each state and local and other authorities. If the expression "Other authorities" was to be read *"ejusdem generis"* with those named authorities, Board could not be covered under the definition of "other authorities". Hence no writ could be issued against Board for violation of Articles 14 and 16 of the Constitution in support of its argument board relied upon the judgment of Madras High Court in the case of *University of Madras* v. *Shantha Bai,* wherein university was considered as state aided institution and not state maintained institution, not subject to writ jurisdiction.

But the Supreme Court held that the High Court have erred in applying the principle of *ejusdem generis* while interpreting the term other authorities under Article 12.

Justice Bhargava tried to interpret term other authorities as follows:

> *'The ejusdem generis rule is one to be applied with caution and not pushed too far.... To invoke the application of the ejusdem generis rule there must be a distinct genus or category. The specific words must apply not to different objects of a widely differing character but to something which can be called a class or kind of objects. Where this is lacking, the rule cannot apply, but the mention of a single species does not constitute a genus.'*[36]

Maxwell in his book on "Interpretation of Statutes" explained the principles by saying: But the general word which follows particular and specific words of the same nature as itself takes its meaning from them and is presumed to be restricted to the same genus as those words.... Unless

36. AIR 1967 SC 1857, p. 1862.

there is a genus or category, there is no room for the application of the *ejusdem generis* doctrine.

The ratio laid down in the case of *United Towns Electric Co.* v. *Attorney General for Newfoundland*[37] was considered by the Supreme Court. In that case, the Privy Council held that in their opinion, there is no room for the application of the principle of *ejusdem generis* in the absence of any mention of a genus, since the mention of single species—for example, water rate—does not constitute a genus. In Article 12 of the Constitution the bodies specifically named are the Executive Governments of the Union and the State, the legislatures of the Union and the States, and local authorities. We are not unable to find any common genus running through these named bodies, nor can these bodies be placed in one single category on any rational basis. The doctrine of *ejusdem generis* could not, therefore, be applied to the interpretation of the expression "other authorities" in this article.

With these observations Justice Bhargava held that the expression "other authorities" in Article 12 includes all Constitutional or Statutory authorities on whom powers are conferred by law. It is not at all material that some of the powers conferred may be for the purpose of carrying on commercial activities.

Under the Constitution, the state is itself envisaged as having the right to carry on trade or business as mentioned in Article 19(1)(g). In Part IV, the "State" has been given the same meaning as in Article 12 and one of Directive Principles laid down in Article 46 is that the State shall promote with special care the educational and economic interests of the weaker sections of the people. The State, as defined in Article 12, is thus comprehended to include bodies created for the purpose of promoting the educational and economic interests of the people. The State, as constituted by our Constitution, is further specifically empowered under Article 298 to carry on any trade or business. The circumstance that the Board under the Electricity Supply Act is required to carry on some activities of the nature of trade or commerce does not, therefore, give any indication that the Board must be excluded from the scope of the word "State" as used in Article 12. On the other hand, there are provisions in the Electricity Supply Act which clearly show that the powers conferred on the Board include power to give directions, the disobedience of which is punishable as a criminal offence. In these circumstances, the Supreme Court did not consider it necessary to examine the cases cited on behalf of the appellant Board that it could not be held to be an agent or instrument of the Government. The Board was clearly an authority to which the provisions of Part III of the Constitution were applicable.

Justice J.C. Shah though agreed with the order proposed by Justice Bhargava, he differed slightly regarding interpretation of the term "other authorities". According to Justice J.C. Shah every constitutional or statutory

37. (1939)1 All.E.R. 423.

authority on which powers are conferred by law cannot be designated as other authority within the meaning of Article 12. The expression "authority" in its etymological sense, means a body invested with power to command or give an ultimate decision or enforces obedience or having a legal right to command and be obeyed. But as majority supported view taken by **Justice Bhargava** regarding interpretation of other authority, the following ratio was laid down by the Supreme Court:

> *'Authorities constitutional or statutory invested with power by law not sharing the sovereign power do not fall within the expression "State" as defined in Article 12. Those authorities which are invested with sovereign power, i.e. power to make rules or regulations and to administer or enforce them to the detriment of citizens and others fall within the definition of "State" in Article 12, and constitutional or statutory bodies which do not share that sovereign power of the State are not, "State" within the meaning of Article 12 of the Constitution.'*

Justice Bhargava took into consideration the meaning of the term "authority" as well as the expression "other authority" and observed,

> *'5. The meaning of the word "authority" given in Webster's Dictionary, which can be applicable, is a "public administrative agency or corporation having quasi-governmental powers and authorised to administer a revenue-producing public enterprise." The dictionary meaning of the word "authority" is clearly wide enough to include all bodies created by a statute on which powers are conferred to carry out governmental or quasi-governmental functions. The expression "other authorities" is wide enough to include within itself authority created by a statute and functionaries within the territory of India, or under the control of the Government of India. I do not see any reason to narrow down the meaning in the context in which the terms "other authorities" are used in Art. 12 of the Constitution.'*[38]

This judgment was considered as a turning point in the interpretation of Article 12 of the Constitution, more particularly the term "other authorities". It was made specifically clear by the Supreme Court that the principle of *ejusdem generis* was wrongly applied by several High Courts while interpreting the term "other authorities". It was further held that the expression "other authorities" in Article 12 includes all Constitutional or statutory authorities on whom powers conferred by law. The opinion given in the case of *Ujjam Bai* v. *State of U.P.*[39] by Justice Ayyangar was confirmed. This judgment made it clear that even the autonomous authorities which do not come under the control of

38. AIR 1967 SC 1857, p. 1862.
39. AIR 1962 SC 1621.

Government, can as well be included in the definition of "other authorities". In this sense, the judgment rendered by the Supreme Court in the case of *K.S. Ramamurthy Raddiar* v. *The Chief Commissioner, Pondicherry*[40] was confirmed. This was an exhaustive and detailed interpretation given by the Supreme Court upon the term "other authorities" by which the scope of Article 12 was widened.

The principle laid down in this case constituted base of the further expansion of the definition of "State" under Article 12 in the case of *Sukhdev* v. *Bhagatram, International Airport Authority* case and *Ajay Hasia* v. *Khalid Mujib.*

2. Bihar State Electricity Board

Rohtas Industries v. Bihar State Electricity Board[41]

Two writ petitions were filed before the High Court of Patna contending that the provisions contained in the Terrif Notification of 1979 for the levy of fuel surcharge was devoid of legal sanction and was arbitrary and void. The charge of arbitrariness leveled against the imposition of fuel surcharge was based on the ground that only consumers of low tension industrial service, high tension service, extra high tension service, and railway traction service had been singled out for being subjected to a levy of surcharge, while consumers of electricity for domestic, commercial and irrigation purposes were left unaffected by any such burden.

A point was taken into consideration that the Bihar State Electricity Board is incorporated under Section 12 of the Electricity (Supply) Act, 1948. The general powers and duties of the Board are set out in Section 18. Thereunder the Board has the duty, *inter alia,* to arrange for the supply of electricity that may be required within the State and for the transmission and distribution of the same in the most efficient and economic manner, with particular reference to those areas which are not, for the time being, supplied or adequately supplied with electricity. It was held that the power to classify the consumers into different categories and to fix differential tariffs has thus been conferred on the Board by the Section itself. Thus, where the State Electricity Board had levied the fuel surcharge by its Tariff Notification on the consumers receiving high tension supply to their factories, while, the consumers of the electricity for domestic, commercial and irrigation purposes were left unaffected by such burden, the imposition of fuel surcharge on the consumers could not be said to be arbitrary and violative of Article 14. Hence the Special Leave petition filed by the appellant was dismissed on merits.

In this case Justice D.A. Desai while giving judgment indirectly held in the beginning itself that the Bihar State Electricity Board is "State" within

40. AIR 1963 SC 1464.
41. AIR 1984 SC 657.

meaning of Article 12 of the Constitution and it is a duty of the Board to act reasonably and not arbitrarily. Further, after perusal of the facts of the case, no arbitrariness was found to have been done by the Board. Hence, the Supreme Court declined to interfere.

3. Surya Narayan Yadav and Others v. Bihar State Electricity Board and others[42]

In the year 1985 the concept of "State" became clear and tests have been formulated in various decisions. Hence, it was not tough for the Supreme Court to declare Bihar State Electricity Board as "State" under Article 12. In the case of *Surya Narayan Yadav and Others* v. *Bihar State Electricity Board and others,* the question involved was regarding regularization of the trainee engineers of Bihar State Electricity Board, wherein the apex court, without hesitation held the same as "State".

This judgment is nothing but an extension to the judgment of Rajasthan Electricity Board case. Since the status of Electricity Board has been made so clear and unambiguous, that the Supreme Court had no trouble at all in declaring Bihar State Electricity Board as "State" under Article 12.

4. W.B. State Electricity Board v. Desh Bandhu Ghosh[43]

The first respondent herein, a permanent employee of the West Bengal Electricity Board filed the writ petition out of which the appeal arose in the Calcutta High Court to quash an order dated March 22, 1984 of the Secretary, West Bengal State Electricity Board terminating his services as Deputy Secretary with immediate effect on payment of three months' salary in lieu of three months' notice. The Regulation 34 read with Regulation 33 of the West Bengal Electricity Board provided for the termination of services of both permanent and temporary employees of the Board on attaining the age of superannuation, as a result of the disciplinary action, etc. The Supreme Court held that the Regulations 34 and 33 conferred totally arbitrary powers to the Board, which was capable of vicious discrimination.

It was held that Article 14 has been interpreted in several decisions of the Supreme Court and conferment and exercise of arbitrary power on and by the State or its instrumentalities have been frowned upon and struck down by the Supreme Court as offending Article 14.

With this observation by taking into consideration the well established position in law that the Electricity Boards are covered within the definition of "State" and they cannot act arbitrarily, the Supreme Court dismissed the appeal filed by the West Bengal State Electricity Board and confirmed the judgment of the High Court.

42. AIR 1985 SC 941.
43. AIR 1985 SC 722.

4.3 *MANDAMUS* AGAINST GOVERNMENT COMPANIES

ENGLISH CASES

Rex v. Barton and Immingham Light Railway Company[44]

A light railway company under the powers conferred by an order made under the Light Railways Act, 1896, and incorporating the Lands Clauses Acts, took compulsorily certain lands in the occupation of a tenant from year to year. A single arbitrator was appointed under section 121 of the Lands Clauses Consolidation Act, 1845, as amended by Sec. 13 of the Light Railways Act, 1896, to assess the amount of compensation payable in respect of the tenant's interest. The arbitrator duly made his award and tendered it to the company under Sec. 35 of the Lands Clauses Consolidation Act, 1845. The company refused to take up the award on the ground that the matter was governed by the Arbitration Act, 1889, and not by the Lands Clauses Consolidation Act, 1845.

It was held by the Court of King's Bench that section 13 of the Light Railways Act, 1896, affected only the assessment of the amount of compensation; that the process of enforcing the award remained, as formerly, under the Lands Clauses Consolidation Act, 1845; and consequently that a writ of *mandamus* would issue ordering the light railway company to take up the award.

Rex v. Wilts and Berks Canal Company[45]

Rule *Nisi* was obtained at the instance of the Berkshire County Council, calling upon the respondents, the Wilts and Berks Canal Company, to show cause why a writ of *mandamus* should not issue, directed to them, commanding them to repair and do all the things necessary to repair and maintain a certain bridge over the Wilts and Berks Canal, which carried the main road between the town of Abingdon and the village of Drayton, at Caldecott, in the county of Berks, and was known as the Drayton Road Bridge, and the structure wing and parapet walls and side banks of such bridge, and the banks supporting the approaches thereto, so that the bridge might be made suitable and fit for carrying the main road and the persons and traffic using such main road, on the grounds that the respondents were liable to do such repairs and that the bridge was out of repair and unsafe.

It was argued that the terms of the rule nisi are so vague that the respondents would not know what they were required to do if the Court ordered the writ of *mandamus* to issue. The Court will not enforce a duty so vague as that of repairing a bridge by a prerogative writ of *mandamus*. But by disbelieving the contention, it was said that by the prerogative writ of *mandamus* the Court will compel a system of drainage to be carried out. That is of a much more indefinite nature than the repair of a bridge. The

44. (1912) 3 K.B. 72.
45. (1912) 3 K.B. 623.

work mentioned in the rule is of a specific kind. If the *mandamus* issued and the applicants thought the required works had not been carried out they could show in what respects there had been non-compliance by means of an affidavit.

Lastly, by allowing writ of *mandamus* **Lord Alverstone C.J.** made the following observations,

> *"The only doubt which I have had—but it seems to me not to be sufficient to prevent the rule for the mandamus being made absolute, leaving the respondents the right of raising the question on return if they are so advised to do—is whether the duty of repairing a bridge is of too uncertain a nature to be enforced by the prerogative writ of mandamus. The rule will be made absolute, and if the respondents are so advised they can raise the question upon the return."*

The other two judges, Channell and Avory, J.J. totally agreed with the view of Lord Alverstone, C.J. for the issuance of writ of *mandamus*.

INDIAN CASES

1. Bharat Petroleum

Som Prakash v. Union of India[46]

In the year 1080, in the *Som Prakash* v. *Union of India the Supreme Court* had an occasion to decide as to whether Bharat Petroleum Corporation Ltd., a Government Company is "State" under Article 12 of the Constitution of India. The task was before three judges' Bench consisting of justice Krishna Iyer, Justice Chinnappa Reddy and Justice R.S. Pathak. As a matter of fact the issue was relating to a poor employee's pension on retirement and the legality of the deductions effected by the employer. The petitioner directly preferred a writ petition under Article 32 of the Constitution before the Supreme Court. But a big legal question was that the Bharat Petroleum Corporation Limited vide Certificate of Incorporation dated 1-8-1977, a government company was subject to the issuance of writ under Article 32 or not. This is one of the classic judgments of Justice Krishna Iyer pronounced on 13-11-1980, i.e. the day on which Justice Bhagwati pronounced judgment of *Ajay Hasia* v. *Khalid Mujid*. The former judgment covered Government Company within the definition of "State" while later judgment laid down the ratio that writ can be issued even against the society registered under the Societies Registration Act. Both the above mentioned judgments are historic in a sense that they have taken a step to expand the scope of Article 12 of the Constitution of India by widening the meaning of "State".

This writ petition came up for hearing soon after the pronouncement of judgment of Airport Authority Case, where the Supreme Court took the

46. AIR 1981 SC 212).

stand that statutory corporations or government departments are subject to the writ jurisdiction under Article 12. But this judgment was silent regarding the inclusion of government company within the ambit of "State". By taking into consideration this fact, preliminary objection was raised on behalf of the respondent company that Bharat Petroleum was neither a government department nor a statutory corporation and therefore the Court should not entertain the writ petition under Article 32.

In order to understand the ratio it is necessary to throw some highlights on the facts of the case. The petitioner was employed as a clerk in the Burmah Shell Oil Storage Limited and retired after qualifying for a pension on April 1, 1973. The employer undertaking was statutory taken over by force of the Burmah Shell (Acquisition of Undertakings in India) Act, 1976. Therefore, the Central Government, acting under the statute, took necessary steps for the vesting of the Undertaking in itself and vested in the second respondent, the Bharat Petroleum Corporation Limited as per provisions of section 7(1) of the Act and became the statutory successor of the petitioner's employer. His pensionary rights, such as he had, therefore, became claimable from the Bharat Petroleum. Could a writ issued against Bharat Petroleum for getting pensionary and other benefits? This was the precise question involved in the case.

Justice Krishna Iyer tried to favour the expanded meaning of "state" as interpreted in prior judgment and he was of the opinion that Bharat Petroleum is a double of Bharat Sarkar (Central Government). In support of his conclusion he observed in paragraph 27 of his judgment,

> *".....Jurisprudence bearing on corporate personality is not myth but reality. What we mean is that corporate personality is a reality and not an illusion or fictitious construction of the law. It is a legal person. Indeed, 'a legal person' is any subject-matter other than a human being to which the law attributes personality. "This extension, for good and sufficient reasons, of the conception of personality ...... is one of the most noteworthy feats of the legal imagination." Salmond, Jurisprudence, 10th Edn., pp. 324-25. Corporations are one species of legal persons invented by the law and invested with a variety of attributes so as to achieve certain purposes sanctioned by the law. For those purposes, a corporation or company has a legal existence of its own. The characteristics of corporations, their rights and liabilities, functional authority and juristic status, are jurisprudentially recognized as of a distinct entity even where such corporations are but State agencies or instrumentalities. For purposes of the Companies Act, 1956, a government company has a distinct personality which cannot be confused with the State. Likewise, a statutory corporation constituted to carry on a commercial or other activity is for many purposes a distinct juristic entity not drowned in the sea of State, although, in substance, its existence may be but a projection of the State. What we wish to emphasise is that merely because a company or other legal person has functional ad jural individuality for certain purposes and in certain areas of law, it does not*

necessarily follow that for the effective enforcement of fundamental rights under our constitutional scheme, we should not scan the real character of that entity and if it is found to be a mere agent or surrogate of the State, in fact owned by the State and in effect an incarnation of the State, constitutional lawyers must not blink at these facts and frustrate the enforcement of fundamental rights despite the inclusive definition of Article 12 that any authority controlled by the Government of India is itself State. Law has many dimensions and fundamental facts must govern the applicability of fundamental rights in a given situation."[47]

It was observed therein that the test formulated for determining whether an authority is "State" or not is not as to whether the corporation is created by a statute or under a statute. The true test is functional. Not how the legal person is born but why it is created. Apart from discharging functions or doing business as the proxy of the State, wearing the corporate mask there must be an element of ability to affect legal relations by virtue of power vested in it by law.

The Supreme Court made careful study of various provisions of the Burmah Shell (Acquisition of Undertakings in India) Act, 1976.

Study of Section 7 signifies that the company should step into the shoes of the executive power of the State. The legislative milieu in which the second respondent came to be the successor of Burmah Shell suggests that the former is more than a mere company registered under the Companies Act, 1956. It has a statutory flavour acquired under Section 7 of the aforesaid Act. Sections 9 and 10 disclose that provident, superannuation and welfare funds of the employees, conditions of service, adjudication of service disputes are regulated statutorily unlike in the case of private companies. Section 12 discloses statutory character of the government company. Thus, by careful study of the various provisions it can be concluded with hesitation that the Bharat petroleum is not a mere company but much more than that and has a statutory flavour in its operation and functions, in powers and duties and in its personality. It is a limb of government, an agency of the State, a vicarious creature of statute working on the wheels of the Acquisition Act.

The arguments made on behalf of the respondent company that the recent trend of rulings of this court broadened the concept of 'authorities' under Article 12 and hence they were required to be placed before larger bench for the reconsidering the issue. The Supreme Court while refusing to do so not only justified the ratio laid down by it in the cases of U.P. Warehousing Corporation as well as Airport Authority but observed:

".... rulings of this Court are calculated to settle the law and not to unsettle it by reconsideration is season and out merely because it hurts one part or the other or tastes sour for one Judge or the other."

---

47. AIR 1981 SC 212, p. 218.

Justice Krishna Iyer has in this judgment openly supported the extended meaning of Article 12 and supported the enlargement of Article 12. While doing so he observed,

> *"......It is well known, and surely within the erudite and experienced ken of our 'founding fathers' that Government embarks on myriad modern commercial activities by resort to the jurisprudential gift of personification through incorporation. This contrivance of carrying business activities by the State through statutory corporations, government companies and other bodies with legal personality, simplifies and facilitates transactions and operations beyond the traditional and tardy processes of governmental desks and cells noted for their red tape exercise and drowsy dharma. But to use the corporate methodology is not to liberate the State from its basic obligation to obey Part III. To do the mantle of company is to free the State from the inevitable constraints of governmental slow-motion, not to play tunt with the great rights. Otherwise, a cunning plurality of corporations taking over almost every State business—the post and the rail-road, the T.V. and the radio, every economic ministry's activity, why, even social welfare work will cheat the people of Part III rights by the easy plea: "No admission for the bill of rights; no State here". From Indian Posts and Telegraphs Limited to Indian Defence Manufacture Limited from Social Welfare Board to Backward Classes Corporation, the nation will be told that 'the State has ceased to be, save for the non-negotiable sovereign functions'; and fundamental rights may suffer eclipse only to be view in museum glass cases. Such a situation will be a treachery on the founding fathers, a mockery of the Constitution and a government by puppetry because the crowd of corporations which have carved out all functions will still be controlled completely by the switch boards of bureaucrats and political bosses from remote control rooms in Government Secretariats. The extended definition in Article 12 is not to be deadened but quickened by judicial construction. Before our eyes the corporate phenomenon is becoming ubiquitous. What was archaicly done yesterday by Government departments is alertly executed today by government companies, statutory corporations and like bodies and this tribe may legitimately increase tomorrow. This efficiency is not to be purchased at the price of fundamental rights....."*[48]

Here Justice Krishna Iyer also remained the quotation made by Justice Methew in the case of *Punnen Thomas* v. *State of Kerala*[49]:

> ***"What's in a name? that which we call a rose.***
> ***By any other name would smell as sweet.***
> **(Romeo and Juliet II, ii 43)**
> *And the State is fragrant with fundamental rights whatever the legal hue*

48. AIR 1981 SC 212, p. 222.
49. AIR 1969 Ker. 81 (FB).

or jural cloak of its surrogate. And, to alter the imagery, Maricha is Ravana, the misleading golden deer mask notwithstanding !"

In this judgment Justice Krishna Iyer discussed at large the validity and propriety of the ratio laid down qua Article 12 in the cases of *Rajasthan Electricity Board case, Sukhdev* v. *Bhagatram's case, International Airport Authority case, Praga Tools case* and *Hindustan Steel case* and in held that Bharat Petroleum is "State" within the meaning of Article 12 of the Constitution. He negatived the argument that Justice Bhagwati had unnecessarily extended the scope of Article 12 and hence the same should be considered as obiter dicta. In this judgment Justice Krishna Iyer (Supported by Justice Chinnappa Raddy) gave the following preponderant considerations for pronouncing an entity as State, agency or instrumentality:

(i) financial resources of the State being the chief funding source,
(ii) functional character being the governmental in essence,
(iii) plenary control residing in Government,
(iv) prior history of the same activity having been carried on by Government and made over to the new body, and
(v) some element of authority or command.

It is observed that if any of the above conditions is satisfied, it is quite immaterial whether the legal person is a corporation created by a statute as distinguished from under a statute. Careful study of Airport Authority and Bharat Petroleum it can be understood that the former is created by a statute while later is recognized by and clothed with rights and duties by the statute. Applying this criteria, there is enough material to hold Bharat Petroleum as State.

In this case Justice R.S. Pathak took slight different view but in terms supported the ratio of the majority decision of Justice Krishna Iyer. He raised some doubts as to whether the Bharat Petroleum Corporation Limited was a "State" within the meaning of Article 12 or not. Justice Pathak said that the provisions of the Burmah Shell (Acquisition of Undertakings in India) Act, 1976 would be made applicable to any Government Company and they did not alter the basic nature of that company. Such provisions could be applied to private corporation as well, if the act had selected one for vesting the undertaking in it. Would that have made the private corporation a "State"? Hence, according to him, it is very hard to digest the ratio that Bharat Petroleum, a government company is "State".

But he showed his helplessness in the light of the decision taken by the Airport Authority case and observed that this bench is bound to follow the guidelines given by Justice Bhagwati in the Airport Authority case. By applying these guidelines to the present case he confessed that he had no other alternative but to declare Bharat Petroleum as "State". At the same time he desired that he would have welcomed wide debate upon the burning issue of "State" under Article 12.

In the year 1981, there was drastic change in the definition of Article 12, by this judgment as well as the judgment of Ajay Hasia's case. Both have been pronounced on the same day opening a flood gate of writ petitions before High Courts as well as the Supreme Court. Former allowed to prefer writ petitions against the Government Companies whereas the later judgment covered the Societies registered under the Societies Registration Act within the ambit of "State" under Article 12. In both these judgments the Supreme Court gave guidelines and included various authorities within the ambit of Article 12 of the Constitution.

2. Central and Industrial Development Corporation (CIDC) of Maharashtra Ltd.

Star Enterprises v. Central and Industrial Development Corporation of Maharashtra Ltd. and Others[50]

While dealing with the matter relating to the rejection of tenders of the highest bid without assigning any reasons, three judges' Bench of the Supreme Court had in the case of *Star Enterprises* v. *Central and Industrial Development Corporation of Maharashtra Ltd. and Others* an occasion to enter into the question as to whether City and Industrial Development Corporation of Maharashtra Ltd. (C.I.D.C. of Maharashtra Ltd.), a government company constituted as Development Authority under State Town Planning Act was covered by the definition of "State" under Article 12 or not.

Three appellants initially challenged the rejection of their highest offers in response to invitation by public tender without assigning any reason before the Bombay High Court on the ground that the same was arbitrary, unconstitutional and contrary to Rule of Law.

The respondent, a government company within the meaning of Section 617 of the Companies Act has been constituted as the New Town Development Authority under sub-section (3)(A) of section 113 of the Maharashtra Regional Town Planning Act, 1966. The respondent company was empowered to dispose land vested in it and the respondent has formulated with the approval of the State Government under Section 159 of the said Act a code for regulating, *inter alia*, disposal of land. Regulation 4 is reproduced herebelow:

4. The Corporation may dispose of plots of lands by putting auction or considering the individual applications as the corporation determines from time to time.

The normal practice adopted by the corporation was to invite tenders for the disposal of the specified plots which the corporation chooses to assign according to the terms and conditions for lease of plots for mercantile use. As per the contention of the appellants, they gave the highest offers, still however, their tender was rejected without assigning the reason. It was undisputed fact that the scheme which was operating

50. (1990)3 SCC 280.

provided that the respondent No. 1 reserves the right to amend, revoke or modify the scheme at its discretion as well as to reject any or all offers for allotment without assigning any reason. The respondent No. 1 defended by taking shelter of this provision and said that in exercise of this power the highest tenders had not been accepted.

Here the prime contention of the appellant was that the respondent is "State" under Article 12 of the Constitution and conferment of naked and unguided power as referred to above is arbitrary and contrary to the provisions of Article 14 of the Constitution; and since there is no prescribed norm or guideline and the power is unregulated and unfettered and the highest offer after complying with the prescribed requirement is liable to be rejected without assigning any reasons, citizens are likely to be affected by exercise of such uncanalised power. Thus appellant contented that the procedure adopted by the respondent No. 1 was contrary to the Rule of Law and it being "State" cannot act arbitrarily.

The Supreme Court without any hesitation accepted the above mentioned contention of the council appearing for the appellant that the respondent is "State" under Article 12 and conferment of naked and unguided power as referred to above is arbitrary and contrary to the provisions of Article 14 of the Constitution. It was also observed by the Supreme Court that in absence of prescribed norms and guideline the power was unregulated and unfettered. It was quite strange that the highest offer of tender, after complying with the prescribed requirement were rejected without assigning any reasons. An instrumentality of the State as has been laid down by this Court in a series of authoritative decisions beginning with *R.D. Shetty* v. *International Airport Authority of India*, and in *Ajay Hasia* v. *Khalid Mujib* and a number of decisions thereafter has to act within the ambit of Rule of Law and would not be allowed to conduct itself arbitrarily and in its dealing with the public would be liable to judicial review. The appellants had not made any allegations of *mala fide* on the part of the respondent, but insisted that its activities should be transparent. It was incumbent on the part of the respondent No. 1 to assign reasons for rejecting the tenders and to communicate the same to the citizens. The Supreme Court also said that even in absence of any rules, it was in the interest of the respondent to act fairly and assign reasons for the acceptance or rejection of the offer of tenders as it is "State" cannot act arbitrarily.

The Supreme Court has, by this judgment not only declared CIDC of Maharashtra, a government company "State" being the instrumentality of the government, but declared that the respondent company, being "State" under Article 12 of the Constitution cannot frame rule or schemes as it desires. It must develop an atmosphere of credibility and trust. While dealing into the commercial field, it must act fairly, within the ambit of Rule of Law. Both the landmark judgments mentioned herein above have been followed in this case.

3. Central Inland Water Transport Corporation

Central Inland Water Transport Corporation v. Brijo Nath[51]

In the case of *Central Inland Water Transport Corporation* v. *Brijo Nath* the Supreme Court had an occasion to decide whether the aforesaid corporation falls within the definition of "State" under Article 12 of the Constitution or not. This is a landmark judgment pertaining to service contracts. One of the rules of the Government Corporation empowering it to terminate services of its permanent employees by giving notice or pay in lieu of notice period was under challenge as it was alleged to be violative of Article 14 and directive principles contained in Articles 39(a) and 41.

A company carrying on the business of maintenance and running of river services entered into a scheme of Agreement with the Central Water Transport Corporation Ltd., a Government Company owned by Central Government and two State Governments. The scheme was approved by the High Court and the company was dissolved by the order of the High Court. A sub-clause in the rules provided for termination of services of the officers by giving three months' notice. The clause in the rule was struck down by the High Court and the Supreme Court in appeal approved the decision of the High Court by observing that considering the inequality in the bargaining power of the parties the clause in the contract of employment was void under Sec. 23 of the Contract Act as opposed to public policy, besides being *ultra vires* Art. 14.

The following arguments were raised on behalf of the appellant Corporation while challenging the judgment of the High Court:

(1) A Government company stands on a wholly different footing from a statutory corporation for while a statutory corporation is established by a statute, a Government company is incorporated like any other company by obtaining a certificate of incorporation under the Companies Act and, therefore, a Government company cannot come within the scope of the term "the State" as defined in Article 12 of the Constitution.

(2) A statutory corporation is usually established in order to create a monopoly in the State in respect of a particular activity. A Government Company is, however, not established for this purpose.

(3) The Corporation does not have the monopoly of inland water transport but is only a trading company as is shown by the objects clause in its Memorandum of Association.

(4) Assuming a Government company is "the State" within the meaning of Article 12, a contract of employment entered into by it is like any other contract entered into between two parties and a term in that contract cannot be struck down under Article 14 of the Constitution on the ground that it is arbitrary or unreasonable or unconscionable or one-sided or unfair.

---

51. AIR 1986 SC 1571.

The respondents opposed the arguments of the appellant corporation and justified the order of the High Court. They contended as follows:

(1) The definition of the expression "the State" given in Article 12 is wide enough to include within its scope and reach a Government Company.
(2) A State is entitled to carry on any activity, even a trading activity, through any of its instrumentalities or agencies, whether such instrumentality or agency be one of the Departments of the Government, a statutory corporation, a statutory authority or a Government company incorporated under the Companies Act.
(3) Merely because a Government company carries on a trading activity or is authorised to carry on a trading activity does not mean that it is excluded from the definition of the expression "the State" contained in Article 12.
(4) A Government company being "the State" within the meaning of Article 12 is bound to act fairly and reasonably and if it does not do so, its action can be struck down under Article 14 as being arbitrary.
(5) A contract of employment stands on a different footing from other contracts. A term in a contract of employment entered into by a private employer which is unfair, unreasonable and unconscionable is bad in law. Such a term in a contract of employment entered into by the State is, therefore, also bad in law and can be struck down under Article 14.

While declaring aforesaid rule *ultra vires* and opposed to public policy, the Supreme Court also discussed in detailed as to whether Central Inland Water Transport Corporation Ltd., a Government Company constituted under Sec. 617 of the Companies Act is "the State" within meaning of Article 12.

The following important factors were found out by the Supreme Court about the Central Inland Water Transport Corporation:

(1) The Corporation is a Government Company under Sec. 617 of the Companies Act, 1956.
(2) As all the shares of the Corporation are held by different Governments, viz. the Government of India and Governments of West Bengal and Assam, the Corporation is not only a Government company as said in Sec. 617 but it is wholly owned by a Central Government and two State Governments.
(3) The following are the main objects of the company:
    (a) maintaining and running river services with ancillary function of maintenance and operation of river-site jetty and terminal;

(b) constructing vessels of various sizes and descriptions;
(c) repairing vessels of various sizes and descriptions;
(d) undertaking general engineering activities.

(4) As per Article 51 of the Article of Association of the corporation, the President of India has the power to issue from time to time such directions or instructions as he may consider necessary in regard to the affairs or the conduct of the business of the Corporation. Further this article gives powers to the President of India to give instructions to the Corporation in the matters involving national security or public interest and the Directors of the Corporation are bound to comply with and give immediate effect to such directions.

(5) The Company is managed by the Chairman and Board of Directors appointed by the Central Government and removable by it.

(6) The Company is financed entirely by these three Governments viz. the Central Government and the State Governments of West Bengal and Assam.

(7) The activities carried on by the Corporation are of vital national importance, of great importance to public interest, concern and welfare.

(8) The Annual Report of the year 1984-85 of the Government of India, Ministry of Shipping and Transport, states in para. 6.1.2 as follows:

> *"the Inland Water Transport Directorate is an attached office of this Ministry headed by a Chief Engineer-cum-Administrator. ...... The Ministry has also under its control a public sector undertaking, namely, the Central Inland Water Transport Corporation, which is the only major company in inland water transport in the country."*

As per the above facts and the provisions mentioned in the Memorandum of Association and the Article of Association clearly show that not only is the Corporation a Government Company of which all the shares were and are owned by the Central Government and two State Governments but is a Government Company which is under the complete control and management of the Central Government. In other words, we can say that in every respect it is thus a veil behind which the Central Government operates through the instrumentality of a Government Company. For the purposes of Article 12 one must necessarily see through the corporate veil to ascertain whether behind that veil is the face of an instrumentality or agency of the state. The Central Inland Water Transport Corporation, squarely falls within these observations and it also satisfies the various tests which have been laid down. Merely because it has so far not the monopoly of inland water transportation is not sufficient to divest it of its character of an instrumentality or agency of the State. It is nothing but the Government operating behind a corporate veil, carrying out a governmental activity and governmental functions of vital public importance.

It has been observed by **Justice Madon** while delivering judgment,

'Thus, in the face of so much evidence it is ridiculous to describe the Corporation is a trading company as the Appellants have attempted to do. What has been set out above is more than sufficient to show that the activities of the Corporation are of great importance to public interest, concern and welfare and are activities of the nature carried on by a modern State and particularly a modern Welfare State.'

The Supreme Court by quoting the ratio laid down in the cases of *Sukhdev Singh* v. *Bhagatram, The International Airport Authority case* and *Ajay Hasia's case* observed that now it is well established law that an instrumentality or agency of the State being "the State" under Article 12 of the Constitution is subject to the Constitutional limitations and its actions are state actions and must be judged in the light of the Fundamental Rights guaranteed by Part III of the Constitution. The actions of an instrumentality or agency of the State must, therefore, be in conformity with Article 14 of the Constitution.

At the end, the Supreme Court declared the Central Inland Water Transport Corporation Ltd., as instrumentality/agency of the state and subsequently struck down the rule under challenge as being violative of Article 14 of the Constitution and confirmed the judgment of the High Court.

4. Steel Authority of India Ltd.

Balbir Kaur v. Steel Authority of India Ltd.[52]

The Division Bench comprising of Justice S.B. Majmudar and Justice U.C. Banerjee clearly opined that the Steel Authority of India Ltd. is covered within the ambit of "State" under Article 12 of the Constitution of India and hence it is amenable for the writ jurisdiction.

Steel Authority of India Ltd. v. National Union Water Front Workers[53]

In the above case, a question for consideration before a bench of five judges of the Supreme Court was regarding who should be the appropriate government, central or state government for the purpose of Contract Labour (Regulation and Abolition) Act. But an attempt was made to get help by arguing that the Steel Authority of India Ltd. was a Government Company and hence covered within the definition of "State" under Article 12 of the Constitution. Here the Supreme Court impliedly accepted that the Steel

52. AIR 2000 SC 1596.
53. AIR 2001 SC 2571.

Authority of India Ltd. was an instrumentality or agency of the Government and hence "State" under Article 12 of the Constitution. But at the same time it was of the opinion that since the matter before it was under the Contract Labour (Regulation and Abolition) Act and the point of consideration was to determine under whose authority the establishment carried on industry. Concept of Article 12 was out of question. The real test was not whether the establishment was instrumentality of Government under Article 12 of the Constitution. The observations made in para. 37 of the judgment given by **Justice Syed Shah Mohammed Quadri** categorically said,

> '37. *We wish to clear the air that the principle, while discharging public functions and duties the Government Companies/Corporations/Societies which are instrumentality or agencies of the Government must be subjected to the same limitations in the field of public law—constitutional or administrative law—as the Government itself, do not lead to the inference that they become agents of the Center/State Government for all purposes so as to bind such Government for all their acts, liabilities and obligations under various Central and/or State Acts or under private law.*'

5. Hindustan Steel Works Construction Ltd.

Hindustan Steel Works Construction Ltd. v. State of Kerala[54]

In the case of *Hindustan Steel Works Construction Ltd.* v. *State of Kerala* the point of consideration before the Supreme Court was as to whether a government company or a statutory corporation undertaking construction work should necessarily be a department or establishment of the Government or not. It was held by the Supreme Court that it is not necessary for any government company to be a department of Government. It may be an instrumentality or agency of the government only.

Looking to the facts of the case, the appellant company entered into an agreement with the Greater Cochin Development Authority (GCDA) for construction of a stadium subject to the stipulation that the sub-contractors to be employed by the appellant for execution of the contract were to be approved by GCDA. The appellant commenced the work and from time to time engaged different contractors. GCDA started making deduction from the part-payment of the bills raised by the appellant at the rate of 1% on account of contribution under the Kerala Construction Workers' Welfare Funds Act, 1989 (Act No. 20 of 1989) (Welfare Funds Act). The appellant unsuccessfully challenged the deduction before the High Court on the ground that, being a government company wholly owned and controlled by the Central Government, it was excluded from the purview of the Welfare Fund Act.

While dealing with the point of instrumentality or agency of the "State", the Supreme Court observed that the appellant company can not be held to be a department of the Government. There may be deep and

54. AIR 1997 SC 2275.

pervasive control of the Government over the appellant company and the appellant company, on such account may be an instrumentality or agency of the Central Government and as such a "State" within the meaning of Article 12 of the Constitution. Even then it can not be held to be a department or establishment of the Government in all cases. Section 2(c) and (e) of the Welfare Funds Act clearly shows that the legislature has not intended to exclude the government company or the statutory corporations from the purview of the Welfare Funds Act. The establishment of a Government only connotes in its plain meaning, an establishment directly run by the Government and not through the agency or instrumentality of the Government. The Welfare Funds Act is essentially an Act to protect the interest of and welfare of the labourers. Unless expressly the instrumentality or agency of the Government is kept outside the purview of the said Act, it would not be proper to interpret the said Act in wide amplitude by removing the corporate veil so as to exclude such instrumentality or agency from the purview of the said Act. By making these observations the Supreme Court rejected the appeal.

In this case, the Supreme Court though declared Hindustan Steel Works Construction Ltd. as "State" under Article 12, it specifically made it clear that there was no case of enforcement of fundamental rights against an action of the government. On the contrary, the question of protecting the welfare of the employees *vis-a-vis* the instrumentality or agency of the Central Government under the Welfare Funds Act is to be kept in mind. Hence the Supreme Court dismissed the appeal. However, the fact remains that the appellant company was declared as instrumentality or agency by following Ajay Hasia's case and held to be "State" under Article 12 of the Constitution.

6. Modern Food Industries (India) Ltd.

Ram Chandra Sharma v. Modern Food Industries (India) Ltd.[55]

In the case of *Ram Chandra Sharma* v. *Modern Food Industries (India) Ltd.*, a worker filed a writ petition against the said company to challenge his supersession before the High Court. But the High Court rejected the writ petition on the ground that the same was not maintainable as the respondent company is not "State" under Article 12 of the Constitution of India.

In an appeal by the petitioner, the Supreme Court set aside the view of the High Court and observed that the writ petition was maintainable as Modern Food Industries (India) Ltd. is "State" under Article 12. The Supreme Court by this decision confirmed the ratio laid down by the Gujarat High Court in the case of *Modern Food Industries (India) Ltd.* v. *M.D. Juvekar.*[56] The Supreme Court, with this observations regarding maintainability of the writ petition, sent the case back to the Gujarat High Court for giving the decision on merits.

55. (1998) 8 SCC 719.
56. (1988)1 G.L.H. 232.

7. Project and Equipment Corporation of India

A.L. Kalra v. Project and Equipment Corporation of India[57]

In the year 1984, despite the well settled law regarding the inclusion of any body/authority as instrumentality or agency of the state under Article 12 of the Constitution, the case of *A.L. Kalra* v. *Project and Equipment Corporation of India* traveled before the Supreme Court as the Division Bench of the Delhi High Court summarily rejected a writ petition challenging dismissal order filed by the appellant on the ground that Project and Equipment Corporation was not an instrumentality of the State as defined in Article 12 of the Constitution and hence writ petition against it was not maintainable. The aggrieved employee-appellant challenged the order of the Delhi High Court before the Supreme Court by way of filing Special Leave to Appeal.

A bench consisted of Justice D.A. Desai, Justice O. Chinnapa Reddy and Justice A. Varadarajan had an occasion to decide this matter. While delivering judgment for himself and for other two judges, Justice D.A. Desai went into the history and constitution of the respondent Project and Equipment of India Ltd. and found out as follows:

(1) That the Respondents, the Project and Equipment Corporation of India Ltd., since its formation in the year 1971 a wholly owned subsidiary company of State Trading Corporation (STC), a Government of India Undertaking up to 1976 when it was separated and since then it functions as a Government of India undertaking.

(2) The appellant joined as Upper Division Clerk in the STC in the year 1963. In the year 1969 he was promoted as Assistant and earned a further promotion in the year 1974 as Accountant. On setting up of the Corporation, the appellant exercising his option came to be transferred as Accountant to the Project and Equipment Corporation of India Ltd. in the year 1976.

(3) A departmental inquiry was initiated against the appellant regarding an alleged misconduct and he was after the report of the Enquiry officer dismissed from the service. Against the order of the disciplinary authority, the appellant filed a departmental appeal. The same was rejected.

(4) The appellant challenged the orders passed by the disciplinary authority and appellate authority by way of filing writ petition before the division bench of the Delhi High Court.

(5) The Delhi High Court, without entering into the merits of the case, dismissed the writ petition in limine by observing that the respondent company was not an instrumentality of the state under Article 12 of the Constitution.

57. AIR 1984 SC 1361.

Initially, Justice D.A. Desai has painfully said that it was unfortunate that the matter came up before the Supreme Court for the settlement of such trivial and undisputed issue as to whether Project and Equipment Corporation of India Ltd. was an instrumentality of the state under Article 12 or not. He observed in the first paragraph itself,

> *'Failure to adjust the antenna to the operative channel and dipping the head like the proverbial ostrich in the sand so as not to view the changing kaleidoscope of the law can alone be said to be responsible for this trivial matter to be brought to this court.'*

But the respondent did not take the contention before the Supreme Court that the Project and Equipment Corporation of India Ltd. was not instrumentality of the State under Article 12. On the contrary, in para. 2(vi) of the counter-affidavit filed by the officer on behalf of the respondents it was unambiguously stated that 'respondent Corporation is advised not to dispute the maintainability of the petitioner's petition as regards applicability of Article 12 of the Constitution. Further in Para. 5.1 of the same affidavit it was stated that as regards the assertion of the appellant that the respondent-Corporation is an instrumentality of the Central Government and hence within Article 12 of the Constitution, the respondent-Corporation does not dispute the same. The same statement was reiterated in another affidavit filed on behalf of the respondent.

This concession absolved the Supreme Court from the obligation to examine the status and character of the respondent, Corporation to determine whether it is an instrumentality of the State and therefore comprehended in the expression "other authorities" in Article 12 of the Constitution. Hence, it became clear and undisputed that the writ petition under Article 32 and Article 226 of the Constitution against the respondent-Corporation is maintainable.

The Supreme Court also observed here that apart from the concession given by the respondent—Corporation regarding maintainability of the writ petition, the tests collated in the decision of the Constitutional Bench of the Supreme Court in *Ajay Hasia* v. *Khalid Mujib* (AIR 1981 SC 487) for determining whether a particular body is an instrumentality of the State are fully satisfied and therefore on precedent and concession it is satisfactorily established that the respondent—Project and Equipment Corporation of India Ltd. is an instrumentality of the State within the meaning of the expression "other authority" under Article 12 of the Constitution and is amenable to the writ jurisdiction.

8. Indian Oil Corporation

Mahabir Auto Stores v. Indian Oil Corporation[58]

In the above mentioned case the Supreme Court followed the

58. AIR 1990 SC 1031.

guidelines and ratio laid down in the cases decided earlier. It had no hesitation to declare Indian Oil Corporation, a government company to declare as "State" under Article 12 of the Constitution of India. It took into consideration the cases of *Ajay Hasia* v. *Khalid Mujib* and *Som Prakash* v. *Union of India* and heavy reliance was put on both of these cases.

9. United India Insurance Company Ltd.
Biman Krishna Bose v. United India Insurance Company Ltd.[59]

In the case of *Biman Krishna Bose* v. *United India Insurance Company Ltd.*, point for consideration before the Supreme Court was whether the above mentioned insurance company was covered under the ambit of "Other authorities" as defined in Article 12 of the Constitution or not. In this case as a matter of fact, arbitrariness on the part of the company was challenged and it was argued that the company, being the "State" under Article 12 must act fairly.

It was held by the Supreme Court,

> *"A perusal of the provisions of the General Insurance Business (Nationalisation) Act, 1972 makes it evident that it is only the acquiring companies which have exclusive privilege of carrying on the general insurance business in India, under the supervision and control of General Insurance Corporation of India. Excepting the acquiring companies, no other company in the private sector has a right and privilege to carry on general insurance business in India and to that extent the acquiring companies have a monopoly over such business...."*

The Supreme Court criticized the arbitrary action of the insurance company and observed that it ought to have acted fairly by making following observations in para. 3 of the judgment:

> *"Thus, even in an area of contractual relations, the State and its instrumentalities are enjoined with the obligation to act with fairness and in doing so can take into consideration only the relevant materials. They must not take any irrelevant and extraneous consideration while arriving at a decision. Arbitrariness should not appear in their actions or decisions...."*

In addition to the observations made herein above the Supreme Court also added that the Government Company having monopoly business with right and privilege to carry on such business to the exclusion of others. Hence it would have acquired the trapping of the "State". In the same paragraph 3 of the judgment, following was the important observation of the Supreme Court:

---

59. (2001) 6 SCC 477.

"Under Sec. 24 of the General Insurance Business (Nationalisation) Act, 1972 the acquiring companies were given the exclusive privilege to carry on general insurance business in India. Under Sec. 3(a) of the Act, an acquiring company has been defined to mean any Indian insurance company in which any other company has been merged in pursuance of the amalgamation scheme formulated under the Act. The respondent Insurance Company is one of such acquiring companies. A perusal of the provisions of the Act makes it evident that it is only the acquiring companies, which have exclusive privilege of carrying on the general insurance business in India, under the supervision and control of General Insurance Corporation of India. Excepting the acquiring companies, no other company in the private sector has a right and privilege to carry on general insurance business in India and to that extent the acquiring companies have a monopoly over such business. In such a situation, acquiring companies have the trappings of "the State" being other authorities under Article 12 of the Constitution of India and are expected to act fairly and reasonably."

In the above case, it appears that the Supreme Court had no confusion while declaring the United India Insurance Company Ltd., as "the State" under Article 12 of the Constitution because it had a monopoly business and looking to the guidelines given in the case of *Ajay Hasia* v. *Khalid Mujib*, this was a fit case for declaring the company as instrumentality or agency of the State.

10. Mysore Paper Mills Ltd.

Mysore Paper Mills Ltd. v. Mysore Paper Mills Officers' Association[60]

A question for consideration before the Supreme Court, in the case of *Mysore Paper Mills Ltd.* v. *Mysore Paper Mills Officers' Association* was whether a government company, i.e. Mysore Paper Mills Ltd. could be considered as instrumentality or agency so as to fall within the ambit of Article 12 of the Constitution of India or not. The case came up before the Supreme Court by way of appeal against the judgment of a Full Bench of the High Court of Karnataka. The petitioner by way of filing writ petition in fact challenged transfer order. An appeal was filed against the interim stay order granted by the learned single Judge of the High Court. The following two points were raised before the Division Bench: (1) The writ petitions filed were not maintainable against the appellant-company, since it is not a "State" or other authority within the meaning of Article 12 of the Constitution of India, and (2) the order of transfer was not required to be stayed as there were no allegations of *mala fide*.

The division bench of Karnataka High Court while answering the question as to whether an appellant-company was "State" under Article 12 of the Constitution of India or not, made following conclusions:

60. AIR 2002 SC 609.

(a) That the appellant-company is a governmental company as per Sec. 617 of the Companies, Act, 1956.

(b) The declared objects of the company viz. 1, 1A, 3, 4, 4A, 5, 5A and 5B establish that the company has been entrusted with an important function of public interest closely related to governmental functions and it enjoys a monopoly status, which is state conferred.

(c) The functions entrusted to the appellant-company go to show that the Government operates behind a corporate veil carrying out governmental functions of vital importance and, therefore, there is no difficulty in identifying the appellant-company to be "State" within the meaning of Article 12 of the Constitution of India.

(d) The summarized balance sheets for the year 1993-94, 1994-95 and 1995-96 disclosed that the State of Karnataka and the financial institutions controlled and belonging to Government of India have contributed more than 97% of the share capital.

(e) The business of the company which has to be managed by the Board of Directors (Art. 114 of the Articles of Association) shall have the Chairman of the Board and Managing Director (Art. 119) and four Directors of whom one will be the Chairman will be nominated by the Government of Karnataka who shall not retire by rotation or be removed from office except under the orders of the Government of Karnataka (Art. 94). The Directors to whom the management is entrusted shall not be more than 12 or less than 9, inclusive of the Government nominees and nominees of the Financial Institutions noticed under Art. 94-A and not only such nominees of Financial Institutions hold office so long as moneys remain owed to those institutions or those institutions hold debentures in the company as a result of direct subscription or private placement, but the Board also has no power to remove them during such period.

(f) The appellant-company is found to be under the control of the Government of Karnataka—sometimes directly and sometimes through the machinery of Karnataka State Bureau of Public Enterprises in respect of matters entrusted to it; as disclosed from the book published by the Department of Personnel and Administration Reforms of the Government of Karnataka.

(g) Apart from the Directors who are nominees of the Government and the Financial Institutions controlled by the Central Government even the elected Directors were also to be nominated by the Government of Karnataka and one cannot become a Director of the appellant-company without the concurrence or nomination by the Government.

(h) Appointment of several officers, playing vital role in the day-to-day administration of the company can be done only with the prior permission or approval of the Government of Karnataka. The General Manager also may be appointed on such terms and remunerations as may be fixed, only subject to the approval of the Government of Karnataka.

(i) For any investment or expenditure above 25 lakhs the approval of Government of Karnataka is required. Any revision of pay scales and allowances of employees and officers also have to be done only with the approval of the KSBPE. Recruitments to posts carrying pay scales above Rs. 4700/- can only be with the permission of the Government and reservation policies under Art. 16(4) of the Constitution are also applicable to recruitments by the company. Deputation to Government and *vice-versa* is also permitted. All foreign tours of officers have to be approved by the Government.

(j) All loans taken by the appellant-company are guaranteed by the Government of Karnataka.

(k) The Company Secretary of the appellant- company has in his communication Annexure "G" declared that the same is an undertaking under the control of the Government of Karnataka.

By making above observations the Full Bench of Karnataka High Court inevitably came to the conclusion that the appellant-company is run as part or an enterprise of the State Government and that everyone of the scheme of the company are also to be approved by the Government. Total financial control of the company by the Government has also been found. Therefore, the company is an authority and instrumentality or agency of the State, so as to attract Article 12 of the Constitution of India.

The Supreme Court referred to the guidelines given in the cases of *Ajay Hasia* v. *Khalid Mujib* as well as the case of International Airport Authority and summarized numerous cases on the issue of "other authorities" under Article 12 of the Constitution and also demonstrated as to how the appellant company falls within the definition of "State" under Article 12. It has been observed in para. 11 of the judgment by **Justice Raju**,

> *'11. A careful consideration of the principles of law noticed supra and the factual details not only found illustrated from the memorandum as well as Articles of Association of the appellant but enumerated from the day-to-day running of the business and administration of the company leave no room for any doubt as to the identity of the appellant-company being "other authority" and consequently "the State" within the meaning of Art. 12 of the Constitution of India. The said definition has a specific purpose and that is Part III of the Constitution and not for making it a Government or department of the Government itself. This is the inevitable consequence of the "other authorities" being entities with independent status distinct from the State and this fact alone does not militate against such entities or institutions being agencies or instrumentalities to come under the net of Art.*

> *12 of the Constitution. The concept of instrumentality or agency of the Government is not to be confined to entities created under or which owes its origin to any particular status or order but would really depend upon a combination of one or more of relevant factors, depending upon the essentiality and overwhelming nature of such factors in identifying the real source of governing power, if need be, by piercing the corporate veil of the entity concerned.'*

The main point of consideration in this judgment is the observation of the Supreme Court that the concept of instrumentality or agency of the Government is not to be confined to entities created under or which owes its origin to any particular statute or order but would really depend upon a combination of one or more of relevant factors, depending upon the essentiality and overwhelming nature of such factors in identifying the real source of governing power, if need be, by piercing the corporate veil of the entity concerned. Moreover, the Supreme Court accepted the reasoning given by the Full Bench of Karnataka High Court and held that the appellant-company is nothing but instrumentality and agency of the State Government and therefore, is "State" within the meaning or Article 12 of the Constitution of India.

11. Export Credit Guarantee Corporation of India Ltd.

ABL International Ltd. v. Export Credit Guarantee Corporation of India Ltd.[61]

The question arose in an appeal filed before the Supreme Court in the above case was whether a writ petition under Article 226 of the Constitution of India was maintainable to enforce a contractual obligation of the State or its instrumentality, by an aggrieved party or not. At the same time another question was regarding the status of the respondent as to whether the respondent was an instrumentality of "State" under Article 12 of the Constitution of India or not. The matter was pertaining to the contract of insurance. The single judge of the High Court allowed the writ petition. But in an appeal the division bench of the High Court reversed the judgment of the learned single Judge and refused to interfere on the ground that there were so many disputed questions of facts. Being aggrieved by the judgment of the Division Bench, the appellants preferred appeal before the Supreme Court. The first hurdle was regarding the maintainability of the writ petition.

The Supreme Court observed that the Export Credit Guarantee Corporation of India was a company registered under the Companies Act and was wholly owned by the Government of India. The total subscribed share capital of this company was 2,50,000 shares out of which 2,49,998 shares are held by the President of India while one share each is held by the President of India while one share each was held by the Joint Secretary,

61. (2004) 3 SCC 553.

Ministry of Commerce and Industry and Officer on Special duty, Ministry of Commerce and Industry respectively. The objects enumerated in the Memorandum of Association of the first respondent, company at paragraph 10 said,

> *'To undertake such functions as may be entrusted to it by the Government from time to time, including grant of credits and guarantees in foreign currency for the purpose of facilitating the import of raw materials and semi-finished goods for export.'*

The contents of Para. 11 gave specific and clear picture by saying,

> *'To act as agent of the Government, or with the sanction of the Government on its own account, to give the guarantees, undertake such responsibilities and discharge such functions as are considered by the Government as necessary in national interest.'*

The Supreme Court, with the observation of the above clauses came to the conclusion that the Company was wholly a Government-owned company, it discharges the functions of the Government and acts as an agent of the Government even when it gave guarantees and it had a responsibility to discharge such functions in the national interest. In the background it would be futile to contend that the actions of the first respondent impugned in the writ petition did not have a touch of public function or discharge of public duty.

The Supreme Court gave the following three legal principles in paragraph 27 of its judgment:

- In an appropriate case, a writ petition as against a State or an instrumentality of a State arising out of a contractual obligation is maintainable.
- Merely because some disputed questions of fact arise for consideration, same cannot be a ground to refuse to entertain a writ petition in all cases as a matter of rule.
- A writ petition involving a consequential relief of monetary claim is also maintainable.

In support of its view, the Supreme Court took support of the ratio laid down in the cases of *Gujarat State Financial Corporation* v. *Lotus Hotel* and also of the case of *R.D. Shetty* v. *International Airport Authority*. It clarified that the instrumentality of the State which would be "other authority" under Article 12 could not commit breach of a solemn undertaking or promise and put itself in a disadvantageous position. The Supreme Court also held that on a given set of facts if "the State" acts in an arbitrary manner even in a matter of contract, an aggrieved party can approach the court by way of writ under Article 226 of the Constitution and the Court depending on facts of the case was empowered to grant the relief. The Supreme Court clarified the position of maintainability in affirmative by saying,

> *'when an instrumentality of the State acts contrary to public good and public interest, unfairly, unjustly and unreasonably, in its contractual, constitutional or statutory obligations, it really acts contrary to the constitutional guarantee found in Article 14 of the Constitution. Therefore, once the State or an instrumentality of the State is a party, it has an obligation in law to act fairly, justly and reasonably to a contract which is the requirement of Article 14 of the Constitution.'*

The Supreme Court also put reliance on the judgment of *Anadi Mukta Sadguru S.M.V.S.J.M.S. Trust* v. *V.R. Rudani case* by saying that the writ petition under Article 226 of the Constitution of India could be invoked when the authority or the person either performs public function or discharges public duty. The appeal was ultimately allowed with costs justifying the decision of the learned single Judge of the High Court.

4.4 *MANDAMUS* AGAINST SOCIETIES REGISTERED UNDER THE SOCIETIES REGISTRATION ACT AND CONTROLLED BY STATE

1. Regional Engineering College, Srinagar, a society registered under the J. & K. Societies Registration Act, 1898

Ajay Hasia v. Khalid Mujib[62]

In the year 1981, five judges' Constitutional Bench had an opportunity to examine as to whether a regional Engineering College, Srinagar, run by a society registered under the Jammu and Kashmir Registration of Societies Act, 1898 was covered within the definition of "State" under Article 12 of the Constitution of India or not.

In the above mentioned case the procedure of giving admission to the students in Engineering College by *viva-voce* test was challenged. The respondent college alongwith other defences took a preliminary objection that the college was run by a registered society under J. & K. Registration of Societies Act, 1898 and hence it was not covered under the definition of "State" under Article 12 of the Constitution. Therefore, writ petition seeking relief in the nature of *mandamus* and/or *certiorari* was not maintainable. Thus, the Supreme Court had an occasion to examine as to whether a writ was maintainable against a registered society was maintainable or not.

Again, **Justice Bhagwati** took a task to ascertain the issue before the Supreme Court. He examined the various clauses of the Memorandum of Association of the Society and came to the conclusion that there was deep and pervasive control of the Central as well as State Government over the

62. AIR 1981 SC 487.

management and function of the society. The Government looked after the procedure of appointment, terms of service and termination procedure of the employees of the society. As observed in the case of *Sukhdev* v. *Bhagatram*, a corporation may be created in one of two ways. It may be either established by statute or incorporated under law such as the Companies Act, 1956 or the Societies Registration Act (as in this case). While giving reasons for considering a registered society under the ambit of "State" Justice Bhagwati also discussed regarding the status of Corporations, Government Companies, etc. and firmly observed in paragraph 7 of the Judgment as under:

> *'.........It is undoubtedly true that the corporation is a distinct juristic entity and it carries on its functions on business principles with a certain amount of autonomy which is necessary as well as useful from the point of view of effective business management, but behind the formal ownership which is cast in the corporate mould, the reality is very much the deeply pervasive pressure of the Government. It is really the Government which acts through the instrumentality or agency of the corporation and the juristic veil of corporate personality worn for the purpose of convenience of management and administration cannot be allowed to obliterate the true nature of the reality behind which is the Government. Now it is obvious that if a corporation is an instrumentality or agency of the Government, it must be subject to the same limitations in the field of constitutional law as the Government itself, though in the eye of law it would be a distinct and independent legal entity. If the Government acting through its officers is subject to certain constitutional limitations, it must follow a fortiori that the Government acting through the instrumentality or agency of a corporation should equally be subject to the same limitations. If such a corporation were to be free from the basic obligation to obey the Fundamental Rights, for in that event the Government would be enabled to override the Fundamental Rights by adopting the stratagem of carrying out its functions through the instrumentality or agency of a corporation, while retaining control over it. The Fundamental Rights would then be reduced to little more than an idle dream or a promise of unreality. It must be remembered that the Fundamental Rights are constitutional guarantees given to the people of India and are not merely paper hopes or fleeting promises and so long as they find a place in the Constitution, they should not be allowed to be emasculated in their application by a narrow and constricted judicial interpretation. The courts should be anxious to enlarge the scope and width of the Fundamental Rights by bringing within their sweep every authority which is an instrumentality or agency of the Government or through the corporate personality of which the Government is acting, so as to subject the Government in all its myriad activities, whether through natural persons or through corporate entities, to the basic obligation of the Fundamental Rights. The Constitutional philosophy of a democratic socialist republic requires the Government to undertake a multitude of socio-economic*

operations and the Government, having regard to the practical advantages of functioning through the legal device of a corporation embarks on myriad commercial and economic activities by resorting to the instrumentality or agency of a corporation, but this contrivance of carrying on such activities through a corporation cannot exonerate the Government from implicit obedience to the Fundamental Rights. To use the corporate methodology is not to liberate the Government from its basic obligation to respect the Fundamental Rights and not to override them. The mantle of a corporation may be adopted in order to free the Government from the inevitable constraints of red-tapism and slow motion but by doing so the Government cannot be allowed to play truant with the basic human rights. Otherwise it would be the easiest things for the government to assign to a plurality of corporations almost every State business such as Post and Telegraph, TV and Radio, Rail Road and Telephone—In short, every economic activity—and thereby cheat the people of India out of the Fundamental Rights guaranteed to them. That would be a mockery of the Constitution and nothing short of treachery and breach of faith with the people of India, because, though apparently the corporation will be carrying out these functions, it will in truth the reality be the Government which will be controlling the corporation and carrying out these functions through the instrumentality or agency of the corporation. We cannot by a process of judicial construction allow the Fundamental Rights to be rendered futile and meaningless and thereby wipe out Chapter III from the Constitution. That would be contrary to the constitutional faith of the post-Maneka Gandhi era. It is the Fundamental Rights which along with the Directive Principles constitute the life force of the Constitution and they must be quickened into effective action by meaningful and purposive interpretation. If a corporation is found to be a mere agency or surrogate of the Government, "in fact owned by the Government, in truth controlled by the Government and in effect an incarnation of the Government," the court must not allow the enforcement of Fundamental Rights to be frustrated by taking the view that it is not the government and therefore not subject to the constitutional limitations. We are clearly of the view that where a corporation is an instrumentality or agency of the government, it must be held to be an 'authority' within the meaning of Article 12 and hence subject to the same basic obligation to obey the Fundamental Rights as the government.'[63]

Moreover, in this case Supreme Court gave a guideline to ascertain as to whether any institution is "State" or not.

These guidelines or tests gathered from this decision are summarized herein:

---

63. AIR 1981 SC 487, p. 493.

Guidelines

1. **If the entire share capital of the corporation is held by the government, it would go a long way towards indicating that the corporation is an instrumentality or authority of the government.**
2. **Where the financial assistance of the State is so much as to meet almost entire expenditure of the corporation it would afford some indication of the corporation being impregnated with government character.**
3. **Whether the corporation enjoys monopoly status which is State conferred or State protected.**
4. **Existence of deep and pervasive State control may afford an indication that the corporation is a State agency or instrumentality.**
5. **If the function of the corporation are of public importance and closely related to government functions, it would be a relevant factor in classifying a corporation as an instrumentality or agency of government.**
6. **If a department of government is transferred to corporation, it would be a strong factor supporting this inference of the corporation being an instrumentality or agency of government.**

This judgment can be considered as a model judgment for the purpose of ascertaining as to whether any entity is instrumentality or agency of the government or not. Every case wherein a dispute arose regarding the issue of party involved there is instrumentality or agency or it falls within the definition of "State" under Article 12 or not, its constitution, functions, rules, regulations, powers assigned to it, scope of financial assistance, governmental control, etc. are minutely observed and thereafter they are compared with the guidelines given in Ajay Hasia's case by the Supreme Court. Thus, after the above six guidelines it has become very easy for the Supreme Court to ascertain as to whether any entity is "State" under Article 12 or not.

2. Indian Statistical Institute

B.S. Minhas v. Indian Statistical Institute[64]

In the case of *B.S. Minhas* v. *Indian Statistical Institute*, the petitioner filed writ petition under Article 32 of the Constitution of India in order to challenge the appointment of respondent No. 4, as the director of the Indian Statistical Institute. The respondent Institute regarding maintainability of writ petition against it took a preliminary objection. According to the respondent, Indian Statistical Institute is not covered within the meaning of "other authorities" under Article 12 of the Constitution of India.

64. (1983)4 SCC 588.

While deciding the issue, Division Bench of Justice Bhagwati and Justice R.B. Mishra put total reliance of the guidelines given by the Supreme Court in the case of Ajay Hasia.

The Supreme Court observed that the Indian Statistical Institute is a society registered under the Societies Registration Act. The Indian Statistical Institute Act, 1959, governs it. Following points were observed by the Supreme Court:

1. The control of the Institute completely vests in the Union of India.
2. It is wholly financed by the Union of India.
3. All the functions of the Institute are controlled by the Union of India. The apex court took into consideration provisions of various sections of the Indian Statistical Institute Act, 1959. As per Section 8 of the Act committees appointed by the Central Government settle the annual work programmes of the Institute and general financial estimates in respect of such work. No research or training programmes without approval of the Central Government. Thus, the provisions of the act by which the Institute came into existence shows deep and pervasive control of the Central Government over it.
4. The Institute has been declared as an "Institution of National Importance" under the Act. Apart from conducting training and research programmes the Institute is empowered under Sec. 4 of the act to grant degrees and diplomas in statistic. Hence, it can be understood that the duties discharged by the institute is of public nature and of general importance.
5. As per the provisions of section 5 of the Act, the Central Government pays to the Institute the sum of money by way of grant, loan or otherwise in each financial year. The Institute entirely depends upon the financial assistance of the Central Government.
6. Audit of the accounts of the Institute is done by the qualified auditors and the Central Government selects auditors after consultation with the Comptroller and Auditor-General of India.
7. The Institute is restricted by Sec. 7 of the Act to alter, extend or abridge its memorandum or rules or regulations and to sell or otherwise dispose of its property except previous approval of the Central Government.
8. The Central Government has power to constitute a committee for reviewing and evaluating the work done by the Institute and the progress made by it.
9. The provision of Section 11 empowers the Central Government to issue directions to the Institute. Further, Section 12 of the Act authorizes the Central Government to assume control over the Institute under certain circumstances.

Arguments on behalf of the Institute regarding maintainability of the petition:

Advocate appearing for the respondent Institutes opposed the petition on three grounds viz.:

(i) That the petition is not maintainable under Article 32 of the Constitution as respondents Nos. 1 and 2 are not "state" or "other authority", within the meaning of Article 12 of the Constitution.

(ii) (a) Even assuming, though not conceding, that there has been a violation of bye-law 2 (i.e. procedure for appointment of a Director), no writ can lie to correct the same as the alleged bye-law has no statutory basis inasmuch as by the Indian Statistical Institute Act, 1959 Parliament only declared the Indian Statistical Institute, as an institution of natural importance and if it has made bye-law 2 for its guidance, such bye-law cannot be said to have any statutory force.

(b) The bye-laws not being statutory the respondents are under no obligation to observe the procedure laid down in the bye-laws.

(iii) In any case the petitioner was duly and properly considered for selection to the post of Director and, therefore, he could not possibly make any grievance about violation of bye-law 2.

The advocate appearing on behalf of the petitioner contended that it is quite evident from the provisions of the Indian Statistical Institute Act, 1959 that the Central Government has deep and pervasive control over the Institute and, therefore, to all intents and purposes, it is an instrumentality of the Central Government and as such is an "authority" within the meaning of Article 12 of the Constitution. It is, therefore, subject to the constitutional obligations under Articles 14 and 16 of the Constitution. The learned council also relied upon the view taken by the Supreme Court in the case of Ajay Hasia and argued that as per the observations made therein, the expression "other authorities" must be given a broad and liberal interpretation, where constitutional fundamentals vital to the maintenance of human rights are at stake and functional realism and not facial cosmetics must be the diagnostic tool, for constitutional law must seek the substance and not the form. In the above judgment, the apex court pointed out that the Government may act through the instrumentality or agency of judicial persons to carry out its functions, since, with the advent of the welfare State, its new tasks have increased manifold and such juridical persons acting as instrumentality or agency of the Government must therefore be subject to the same discipline of fundamental rights as the State.

The advocate for the petitioner also argued that the bye-law had a statutory force and assuming for a while, the bye-law was not statutory, even then the respondent No. 1 was bound to comply with it. For that he relied upon the ratio laid down in the case of *R.D. Shetty* v. *International Airport Authority case.*

The learned council for the petitioner also quoted the rule enunciated by **Justice Frankfurter** in **Vitarelli v. Seaton**[65], where the learned judge said:

> *'An executive agency must be rigorously held to the standards by which it professes its action to be judged. ...... Accordingly, if dismissal from employment is based on a defined procedure, even though generous beyond the requirements that bind such agency, that procedure must be scrupulously observed.... This judicially evolved rule of administrative law is now firmly established and, if I may add, rightly so.* ***He that takes the procedural sword shall perish with the sword.'***

The Supreme Court in this case was fully convinced that the Indian Statistical Institute is an "authority" within the meaning of Article 12 of the Constitution and hence, the writ petition filed by the petitioner was maintainable.

It is submitted here that the task of the Supreme Court has become easier after the guidelines of Ajay Hasia's case. Moreover, in this case, Division Bench consisted of Justice Bhagwati, who dictated the landmark judgment of Ajay Hasia's case. The exercise which the apex court has done in this case for deciding the issue as to whether respondent No. 2 is "State" or not is just to concentrate upon the Act by which the Institute came into existence. The Supreme Court thereafter compared the provisions of the act alongwith the guidelines of Ajay Hasia's case and decided the issue.

The Supreme Court has decided the issue regarding the enforceability of bye-laws in the case of International Airport Authority case as well as *Sukhdev* v. *Bhagatram.*

3. Sainik School Society

All India Sainik School Employees' Association v. Defence Minister–*cum*-Chairman, Board of Governors' Sainik School Society[66]

A Sainik School Society was a "State" under Article 12 of the Constitution of India or not. This was a question for consideration in a writ petition filed under Article 32 of the Constitution of India by the All India Sainik School Employees Association through its President in the case of *A.I.S.S.E. Association* v. *Defence Minister-cum-Chairman, B.O.G., S.S. Society.*

It is pertinent to note that the Sainik School Society is a society registered under the Societies Registration Act, 1860. As per the memorandum of association of the society, the main object of it was to establish Sainik Schools in various parts of India providing special school education of a high standard with the aim of preparing boys academically

65. (359 US 535).
66. A.I.R. 1988 SC 88.

and physically for entry into National Defence Academy and other walks of life. Eighteen schools were established for that purpose in different States of the country. In the above mentioned writ petition, the petitioner asked for a writ of *mandamus* to the respondent No. 1 herein and Union of India following reliefs:

1. to implement the recommendations of the Fourth Pay Commission in the Sainik Schools and to extend all the benefits already given to employees of the Kendriya Vidyalayas by way of implementing the recommendations of the Chattopadhya Commission;
2. to give to the employees of the Sainik School Society the differential wages in terms of the Third Pay Commission between 1973 and 1978;
3. to direct that the employees of the Sainik Schools shall have the benefits of leave travel concession, house rent, pension, group insurance, contributory provident fund, pensionery benefits and gratuity in the same pattern as obtaining in Kendriya Vidyalaya Sangathan or given to Defence Service Officers working in the Sainik Schools; and
4. enhance the age of superannuation to 60 years in the case of Kendriya Vidyalaya employees.

In reply to the notice issued by the Supreme Court to the respondents a preliminary objection was raised regarding maintainability of the writ petition as the Society was not an instrumentality of the State. On the other hand it was the contention of the petitioner that the Sainik School Society was "State" within the meaning of Article 12 of the Constitution of India and is accordingly amenable to claim and enforcement of fundamental rights. The following important points were taken upon inquiry made to the respondent No. 1:

(a) The entire capital expenditure on land, building, furniture and educational equipment and the major portion of the recurring expenditure is borne by the concerned State Government/Union Territory Administration of the places where the School is located.
(b) Maintenance, additions and replacements are also the obligation of the respective State Governments.
(c) The Principal, the Head-Master, the Registrar and an Army Physical Training Corp/National Cadet Corp Instructor posted in every School are paid out of the Defence Budget.
(d) All other expenses are met out of the fees payable by the parents or taken out of the scholarships paid by the State/Central Government to the students.

(e) The quantum of the fees/scholarships is fixed by the Board of Governors from time to time taking into consideration the financial position.

During pendency of the writ petition Board of Governors decided to extend certain advantages and benefits to the employees of the Sainik School employees.

In order to consider the question as to whether Sainik School Society is "State" or note, the tests given by the Supreme Court in the case of *Ajay Hasia* v. *Khalid Mujib and International Airport Authority case* were applied. The Supreme Court observed after application of such tests to the present case that the Sainik School Society was undoubtedly "State" under Article 12 of the Constitution and was amenable to the writ jurisdiction. In the case of *Ajay Hasia* v. *Khalid Mujib* (discussed above) a question involved was on the same line that a private engineering college run by a society registered under the Societies Registration Act was "State" or not. The apex court observed that it can not be doubted that the Sainik School Society is also "State". The entire funding is by the State Government and the Central Government/ The overall control vests in the governmental authority. The main object of the Society is to run schools and prepare students for the purpose of feeding the National Defence Academy. Defence of the country is one of the regal functions of the State.

On the facts it was held that being "State" under Article 12, the Sainik School is bound to act reasonably and provisions of Article 14 can be applied. At the same time Supreme Court also clarified that there was no discrimination to the employees of Sainik Schools as the treatment given to the employees thereof can not be compared with that of employees of Kendra Vidyalaya School. Further it expressed that the violation of constitutional rights, other than fundamental rights is no ground for entertaining writ petition under Article 32 of the Constitution. The Supreme Court quoted a following passage from paragraph 12 of Ajay Hasia's case:

> *'It is also necessary to add that merely because a juristic entity may be an authority and therefore State within the meaning of Article 12, it may not be elevated to the position of State for the purpose of Articles 309, 310 and 311 which find a place in Part XIV. The definition of State in Article 12 which includes an authority within the territory of India or under control of the Government of India is limited in its application only to Part III and by virtue of Article 36, to Part IV: it does not extend to the other provisions of the Constitution and hence a juristic entity which may be State for the purpose of Parts III and IV would not be so for the purpose of Part XIV or any other provisions of the Constitution.'*[67]

67. Ajay Hasia *v.* Khalid Mujib AIR 1981 SC 481, p. 497.

By making the above observation as the basis the Supreme Court gave certain directions to the respondents. At the same time it has laid down a ratio that the Sainik School Society falls within the definition of "State" under Article 12 of the Constitution.

4. Indian Council for Agricultural Research (I.C.A.R.)

P.K. Ramchandran Iyer v. Union of India[68]

In the case of *P.K. Ramchandran Iyer* v. *Union of India*, a writ petition under Article 32 was preferred before the Supreme Court relating to the revision of pay scales of the posts of professors working in Indian Council of Agricultural Research (ICAR) and Indian Veterinary Research Institute (IVRI). The preliminary contention raised by the advocate appearing on behalf of the respondent ICAR is a society registered under the Societies Registration Act and hence neither ICAR nor its affiliates IVRI was covered within the definition of "State" under Article 12 of the Constitution and hence writ petition under Article 32 was not maintainable. Thus, the prime question for consideration before the Supreme Court Bench consisted by Justice D.A. Desai and Justice V. Balakrishna Eradi was whether ICAR and IVRI were "State" under Article 12 or not.

Justice D.A. Desai, went into the brief history of the initial set-up and development into the present position of ICAR and came to the conclusion that it was a society registered under the Societies Registration Act but substantially when set-up it was an adjunct of the Government of India and it had not undergone noteworthy change. On the advent of the provincial autonomy under the Government of India Act, 1919, "agriculture" and "animal husbandry" came under the heading "transferred subject" with the result came within the exclusive jurisdiction of the Provincial Government. In the year 1926 the Royal Commission on Agriculture, in its report recommended the setting-up of Imperial Council of Agricultural Research. Acting upon the recommendation, the Government of India initiated the process to set-up a council. By its Resolution dated May 23, 1929, the Central Government directed that Imperial Council of Agricultural Research should be registered as a Society under the Registration of Societies Act, XXI of 1860. The Resolution further provided that with respect to the grant to be made to the Council to meet the cost of staff, establishment, etc., the Government of India decided that for reasons of administrative convenience it should be in the same position as a department of the Government of India Secretariat. Thus, the Imperial Council of Agricultural Research was set-up in June 1929. In July 1929, ICAR was registered as a society with its office in the Secretariat as an attached office of the Secretariat. By the Resolution dated August 4, 1930, Government of India directed that for the reasons of administrative convenience "the Governor-General in Council has now decided that the Imperial Council of Agricultural Research Department, as the Secretariat of the Council will henceforth be designated,

68. AIR 1984 SC 541.

should be a regular department of the Government of India Secretariat under the Honourable Member in charge of the Department of Education, Health and Lands." A proposal to the then Viceroy was made on 29th December 1937 stating therein that the position of the ICAR as a Department of the Government in which it was recommended that ICAR should not only be maintained as a distinct entity independent of the Government of India and with a view to achieving this position, the office of the ICAR should not in future be a Department of the Government of India but it should be an attached office. On January 14, 1938, the proposal was approved by the Viceroy. On 5th January, 1939 the status of the ICAR was modified by the Resolution of the Government of India to one of an attached office of the Government of India.

On the advert of independence the Imperial Council of Agricultural Research was redesignated as Indian Council of Agricultural Research. With effect from 1st April, 1966, administrative control over IARI and IVRI and other institutes was transferred to ICAR simultaneously placing the Government staff of the institutes at the disposal of ICAR as on foreign service. The Government of India enforced the new rules framed by the ICAR effective from January 10, 1966 keeping Rule 18 in abeyance. With the change in the status of the ICAR, Department of Agricultural Research and Education was set-up in the Ministry of Agriculture and it came into existence on 15-12-1973. The said Department was established to have link between the ICAR and the Government. The Rule 18 of the ICAR rules which was kept in abeyance on 10th January, 1966 was brought into operation in its entirely effective from April 1, 1974. The consequence of Rule 18 becoming operative was that the Secretariat if ICAR ceased to be an attached office of the Ministry of Food and Agriculture and the society shall function as "wholly financed and controlled by the Society". Till Rule 18 was kept in abeyance, recruitment to ICAR was done through the Union Public Service Commission. Rule 18 provides that "the Society shall establish and maintain its own office, Research Institutes and Laboratories. The appointment to the various posts under the Society's establishment was to be made in accordance with the governing body with the approval of the Government of India".

In these circumstances, after having perused the very birth of the society and its continued existence over half a century and its present position the Supreme Court observed that no one in doubt that ICAR was almost an inseparable adjunct of the Government of India having an outward from being a Society, it could be styled as a Society set-up by the State and, therefore, would be an instrumentality of the State.

Further the Supreme Court found out certain characteristics of the ICAR, which clearly indicated that it was an instrumentality of the state. They are:

(1) It was started as a Department of the Government of India, having an office in the Secretariat, even though it was a Society registered under the Societies Registration Act.

(2) It was wholly financed by the Government of India. Its budget was voted upon as part of the expenses incurred in the Ministry of agriculture.

(3) Even when its status underwent a change, it was declared as an attached office of the Government of India.

(4) The control of the Government of India permits through all its activities and it is the body to which the Government of India transferred Research Institutes set-up by it.

(5) In order to make it financially viable, a cess was levied meaning thereby that the taxation power of the State was invoked, and the proceeds of the tax were to be handed over to ICAR for its use.

(6) At no stage, the Government of India ever flinched and since its inception it was set-up to carry out the recommendations of the Royal Commission on Agriculture.

Case of Sabhajit Tewary Distinguished

On behalf of the respondent it was argued that the Council of Scientific and Industrial Research (CSIR), a society registered under the Societies Registration Act and having an identical set-up as well as the constitution was not held to be an instrumentality of the state or "other authority" under Article 12 in the case of Sabhajit Tewary's case[69]. (facts of the case discussed separately.) The Supreme Court, while discussing the status of CSIR referred some cases which have held that the companies incorporated under the Companies Act and the employees of these companies do not enjoy the protection available to Government servants as contemplated in Art. 311. But Justice Desai, in his sarcastic language distinguished the aforesaid judgment from the present case by saying that,

> *'much water has flown down in Jamuna since the dicta in Sabhajit Tewary's case and conceding that it is not specifically overruled in later decision, its ratio is considerably watered down so as to be a decision confined to its own facts. The case is wholly distinguishable on the facts apart from the later indicia formulated by the Court for ascertaining whether a body is "other authority" within the meaning of Article 12. A mere comparison of the history of ICAR as extensively set out hereinbefore and the setting up of CSIR would clearly show that ICAR came into existence as a department of the Government, continued to be an attached office of the Government even though it was registered as a society and wholly financed by the Government and the taxing power of the state was invoked to make it financially viable and to which independent research institutes set-up by the Government were transferred. None of these features was present in the case of CSIR and, therefore, the decision in Sabhajit Tewary's case would render no assistance and would be clearly distinguishable.'*

69. Sabhajit Tewary *v.* Union of India, AIR 1975 SC 1329.

Moreover, Justice Desai relied upon the ratio as well as the guidelines given by the Supreme Court in the decisions of *Sukhdev* v. *Bhagatram, International Airport Authority case, U.P. Warehousing Corporation* v. *Vijay Narayan's case* and at last the case of *Ajay Hasia* v. *Khalid Mujib* and declared ICAR as instrumentality of the state and therefore covered in the expression "other authority" in Article 12.

In the present case the task of the Supreme Court was easy as compared to other cases of societies registered under the Societies Registration Act because of the distinguished facts of the constitution and development of ICAR. It was a society registered under the Societies Registration Act, but it was given a status as the department of the government and therefore it was inseparable from the government. It was fulfiling almost all the guidelines given in the case of *Ajay Hasia* v. *Khalid Mujib* by the Supreme Court.

5. Children's Aid Society, Bombay
Sheela Barse v. Secretary, Children Aid Society[70]

The case was arisen out of appeal by special leave by the appellant, who was a free lance journalist by profession and a member of the Maharashtra State Legal Aid and Advice Committee. By this appeal the appellant sought to challenge the judgment of the Bombay High Court. The Children's Aid Society, Bombay was running remand Homes and Observation Homes for children. It was a society registered under the Societies Registration Act, 1860 and was treated as a public trust. It received grants from the State.

The appellant, earlier made grievances before the Bombay High Court by way of writing a letter about the working of the New Observation Home located at Mankhurd which was maintained and managed by the Children's Aid Society, Bombay. The Bombay High Court treated a letter as a writ petition and called upon the society by notice. The following were the main grievances:

- Delay in repatriation or restoration of children to their parents in respect of whom orders for repatriation were made by the Juvenile Court.
- Non-application of mind in the matter of taking children into custody and directing production before the Juvenile Court.
- Absence of proper follow-up action after admission of the children in the Observation Homes, in particular, grievance was made that the Child Welfare Officers were not performing their duties and such failure led to continued detention of children without any justification.
- Detention in such circumstances was illegal and the condition very often resulted in harassment to the children detained.

70. AIR 1987 SC 656.

Society denied the allegation raised by the petitioner. The High Court went into considerable detail and found some of the allegations are correct and gave necessary directions. But in appeal the appellant contended that the High Court failed to appreciate certain points advanced by her. After having heard the appellant, the Supreme Court passed further necessary directions regarding the employment of children in children's home, role of Juvenile Court, etc.

However, the more important here for the study of this research was that the Supreme Court directed to treat 'Children Aid Society' as a "State" within the meaning of Article 12. **Bhagwati, C.J.** in his judgment in paragraph 12 stated,

> '12. *We agree with the appellant that the respondent-Society should have been treated as a State within the meaning of Article 12 as it is undoubtedly instrumentality of the State on the basis of the test laid down by this Court. The respondent-Society has, therefore, to regulate its activities not only in accordance with the statutory requirements but also act in a manner satisfying the requirements of the Constitutional provisions in Articles 21 and 24 as also the Directive Principles of the State Policy.*'

6. Council of Scientific and Industrial Research
Sabhajit Tewary v. Union of India[71]

Note: Overruled in the case of *Pradeep Kumar Biswas* v. *Indian Institute of Chemical Biology*—(discussed later)[72]

The Five Judges' Bench of the Supreme Court had an occasion to decide in the case of *Sabhajit Tewary* v. *Union of India* as to whether Council of Scientific and Industrial Research is a "State" under Article 12 of the Constitution or not. The Bench was constituted of the same five judges who delivered a landmark judgment in the case of *Sukhdev* v. *Bhagatram.* Surprisingly the Bench held unanimously that the aforesaid Council was not "State" under Article 12. In fact this is a very short judgment. The reasons given in it are neither convincing nor sufficient for not declaring the Council as "State". Still, however, the defence is taken while arguing number of the cases on the issue of its inclusion as "State".

As per the facts of the case, the petitioner was a junior steno-grapher, who filed a writ petition against the Council of Scientific and Industrial Research on the ground that his fundamental rights under Articles 14 and 16 are violated due to the recommendations of the Finance Sub-Committee of the Council. Therefore, in order to entitle the petitioner to impeach the circular on the ground of infringement of Articles 14 and 16 of the Constitution, he had to establish that the Council of Scientific and Industrial Research was an authority within the meaning of Article 12 of the Constitution.

---

71. AIR 1975 SC 1329.
72. (2002) 5 SCC 111.

On the above mentioned issue, the Supreme Court entered into the constitution and function of the Council and observed as follows:

1. The Council of Scientific and Industrial Research (CSIR) is a society registered under the Societies Registration Act.
2. The Prime Minister of India is the *ex-officio* President of the Society under Rule 3 of the Society.
3. As per Rule 30, the Government of India has power to appoint some members in the Council.
4. The Government of India can terminate the membership of any member or at one and the same time of all members other than the ex-officio members of the Governing Body.
5. The Governing Body has the management of all the affairs and funds of the Society under Rule 45.
6. The Governing Body is not competent to frame, amend or repeal bye-laws, which are not inconsistent with the rules without previous approval of the Government of India.

By taking into consideration all the above mentioned points it was argued on behalf of the petitioner that the Council was "State" under Article 12 and therefore the writ petition challenging infringement of the fundamental rights under Articles 14 and 16 was maintainable. Unfortunately, the Supreme Court distinguished the Council with the Statutory Corporations like LIC, ONGC and IFC. It was held by the Supreme Court that the Council had no statutory character like aforesaid Corporations. The points argued by the petitioner were, in the eyes of the Supreme Court not sufficient to designate the Council as "State". It is observed by the apex court:

> '...... *The Society does not have a statutory character like the Oil and Natural Gas Commission, or the Life Insurance Corporation or Industrial Finance Corporation. It is a society incorporated in accordance with the provisions of the Societies Registration Act. The fact that the Prime Minister is the President or that the Government appoints nominees to the Governing Body or that the Government may terminate the membership will not establish anything more than the fact that the Government takes special care that the promotion, guidance and co-operation of the scientific and industrial research, the institution and financing of specific researches, establishment or development and assistance to special institutions or departments of the existing institutions for scientific study of problem affecting particular industry in a trade, the utilisation of the result of the researches conducted under the auspices of the Council towards the development of industries in the country are carried out in a responsible manner.*'

After having made these observations, the Supreme Court tried to compare the Council of Scientific and Industrial Research, a society registered under the Societies Registration Act with the companies constituted under the Companies Act. Moreover, the Supreme Court observed that the employees of the companies like Praga Tools Corporation, Heavy Engineering Corporation Ltd., and the Hindustan Steel Ltd. did not enjoy the protection available to Government servants under Article 311. The aforesaid companies are having separate statutory character from that of the Government. In the same manner, according the apex court, the Council, being a registered society, had an independent existence from the Government. Hence, the Council was not declared as "State" under Article 12 of the Constitution.

The Supreme Court rejected the petition filed by the petitioner by making observation that the Council of Scientific and Industrial Research was not an authority within the meaning of Article 12 of the petition. While deciding this case, the Supreme Court wrongly compared a registered society with the companies. The Supreme Court had also erred in coming to the conclusion that the Council was separate from the department of the Government, no writ could be issued against it. Further, the writ of *mandamus* can be issued for the violation of fundamental rights. The same may not be issued in the event of violation of Article 311 of the Constitution, which is not a fundamental right. This aspect has been completely brushed aside by the Supreme Court while deciding the case of Sabhajit Tewary. The same bench of the Supreme Court had, in the case of *Sukhdev* v. *Bhagatram* a task to decide whether LIC, ONGC and IFC, the statutory corporations are "State" under Article 12 or not. These two cases of *Sabhajit Tewary and Sukhdev* v. *Bhagatram* were pending. The Supreme Court in the case of *Sukhdev* v. *Bhagatram* showed the boldness and courage to develop a new law relating to the issuance of writ of *mandamus* against statutory corporation. But surprisingly, the Bench consisting of the same judges, at the same time failed to develop the new law for issuance of writ against a registered society. Hence, the judgment of Sabhajit Tewary is not considered to be good law. The reliance of this judgment is not considered and disbelieved by the Supreme Court in number of the cases thereafter. Thus, though the judgment of Sabhajit Tewary has not been specifically overruled, the effect of this judgment is indirectly nullified and watered down by the Supreme Court in number of judgments. The observations made by the Supreme Court while distinguishing the case pending for the decision from Sabhajit Tewary's case are relevant. Some of them are reproduced hereunder:

In the case of International Airport Authority (AIR 1979 SC 1628) the Supreme Court in para. 31 made the observation that the tests or guidelines for declaring any institution or authority as "State" was not given. There was no discussion regarding the principle of "State". It was observed:

> *'Lastly, we must refer to the decision in Sabhajit Tewary v. Union of India , where the question was whether the Council of Scientific and industrial*

Research was an 'authority' within the meaning of Article 12. The Court no doubt took the view on the basis of facts relevant to the constitution and functioning of the Council that it was not an 'authority', but we do not find any discussion in this case as to what are the features which must be present before a corporation can be regarded as an 'authority' within the meaning of Art. 12. This decision does not lay down any principle or test for the purpose of determining when a corporation can be said to be an 'authority'.....'

In the case of *Ajay Hasia* v. *Khalid Mujib,* the Supreme Court tried to point out that the point for consideration in Sabhajit Tewary's case was whether council for scientific and Industrial Research was an agency or not. The Supreme Court held that the council was not an agency of the Government and therefore not an "authority" under Article 12 of the Constitution. Unfortunately, argument was not made, nor the Supreme Court considered the fact that the Council was a society registered under the Societies Registration Act. Had it been, it would be a different ratio laid down by the Supreme Court in Sabhajit Tewary's case. While distinguishing the ratio laid down in Sabhajit Tewary's case, the Supreme Court (per Bhagwati, J.) observed in the case of Ajay Hasia (AIR 1981 SC 487 Para. 13) as follows:

'The learned counsel appearing on behalf of the respondents Nos. 6 to 8, however, relied strongly on the decision in Sabhajit Tewary v. Union of India (AIR 1975 SC 1329) and contended that this decision laid down in no uncertain terms that a society registered under the Societies Registration Act, 1860 can never be regarded as an "authority" within the meaning of Article 12. This being a decision given by a Bench of five Judges of this Court is undoubtedly binding upon us but we do not think it lays down any such proposition as is contended on behalf of the respondents. The question which arose in this case was as to whether the Council of Scientific and Industrial Research which was juridically a society registered under the Societies Registration Act, 1860 was an "authority" within the meaning of Article 12. The test which the Court applied for determining this question was the same as the one laid down in the International Airport Authority's case and approved by us, namely, whether the Council was an instrumentality or agency of the Government. The Court implicitly assented to the proposition that if the Council were an agency of the Government, it would undoubtedly be an "authority". But, having regard to the various features enumerated in the judgment, the Court held that the Council was not an agency of the Government and hence could not be regarded as an "authority". The Court did not rest its conclusion on the ground that the Council was a society registered under the Societies Registration Act, 1860, but proceeded to consider various other features of the Council for arriving at the conclusion that it was not an agency of the Government and therefore not an "authority". This would have been totally unnecessary if the view

of the Court were that a society registered under the Societies Registration Act can never be an "authority" within the meaning of Art. 12.'

In the case of *P.K. Ramchandran Iyer* v. *Union of India*,[73] while deciding the issue as to whether Indian Council for Agricultural Research (ICAR) as "State", **Justice D.A. Desai** made observation regarding the case of Sabhajit Tewary as under:

'...much water has flown down in Jamuna since the dicta in Sabhajit Tewary's case and conceding that it is not specifically overruled in later decision, its ratio is considerably watered down so as to be a decision confined to its own facts. The case is wholly distinguishable on the facts apart from the later indicia formulated by the Court for ascertaining whether a body is "other authority" within the meaning of Article 12. A mere comparison of the history of ICAR as extensively set out hereinbefore and the setting up of CSIR would clearly show that ICAR came into existence as a department of the Government, continued to be an attached office of the Government even though it was registered as a society and wholly financed by the Government and the taxing power of the state was invoked to make it financially viable and to which independent research institutes set-up by the Government were transferred. None of these features was present in the case of CSIR and, therefore, the decision in Sabhajit Tewary's case would render no assistance and would be clearly distinguishable.'

From the observations of the Supreme Court in the above mentioned cases regarding the ratio laid down in Sabhajit Tewary's case, it becomes apparently clear that the same is not considered as good law. This ratio has not been specifically overruled in later judgments, but at the same time, the observations of later judgments of the Supreme Court have practically nullified the effect of Sabhajit Tewary's case. The Supreme Court failed to consider the pertinent point as to whether society registered under the Societies Registration Act, 1860 was instrumentality or agency or not.

Status of Council for Scientific and Industrial Research (CSIR) after the case of:

Pradeep Kumar Biswas v. Indian Institute of Chemical Biology[74]

As observed in the comments of the above mentioned case of *Sabhajit Tewary* v. *Union of India* that it was not considered to be a good law laid down by the Supreme Court. Further the Supreme Court has thereafter, in number of cases expressed the same opinion as well. In the case of *Sukhdev* v. *Bhagatram, International Airport Authority* case the Supreme Court distinguished the case of Sabhajit Tewary. Moreover, in the case of P.K.

73. AIR 1984 SC 541.
74. (2002)5 SCC 111.

Ramchandran Iyer, the Supreme Court (Per Justice D.A. Desai) held that the law laid down in the case of Sabhajit Tewary has been much more watered down and distinguished the same. But till the year 2002 the ratio of Sabhajit Tewary's case was not specifically overruled. Hence, in number of cases before the apex court the aforesaid case was taken by the parties as a defence. Lastly, in the case of *Pradeep Kumar Biswas* v. *Indian Institute of Chemical Biology*, again before the bench of seven judges of the Supreme Court a question came for the consideration as to whether the CSIR was "State" or not. In other words, the ratio laid down in the case of Sabhajit Tewary was proper or not. The bench of seven judges, by majority specifically overruled the ratio laid down in the year 1975 in the case of Sabhajit Tewary and held that the CSIR falls within the definition of "other authorities" and hence "State" within meaning of Article 12.

The following factual aspects were taken into consideration by the Supreme Court:

The appellants filed a writ petition before the Calcutta High Court to challenge the termination of their services by the respondent which is a unit of the Council of Scientific and Industrial Research (CSIR). They also sought an interim order but that was refused by the High Court on the *prima facie* view that in view of the Supreme Court's decision in Sabhajit Tewary case, the writ petition itself was not maintainable. The appellants approached the Supreme Court. A two-judge Bench of the Supreme Court took the view that in view of subsequent decisions of the Supreme Court, Sabhajit Tewary's case required reconsideration, and, therefore, referred the matter to the Constitution Bench comprising of seven Judges.

On 27-4-1940, the Board of Scientific and Industrial Research and on 1-2-1941, the Industrial Research Utilisation Committee were set-up by the Department of Commerce, Government of India with the broad objective of promoting industrial growth in the country. On 14-11-1941, the Legislative Assembly for constituting the Industrial Research Fund for the purpose of fostering industrial development passed a Resolution. The Government of India accepted this resolution. For the purpose of co-ordinating and exercising administrative control over the working of the said two research bodies and to oversee the proper utilisation of the Industrial Research Fund, by a further Resolution dated 26-9-1942, the Government of India decided to set-up a Council of Industrial Research on a permanent footing which would be a registered society under the Registration of Societies Act, 1860. Pursuant to the Resolution, on 12-3-1942 CSIR was duly registered. The Governing Body of the Society framed bye-laws and rules in 1942 which have been subsequently revised and amended. Unquestionably this shows that CSIR was "created" by the Government to carry on in an organized manner what was being done earlier by the Department of Commerce of the Central Government. In fact the two research bodies which were part of the Department of Commerce have since been subsumed in CSIR.

The resolution dated 26-9-1942 enumerated the functions of CSIR. The objects which have been incorporated in the memorandum of association of CSIR manifestly demonstrate that CSIR was set-up in the national interest to further the economic welfare of the society by fostering planned industrial development in the country. Such a function is fundamental to the governance of the country.

Unlike other registered societies governed by Sec. 14 of the Societies Registration Act, 1860, on the winding up or dissolution of CSIR, any property remaining after payment of all debts shall have to be dealt with "in such manner as the Government of India may determine". CSIR is therefore both historically and in its present operation subject to the financial control of the Government of India. The assets and funds of CSIR though nominally owned by the Society are in the ultimate analysis owned by the Government.

The Council of Scientific and Industrial Research is a society registered under the Societies Registration Act. By taking into consideration the Rules and Regulations, 1999 of CSIR, the dominant role played by the Government of India in the Governing Body of CSIR is evident. The Government of India appoints the Director General who is *ex-officio* Secretary of the Society. [Rule 2(iii)] Furthermore, the President nominates the members of the Governing Body who are not there *ex-officio* and he can also terminate their membership and the Prime Minister is the *ex-officio* President of CSIR. The contention that although the Prime Minister was *ex-officio* President of the Society the power exercised by the Prime Minister was as President of the Society, is erroneous. An *ex-officio* appointment means that the appointment is by virtue of the office; without any other warrant or appointment than that resulting from the holding of a particular office. Powers may be exercised by an officer, in this case the Prime Minister, which are not specifically conferred upon him, but are necessarily implied in his office (as a Prime Minister), these are *ex-officio*.

The control of the Government in CSIR is ubiquitous. The Governing Body is required to administer, direct and control the affairs and funds of the Society and, under Rule 43, has authority "to exercise all the Powers of the Society subject nevertheless in respect of expenditure to such limitations as the Government of India may from time to time impose. The Governing Body also has the power to frame, amend or repeal the bye-laws of CSIR but only with the sanction of the Government of India. Bye-law 44 had provided, "any alteration in the bye-laws shall acquire the prior approval of the Governor-General-in-Council". Under Rule 41, the President may review/amend/vary any of the decisions of the Governing Body and pass such orders as considered necessary which would binding on the Governing Body. Moreover, decisions of the President on questions referred by the Chairman are binding on the Governing Body. Under this rule the subjugation of the Governing Body to the will of the Central Government is complete.

Before the seven Judges' Bench the following two questions were involved:

- whether CSIR was a State within the meaning of Article 12, and
- if yes, whether the Supreme Court should reverse the decision to the contrary in Sabhajit Tewary's case, which had stood for over a quarter century.

Answering both the questions in affirmative majority opinion was as follows:

It has summarized the statement of law in Rajasthan Electricity Board's case,

> *'The State, as defined in Article 12, is thus comprehended to include bodies created for the purpose of promoting the educational and economic interests of the people.'*[75]

The Supreme Court took into consideration the situation prevailing at the stage of development of case laws while defining the term "State" under Article 12 and observed in para. 11 of its judgment as follows:

> *'11. Initially the definition of State was treated as exhaustive and confined to the authorities or those which could be read ejusdem generis with the authorities mentioned in the definition of Article 12 itself. The next stage was reached when the definition of "state" came to be understood with reference to the remedies available against it. For example, historically, a writ of mandamus was available for enforcement of statutory duties or duties of a public nature. Thus, a statutory corporation, with regulations framed by such corporation pursuant to statutory powers was considered a State, and the public duty was limited to those which were created by statute.'*

The picture that emerges from the case-law is that the tests formulated in Ajay Hasia's case in the year 1981, for determining as to when a corporation can be said to be an instrumentality or agency of the Government are not a rigid set of principles so that if a body falls within any one of them it must, ex hypothesi, be considered to be a State within the meaning of Article 12. The question in each case would be—whether in the light of the cumulative facts as established, the body is financially, functionally and administratively dominated by or under the control of the Government. Such control must be particular to the body in question and must be pervasive. If this is found then the body is a "State" within Article 12. On the other hand, when the control is merely regulatory whether under statute or otherwise, it would not serve to make the body a "State".

By taking into consideration the facts of the case as well as the settled judicial position, there can be no doubt that the conclusion reached in Sabhajit Tewary's case not declaring CSIR as "State" under Article 12

---

75. Electricity Board, Rajasthan *v.* Mohan Lal, AIR 1967 SC 1857, Para. 45.

was erroneous. If the decision of Sabhajit Tewary had sought to lay down as a legal principle that a society registered under the Societies Registration Act or a company incorporated under the Companies Act is, by that reason alone, excluded from the concept of State under Article 12, it is a principle which has long since been discredited. Had the facts been closely scrutinized in the proper perspective, it could have led and can only lead to the conclusion that CSIR is a "State" within the meaning of Article 12.

While dealing with the question as to whether CSIR is a "State" or not, the Supreme Court went into the wider issue and discussed in detail the need for expanding the judicial definition of "State" under Article 12.

It observed that the significance of Article 12 lies in the fact that it occurs in Part III of the Constitution which deals with fundamental rights. The various articles in Part III have placed responsibilities and obligation on the "State" *vis-à-vis* the individual to ensure constitutional protection of the individual's rights against the State, including the right to equality under Article 14 and equality of opportunity in the matters of public employment under Article 16 and most importantly, the right to enforce all or any of these fundamental rights against the "State" as defined in Article 12 either by way of filing writ under Article 32 or under Article 226.

While deciding the issues involved in this case, the Supreme Court discussed the development in judicial decisions regarding the definition of "state" under Article 12. The Apex Court took the view that in the recent years the Courts have entertained the case where there was arbitrariness and violation of Articles 14 and 16. At the same time it became necessary to widen the scope of "State" under Article 12 also. This fact is mentioned by the majority judgment by **Justice Ruma Pal** in paragraph 9 as under:

> *'9. The range and scope of Article 14 and consequently Article 16 have been widened by a process of judicial interpretation so that the right to equality now not only means the right not to be discriminated against but also protection against any arbitrary or irrational act of the state. It has been said that,*
> *"Articles 14 and 16 strike at arbitrariness in State action and ensure fairness and equality of treatment.".....'*

The range and scope of Article 14 and consequently Article 16 have been widened by a process of judicial interpretation so that the right to equality now not only means the right not to be discriminated against but also protection against any arbitrary or irrational act of the State. Keeping pace with this broad approach to the concept of equality under Articles 14 and 16, courts have whenever possible, sought to curb an arbitrary exercise of power against individuals by "centers of power", and there was correspondingly an expansion in the judicial definition of "State" in Article 12.

The Constitution has to be an extent defined the word "State" in Article 12 itself as including "the Government under the control of the

Government of India". That an "inclusive" definition is generally not exhaustive is a statement of obvious and so far as Article 12 is concerned, has been so held by the Supreme Court. The words "State" and "authority" used in Article 12 therefore remain among "the great generalities of the Constitution" the content of which has been and continues to be supplied by courts from time to time.

> *'10. Keeping pace with this broad approach to the concept of equality under Articles 14 and 16, courts have whenever possible, sought to curb an arbitrary exercise of power against individuals by "centers of power", and there was correspondingly an expansion in the judicial definition of "State" in Article 12.'*

Observations of **Justice Ruma Pal (for majority)**:

After having discussed in detail all the cases relevant to the term "State" under Article 12, starting from Rajasthan Electricity Board case to the case of *Mysore Paper Mills Ltd.* v. *Mysore Paper Mills Officers' Association* Justice Ruma Pal observed in para. 40 of the judgment making a position specifically clear as to when a body can fall within the definition of the state. Paragraph 40 is reproduced here below:

> *'40. The picture that ultimately emerges is that the tests formulated in the case of Ajay Hasia are not a rigid set of principles so that if a body falls within any one of them it must, ex-hypothesi, be considered to be a State within the meaning of Article 12. The question in each case would be—whether in the light of the cumulative facts as established, the body is financially, functionally and administratively dominated by or under the control of the Government. Such control must be particular to the body in question and must be pervasive. If this is found then the body is a State within Article 12. On the other hand, when the control is merely regulatory whether under statute or otherwise, it would not serve to make the body a State.'*

After having made these observations and going into the facts relating to the formation, objects and functions of CSIR, Justice Ruma Pal came to the conclusion that CSIR falls within the range of Article 12 of the Constitution.

Apart from the above facts, a new fact relating to CSIR came to light that on 31-10-1986 in exercise of the powers conferred by sub-section (2) of Section 14 of the Administrative Tribunals Act, 1985, the Central Government specified 17-11-1986 as the date on and from which the provisions of sub-section (3) of Section 14 of the 1985 Act would apply to CSIR "being the Society owned and controlled by Government". This notification issued by the Central Government made task of the majority in this case easier than before for reversing the Sabhajit Tewary's judgment.

The learned Attorney-General contended that the notification was not conclusive of the fact that CSIR was a State within the ambit of Article 12 and that even if an entity is not a State within the meaning of Article 12, it is open to the Government to issue a notification for the purpose of ensuring the benefits of the provisions of the Act to its employees.

By disbelieving the argument of the Attorney-General, the Supreme Court came to the conclusion that it is clear while reading Article 323-A of the Constitution and Section 14 of the Administrative Tribunals Act, 1985 that no notification under Section 14(2) of the aforesaid Act could have been issued by the Central Government unless the employees of CSIR were either appointed to public services and posts in connection with the affairs of the Union or of any State or of any local or other authority within the territory of India or of any corporation owned or controlled by the Government.

It has been further observed by the Supreme Court in paragraph 21 of the judgment while thinking to reverse the precedent laid down in Sabhajit Tewary's case as follows:

> '21. *Normally, a precedent like Sabhajit Tewary which has stood for a length of time should not be reversed, however erroneous the reasoning if it has stood unquestioned, without its reasoning being "distinguished" out of all recognition by subsequent decisions and if the principles enunciated in the earlier decision can stand consistently and be reconciled with subsequent decisions of the Supreme Court. Sabhajit Tewary case fulfils both these conditions. Yet, since on a re-examination of the question the Supreme Court has come to the conclusion that the decision in Sabhajit Tewary case was plainly erroneous, it is the duty of the Supreme Court to say so and not perpetuate the mistake.*'

Further, the Supreme Court also observed in paragraph 61 on this issue and boldly expressed the opinion that there is nothing in the Constitution that prevents the Supreme Court from reversing earlier ratio of it, if it is erroneous. The contents of paragraph 61 is reproduced here below:

> '61. *Should Sabhajit Tewary still stand as an authority even on the facts merely because it has stood for 25 years? We think not. Parallels may be drawn even on the facts leading to an untenable interpretation of Article 12 and a consequential denial of the benefits of fundamental rights to individuals who would otherwise be entitled to them and "[t]here is nothing in our Constitution which prevents us from departing from a previous decision if we are convinced of its error and its baneful effect on the general interests of the public". (Bengal immunity Co. Ltd. v. State of Bihar, AIR 1955 SC 661).*
>
> *Since on a re-examination of the question we have come to the conclusion that the decision was plainly erroneous, it is our duty to say so and not to perpetuate our mistake.*'

Thus, finally, majority held that Sabhajit Tewary decision must be and is in the circumstances overruled.

Dissenting Minority opinion of R.C. Lahoti, J. (as he then was) (for himself and on behalf of Doraiswamy Raju, J.)

Both the above named judges were not of the opinion to reverse or overrule the ratio laid down in Sabhajit Tewary's case. According to their opinion an instrumentality or agency of State is not necessarily an authority within the meaning of Article 12. To be an authority, the entity should have been created by or under a statute and should be functioning with liability or obligations to the public. Moreover, in the former case the statute creating it, and in the later case some other statute, should vest it with power to make law within the meaning of Article 13(2) governing its relationship with other people or the affairs of the people. In either case it should be entrusted with functions, which are governmental or closely associated therewith by being of public importance or fundamental to the life of the people.

Here the minority opinion, consisting of two judges, viz. Justice R.C. Lahoti and Justice Raju not only refused to declare CSIR as "State" but gave strong reasoning for not reversing the ratio laid down by the Supreme Court in the case of Sabhajit Tewary. By making distinction between instrumentality or agency on one hand and authority on the other hand they took a view that an entity may be instrumentality or agency but not necessarily be therefore, and authority under Article 12 of the Constitution. The following conclusions were made by the minority:

(1) simply by holding a legal entity to be an instrumentality or agency of the State it does not necessarily become an authority within the meaning of "other authority" under Article 12. To be an authority, the entity should have been created by a statute or under a statute and functioning with liability and obligations to the public. Further, the statute creating the entity should have vested that entity with power to make law or issue binding directions amounting to law within the meaning of Article 13(2) governing its relationship with other people or the affairs of other people—their rights, duties, liabilities or other legal relations. If created under a statute, then there must exist some other statute conferring on the entity such powers. In either case, it should have been entrusted with such functions as are governmental or closely associated therewith by being of public importance or being fundamental to the life of the people and hence governmental. Such authority would be the State, for, one who enjoys the powers or privileges of the State must also be subjected to limitations and obligations of the State. It is this strong statutory flavour and clear indicia of power—Constitution or statutory and its potential or capability to act to

the detriment of fundamental right of the people, which makes it an authority; though in a given case, depending on the facts and circumstances, an authority may also be found to be an instrumentality or agency of the State and to that extent they may overlap. Tests 1, 2 and 4 in Ajay Hasia enable determination of governmental ownership or control. Tests 3, 5 and 6 are "functional" tests. The propounder of the tests himself has used the words suggesting relevancy of those tests for finding out if an entity was instrumentality or agency of the State. Therefore, the question whether an entity is an "authority" can not be answered by applying Ajay Hasia Tests.

(2) The tests laid down in Ajay Hasia case are relevant for the purpose of determining whether an entity is an instrumentality or agency of the State. Neither all the tests are required to be answered in the positive nor a positive answer to one or two tests would be suffice. It will depend upon a combination of one or more of the relevant factors depending upon the essentially and overwhelming nature of such factors in identifying the real source of governing power, if need be by removing the mask or piercing the veil disguising the entity concerned.

Therefore, CSIR is not an "authority" so as to fall within the meaning of the expression "other authorities" under Article 12. It has no statutory flavour—neither it owes its birth to a statute nor is there any other statute conferring it with such powers as would enable it being branded an authority. The indicia of power is absent. It does not discharge such functions as are governmental or closely associated therewith or being fundamental to the life of the people.

All the tests given in Ajay Hasia's case can not be fulfilled completely so as to designate CSIR as an "authority" under Article 12. The following conclusions are given by the minority:

(a) The Government does not hold the entire share capital of CSIR. It is not owned by the Government.

(b) The government funding is about 70% and grant by the Government of India is one out of five categories of avenues to derive funds. CSIR need not have to take permission from the Government in order to generate income from other sources.

(c) The Governing Body does not consist entirely of government nominees. The membership of the Society and the manning of its Governing Body—both consist substantially of private individuals of eminence and independence.

(d) There is no provisions in the rules or the bye-laws that the Government can issue such directives as it deems necessary to CSIR and later is bound to carry out the same.

(e) The functions of CSIR can not be regarded as governmental or of essential public importance or as closely related to governmental functions or being fundamental to the life of the people or duties and obligations to the public at large.

(f) CSIR was never a department of the Government.

(g) The membership of the Society and the Governing Body of the Council may be terminated by the President, not by the Government of India. The Governing Body is headed by the Director General of CSIR and not by the President of the society (i.e. the Prime Minister).

Thus, the Board and Committee taken over by CSIR, did not discharge the functions of regal, governmental or sovereign nature. Hence, CSIR is not offspring or the blood and bones or the voice and hands of the Government.

However, the following points go against the view taken by the minority:

(a) The Prime Minister of India is the President of the Society and members of the Government Body are persons appointed *ex-officio* by virtue of their holding some office under the Government also.

(b) There is some element of control exercised by the Government in matters of expenditure such as on the quantum and extent of expenditure more for the reason that the Government of India and the later wishes to see that its money is properly used and not misused also grant financial assistance.

(c) The President is empowered to review, amend and vary any of the decisions of the Governing Body which is in the nature of residual power for taking corrective measures vesting in the President but then the power is in the President in that capacity and not as Prime Minister of India.

(d) On winding up or dissolution of CSIR, any remaining property is not available to members but "shall be dealt with in such manner as Government of India may determine".

All the above mentioned points are considered by the minority and also conceded that there is no doubt, some element of control of the Government but not a deep and pervasive control. To some extent, it may be said that the Government's presence or participation is felt in the Society but such presence cannot be called a brooding presence or the overlordship of the Government. Moreover, the tests in Ajay Hasia case are not substantially or on essential aspects even satisfied to call CSIR an instrumentality or agency of the State. A mere governmental patronage, encouragement, push or recognition would not by itself make an entity "the State".

While responding to the last point taken by the majority regarding the notification under Section 14(2) of the Administrative Tribunals Act, it is observed by the minority that though the same issued in 1986, was not relied on or referred to in the pleadings of the appellants before the High Court or the Supreme Court. It is quite strange that just during the course of hearing, the notification was taken out from the brief of the counsel and shown to the Court and the opposite counsel. Minority failed to understand as to how the Court could take cognizance of the document shown during the course of the argument, even without giving an opportunity to explain to the other side. A positive finding recorded on material available that CSIR is not a society "owned or controlled by Government" can not be ignored solely by relying on the contents of the notification wherein the user of the relevant expression has been mechanically copied but is unsupportable.

Further, the minority opinion dissented for the application of the tests laid down in Ajay Hasia's case. Further the burden to prove an entity having an independent legal existence to be an instrumentality or agency of the State lies on the person making such allegation. Therefore, the minority opinion was in favour of upholding the ratio laid down in Sabhajit Tewary's case by not declaring CSIR "State".

Summarizing the entire picture regarding the case-laws regarding the issue of the term "State" under Article 12 of the Constitution, after the case of Pradeep Kumar Biswas, it appears that the Supreme Court has at last corrected the error made by it by not declaring CSIR as "State" under Article 12 in Sabhajit Tewary's case. If we peruse the period between the year 1975 and the year 2001 (period between both these decisions), the Supreme Court has in number of cases distinguished the ratio laid down in Sabhajit Tewary's case. But in no decision it was specifically overruled by the apex court. Thus, every time a ratio of Sabhajit Tewary's case was taken as a defence by the institutions and every time, the Supreme Court had to decide the issue by distinguishing the above case. But, after the case of Pradeep Kumar Biswas, the Supreme Court has by overruling the decision of Sabhajit Tewary, by majority of 5: 2 declared CSIR as "State" within the meaning of Article 12.

Here it appears that the minority opinion is not a balanced one as on one hand the minority concedes that there is some element of governmental control over the CSIR and again says that such a narrow element of control is not sufficient to declare CSIR as "State". This view brushes aside the fact that the Prime Minister is *ex-officio* President of CSIR and other governmental officers are present therein. The government is giving about 70% of the grant to CSIR. The property of CSIR would be disposed as per the desire of the government. Still, however, minority, just to save the judgment of Sabhajit Tewary from being reversed said that the control of government is not deep and pervasive so as to designate an entity as "State". The minority opinion failed to appreciate the fact that ratio laid down in Sabhajit Tewary has been distinguished and impliedly brushed away by the judgments of *International Airport Authority case, Ajay Hasia case,*

Som Prakash Rekhi, P.K. Ramchandran Iyer, B.S. Minhas v. *Indian Statestical Institute* and in number of other cases. Merely because of the fact that a bench of five judges pronounces the judgment of Sabhajit Tewary and it stands for more than 25 years, it cannot be said that it should not be interfered with. On the other hand, it is a bold view taken by the majority that it at last corrected the wrong precedent established in the case of Sabhajit Tewary by reversing it. This is perhaps a land-mark judgment in the field of definition of "State" under Article 12 of the Constitution after the case of *Ajay Hasia* v. *Khalid Mujib*. The majority has probably committed error while coming to the conclusion that one or more tests laid down in Ajay Hasia's case are fulfilled, an entity can not for the sole reasons declared as "State". By deciding this issue, the majority has curtailed the definition of "State" under Article 12 of the Constitution.

CSIR Scientific Workers Association v. Union of India[76]

In the present case the ratio laid down in the former case of CSIR viz. *Pradeep Kumar Biswas* v. *Indian Institute of Chemical Biology* was simply followed and it was held by the Supreme Court that in view fact that decision of Sabhajit Tewary was overruled by the seven judges Bench of the Supreme Court in the year 2002 in Pradeep Kumar Biswas case, the Supreme Court held CSIR as an "authority" under Article 12 and hence amenable to writ jurisdiction of the High Court under Article 226. Thus, in the present case the Supreme Court reiterates the view of Pradeep Kumar Biswas case (discussed herein above).

8. Institute of Constitutional and Parliamentary Studies

Tekraj v. Union of India[77]

The question arisen before the Supreme Court in the case of *Tekraj* v. *Union of India* while deciding whether Institute of Constitutional and Parliamentary Studies (ICPS) is "State" or not was that the guidelines/tests given in the case of Ajay Hasia and other cases decided on the similar lines for determining any authority within the ambit of "State" under Article 12 of the Constitution should be followed blindly by declaring all the societies registered under the Societies Registration Act or not. While giving guidelines for declaring any authority as "State" under Article 12, in the case of *Ajay Hasia* v. *Khalid Mujib*, Justice Bhagwati observed,

> *'The tests for determining as to when a corporation can be said to be an instrumentality or agency of Government may now be culled out from the judgment in the International Airport Authority's case. These tests are not conclusive or clinching, but they are merely indicative indicia which have to be used with care and caution because while stressing the necessity of a wide meaning to be placed on the expression "other authority", it must be*

76. (2003) 9 SCC 289.
77. AIR 1988 SC 469.

realized that it should not be stretched so far as to bring in every autonomous body which has some nexus within the sweep of the expression. A wide enlargement of the meaning must be tempered by a wise limitation...'

A case was arisen out of the suspension and thereafter Dismissal of employee of Institute of Constitutional and Parliamentary Studies. Initially the appellant before learned single judge before the Delhi High Court challenged the dismissal order. Learned Single Judge rejected the writ petition by holding that the respondent society was not "State" within the ambit of Article 12 of the Constitution and hence writ is not maintainable against it. In a Letters Patent Appeal before the Division Bench of the Delhi High Court the appellant filed an appeal, but the Division Bench also rejected the Letters Patent Appeal by confirming the decision of a learned single Judge. Being aggrieved by both the judgments, the applicant approached the Supreme Court by way of special leave under Article 136 of the Constitution of India.

The advocate appearing for the Institute during the course of argument stated that irrespective of the fact as to whether the Institute was "State" under Article 12 or not, the employer was prepared to give a fresh opportunity to the applicant to meet the charges so as to dispel from his mind the feeling that he had not been given reasonable opportunity to defend his case. The Supreme Court might have disposed of the appeal based on the statement made by the council of the Institute, but alongwith making the statement, the counsel for the Institute requested the Division Bench of the Supreme Court to enter into the merits of the issue as to whether ICPS constitutes "State" within constitutional meaning of the term. The counsel appearing on behalf of the Union of India also wanted the question to be decided. Hence, the main and the sole question for consideration before the Supreme Court was whether ICPS was "State" or not. For the appropriate consideration of the issue it became necessary to look into the constitution of the body, the purpose for which it has been created, the manner of its functioning, including the made of its funding and the broad features which had been founded by the Supreme Court in several decisions to be relevant in the matter of determining a dispute. As per Article 12 of the Constitution, ICPS can be declared "State" only if it is found to be an authority within the territory of India or under the control of the Government of India.

Constitution of ICPS

ICPS is a society registered under the Societies Registration Act, 21 of 1860, and was registered on 9th March,. 1965. The Institute consists of a President, five vice-presidents and 13 members, in all 19 in numbers. The first President of the Institute was the then Speaker of Lok Sabha. Following five were the first Vice-Presidents viz. the then Minister of Railways, Minister of Law and Social Security, Minister of Communication and

Parliamentary Affairs, a former Chief Justice of India and a former Attorney General of India. The First 13 members were from the then Ministers, Members of Parliament and other distinguished personalities.

Objects of the Society

From the objects of the ICPS it is very easy to come to the conclusion that the said institute is an instrumentality or agency of the government or not. The following *inter alia* are the objects:

(1) to promote and provide for constitutional and parliamentary studies with special reference to comparative studies in constitutional systems of various countries and working of the Indian Constitution and parliamentary and governmental institutions in their various aspects;
(2) to undertake study of courses and fundamental research relating to developments in constitutional law, conventions and practices, parliamentary procedure, legislative drafting, trends in judicial interpretation and allied matters;
(3) to organise *inter alia* training programmes in constitutional problems and matters of current parliamentary importance;
(4) to set-up a legislative research and reference service for the benefit of all interested members of the Union Parliament and State Legislatures irrespective of their party affiliations;
(5) to undertake and provide for the publications of a journal and of research papers and of books and brochures with a view to disseminate democratic values and to foster broad-based civic education and awareness, and in particular, to promote study of constitutional and parliamentary affairs;
(6) to establish and maintain libraries and information services to facilitate the study of constitutional and parliamentary subjects and spread information in regard thereto;
(7) to invite as and when feasible, scholars who may or may not be members of the Society, to take advantage of the facilities offered by the Society and to benefit the Society by their knowledge and experience; and
(8) to institute appropriate fellowships, offer prizes and arrange scholarships and stipends in furtherance of the objects of the society.

One of the important provision included in the memorandum of Association of the society was to accept gifts, donations and subscriptions in cash and securities and of any property either movable or immovable. The rule classified the members under heads like Founder Members, Life Members, Honorary Members, Ordinary Members, Corporate Members and Associate Members. Ordinary membership would extend to Members of Parliament or of any State Legislature or those who have been or members of the judiciary or advocates of the Supreme Court or the High Courts or persons employed in public service or persons engaged in teaching of study of social sciences particularly of political science, Law or subjects related thereto. In the category of Honorary members were the President, the Vice-President and the Prime Minister of India.

Though memorandum permitted receipt of gifts and donations from outside, it is not disputed that the main source of income of the Society has been the annual Central Government Grant.

In the light of the above mentioned facts, the Supreme Court had to decide the status of ICPS. Looking to the constitution, object, status and activities of the Institution, the Supreme Court was of the opinion that ICPS is not an instrumentality or agency of the government and hence not "State" within meaning of Article 12 of the Constitution. Merely because of the fact that the Institute is dependant almost entirely upon the annual grant given by the Central Government, ICPS can not be declared as an instrumentality or agency of the government. For declaring that the Supreme Court dealt with and distinguished various judgments starting from the Rajasthan Electricity Board to P.K. Ramchandran Iyer's case and demonstrated that the ratio laid down in all these cases was not applicable in the case under consideration.

Justice Ranganath Mishra while coming to the conclusion has effectively discussed the extracts and ratio laid down by the Supreme Court in various cases.

Case of *Rajasthan Electricity Board* v. *Mohan Lal* was the first judgment rendered by the Constitutional Bench of the Supreme Court regarding the scope and meaning of the term "other authorities" under Article 12 of the Constitution. While declaring Rajasthan Electricity Board falls within the term "other authorities" the majority opinion given by Justice Bhargava took into consideration the meaning of the term 'authority' as well as the expression "other authority" and observed,

> *"The meaning of the word 'authority' given in Webster's Dictionary, which can be applicable, is a "public administrative agency or corporation having quasi-governmental powers and authorised to administer a revenue-producing public enterprise." The dictionary meaning of the word 'authority' is clearly wide enough to include all bodies created by a statute on which powers are conferred to carry out governmental or quasi-governmental functions. The expression "other authorities" is wide enough to include within itself authority created by a statute and functionaries within the territory of India, or under the control of the Government of India. I do not see any reason to narrow down the meaning in the context in which the term "other authorities" are used in Art. 12 of the Constitution."*

It was held by majority in this case that the doctrine of *ejusdem generis* is not applicable while interpreting the term "other authorities".

Prior to the Rajasthan Electricity Board's case, the issue regarding "other authorities" arose in the case of *Smt. Ujjam Bai* v. *State of U.P.*, wherein it was held by Justice Ayangar that the term "other authorities" cannot be read *ejusdem generis* with the earlier categories given in Article 12 of the Constitution viz. Union or State Governments, Parliament or State Legislatures. But in this case the Supreme Court gave comparatively narrow meaning of "other authority". Justice Shah in above case observed that authorities, constitutional or statutory invested with powers by law but not sharing the sovereign power do not fall within the expression "State" as defined in Article 12. He further added that those authorities which are invested with sovereign powers, i.e. power to make rules and regulations and to administer or enforce them to the detriment of citizens and others fall within the definition "State" in Art. 12 and constitutional or statutory bodies which do not share that sovereign power of the State are not, in his view, "State" within the meaning of Article 12 of the Constitution.

Case of *Sabhajit Tewary* v. *Union of India* (AIR 1975 SC 1329) was one where the status of the Council of Scientific and Industrial Research was required to be examined by the Supreme Court. The Supreme Court took note of the fact that the Council was a society registered under the Societies Registration Act. Under Rule 3, the Prime Minister of India was the ex-officio President of the society and under Rule 30 the governing body consisted of persons appointed by the Government of India representing the administrative Ministry under which the Council of Scientific and Industrial Research is included and the Ministry of Finance. The Supreme Court here declared the council not to be "State" under Article 12 of the Constitution. In this view this judgment is very important for the present case. The Supreme Court in Sabhajit Tewary's case (per Ray C.J.) observed:

> *"Extracting the features as aforesaid it was contended that these would indicate that the Council of Scientific and Industrial Research was really an agency of the Government. This contention is unsound. The Society does not have a statutory character like the Oil and Natural Gas Commission or the Life Insurance Corporation or Industrial Finance Corporation. It is a society incorporated in accordance with the provisions of the Societies Registration Act. The fact that the Prime Minister is the President or that the Government appoints nominees to the governing body or that the Government may terminate the membership will not establish anything more than the fact that the Government takes special care that the promotion, guidance and co-operation of scientific and industrial research, the institution and functioning of specific researches, establishment or development and assistance to special institutions or departments of the existing institutions for scientific study of problems affecting particular industry in a trade, the utilization of the result of the researches conducted under the auspices of the Council towards the development of industries in the country are carried out in a responsible manner.*

> *This Court has held in Praga Tools Corporation v. C.V. Imanual (AIR 1969 SC 1306), Heavy Engineering Mazdoor Union v. State of Bihar (AIR 1970 SC 82) and in S.L. Agarwal v. General Manager, Hindustan Steel Ltd. (1970) 3 SCR 363 that the Praga Tools Corporation, Heavy Engineering Mazdoor Union and Hindustan Steel Ltd. are all companies incorporated under the Companies Act and the employees of these companies do not enjoy the protection available to Government servants as contemplated in Art. 311. The companies were held in these cases to have independent existence of the Government and by the law related to corporations. These could not be held to be departments of the Government."*

The status of Life Insurance Corporation, Oil and Natural Gas Corporation and Industrial Finance Corporation. as declared by the Supreme Court in the case of *Sukhdev* v. *Bhagatram* (AIR 1975 SC 1331) has been mentioned in the present case. The ratio laid down and tests given in the case of *International Airport Authority, Ajay Hasia* v *Khalid Mujib* and *Som Prakash* v. *Union of India* have been considered by the Supreme Court in the paras. 7-10 in this case. The status of Indian Statistical Institute and Indian Council of Agricultural Research was discussed in detail. The Supreme Court declared former to be "State" within the meaning of Article 12 whereas the later was not found to be "State".

After having discussed all above cases the Supreme Court in this case came to the conclusion that there cannot indeed be a strait jacket formula for declaring any authority/institute as "State". It is not necessary that all the tests given in Airport Authorities case or Ajay Hasia's case should be satisfied for reaching the conclusion either for or against holding an institution to be "State". In a given case some of the features may emerge so boldly and prominently that a second view may not be possible. There may yet be other cases where the matter would be on the border-line and it would be difficult to take one view or the other outright.

The Supreme Court thereafter discussed regarding need to establishment of the Institute of Constitutional and Parliamentary Studies. It observed,

> *"Democracy pre-supposes certain conditions for its successful working. It is necessary that there must be a deep sense of understanding, mutual confidence and tolerance and regard and acceptance of the views of others. In the early years of freedom, the spirit or sacrifice and a sense of obligation to the leadership that had helped the dream of freedom to materialize had been accepted. The emergence of a new generation within less than two decades of independence gave rise to a feeling that the people's representatives in the Legislatures required the acquisition of the appropriate democratic ideas and spirit. ICPS was born as a voluntary organization to fulfil this requirement. At the inception it was certainly not a governmental organisation and it has not been the case of parties in their pleadings nor have we been told at the bar during the long arguments that had been*

advanced that the objects of ICPS are those which are a State obligation to fulfil. The Society was thus born out of a feeling that there should be a voluntary association mostly consisting of members of the two Houses of Parliament with some external support to fulfil the objects which were adopted by the Society."

The Supreme Court has taken into consideration the constitution of ICPS and observed that the then Speaker of Lok Sabha was the First President, some of the then Ministers were Vice-Presidents and other Members of Parliaments and Members of State Legislature were also the members of the ICPS. But individual Members of Parliament and the corporate body known as Parliament are certainly two different concepts. Services of some of the employees of Parliament were lent to the Society. While Article 12 refers to Parliament as such, a few Members of Parliament cannot be considered as Parliament so as to constitute that body as referred to in Article 12. The Speaker and the Minister who joined as Vice-Presidents of the Society were there in their individual capacities and not as Ministers, though designations were indicated. In the category of Vice-Presidents, Executive Chairman, Treasurer and members, there were many people who were really not a part of Government as such and some of them did not belong to Parliament.

Apart from that none of the objects of the ICPS specified hereinbefore was governmental business but they all were certainly the aspects which were expected to equip Members of Parliament and the State Legislatures with the requisite knowledge and experience for better functioning. Many of the objects adopted by the Society were not confined to the two Houses of Parliament and were intended to have an impact on society at large.

The Memorandum of the society was also very important for the consideration of its status as it permitted acceptance of gifts, donations and subscriptions. There is material to show that the Ford Foundation, a US-based Trust, had extended support for sometime. Undoubtedly, the annual contribution from the Central Government has been substantial and it would not be wrong to say that they perhaps constitute the main source of funding. The Supreme Court has also observed here that if the Society's affairs were really intended to be carried on as part of Lok Sabha or Parliament as such, the manner of its functioning would have been different. The accounts of the Society are separately maintained and subject to audit in the same way as the affairs of societies receiving Government grants are to be audited. The Government usually impose certain conditions and restrictions when grants are made. No exception has been made in respect to the Society and the mere fact that such restrictions are made is not a determinative aspect.

Thus, by taking into consideration the constitution, object and memorandum of the society the apex court came to the conclusion that ICPS is not "State" under Article 12, though the Supreme Court has treated many societies registered under the Societies Registration Act as "State". But in each of those cases it would appear on analysis that either governmental business had been undertaken by the Society or what was expected to be the public obligation of the "State" had been undertaken to be performed as a part of Society's function. In a welfare state, as has been pointed out on more than one occasion by the Supreme Court, Governmental control is very pervasive and in fact touches the aspects of social existence. In the absence of a fair application of the tests to be made, there is possibility of turning every non-governmental society into an agency or instrumentality of the State. That obviously would not serve the purpose and may be far from reality. Thus without any ambiguity or doubt the Supreme Court observed that the ICPS is neither instrumentality nor agency of the state so as to come within the purview of "other authorities" in Article 12 of the Constitution.

9. Grih Kalyan Kendra

Grih Kalyan Kendra Workers' Union v. Union of India[78]

A writ petition under Article 32 of the Constitution of India was preferred before the Supreme Court filed by the petitioner—Grih Kalyan Kendra Workers' Union on behalf of the employees of the Grih Kalyan Kendra for a declaration that the Grih Kalyan Kendra wherein the workers are employed is "State" within the meaning of Article 12 of the Constitution of India and for the issuance of a writ of *mandamus* directing the Union of India and the respondents to pay regular pay scales in parity with other employees performing similar work under the Union of India like New Delhi Municipal Committee and other Departments of Delhi Administration.

Grih Kalyan Kendra is a society registered under the Societies Registration Act, 1860. Its objectives as set out in the Memorandum of Association are as follows:

(a) To promote social, economic, cultural and educational activities for the betterment of the Central Government employees and their families;
(b) To impart technical and vocational training in home crafts and other household arts for useful utilisation of leisure time; and
(c) To organise and promote economic activities that may provide opportunities for gainful employment to families of Central Government employees for supplementing family incomes.

The Kendra has been conducting the following activities:

(i) holding of craft classes for training in cutting, tailoring and embroidering for the house-wives and grown-up girls during their leisure hours;

78. AIR 1991 SC 1173.

(ii) imparting nursery education for children in the age group of 3 to 7 years;

(iii) running of crèches or day-care centers for children between the age of 90 days and 7 years;

(iv) providing the recreational facilities like T.V. shows, libraries, gymnasia and in-door games and sports at the Samaj Sadans (Community Halls); and

(v) conducting stitching of liveries for class III (Group C) and class IV (Group D) employees of Government Departments and Public Sector Undertakings.

The Grih Kalyan Kendra is a welfare organisation working under the aegis of the Department of personnel and Administrative Reforms, Ministry of Home Affairs. The purpose and object of establishing the Kendras were to help needy Government servants especially those belonging to the lower income group by providing to their departments opportunity of gainful work or training during their leisure time. It was contended by the petitioner that the Grih Kelyan Kendra is a "State" within the meaning of Article 12 of the Constitution and therefore the respondents are under constitutional obligation to prescribe similar scales of pay as applicable to the employees of New Delhi Municipal Corporation (NDMC) and other Departments of the Delhi Administration. The petitioner has claimed relief for declaring the Kendra to be an instrumentality of State and for the issue of a direction directing the respondents to pay equal pay as paid to the similar employees doing similar work in NDMC and other Departments of the Delhi Administration.

The Supreme Court, without making firm decision for declaring the Kendra as "State" under Article 12, went upon the assumption that the Grih Kalyan Kendra is an instrumentality of State and further held that the writ petition filed by the petitioner claiming equal pay for equal work was not tenable in the eyes of law. Hence the matter was rejected on merits and therefore it was not necessary to declare the Kendra as "State" within the meaning of Article 12. It was held by the Supreme Court (K.J. Singh, J.) answering the question whether the Kendra is "State" or not,

> '...*We do not think it necessary to consider this question in detail as in our opinion given on an assumption that the Grih Kalyan Kendra is an instrumentality of a State within the meaning of Article 12 of the Constitution and the petitioners are entitled to enforce their fundamental rights of the petitioners. We according proceed on the assumption that the Grih Kalyan Kendra is a State for the purposes of Chapter IV of the Constitution and consequently this petition under Article 32 was maintainable and the petitioners are entitled to invoke the jurisdiction of this Court for the enforcement of their fundamental right founded on the principle of equal pay for equal work.*'

10. Rajasthan Adult Education Association

Rajasthan Adult Education Association v. Ashoka Bhatacharya[79]

The appellant was a society registered under the Societies Registration Act. It was established with the main object of creating atmosphere of adult education, which includes imparting education for women in rural parts of the State of Rajasthan. The respondent was appointed temporarily as programme Assistant in district IDARAS. Her appointment was for a period of three months, which was extended for the period of six months. A letter from the appellant dated May 1, 1989 informed the respondent informed that her service was not required.

The respondent thereupon filed a writ petition under Article 226 of the Constitution before the High Court challenging her termination from service as Temporary Programme Assistant on the grounds that her termination was without complying with the provisions of section 25-F of the Industrial Disputes Act, 1947. The appellant appeared and opposed the petition on the ground of maintainability by taking the preliminary objection that it was not covered within the definition of "State" under Article 12 and it was not 'industry' and therefore, the Industrial Disputes Act was not applicable to it.

But the High Court said that keeping aside the objections, the respondent ought to have given a reasonable opportunity to the petitioner to present her case before termination. Being aggrieved by the judgment of the High Court, the Association preferred appeal before the Supreme Court. The Supreme Court instead of going into the question of instrumentality or agency under Article 12, went into the facts of the case and observed that during a period of probation, the petitioner was told to improve her work. But even thereafter her work was not found up to the mark. Thus, in view of the Supreme Court, the termination of the employee was not by way of punishment, but it was termination simpliciter. The appellant was within its right to terminate temporary employment of the petitioner.

Lastly, Supreme Court said that as the matter was disposed on factual aspects, it was not necessary to enter into the wider question as to whether the appellant was amenable to writ jurisdiction as being covered within the definition of "State" or not. Hence the question was kept open.

11. Indian Red Cross Society

Surjit Singh Gandhi v. Indian Red Cross Society and others[80]

The appellant in this case initially preferred writ petition before the High Court of Punjab and Haryana. The said petition was dismissed by the High Court being not maintainable. The appellant was an employee of St. John Ambulance Association which does not satisfy the tests laid down by the Supreme Court within the meaning of the expression in Article 12 of the Constitution.

79. AIR 1998 SC 336.

80. (1998) 8 SCC 450.

In appeal the Supreme Court felt that the High Court in its decision did not give much emphasis and reasoning as to whether the Indian Red Cross Society was "State" under Article 12 or not. Therefore, the decision of the High Court was quashed and set aside. At the same time the Supreme Court directed to restore the writ petition filed by the petitioner and directed the High Court to hear afresh and decide the petition without prejudice to the earlier decision nor with the direction of the Supreme Court, giving liberty to all the parties to put their contentions.

Thus, the question whether Indian Red Cross Society is "State" or not was not decided by the Supreme Court.

12. A Society Registered under the T.N. Cooperative Societies Act, 1961

A. Umarani v. Registrar, Co-operative Societies[81]

This was case regarding the directions issued by the Government of Tamil Nadu State by its order to the Co-operative Society to regularize the services of the employees of the Co-operative Society. The appointment of aforesaid employees was made in flagrant violation of the mandatory provisions of the Tamil Nadu Cooperative Societies Rules, 1988.

In a writ petition filed under Article 226 of the Constitution of India before the High Court a preliminary objection was taken by the Society was that it was not "State" under Article 12 of the Constitution of India and hence writ is not maintainable against it. The Supreme Court, finally gave the opinion to the effect that when the action of the cooperative society is violative of mandatory statutory provisions, the writ petition is maintainable. However, the apex court found it fit not to give any opinion as to whether the respondent society is "State" under Article 12 of the Constitution of India or not.

13. U.P. Rajya Karamchari Kalyan Nigam (Corporation) (A Society registered under the Societies Registration Act)

Virendra Kumar Srivastava v. U.P. Rajya Karamchari Kalyan Nigam[82]

The appellant was the original petitioner who preferred the respondent from one of its stores terminated a writ petition before the Allahabad High Court under Article 226 of the Constitution of India as his services from the post of Salesman. A preliminary objection taken by the respondent Corporation regarding the maintainability of writ petition that it did not fall in the definition of "State" under Article 12 of the Constitution. The High Court dismissed the writ petition of the petitioner as not maintainable.

Being aggrieved by the dismissal order, the petitioner preferred appeal before the Supreme Court. After passing of the impugned judgments

81. (2004)7 SCC 112.
82. AIR 2005 SC 411.

by the High Court, the scope of Article 12 came up for consideration before a Constitution Bench comprising seven Judges of the Supreme Court in the case of *Pradeep Kumar Biswas* v. *Indian Institute of Chemical Biology* (already discussed above in detail). The seven Judges' Bench in the case of Pradeep Kumar Biswas (supra) overruled the decision of five-Judge Constitution Bench in the case of *Sabhajit Tewary* v. *Union of India* (AIR 1975 SC 1329). Moreover, by explaining and relying on Constitution Bench decision in the case of *Ajay Hasia* v. *Khalid Mujid* (AIR 1981 SC 487) by a majority of five against two the Supreme Court has laid down a multiple test for determining whether a particular Corporation or Body can be held to be included within the definition of "State" under Article 12 of the Constitution. For majority following opinion was given by Ruma Pal, J. in the case of Pradeep Kumar Biswas:

> *'...The picture that ultimately emerges is that the tests formulated in Ajay Hasia's case (supra) are not a rigid set of principles so that if a body falls within any one of them it must, ex hypothesi, be considered to be a State within the meaning of Article 12. The question in each case would—* ***whether in the light of the cumulative facts as established, the body is financially, functionally and administratively dominated by or under the control of the Government. Such control must be particular to the body in question and must be pervasive.'***

From the above proposition it can be concluded that mere fulfilment of any one of the tests of Ajay Hasia's case is not sufficient to constitute any body as "State", it must be established that the body is either financially, functionally or administratively dominated by or under the control of the Government.

The following points were considered by the Apex Court:

The Corporation herein has not been created by any statute. It is merely a society registered under the Societies Registration Act, 1860. Therefore, the enquiry herein was confined to the decision as to whether the present Corporation is an "instrumentality" or "agency" of the state and can claim the status of "State" as defined in Article 12 of the Constitution.

Administrative Control: The careful study of the respondent Nigam clearly revealed that the objects of the Corporation (Nigam) and the provisions of the Memorandum of Association and Rules of the Corporation clearly go to show that the administrative control of the Corporation vests in executive officers representing different departments of the State.

Financial Control: The financial control of the Corporation is to large extent with the State Government. Admittedly, therefore, there is total financial support to the Corporation of the State of U.P. although it is expected that the Corporation will generate sufficient amount to be able to run on "no-profit-no-loss" basis.

Functional Control: There is complete functional control of the Corporation by the State which is evident from the fact that executive officers of the State are *ex-officio* members and office-bearers of the Corporation. As observed in the minority view in the case of Pradeep Kumar Biswas, (2002) 5 SCC 11 if the corporate mask of the registered society is removed it clearly exposes the real nature of the Corporation as an entity of the State.

Therefore, on a detailed examination of the administrative, financial and functional control of the Corporation there is no doubt that it is nothing but an "instrumentality and agency of the State" and the control of the State is not only "regulatory" but it is "deep and pervasive" in the sense that it is formed with the object of catering to the needs of the government employees as a supplement to their salaries and other perks. Even day-to-day functioning of the Corporation is watched, supervised and controlled by the various departmental authorities of the State particularly the Department of Food and Civil Supplies. The multiple test indicated to be applied both by the majority view (Para. 17) and minority view of Pradeep Kumar Biswas, is fully satisfied in this case for coming to a conclusion that the Corporation is covered as an "agency and instrumentality of the State" in the definition of "State" under Article 12 of the Constitution. It is, therefore, amenable to the writ jurisdiction of the High Court under Article 226 of the Constitution.

Before appreciating the present case Dharmadhikari, J. took into consideration the minority judgment given by R.C. Lahoti, J. (as he then was) in the case of Pradeep Kumar Biswas. Dharmadhikari, J. was of the opinion that both majority as well as minority opinion were relevant in order to decide the case.

In Minority opinion, per R.C. Lahoti, J. (as he then was) in Pradeep Kumar Biswas's case it was held that the tests laid down in the case of Ajay Hasia were not relevant only for the purpose of determining whether an entity is 'an instrumentality or an agency of the State'. For Minority, in Pradeep Kumar Biswas's case **Lahoti, J.** (as he then was) said,

> '.... *Simply by holding a legal entity to be an instrumentality or agency of the State it does not necessarily become an authority within the meaning of "other authorities" in Article 12. To be an authority, the entity should have been created by a statute or under a statute and functioning with liability and obligations to the public......*
>
> ....
>
> *The tests laid down in the case of Ajay Hasia (supra) are relevant for the purpose of determining whether an entity is an instrumentality or agency of the State. Neither all the tests are required to be answered in the positive nor a positive answer tone or two tests would suffice. It will depend upon a combination of one or more of the relevant factors depending upon the essentiality and overwhelming nature of such factors in identifying the real source of governing power, if need be by removing the mask or piercing the veil disguising the entity concerned. When an entity has an independent legal existence, before it is held to be the State, the person alleging it to be*

so must satisfy the Court of brooding presence of the Government or deep and pervasive control of the Government so as to hold it to be an instrumentality or agency of the State.'

In the background of both the minority and majority views expressed in Pradeep Kumar Biswas's case, the Supreme Court applied the tests for determining as to whether U.P. Rajya Karamchari Kalyan Nigam was "State" under Article 12 or not. The following points were taken into consideration regarding the establishment and objects of the U.P. Rajya Karamchari Kalyan Nigam by the Supreme Court:

1. The Corporation herein was not created by any statute but it was merely a society registered under the Societies Registration Act, 1860. Therefore, the Supreme Court confined its enquiry and decision as to whether the Corporation was an "instrumentality" or "agency" of the State or not.
2. The Corporation was set-up by the Government wholly financed by it for establishing a chain of stores throughout the State for supply of essential commodities to the State Government employees at normal rates.
3. As per clause (3) of the Memorandum of Association of the Corporation, the objects of it were as under:
   (i) To carry on and promote activities aimed at the welfare of the employees of the State Government and to equip itself with capital, credit, means, resources and technical and managerial assistance for this purpose.
   (ii) To provide and help for the welfare of the employees, the places of interests, recreation, sports and medical attendance and to subscribe money to or for, or otherwise help any other charitable and benevolent object which is in the opinion of the Corporation useful to the employees.
   (iii) To establish and run stores, shops, canteens for carrying on retail business in essential commodities of daily use and other consumer goods without profit motive in such localities within the State of Uttar Pradesh as the Board of Directors of the Corporation may decide from time to time.
   (iv) To help by planning sales of the said commodities in a no profit, no loss basis as a whole in maintaining the prices of such commodities at a reasonable level to the advantage of the community as a whole.
   (v) To act as an agent or stockist on behalf of any government or any institution, manufacturer or concern for procurement, supply and distribution of consumer goods.
   (vi) To make or enter into arrangements for transport, processing, manufacturing, grading, packing and distribution of consumer goods.

(vii) To acquire by purchase or on lease or hire or by licence or otherwise, buildings and premises required for the activities of the Corporation.

(viii) To lease or let on hire, mortgage, sale, pledge or transfer by licence or otherwise any lands, buildings or other property movable or immovable.

(ix) To enter into any arrangements with the Union or the State Government or any local authority or any person for the purpose of carrying out the objects of the Corporation or furthering its interests and to obtain from such government or authority or person subsiding, loans, indemnities, grants, contract licences rights, concessions, privileges or immunities which the Corporation may think it desirable to obtain and exercise and comply with any such arrangements, rights privileges and concessions.

(x) To erect buildings or other structures on lands acquired by the Corporation in any nature, whatsoever.

(xi) To accept gifts, donations, etc. of any nature, whatsoever.

(xii) To lend or borrow money on such terms and conditions as it thinks fit.

(xiii) To draw, make, accept, endorse, discount, execute and issue cheques, promissory notes, bills of exchange or other negotiable or transferable instruments.

(xiv) To do all such other matters and things as may appear to be incidental or conductive to the attainment of the above objects or any of them or consequential upon the exercise of its powers or discharge of its duties.

4. Rule 5 of the Association makes it clear that members of the Corporation or the Board who are members by virtue of their offices which they hold in the State shall stand terminated when they cease to hold the office in the State and their successors to that office shall become members.
5. Clause 4 of the Memorandum of Association of the Corporation said that if on the winding up or dissolution of the Corporation there shall remain, after the satisfaction of its debts and liabilities, any property, the same shall not be paid to any of its members or distributed amongst them but subject to the provisions of section 14 of the Act shall be disposed of in such manner as the State Government may determine.
6. Rule 4 of the Rules of Association permitted the Board to admit any employee of the State Government in it with the previous approval of the State Government.
7. As per Rule 6 of the Rules of Association, the Board might give all or any of its powers, subject to its general control and supervision and subject to such restrictions, to any one or more members of the Board. Rule 12 also conferred the delegation of

powers of the Executive Director in favour of any officer of the Corporation or State.

8. The above mentioned rules could be added, amended, varied or repealed by a procedure only after the prior approval of the State Government.

From the above points it became very easy for the Supreme Court to apply the multiple tests to ascertain the character of a body as falling within Article 12 or outside as laid down in Pradeep Kumar Biswas case (supra). The only important thing here is to ascertain whether the nature of financial, functional and administrative control of the State over the body and whether it is dominated by the State Government and the control can be said to be deep and pervasive as described in the minority view in the Pradeep Kumar Biswas case (*supra*).

On detailed examination of the administrative, financial and functional control of the Corporation, the Supreme Court had no doubt that the Corporation was nothing but an "instrumentality and agency of the State" and the control of the State was not only "regulatory" but it was "deep and pervasive" in the sense that it was formed with the object of catering to the needs of the government employees as a supplement to their salaries and other perks. The top executives of the government department *ex-officio* are members and office-bearers of the Corporation. The Corporation was fully supported financially and administratively by the State and its authorities. Even day-to-day functioning of the Corporation was watched, supervised and controlled by the various departmental authorities of the State particularly the Department of Food and Civil Supplies. The multiple tests indicated to be applied both by the majority and minority view in Pradeep Kumar Biswas case (supra) is thus fully satisfied in the present case as per the view of the Supreme Court. Hence, undoubtedly, the Corporation is said to be covered as an "agency and instrumentality of the State" under Article 12 of the Constitution. It is therefore, amenable to the writ jurisdiction of the High Court under Article 12 of the Constitution as per the decision of the Supreme Court. But, so far as granting of relief is concerned, **Dharmadhikari, J.** expressed his views by saying that it would depend upon the facts of each case what relief should be granted even after declaring any body as "State" under Article 12. He observed in the paragraph 27 of the judgment,

> '27. *Before parting with the case, it is necessary for us to clarify that even though a body, entity or Corporation is held to be a "State" within the definition of Article 12 of the Constitution what relief to the aggrieved person or employee of such a body or entity is to be granted is a subject-matter in each case for the Court to determine on the basis of the structure of that society and also its financial capability and viability. The subject of denial or grant of relief partially or fully has to be decided in each particular case by the Court dealing with the grievances brought by an*

> *aggrieved person against the bodies covered by the definition of "State" under Article 12 of the Constitution.'*

The Supreme Court, with these observations held that U.P. Rajya Karamchari Kalyan Nigam as "State" within the meaning of Article 12 of the Constitution and the order of the High Court was quashed and set aside. The case was further sent to the High Court for taking decision on merits of the case.

It is submitted that this was the important case because in all the cases after the year 1981 came for consideration of the fact whether a body was "State" under Article 12 or not, the tests given in the case of *Ajay Hasia* v. *Khalid Mujib* were applied. This is the first case in which the Supreme Court has advanced a step ahead and applied the tests laid down by the Seven Judges Constitutional Bench in the case of Pradeep Kumar Biswas. The tests given in Pradeep Kumar Biswas case are precise, accurate and in a narrow circumference than that were in Ajay Hasia's case.

4.5 *MANDAMUS* AGAINST UNIVERSITIES AND EDUCATIONAL INSTITUTIONS

English Law

So far as the issuance of *mandamus* against the Colleges and other educational institutions are concerned, Halsbury's Laws of England specifically barred the jurisdiction of the court. It is observed in Halsbury's Laws of England as under:

> *'1302. No mandamus will lie to the provost and fellows of a college to restore an individual to a fellowship, or to the benchers of any of the inns of court to compel them to admit a certain person as a student of the society, or to call a student to the Bar. Such societies have absolute discretion as to the management of their own affairs, and there is accordingly no legal right that can be enforced against them by mandamus.'*[83]

By following the above principles the case of *The King v. Benchers of Lincoln's Inn*,[84] was decided wherein the writ of *mandamus* was not issued. In this case, petitioner Mr. Wooler made an application at the Steward's office of the Society of Lincoln's Inn to have his name enrolled as a member of that society and left a paper containing his name, etc. conformably to the regulations of the society. The Benchers rejected his application. He applied for an opportunity to be heard but he was rejected. He then applied to the High Court for a rule calling upon the Masters, Treasurers, and Benchers of Lincon's Inn to show cause why a writ of *mandamus* should not issue commanding them to admit him as a member of their society for the

---

83. Halsbury's Laws of England, Hailsham's Edition, Vol. 9, Para 1302.
84. (1825) 107 E.R. 1277.

purpose of qualifying himself to be called to the Bar. The application was dismissed mainly on the ground that he had no inchoate right to be admitted as a member of the association and there was no obligation on the part of the association to admit him. At page 1279 of the judgment, learned **Chief Justice Abbot** made his following remarks:

> *'It has been argued that every individual has 'prima facie' an inchoate right to be a member of one of those societies for the purpose of qualifying himself to practise as a barrister. If that proposition were established, there would be a sufficient ground for granting a mandamus but I apprehend that there is no such inchoate right. It might as well be said that every individual had an inchoate right to be admitted a member of the College in either of the University or College of Physicians or any other establishment of that nature. But supposing an individual were desirous to practice medicine in London, this court would not grant a mandamus to compel the College of Physicians to admit him as one of their members or as a licentiate. I think therefore that in this case we ought not to grant a mandamus.'*

On the same page **Justice Bayley** added by making following observation supporting the view of Abbot, C.J.,

> *'They make their own rules as to the admission of members and even if they act capriciously upon the subject this Court can give no remedy in such case, because in fact there has been no violation of any right. This case is analogous to that of a college.'*

Thomson v. University of London[85]

It is pertinent to note that in earlier days *mandamus* was not issued normally to a body like a University in England. In the case of *Thomson* v. *University of London*, where it was sought to restrain the University of London from granting, and a certain candidate from receiving, a gold medal for distinction in an examination and the ground of the action was that the plaintiff, who had become entitled to a gold medal in the examination, was entitled to be the sole gold medalist for the year, it was held that such an action would not lie. No *mandamus* could be issued against a University in such circumstances.

R. v. Thomas[86]

Subsequently, *the Queens Bench in England against University as well as Syndicate in appropriate cases issued mandamus.* In the case of *R.* v. *Thomas* it was held that writ of *mandamus* could be issued against a university or syndicate of a university.

85. (1864)10 LT 403.
86. (1892)1 Q.B. 426.

But at the same time it is observed in number of subsequent English cases that the court has power and can issue writ of *mandamus* even in the event of violation of the principles of natural justice.

The King v. Chancellors, Masters and Scholars of the University of Cambridge[87]

In this case, an application for issuing a writ of *mandamus* was taken out of restore one Richard Bentley to his degree of Doctor of Divinity. He had been degraded by the Vice-Chancellor's Court of the University of Cambridge for having been guilty of contempt in speaking approbrious words against the Vice-Chancellor.

One of the grounds of objection raised by Mr. Bentley was that in the Vice-Chancellor's Court he was not summoned which was against natural justice and against law of god and man. The learned Judge observed at page 819 of the judgment,

> *'This is a very proper mandamus for it is to restore a member of a great corporation to a great office, a dignity and a free-hold. First an office that concerns the Government of a corporation and so agreed in the return. And is not the Government of so great an University as Cambridge of as great concern as the Government of a poor borough?'*

In the above mentioned case writ of *mandamus* was only issued on the ground that the petitioner was not summoned in the Court. It was distinguished on the ground that there was no analogy on facts between the two cases.

R. v. Dunsheath[88]

Again in the year 1950, in the case of *R.* v. *Dunsheath,* Lord Goddard, C.J. while refusing to entertain a writ of *mandamus* against a University observed as follows:

> *'It is important to remember that mandamus is neither a writ of right, but that it will be granted if the duty is in the nature of a public duty and specially affects the rights of an individual, provided there is no more appropriate remedy. This Court has always refused to issue a mandamus if there is another remedy open to the party seeking it. This is one of the reasons, no doubt, why, where there is a visitor of a corporate body, the Court will not interfere in a matter within the province of the visitor, and especially this is so in matters relating to educational bodies such as colleges. I see no difference for this purpose between a college and a University. Any question that arises of a domestic nature is essentially one for a domestic forum, and this is supported by all the authorities which deal with visitatorial powers and duties.'*

87. 92 E.R. 828.
88. (1950)2 All E. R. 741.

It was held in that case that the question whether an officer of a University had refused to perform a duty placed on him by the Status of the University was a domestic matter and, therefore, was one essentially for the visitor and the application for *mandamus* should be refused.

Position of *mandamus* against University and Other Educational Institutions in India

Order of *mandamus* under the Specific Relief Act, 1877 *re* G.A. Satesan[89]

The position of Syndicate of the University was in consideration in the case of In *re* G.A. Satesan, in a proceedings initiated under Sec. 45 of the Specific Relief Act, 1877. The following observations were made by the High Court while refusing to issue order of *mandamus*:

The general scheme of the Indian Universities Act, 1904, and the Regulations framed thereunder is, that the Senate should be the Legislative and the Syndicate the Executive Government of the University. The Syndicate is a creature of statute with certain duties imposed upon it by statute and those duties are to be carried out for the benefit of the public at large and especially for the portion of the public, which desires to utilize the educational advantages of the University. It is, therefore, a body amenable to the jurisdiction of section 45 of the Specific Relief Act, if the other conditions for that relief are present. "Public office, I take it means any office created by the legislative or other lawful authority for the purpose of discharging functions which affect the public generally or any particular section thereof. The Universities Act created a public body to carry out certain defined public objects. It created a Corporation vested with powers to carry out various objects for which the University was created. As part of the machinery and for the better carrying out of the public objects contemplated by the Statute, it has by section 15 constituted a body of persons called the Syndicate in whom is vested the executive government of the University. I find it difficult to see why the members of a statutory body so constituted are not persons holding a public office. The ward 'person' in the General Clauses Act of 1868, which was in force at the date of the passing of the Specific Relief Act, is defined as "including any company or association or body of individuals, whether incorporated or not" so that the words "person holding a public office" in section 45 would also include a body of persons holding that office, even though that body has not been incorporated or constituted a Body Corporate.

It was argued by the Advocate-General that the definition in the Civil Procedure Code affords a valuable guide in constituting section 45 of the Specific Relief Act, and that one important test would be whether the person holding a public office receives any emoluments. Reference was also made to *Henley* v. *Mayor of Lyme*, where Best, C.J. was of the opinion that

89. I.L.R. 40 Mas. 125.

every one who was appointed to discharge a public duty and received compensation in whatever shape, whether from the Crown or otherwise, was a public officer. This definition is not exhaustive. Courts in England have issued a *mandamus* against Poor Law Guardians, Town Councilors, Churchwardens, and other purely honorary public officers. There is, so far as I can see, nothing to prevent a person from undertaking public duties without receipt of emoluments. The test is, not whether a man receives any emoluments, but the nature of the acts to perform which he is appointed or which he is legally liable to perform. Neither the Civil Procedure Code nor the Penal Code are in pari- material with the Specific Relief Act and I do not think the definition there given for certain specific purposes in connection with the provisions of those codes can be taken as a general and authoritative definition of the term "public servant".

It was finally held in the above case that where a public body has a discretion which it exercises *bonafide,* the Court in an application for *mandamus* would not constitute itself an appellate authority and go into the discretion by the public body complained against. The case is, however, different where a public body erroneously assumes that it has a discretion, which it does not possess in law and then seeks to defend an application for *mandamus* on the ground that it has exercised a discretion, which Courts ought not to review. Where a Statute expressly or by implication leaves the determination of certain matters to the body corporate created by it, the latter has no power to delegate its authority on matters within its competence to a third person.

The High Courts, however, in the event of violation of principles of natural justice or in the cases where no opportunity was given to the petitioner to present his case, used to issue *mandamus* under the old Specific Relief Act, 1877. In the case of Rudra Narsin Roy (I.L.R. 28 Cal. 479) it was held that where the candidate applies to the Board of Examiners for pleadership, to be allowed to present himself for the examination, to Board, for the time being, should form its own option as to the fitness of such applicant, and should not reject his application on mere ground that a previous application by him in some past years had been rejected. In such cases, it is competent for the High Court to order the Board to consider his present fitness for admission, and if satisfied that he possessed the qualification prescribed by the rules, to allow him to present himself for the examination.

Purno Chundur Dutt[90]

The court held in the case of Purno Chundur Dutt that the court had no jurisdiction to interfere with the discretion of the Board of Examiners and cannot, where there is a discretion imposed on any body, issue a writ of *mandamus* to compel that body to exercise of that discretion "in a manner fair, candid and unprejudiced" and not "arbitrary, capricious or biased,

90. I.L.R. 35 Cal. 915.

much less warped by resentment or personal dislike". The Court of the discretion which the Court has confided in them.

Board of Examiners v. Probhash Chandra Roy (I.L.R. 40 Cal. 588)

In the case of *Board of Examiners* v. *Probhash Chandra Roy,* the petitioner prayed for a declaration under Section 45 of the Specific Relief Act, 1877 that a certain order appearing in the Calcutta Gazette passed by the opposite party or by the local Government was illegal or *ultra vires;* and that the opposite party had acted illegally in not entertaining the petitioner's application and his certificate of character at the ensuing examination for 1913. It was held that there was absolutely no justification in Chapter VIII of the Act for any declaration of that sort, and that no order under section 45 of the Act should be made unless the applicant shows clearly that he has the specific legal right, to enforce which he asks for the interference of the court, that he has claimed to exercise that right and none other, and that his claim has been refused.

Position after Commencement of the Constitution of India

The system of English Court is not prevalent in India and hence the analogy of English decisions will not entirely apply to India. Simultaneously, Courts should be reluctant to interfere with the internal autonomy of academic bodies like Universities, Colleges, etc. In our Constitution, Universities and colleges affiliated to the Universities are covered within the definition of "other authority" under Article 12 of the Constitution of India and therefore writs can be issued against such bodies, institutions in appropriate cases.

4.5.1 *Mandamus* against Universities

Vice-Chancellor, Utkal University v. S.K. Ghosh[91]

This was the first important case answering the question as to whether a writ of *mandamus* can be issued against the University or not. The dispute was arisen in the year 1952 wherein the petitioners were all students of the second year M.B.B.S. class of Shri Ramchandra, Bhanj, Medical College, Cuttack. The examinations were conducted by Board of Examiners, which submitted results to the Syndicate. The Syndicate, instead of approving and publishing the results, passed a resolution canceling the results in Anatomy on the ground of leakage of questions and to hold another examination instead.

The View of Orissa High Court

The petitioners applied to the High Court of Orissa for the issuance of a writ of *mandamus* directing the Syndicate to publish the results of the 1st M.B.B.S. Examination as reported by the Board of Examiners. Allowing the aforesaid writ, Justice Narasimham held,

91. AIR 1954 SC 217.

'The High Court can, in its exercise of its special jurisdiction under Article 226, issue a mandate in the nature of mandamus against a public body created by statute, like the Syndicate of a University compelling it to carry on its duties. A body exercising statutory powers cannot rely on good faith alone for escaping the jurisdiction of the High Court under Article 226. It must be further shown that the statutory powers were exercised reasonably and with due care. The High Court, however, will not interfere with or revise the opinion of an Administrative public body if there is anything on which that body could reasonably have come to its conclusion. But the discretion should be exercised in a judicial spirit, not allowing extraneous considerations to affect their decision. The High Court cannot take upon itself the functions of an appellate Court of fact, scrutinize the materials that were available to the public body and substitute its own discretion and judgment for that of the body. But the writ of mandamus being of the most extensive remedial nature and intended for supplying defects of justice its application should not be refused in cases where there is an abuse of discretion by a responsible statutory body.

An incomplete right may itself suffice for invoking the mandamus jurisdiction of the High Court. Further, where the act, the doing of which is sought to be compelled by mandamus, is the final thing, and if done gives to the relator all that he seeks proximately, then the question whether he is entitled to have that act done may be enquired into by the officer or person to whom the mandamus is sought and is also to be considered by the tribunal which is moved to grant mandamus. Thus, where the approval of the Syndicate is the final act which completes the right of the examinees to a declaration that they passed certain examination, the examinees have a right to apply for a writ of mandamus issued to the Syndicate to approve their results and to publish it.'

In addition to the observations made by **Justice Narasimham,** learned Chief Justice Ray added the following:

'A writ of mandamus cannot in any event be used as a substitute for an appeal or a writ of error to revise or correct the alleged errors by a public body in the proper exercise of its lawful jurisdiction however inequitable and inconsistent its decision it may be. The High Court should not interfere if the errors of law or wrongful conclusion of fact result from a mistaken judgment. A line of distinction however fine should, however, always be drawn between a mistaken judgment and misguided judgment. Where a tribunal, whether administrative or judicial, allows its judgment to be vitiated by lack of reasonableness and care, the decision shall be subject to the superintendence and control by mandamus.

The right claimed by the examiners can be well understood with reference to the duties that the Syndicate have to perform in the circumstances of the instant case. Rights and duties are always correlated. One in whose interest or for whose benefit a public duty is enjoined by law has always the right to enforce the performance of the duty. The position, therefore, is that where the action of a public functionary threatens to violate the plain and imperative duty cast upon them to the substantial prejudice of the rights of the parties and where all other remedies are utterly inadequate, the speedy and the prompt relief of mandamus is undeniable.

Right should not be confused with status. Status may be the result of a perfected right: but the facts that would constitute the status to be declared by certain public authority, when performed, create a title to the status. This title if it is a recognizable one, creates a right though the same until recognized falls short of the status. To illustrate, it may be compared to right as the right to sue for declaration of a status which is as good a right as the right involved in the status itself for the purpose of enforceability. Whatever can be legally enforced is a specific legal right for the protection whereof a writ of mandamus may lawfully issue.'

The Orissa High Court on fact found that the University had acted with undue haste, assumed the existence of certain facts which did not exist, ignored certain facts which did exist, ignored certain papers that were before them and were carried away by the hearsay statement of certain person far beyond the limits to which he himself was prepared to go, in deciding that there was leakage of certain question papers and therefore passing a resolution that the results of that examination should not be published and that the want of notice in the two cases invalidated the resolutions. It was held that the resolution was passed unreasonably and with want of due care and a writ of *mandamus* should be issued on the Syndicate requiring to take immediate steps to publish the results.

View of the Supreme Court

The University preferred appeal before the Supreme Court challenging the judgment and order of the Orissa High Court and the Supreme Court set aside the order of the High Court and the petitioner under Art. 226 preferred by the medical students before the High Court for issue of a writ of *mandamus* was dismissed. While pronouncing the judgment **Justice Bose** made final conclusive comments,

'In our opinion the High Court was wrong in holding that the two resolutions were invalid. Whatever may be thought about each taken separately, the defects if any are, in our judgment, cured when the two are read together and regarded as a whole. The learned judges rightly held that in a mandamus petition the High Court could not constitute itself into a court of appeal from the authority against which appeal was sought, but having said that they went on to do just what they said they could not. The learned Judges appeared to consider that it was not enough to have facts established from which a leakage could legitimately be inferred by reasonable minds but that there must in addition be proof of its quantum and amplitude though they did not indicate what the yard-stick of measurement should be. That is a proposition to which we are not able to assent.'

Further His Lordship also added,

> *'We are not prepared to perpetuate the error into which the learned High Court Judges permitted themselves to be led and examine the facts for ourselves as a court of appeal but in view of the strictures the High Court has passed on the Vice-Chancellor and the Syndicate we are compelled to observe that we do not feel they are justified .... It may be that the matter could have been handled in some other way, as, for example, in the manner the learned Judges indicate, but it is not the function of Courts of law to substitute their wisdom and discretion for that of the persons to whose judgment the matter in question is entrusted by law. The University authorities acted honestly as reasonable and responsible men confronted with an urgent situation are entitled to act.'*

By reversing the judgment of the High Court lastly His Lordships Justice Ray observed,

> *'Substance was not more important than the form and if there was substantial compliance with the spirit and substance of the law, we are not prepared to let an unessential defect in form defeat what is otherwise a proper and valid resolution.'*

Chairman/Director, Combined Entrance Examination v. Osiris Das[92]

The Supreme Court that G.B. Pant University of Agriculture held it in the above case and Technology is an instrumentality of the State and hence it is covered under the definition of "other authority" under Article 12 of the Constitution of India.

It is submitted that the universities are undoubtedly covered within the definition of "State" under Article 12 of the Constitution of India. In the year 1954, Madras High Court held in the case of *State of Madras* v. *Shantha Bai's case* that the University of Madras is not "State" under Article 12. Subsequently, the Supreme Court in Ujjam Bai's case overruled this judgment and thereafter there is consistent ratio laid down by the Supreme Court that University is covered within the definition of "other authority" and hence State under Article 12 of the Constitution.

4.5.2 *Mandamus* against Educational Institutions

Manmohan Singh Jaitla v. Commissioner, Union Territory, Chandigarh and Others[93]

This is a judgment delivered by Justice D.A. Desai deciding the issue as to whether a writ of *mandamus* can be issued against the aided school receiving grants from the government in affirmative.

---

92. (1992) 3 SCC 543.
93. AIR 1985 SC 364.

Here Guru Nanak Khalsa High School, which was an aided school dispensed with the service of the Headmaster of the School and a drawing teacher claiming to exercise power under an agreement executed by each of them with the management of the school. The appellants also made an application to the Deputy Commissioner under Section 3(2) of the Punjab Aided Schools (Security of Service) Act, 1969, but the same was not entertained.

Both the teachers challenged the action of the school before the High Court of Punjab and Haryana under Article 227 of the Constitution of India seeking relief of reinstatement and other consequential reliefs. The School admittedly received 95% of its expenses as grant from the Government. The High Court rejected the writ petition *in limine* but by a speaking order observing that as the school cannot be said to be "other authority" under Article 12 of the Constitution, it was not amenable to the writ jurisdiction of the High Court.

Being aggrieved by the judgment and order of the High Court, the appellant, headmaster preferred Special Leave Petition under Article 136 of the Constitution of India. Alongwith this appeal, the drawing teacher of the same school, preferred a writ petition under Article 32 of the Constitution on rejecting his application by the Deputy Commissioner.

The Supreme Court took into consideration the following important points regarding the School:

1. The school was an aided school receiving aid to the tune of 95% of its expenses.
2. Sec. 3 of the Punjab Aided School (Security of Service) Act, 1969 provided that no employee shall be dismissed or removed or reduced in rank except after an inquiry to be held in the manner prescribed therein.
3. As per sub-section (2) no order of dismissal or removal or reduction in rank of an employee shall take effect unless the Deputy Commissioner has confirmed it.
4. A person could prefer appeal against such order before the Commissioner within 30 days of the order of the Deputy Commissioner under sub-section (5) of the Act.

The Deputy Commissioner in both the cases observed that looking to the terms of the agreement entered into by each of the teachers with the management of the school, it was not open for them to go behind the order and to find out true nature of the order. In view of the Supreme Court, the Deputy Commissioner could not take an easy recourse becoming oblivious to his duties merely to pay lip sympathy to the order made by the management and decline even to examine the allegation of *mala fide* as also the true nature and character of the impugned order. In the aforesaid cases, in the garb of enforcing a term of the agreement what was sought to be done was to impose the penalty of removal. There was also a smell of *malafide*.

In the opinion of the Supreme Court, the High Court wrongly declined to grant any relief on the ground that an aided school is not "other authority" under Article 12 of the Constitution and was therefore not amenable to the writ jurisdiction of the High Court. But the High Court clearly overlooked the point that Deputy Commissioner and Commissioner were statutory authorities operating under the Act of 1969. They were undisputedly quasi-judicial authorities.

Justice D.A. Desai appreciated the matter in a different angle by taking into consideration the guidelines given in the case of *Ajay Hasia* v. *Khalid Mujib Sehravardi* (AIR 1981 SC 487). For that purpose he observed in paragraph 8 of the judgment,

> *"....the aided school receiving 95% of expenses by way of grant from the public exchequer and whose employees have received the statutory protection under the 1969 Act and who is subject to the regulations made by the Education Department of the Union Territory of Chandigarh as also the appointment of Headmaster to be valid must be approved by the Director of Public Instruction, would certainly be amenable to the writ jurisdiction of the High Court. The High Court unfortunately, did not even refer to the decision of the Constitution Bench in Ajay Hasia's case rendered in November 13, 1980 while disposing of the writ petition in 1983. In Ajay Hasia's case, Justice Bhagwati, J. speaking for the Constitution Bench inter alia observed that 'the financial assistance of the State is so much as to meet almost entire expenditure of the corporation, it would afford some indication of the corporation being impregnated with governmental character.' Add to this 'the existence of deep and pervasive State control which may afford an indication that the Corporation is a State agency or instrumentality.' Substituting the words 'public trust' in place of the 'corporation' the reasons will mutatis mutandis apply to the school. Therefore, also the High Court was in error in holding that the third-respondent school was not amenable to the writ jurisdiction of the High Court."*

With the above findings the order passed by the High Court was quashed and set aside in the case of Manmohan Singh and he was directed to reinstate in service as Headmaster alongwith consequential benefits. In the same manner, in another writ petition filed under Article 32 by the drawing teacher Amar Singh was also given reinstatement in service alongwith other benefits. The respondent school management was also directed to pay costs to both the employees in each case at Rs..1500.

Unni Krishnan, J.P. v. State of A.P.[94]

In the famous case of *Unni Krishnan, J.P.* v. *State of A.P.* while answering other questions involved regarding the reservation of payment seats in professional colleges, etc., the Supreme Court also clarified that

94. AIR 1993 SC 2178.

private educational institutions are not instrumentality of State merely by reason of its recognition or affiliation with the University.

Justice Mohan observed it in para. 80 of the Judgment after application of the tests given in the case of *Ajay Hasia* v. *Khalid Mujib* as under:

> *"80. Applying these tests, (given in Ajay Hasia's case) we find it impossible to hold that a private educational institution either by recognition or affiliation to the University could ever be called an instrumentality of State, Recognition is for the purpose of conforming to the standards laid down by the State. Affiliation is with regard to the syllabi and the course of study. Unless and until they are in accordance with the prescription of the University, degrees would not be conferred. The educational institutions prepare the students for the examination conducted by the University. Therefore, they are obliged to follow the syllabi and the course of the study."*

It is necessary to make it clear at this stage that the private educational institutions, though not instrumentality or agency of the state, are amenable to writ jurisdiction under Article 226 of the Constitution of India before High Court, as the duties discharged by such educational institutions are of public nature.

Ganapathi National Middle School v. M. Durai Kannan[95]

In the case of *Ganapathi National Middle School* v. *M. Durai Kannan,* it has been observed by the Supreme Court that the educational institution receiving aid is an instrumentality or education agency of the State imparting education on behalf of the State, which is a fundamental right of the citizens. It is not in dispute in the present case as observed by the Supreme Court that the entire expenditure for the acquisition is being met from the public funds. Under those circumstances, it is clearly a case of public purpose. Hence, a writ petition is maintainable against educational institution.

From the above cases it can be understood that the law regarding issuance of writ against educational institutes is very well settled more particularly, after the judgment of Ajay Hasia's case. The educational institutions which come within any of the tests prescribed in the above mentioned case are covered under the ambit of "State" as defined in Article 12.

Action Group Res. in Environment and Educational Development Society v. Sakky Bai[96]

As per the facts of this case the school building was sold to the appellant and therefore, the school running in the premises was required

95. AIR 1996 SC 1316.
96. (1998) 9 SCC 685.

to be shifted from one place to another. The Manager of the School delivered the possession of the school to the appellant without obtaining permission of the competent authority which was required under the Rules. Hence, the delivery of the possession of the school building to the appellant was in contravention of the Rules.

The respondent herein, belonged to the same locality where the school was running. She preferred writ petition under Article 226 of the Constitution of India before the High Court seeking *mandamus* to the appropriate authority to see that the school must run in the building in question until shifting made in accordance with law. It was held by the High Court that the petitioner had a right to seek for the *mandamus*.

The appellant preferred appeal challenging the decision of the High Court before the Supreme Court. The Supreme Court partly accepted the judgment of the High Court by observing that the High Court was justified in issuing direction that the school shall continue to run in the disputed premises until shifting made in accordance with law. But at the same time, the Supreme Court also observed that it was not just and fair on the part of the High Court in deciding the question of title and legality of the sale deeds by which the building was sold. It was apparently a disputed question of fact and also it was not necessary for the High Court to decide the same. The Supreme Court also held that the directions given by the High Court to the State Government to hold an enquiry under Section 60 of the A.P. Education Act, 1982 was not necessary. With this observation the appeal was disposed of. Hence, the Supreme Court pointed out here that the necessary, relevant and appropriate directions can be given in a writ of *mandamus* by the High Court.

Managing Committee, Sri Lakshmi N.A. College v. Prem Chand (case referred to a larger Bench of the Supreme Court)[97]

The question arose in the above case was regarding the status of the appellant college as to whether it was covered within the definition of "State" under Article 12 of the Constitution or not. The reference of the case of *Unni Krishnan J.P.* v. *State of A.P.* was made. But the Bench of the Supreme Court found the contents of paragraph 76 read with paragraph 77 of Unni Krishnan's judgment ambiguous. Therefore, the matter was referred to a larger bench of three judges in order to decide the question that the College is covered within the definition of "State" under Article 12 of the Constitution or not.

4.6 *MANDAMUS* AGAINST JUDICIARY

As per English Law

***Mandamus* against lower Courts**

Writ of *mandamus* was permissible in England since long against the lower judiciary. This fact can be confirmed from the Halsbury's Laws of

97. (1999) 9 SCC 262.

England in different paragraphs covering lower courts having different jurisdiction in England. All the relevant paragraphs are mentioned here under:

1288. *Mandamus* against County Courts

> *"The writ formerly issued to a county court judge to hear and determine, but now an order in the nature of a mandamus will issue in matters which come within his ordinary jurisdiction. Where, however the matter is one which is not within the ordinary jurisdiction of a county court judge but is specially referred to him by a particular statute, a writ of mandamus, and not an order in the nature of a mandamus, is still the appropriate remedy."*[98]

Thus, the writ of *mandamus,* and in certain cases instead of that order of *mandamus* was issued in England against the County Courts.

1289. *Mandamus* against the courts of Quarter Sessions

> *"The writ (of mandamus) will lie to courts of quarter sessions to hear and determine an appeal in which they have declined jurisdiction. They will be considered to have declined jurisdiction when they have wrongly allowed a preliminary objection on a point of law or practice and consequently refused to hear the case upon the merits as when they have acted upon a supposed rule which is no rule, or under the mistaken belief that there was no jurisdiction, erroneously thinking, for example, that they were precluded from deciding what were the "next practicable sessions"; also when, having heard one side, they have refused to hear the other.*
>
> *Although courts of quarter sessions have discretion to make rules governing their practice, the High Court will interfere to control that discretion, and will issue a mandamus to hear an appeal which has been dismissed for non-compliance with a rule laid down by justices, when justice demands it; or where a rule of sessions is not in accordance with statutory provisions, or is ultra vires.*
>
> *Where sessions have made a false entry in their records, as where it is an entry which they had no power to make, mandamus will lie to compel its erasure.*
>
> *Where a court of quarter sessions refuses to state a case on a point of law, the applicant may apply for a rule calling on the court of quarter sessions and the other party to the proceedings to show cause why a case should not be stated."*[99]

---

98. Halsbury's Laws of England, 2nd Edition, Hailsham's Edition, Vol. 9, Para. 1288.
99. Halsbury's Laws of England, 2nd Edition, Hailsham's Edition, Vol. 9, Para. 1289.

1290. *Mandamus* against Magistrates

"Similarly a mandamus will lie to magistrates who decline to adjudicate in matters within their province. They will be considered to have declined jurisdiction when they have dismissed an information on a point relating to their jurisdiction only, such as that it was necessary to bring all joint-owners before them instead of simply the one against whom the information had been laid also when they have refused to issue summons in consequence of having acted upon considerations which were extraneous and extra-judicial and which they ought not to have taken into account also when they have rejected evidence which was tendered to them, which rejection amounted to a refusal to enter upon an inquiry imposed upon them by status and when they have refused to withdraw a warrant for the arrest of a person by whom, on the admitted fact, no criminal offence has been committed. There is now an alternative remedy by way of a statutory order in the nature of a mandamus which may be directed to justices in respect of the duties of their office."[100]

1294. *Mandamus* against Superior Courts

"The writ of mandamus will not issue to any of the superior courts. Accordingly, no mandamus will go to the House of Lords, the Court of Appeal, or any of the Divisions which make up the High Court of Justice. A Court of Assize is a superior court; and also the Central Criminal Court, whether its jurisdiction is exercised by Her Majesty's judges or the Recorder and Commissioners as justices of sessions and these also, accordingly, are Courts to which the writ will not go.

Apparently, also, the Court will refuse to issue a writ of mandamus to the Privy Council, except, it would seem, when it is sitting as a court of appeal in ecclesiastical matters."[101]

By summarizing all the above paragraphs of the Halsbury's Laws of England it can very well be understood that in England, writ of *mandamus* can be issued against an inferior court, civil or criminal on the following grounds:

(a) that it has declined jurisdiction case of *R. v. Devon, JJ.*[102]

(b) *R. v. Kesteven, JJ.*[103] in the event of refusing to hear the case on merits and wholly allowing preliminary objections.

---

100. Halsbury's Laws of England, 2nd Edition, Hailsham's Edition, Vol. 9, Para. 1290.
101. Halsbury's Laws of England, 2nd Edition, Hailsham's Edition, Vol. 9, Para. 1294.
102. (1924)1 KB 503.
103. (1844) Q.B. 810.

(c) *R. v. Norflok*[104] failing to dispose of a case according to the law of procedure.
(d) *R. v. Norflok,* Quarter Sessions.[105]

Quashing an indictment on the erroneous finding that an incompetent witness had been called before the committing magistrate.

Queen v. The Judges and Justices of the Central Criminal Court[106]

However, *mandamus* cannot be issued upon the Superior Courts. This fact can be supported from the case of *Queen* v. *The Judges and Justices of the Central Criminal Court.*

In the above case, the Recorder of London, upon the trial and conviction of a prisoner charged with larceny, having refused to order the person with whom the stolen property was pledged to restore it to the prosecutor. The prosecutor preferred *mandamus* commanding the Central Criminal Court to pass the order to restore the stolen property to him. The Queen's Bench refused to grant a *mandamus* directed to the Judges and Justices of the Central Criminal Court to compel the Recorder to make such order. The ratio laid down from this case is that *mandamus* cannot be issued to the superior court directing it to pass any judgment in a particular manner.

***Mandamus* against Inferior Courts**

Writ of *mandamus* against lower courts is maintainable subject to certain condition, i.e. if the lower court exceeds its jurisdiction while deciding the case or commits grave error, apparent on the face of it or acts contrary to the principles of Natural Justice, writ of *mandamus* is the appropriate remedy to command and/or direct the lower courts.

In the case of *Rex* v. *Marshland Smith and Fen District Commissioners* the Court of Kings Bench (per Mc Cardie, J.) has discussed the circumstances in which writ of *mandamus* can be issued against the lower courts and observed as follows:

> *"If for example, a jurisdiction be given to an inferior Court all that that Court can be called upon by the High Court to do, save in special circumstances, is to hear and determine the matters brought before it in a regular and proper manner. Hence, a mandamus is granted if jurisdiction has been declined by the inferior Court, to hear and determine only. If the inferior Court has a discretion as to the decision it may give, then if that discretion be exercised bonafide and not arbitrarily or illegally and without reference to extraneous considerations the Court will not control the exercise of that discretion."*

104. (1950) 2 K.B. 558.
105. (1953) 2 All E.R. 346.
106. (1883) Q.B. 479.

Will v. United States[107]

Another underlining principle given regarding the issuance of *mandamus* against the lower Court in the case of *Will* v. *United States* is also on the same line. By putting faith in the lower judiciary, it is observed,

> *"Mandamus is not for controlling the decision of a lower Court, but rather merely to confine the lower Court to the sphere of its discretionary power."*

Position in India after the commencement of the Constitution

4.6.1 *Mandamus* against Lower Judiciary

Budhan Choudhary v. State of Bihar[108]

The inclusive definition of "State" in Article 12 includes the Judiciary under the Constitution of India includes the Judiciary.

But, after the above mentioned judgment, again there was a different view taken by the Supreme Court regarding issuance of writ of *mandamus* against lower judiciary by making observation to the effect that a judicial order could not possibly violate fundamental right.

Ujjam Bai v. State of U.P.[109]

Writ of *mandamus* cannot be issued under Article 32 against judiciary on the ground that a judicial order violated a fundamental right. The petitioner filed writ petition under Article 32 against the assessment order of the Assistant Collector of Customs, who assessed the goods imported under a licence under a different entry and consequently a higher Excise Duty was imposed. The Supreme Court that writ under Article 32 held it as there was no violation of fundamental rights. Moreover, validity of such assessment order can not be challenged by way of a petition under Article 32 of the Constitution. The proper remedy, as observed by the Supreme Court was to file an appeal under the statute or if the error was apparent on the face of the record, then by way of filing a writ of certiorari under Article 226 of the Constitution of India before the High Court. With this observation the Supreme Court rejected the petition.

4.6.2 *Mandamus* against the Decision of the Supreme Court on its Judicial Side

Amirabbas Abbasi Sahebzada Saiyed Muhammed v. State of M.P.[110] (not allowed in this case).

The extract that can be taken from this judgment is that by way of

107. (1967) 19 Law Ed 2d. 305.
108. AIR 1955 SC 191.
109. AIR 1962 SC 1621.
110. AIR 1960 SC 768.

filing writ petition under Article 32 of the Constitution of India relief can be obtained provided there is a violation of fundamental rights. Moreover, the writ of *mandamus* is not maintainable against the order of the Supreme Court itself in a special leave to appeal under Article 136 of the Constitution of India.

The petitioner in this case approached the Supreme Court for seeking relief regarding his alleged right of the petitioner to guardianship of his minor children under the Personal Law. But there was no violation of fundamental right under Part III of the Constitution. Moreover, a petitioner preferred appeal before the High Court against the order of the District Court appointing the second respondent as the guardian of the person and property of the minors and the said appeal was dismissed by the High Court. The dispute was under the Guardian and Wards Act. Against the order of dismissal of the High Court, the petitioner preferred appeal under Article 136 of the Constitution before the Supreme Court and the same was rejected too.

The Supreme Court observed that as the appeal under Article 136 was rejected by it, that order cannot be circumvented by resorting to an application for a writ under Article 32. Further, it was also the opinion of the Supreme Court that relief under Article 32 for enforcement of a right conferred by Chapter III can be granted only on proof of that right and infringement thereof, and if, by the adjudication by a court of competent jurisdiction the right claimed has been negatived, a petition to the Supreme Court under Article 32 of the Constitution for enforcement of that right, notwithstanding the adjudication of the civil court, cannot be entertained.

A.R. Antulay v. R.S. Nayak[111]

In the above case an interesting question of law arose was whether a Supreme Court is empowered to correct its own decision in a writ petition filed under Article 32 of the Constitution of India and give further direction by way of writ of *mandamus*. This question was placed before a bench of seven Judges.

As per the facts of the case, section 7(1) of the Criminal Law Amendment Act, 1952 creates a condition, which is must for the trial of offenders under Section 6(1) of that Act. The offences specified under Section 6(1) are those punishable under Sections 161, 162, 163, 164 and 165-A of the Indian Penal Code and Section 5 of the Prevention of Corruption Act, 1947. Therefore, the order of the Supreme Court transferring the cases filed against the Chief Minister of the State who is alleged to have committed the offences under Ss. 161, 165, 384, 420, 164, 165-A of Penal Code and Section 5 of Prevention of Corruption Act to the High Court was not authorised by law especially when the order was clearly per incurium. It was alleged that the Supreme Court, by its direction could not confer jurisdiction on the High Court to try any case when it did not possess such jurisdiction under the scheme of the 1952 Act.

111. AIR 1988 SC 1531.

The directions issued by the Supreme Court were alleged to have been issued by it without observing the principles of *audi alteram partem.* Therefore, singling out of the accused in such case for a speedier trial by the High Court for an offence of which the High Court had no jurisdiction to try under the Act of 1952 was unwarranted, unprecedented and the directions given by the Supreme Court for the said purpose were not warranted. When that fact is brought to the notice of the Supreme Court, the Supreme Court can remedy the situation or not. This was a question put before the seven judges' Constitutional Bench.

Speaking for the majority view Justice Sabyasachi Mukharji was of the opinion that four valuable rights of the appellant are violated by the direction given by the Supreme Court to transfer the case before the High Court viz.,

The right to be tried by a Special Judge in accordance with the procedure established by law and enacted by Parliament.

The right of revision to the High Court under section 9 of the Criminal Law Amendment Act.

The right of first appeal to the High Court under the same section.

The right to move the Supreme Court under Article 136 thereafter by way of a second appeal, if necessary.

It was held that in rectifying the error, no procedural inhibitions should debar the Supreme Court because no person should suffer by reason of any mistake of the Court. Here no rule of *res judicata* could be made applicable to prevent the Supreme Court from entertaining the grievance and giving appropriate directions. The Supreme Court is not powerless to correct its error which has the effect of depriving a citizen of his fundamental rights and more so, the right to life and liberty. The Supreme Court can do so in exercise of its inherent jurisdiction in any proceeding pending before it without insisting on the formalities of a review application. Hence, the Supreme Court recalled the directions contained in the order in question. While doing so, Justice Sabyasachi Mukharji, reminded the duty of the Court by saying in para. 85 of the judgment,

> *"...The basic fundamentals of the administration of justice are simple. No man should suffer because of the mistake of the Court. No man should suffer a wrong by technical procedure of irregularities. Rules of procedures are the hand-maids of justice and not the mistress of the justice. Ex debito justice, we must do justice to him. If a man has been wronged so long as it lies within the human machinery of administration of justice that wrong must be remedied..."*

It is said that no man is above the law, but at the same time no man can be denied his rights under the Constitution and the laws. In the instant case, the Supreme Court in its anxiety to facilitate the parties to have a speedy trial gave directions without conscious awareness of the exclusive jurisdiction of the Special Courts under the 1952 Act and that being only procedure established by law, there can be no deviation from Article 21 of the Constitution. By giving the directions, the Supreme Court had unintentionally caused the accused the denial of rights under Article 14 of the Constitution by denying the equal protection of law by being singled out for a special procedure not provided for by law.

Further it was observed by Sabyasachi Mukharji, J. that the powers of transfer the criminal case before itself are given to the High Court under section 407 of the Criminal Procedure Code, but the said powers did not permit the High Court to withdraw a case for trial to itself from the Court of Special Judge. It was further contended that there was nothing wrong if the Supreme Court corrects its error. By taking support of the Judgment of Privy Council in *Debi* v. *Habib*[112] which said,

> *"...an abuse of the process of the Court may be committed by the Court or by a party. Where a court employed a procedure in doing something which it never intended to do and there is an abuse of the process of the court it can be corrected."*

Justice Sabyasachi Mukharji in paragraph 106 of the judgment quoted a fair statement that,

> *"106. To err is human, is the oft quoted saying. Courts including the apex one are no exception to own up the mistake when judicial satisfaction is reached does not militate against its status or authority. Perhaps it would enhance both."*

The similar view was taken by Justice Rangnath Misra and said for himself and Justice Oza and Justice Ray that once it was found that the direction transferring the case in question from the Court of Special Judge was not proper, the accused should not suffer. Injustice done should be corrected by applying the principle *actus curiae neminem gravabit*—an act of the Court shall prejudice no one.

Regarding the constitution of larger Bench Justice Ranganath Misra expressed his view that it was not necessary in this case. He added that the practice has developed that a larger Bench is entitled to overrule the decision of a smaller Bench nothwithstanding the fact that each of the decisions is that of the Court. That principle, however, would not apply in the instant case and a Bench of Seven Judges is not entitled to reverse the decision of the Constitution Bench. Overruling when made by a larger Bench of an earlier decision of a smaller one is intended to take away the precedent value of the decision without affecting the binding effect of the decision in the particular case. Here the accused could not get advantage of it. It was also observed that formality of review petition under Article 137 was not needed.

---

112. (1913) ILR 35 All 331.

Minority view of Justice Venkatachaliah

According to minority view it would be wholly erroneous to characterize the directions in question issued by the five judges Bench as a nullity, amenable to be ignored or so declared in a collateral attack. The pronouncements of every Division Bench of the Supreme Court are pronouncements of the Court itself. A larger Bench, merely on the strength of its members cannot undo the finality of the decision of other division Benches. If the decision suffers from an error the only way to correct it, is to go in review petition under Article 137 of the Constitution.

He summarized following points:

(1) In directing a Judge of the High Court to try the case the Supreme Court virtually sought to create a new jurisdiction and a new forum not existent in and recognized by law and has accordingly, usurped Legislative powers, violating the basic tenets of the doctrine or separation of powers.
(2) The directions of transfer of cases were violative of Articles 14 and 21 of the Constitution and they are violative of principles of natural justice.
(3) The contention that the transfer of the case to the High Court involves the elimination of the accused's rights.

In support of minority Justice Ranganathan said that there was nothing wrong on the part of the Supreme Court in giving directions to transfer the trial of the case of the petitioner—accused before the High Court. He said that the court can grant relief where there is some manifest illegality or want of jurisdiction in the earlier order or some palpable injustice is shown to have resulted. Such a power can be traced either to Article 142 of the Constitution or to the powers inherent in the Supreme Court as the apex court and the guardian of the Supreme Court.

Justice Ranganathan further, in support of his contention added the statement of Lord Atkin, "Finality is a good thing but justice is better", (AIR 1933 PC 208) and said, considerations of finality are subject to the paramount consideration of justice, but the remedial action must be appropriate and known to law. Courts are as much human institution as any other and share all human susceptibilities to error. But the same should be corrected in a judicial manner. He quoted words of **Justice Jackson** from the case of **Brown v. Allen,**[113]

> *".... Whenever decisions of one Court are reviewed by another, a percentage of them are reversed. That reflects a difference in outlook normally found between personnel comprising different courts. However, reversal by a higher court is not proof that justice thereby better done. There is no doubt*

113. 1944 US 443 at 540.

that if there were a super-Supreme Court, a substantial proportion of our reversals of State Courts would also be reversed. ***We are not final because we are infallible, but we are infallible only because we are final."***

He also added that the Court can grant relief where there is some manifest illegality or want of jurisdiction in the earlier order or some pulpable injustice is shown to have resulted. Such a power can be traced either to Article 142 of the Constitution or to the powers inherent in the Supreme Court as the apex Court and the guardian of the Constitution. It is, however, indisputable that such power has to be exercised in the "rarest of rare" cases. There is great need for judicial discipline of the highest order in exercising such a power, as any laxity in this regard may not only impair the eminence, dignity and integrity of the Court but may also lead to chaotic consequences. Nothing should be done to create an impression that the Supreme Court can be easily persuaded to alter its views on any matter and that a larger Bench of the Court will not only be able to reverse the precedential effect of an earlier ruling but may also inclined to go back on it and render it ineffective in its application and binding nature even in regard to subsequent proceeding in the same case.

Here it appears that though there is substance in the minority view if we strictly concentrate merely upon the procedural aspect as well as precedents. It is correct that the Supreme Court should not change its view frequently so as to create its credibility. But at the same time we should not forget that the Supreme Court is the highest court of the country and its prime function is to protect the violation of fundamental rights of the people. If the directions of the very Supreme Court violate fundamental rights of the appellant violated then the earlier order should be corrected giving justice to him by deviating all the formalities like review and technicalities like powers of the Supreme Court to give directions, scope of Article 142, etc. Thus, majority view appears to be balanced, reasonable, equitable and proper.

Rupa Ashok Hurra v. Ashok Hurra[114]

In the case of *Rupa Ashok Hurra* v. *Ashok Hurra* the question arising out of a reference made to the Constitution Bench of the Supreme Court was: whether an aggrieved person is entitled to any relief against a final judgment/order of the Supreme Court, after dismissal of review petition, either under Article 32 of the Constitution or otherwise.

While answering the question it was held that final judgment/order passed by the Supreme Court under Article 32 of the Constitution cannot be invoked to challenge the validity of a final judgment/order passed by the Supreme Court after exhausting the remedy of review under Article 137 of the Constitution read with Order XL, Rule 1 of the Supreme Court Rules, 1966.

114. (2002) 4 SCC 388.

Speaking for S.P. Bharucha, C.J., himself, Variava and Patil, JJ., Justice Syed Shah Mohammed Quadri went into the history of writs and expressed his opinion. The following can be the summary of his view:

In English law there are two types of writs: (i) Judicial procedural writs like writ of summons, writ of motion, etc., which are issued as a matter of course; these writs are not in vogue in India, and (ii) substantive writs often spoken of as high prerogative writs like writs of *quo warranto, habeas corpus, mandamus, certiorari* and *prohibition*, etc.; they are frequently resorted to in Indian High Courts and the Supreme Court. In the pre-constitutional era the jurisdiction to issue the prerogative writs was enjoyed only by three chartered High Courts in India, viz. High Courts of Bombay, Calcutta and Madras but with the coming into force of the Constitution, all the High Courts and writs under Article 226 and Article 32, respectively. It is a well-settled principle that the technicalities associated with the prerogative writs in English law have no role to play under our constitutional scheme. Both *certiorari* and *prohibition* are employed for the control of inferior courts, tribunals and public authorities.

Therefore, on principle, a writ of *certiorari* can not be issued to coordinate courts and a *fortiori* to superior courts. Thus, a high Court cannot issue a writ to another High Court, nor can one Bench of a High Court issue a writ to a different Bench of the same High Court; much less to the Supreme Court. Though the judgments/orders of High Courts are liable to be corrected by the Supreme Court in its appellate jurisdiction under Articles 132, 133 and 134 as well as under Article 136 of the Constitution, the High Courts are not constituted as inferior courts in the constitutional scheme. Therefore, the Supreme Court would not issue a writ under Article 32 to a High Court. Further, neither a smaller Bench nor a larger Bench of the Supreme Court can issue a writ under Article 32 of the Constitution to any other Bench of the Supreme Court. Moreover, Article 32 can be invoked only for the purpose of enforcing the fundamental rights conferred in Part III and it is a settled position in law that no judicial order passed by any superior court in judicial proceedings can be said to violate any of the fundamental rights enshrined in Part III. Furthermore, the superior courts of justice do not also fall within the ambit of State or other authorities under Article 12 of the Constitution of India.

Concurring Opinion of Banerjee, J.

Justice Banerjee expressed his view that although the right exists to move the Supreme Court for enforcement of the rights conferred in terms of Article 32 and the language used therein is of widest possible amplitude but as regards the issuance of writs against judicial orders of the Supreme Court, the view seems to be rather well settled in the negative.

4.6.3 *Mandamus* against the Supreme Court on its Administrative Side

Prem Chand Garg v. Excise Commissioner[115]

This was a petition filed under Article 32 before the Supreme Court and it raised an interesting and important question about the validity of one of the Rules made by the Supreme Court in exercise of its power under Article 145 of the Constitution. The impugned Rule was Rule 12 in Order XXXV. It provided that the Court might, in the proceedings to which the said order applies, imposed such terms as the costs and as to the giving of security as it deemed fit. The petitioner and another, partners of M/s. Industrial Chemical Corporation, Ghaziabad, filed petition under Article 32 impeaching the validity of the order passed by the Excise Commissioner refusing permission to the distillery to supply power alcohol to the petitioners. This petition was admitted and a Rule was ordered to be issued wherein the Supreme Court directed the petitioners under the impugned rule that the petitioners should deposit a security of Rs. 2,500 in cash within six weeks. Since the year 1959, this rule was treated as a condition precedent for issuing the rule *nisi* to the respondents. The petitioners found it difficult to raise this amount and so on 24th January 1962, they moved the Supreme Court for modification of said order as to security. The petitioner contended in this petition that the impugned Rule, in so far as it relates to the giving of security, it was *ultra vires* because it contravened the fundamental firth guaranteed under Article 32 of the Constitution.

The Solicitor-General, appearing on behalf of the Registrar of the Supreme Court argued that the rule cannot be said to contravene Article 32 because it is a discretionary rule and it vests discretion in this Court either to make an order as to the giving of the security or not to make it, as it may deem fit according to the circumstances of the case. In support of his contention the learned Solicitor-General relied upon the provisions of Article 145(1)(f) and more particularly on the wide power conferred on the Supreme Court under Article 142(1) of the Constitution of India.

But the majority opinion was that such order could not be justified on the ground that the powers conferred upon the Supreme Court under Article 142(1) are wide and could not be controlled by Article 32. Speaking for majority Justice Gajendragadkar said that on a fair construction of Article 142(1) the Supreme Court has no power to circumscribe the fundamental right guaranteed under Article 32. An order which the Court can make under Article 142 in order to do complete justice between the parties, must not only be consistent with the fundamental rights guaranteed by the Constitution, but it cannot even be inconsistent with the substantive provisions of the relevant statutory laws.

It was also held that the rule providing for making of an order for furnishing security in cases of petitions under Article 32, where the Court is satisfied that in case the petition fails, the petitioner may not be able to

115. AIR 1963 SC 996.

pay the costs of the respondent, cannot also be made under Article 145(1)(f). After all, rules framed under Article 145, are in exercise of the delegated power of legislation, and the said power cannot be exercised so as to affect the fundamental rights.

When the Supreme Court, in the exercise of its statutory rule-making powers, makes rules, which contravene the fundamental rights of citizens, the rule could be held *ultra vires* and appropriate remedy under Article 32 or Article 226 can be given. The Supreme Court lastly held that the provisions of Articles 32 and 142 should be read harmoniously and that the Supreme Court has power even in a writ petition filed under Article 32(1) to make all such orders as it deems proper including an order for security for costs of the respondent. The writ petition was allowed with these observations.

4.6.4 *Mandamus* against High Court on its Judicial side

S.K. Verma v. M.P. High Court and another[116]

Can the Supreme Court, by way of writ petition under Article 32 issue writ of *mandamus* against a High Court or a judge of a High Court? The Supreme Court gave its answer in negative in this case. It has very peculiar facts.

In this case a writ petition was filed under Article 32 before the Supreme Court stating that a learned Single Judge of a High Court heard the first appeal on 17-9-1998 and judgment was reversed. Till the year 2000 the judgment was not pronounced. The petitioner mentioned before the Chief Justice of the High Court stating his grievance but nothing happened.

Hence, the petitioner approached the Supreme Court by way of filing a writ petition under Article 32, directing the learned Single Judge of the High Court to pronounce the judgment by way of issuance of writ of *mandamus*. As a settled principle of law, no writ of *mandamus* can be issued against a High Court on its judicial side. Therefore, the Supreme Court dismissed the writ petition with the hope that the learned Single Judge of the High Court should make it convenient to pronounce the judgment within two weeks of the reopening of the vacation.

4.6.5 *Mandamus* against High Court on its Administrative Side

Pradyat Kumar Bose v. Chief Justice of the High Court of Calcutta[117]

A writ of *mandamus* would lie against Chief Justice of the High Court in its administrative capacity. The appellant was a registrar of the High Court of Calcutta. The Chief Justice of the Calcutta High Court decided to initiate a departmental inquiry against the appellant. He appointed another pusni judge of the High Court as an Enquiry Officer. In a departmental

---

116. (2003)10 SCC 243.
117. AIR 1956 SC 285.

enquiry the charges were found to be proved and hence the appellant was dismissed from the service. He filed a writ petition under Article 226 of the Constitution of India against the Chief Justice of Calcutta High Court. The Calcutta High Court did not entertain the petition.

Being aggrieved by the judgment and order of the Calcutta High Court, the appellant preferred appeal before the Supreme Court. The first objection taken by the appellant was regarding the power of the Chief Justice to remove the registrar. The power to appoint and dismiss the employees of the High Court Staff is given to the Chief Justice. Earlier, the Government of India Act, 1935 specifically vested in the Chief Justice the power of appointment and of framing rules regulating conditions of service including the power of dismissal. The Supreme Court also observed that even on the assumption that Civil Services Rules applied between 1930 and 1935 to the High Court Staff their continuance after 1935 makes a change in the dismissing authority and the power of dismissal is vested in the Chief Justice.

Another argument canvassed by the appellant was that even if the Chief Justice had the power to dismiss; he was not, in exercise of that power competent to delegate to another Judge the enquiry into the charges but should have made the enquiry himself. This contention proceeds on a misapprehension of the nature of the power. It is bad in law on the ground of sub-delegation of power.

> *"It was observed by the Supreme Court while replying the objection. It is well recognized that a statutory functionary exercising such a power cannot be said to have delegated his functions merely by deputing a responsible and competent official to enquire and report. This is the ordinary mode of exercise of any administrative power. What cannot be delegated except where the law specifically so provides—is the ultimate responsibility for the exercise of such power."*

The Supreme Court also relied upon the judgment of the House of Lords in the case of *Board of Education* v. *Rice* (1911 AC 179) and justified the delegation of power to conduct enquiry into another judge. It quoted the passage from page 182 of the same judgment which is reproduced here below:

> *".... A functionary who has to decide an administrative matter, of the nature involved in this case, can obtain the material on which he is to act in such manner as may be feasible and convenient, provided only the affected party has a fair opportunity to correct or contradict any relevant and prejudicial material".*

Hence, the Supreme Court held that there was nothing wrong in appointment of another judge as enquiry officer and the Chief Justice acted upon the finding of another Judge.

The Supreme Court while rejecting the case on merits did not think fit to express any opinion regarding maintainability of a writ petition under Article 226 of the Constitution against the dismissal action taken by the Chief Justice of the High Court of Calcutta. But it reveals from the facts of the case that the appeal by the Supreme Court under Article 32 and writ petition by the Calcutta High Court under Article 226 are dismissed on merits and no relief either in the nature of certiorari nor *mandamus* was granted. At the same time the matter was not rejected on technical grounds of maintainability. Therefore, we can come to the conclusion that writ of *mandamus* is maintainable against the Chief Justice of a High Court on its administrative side.

Ranjit Singh v. Union Territory of Chandigarh[118]

The petitioner was an accused earlier convicted for murder and awarded life imprisonment, committed second murder while he was released on parole. On appeal against his conviction to one under section 302, Indian Penal Code and sentenced him to life imprisonment. The Supreme Court was of the view that since the second murder was committed by the accused within a span of one year of his earlier conviction and that too when he was released on parole the second sentence of imprisonment for life awarded to him should not run concurrently with his earlier sentence is granted to him the later sentence should commence thereafter. The direction of the Supreme Court has to be constructed so as to harmonize with Sec. 427(2) of the Cr.P.C. which is the statutory mandate apart from being the obvious truth. The intended consequence was that the accused would not get any practical benefit of any remission or commutation in respect of his earlier sentence, because of the superimposed subsequent life sentence unless the same corresponding benefit in respect of the subsequent sentence is also granted to the accused. It was in this manner that direction was given for two sentences of life imprisonment not to run concurrently.

The Supreme Court at this juncture observed that it was not a proper remedy to file writ petition under Article 32 of the Constitution in order to challenge a judicial order and observed in paragraph 5:

> *"5. We may straightway mention that the question of grant of relief under Article 32 of the Constitution does not arise on the above facts. The petitioner's incarceration is the result of a valid judicial order and, therefore, there can be no valid claim to the infringement of any fundamental right, which alone can be the foundation for a writ under Article 32 of the Constitution. The only question, it appears, therefore, is about the correct construction of the direction given by this Court in its judgment dated 30-9-1983 in Criminal Appeal No. 418 of 1982."*

118. AIR 1991 SC 2296.

Lastly, the Supreme Court observed that the petition filed for the issuance of writ of *mandamus* under Article 32 of the Constitution is not tenable. If the Supreme Court passes any order entertaining the present writ petition, it would be an order against the order passed by the Supreme Court itself in a writ petition. Hence, the present petition was treated as clarification of the earlier petition filed by the petitioner.

State of Bihar v. Bal Mukund Sah[119]

Recently, in the above case the Supreme Court observed while deciding other important issue that the High Court acting on its administrative side is subject to writ jurisdiction under Article 226 of he Constitution of India. The question arose here was regarding the recruitment of the District Judges and other Judicial Officers, wherein the State Legislature passed an act by which reservation of 50% vacancies in direct recruitment to Subordinate Judiciary was made. The Supreme Court, by majority declared such clause of the Act providing reservation of 50% of vacancies was *ultra vires* Articles 233 and 234 of the Constitution. The State Legislature, totally bypassed the High Court in the matter of recruitment of District Judges and Judicial officers.

While deciding the issue Majmudar, J. in paragraph 52 (at page 704) in the judgment observed,

> "52...... *The effort made by the learned counsel for the appellant State to show that Judicial Service also represents a part of State service and it is a "State" within the meaning of Article 12 amenable to writ jurisdiction under Article 226 so far as the administrative decisions taken by the courts are concerned also cannot solve the problem which is posed for our consideration. The High Court may be an "authority" within the meaning of Article 12, its administrative decisions may be subject to its writ jurisdiction on the judicial side but that does not mean that for recruiting judicial officers for manning the Judicial Services, the say of the High Court can be totally bypassed by enacting provisions like the impugned Act by the State Legislature which, while enacting this statute, was not expected to consult anyone else including the High Court.*"

In these circumstances, the Supreme Court indirectly laid down the ratio that the writ petition under Article 226 of the Constitution of India is maintainable before the High Court against the administrative decision of the High Court itself.

Himansu Kumar Bose v. Jyoti Prakash[120]

Where a judge of a High Court contends that he has not reached the age of superannuation notwithstanding a decision by the Union

---

119. (2000) 4 SCC 640.
120. AIR 1964 SC 1636.

Government to the contrary, communicated to him, and the Chief Justice of the High Court does not allot work to such judge, a rule *nisi* for a *mandamus* should issue, even if there are disputed questions of fact to investigate.

Naresh S. Mirajkar v. State of Maharashtra[121]

The facts of this case are very interesting. The court, by an order directed one of the petitioner, who happened to be reporter, not to publish certain judicial proceedings in the newspaper named 'Blitz'. The petitioner being aggrieved by the order passed by the learned judge moved the Bombay High Court by way of filing writ petition under Article 226 of the Constitution of India by alleging therein that his fundamental right under Article 19(1)(a) was violated by the order of a Judge and was not falling anywhere within the reasonable restrictions defined in Article 19(2) to (6). But the division Bench of the Bombay High Court rejected the writ petition on the ground that the impugned order was a judicial order of the High Court and was not amenable to a writ jurisdiction under Article 226.

The petitioner being aggrieved by the order of the High Court preferred writ petition under Article 32 of the Constitution of India. Nine Judges' constitutional bench was formed to decide the issue as to whether writ can be issued against a judge of a High Court against his judicial order or not.

The Supreme Court, by majority rejected the writ petition by making observation that writ is not maintainable against the judicial order of a judge of a High Court.

Even if a court is 'the State', the Supreme Court has in the above case held that a writ under Article 32 cannot be issued to a High Court of competent jurisdiction against its judicial orders, because no violation of the fundamental rights can be attributed to such orders. In this case Gajendragadkar, C.J. observed,

> *"It is singularly inappropriate to assume, that a judicial decision pronounced by a Judge of competent jurisdiction in or in relation to a matter brought before him for adjudication can affect the fundamental rights of the citizens under Article 19(1). What the judicial decision purports to do is to decide the controversy between the parties brought before the court and nothing more."*

Also minority opinion of Justice Hidayatullah requires consideration. The propositions so far asserted in these subsequent cases are—

(a) A judicial decision or order which violates a fundamental right is void, even though it will be binding on the parties so long as it is not set aside in appropriate proceedings.

---

121. AIR 1967 SC 1.

(b) Though the remedy under Article 32 is not available where the offending Court is the Supreme Court itself, the Court in the exercise of its inherent jurisdiction (para. 105 of Antulay's case) would review and set aside a previous direction given by the Court which offended against a fundamental right, e.g., natural justice, an ingredient of Art. 14 or 21. (para. 60-61, 77, 80-82 of Antulay's case).

Justice Hidayatullah were of the opinion that the principle of not issuing writs against the superior courts is not applicable in our country as a whole. Unlike in England, our country is not having Crown or Queen. Hence, Supreme Court can issue writs against High Courts in the event of violation of fundamental rights. He observed in paragraph 108 of the judgment,

> *"Article 32 makes no exception in favour of the High Court. It refers to the writs of certiorari and prohibition which lie only in respect of judicial acts and although they lie also to bodies and persons who are not courts stricto sensu, they always lie to Courts. As these writs are mentioned in Article 32 and there is no exception in respect of the High Courts we start with a presumption that the High Court may not be excluded. The writ of mandamus may also be issued to Courts and that does not detract from the presumption..."*

As a matter of fact, the issue involved in this case was as to whether the Supreme Court can issue writ of *certiorari* against the judgment and order of the High Court or not. But, Justice Hidayatullah, while delivering his dissenting opinion discussed the situation regarding issuance of writ of *mandamus* as well. In paras. 112 and 113 he observed as follows:

> *112. " Mandamus lies for the enforcement of legal rights when there is no other specific remedy or the other available remedy is not so effective. If often issues to a court to hear and determine a matter pending before it. Such a writ issued also from the Chancery when judgments were delayed, but returnable to the Queen's Bench."*
>
> *113. "As Halsbury tersely puts it (Halsbury's Laws of England, Vol. XI, page 53, para. 109) the three writs of mandamus, prohibition and certiorari are used as a means of controlling inferior courts and those who have legal authority to determine the questions affecting the rights of subjects and having to act judicially. By these three writs inferior courts were compelled to do ample and speedy justice and were kept within their jurisdiction."*

Further he tried to demonstrate that the restriction of issuance of writ by the higher court to the lower court in England was justified as the writ could not be issued to the Queen by a court in which Queen herself was present as the Queen cannot issue writ against herself. But there is no such provision in our Country. The Constitution of India provides for the issuance of writ against the lower courts by the High Court and the Supreme Court. But no satisfactory explanation is possible as to why the Supreme Court should not issue writ to a High Court in the event of violation of fundamental right by it. In para. 118 of his judgment, Hidayatullah, J. tried to throw highlight upon the point that the powers of issuance of writs of the Supreme Court and that of a High Court are not similar. He observed,

> *118. "Although the amendment of Art. 32 has been held to be a less difficult process than the amendment of Art. 226, the guarantee in Art. 32(1) seems to be real till it is repealed or annulled. The provisions of Art. 226 themselves indicate this Article 226 begins by saying, "Notwithstanding anything in Article 32", which shows that the whole of the power must otherwise be with the Court. It indicates an intention to carve out an area for local action by the High Court. This might have made the exercise of the power by the High Court equal to its exercise by this Court but for the existence of Cl.(2) which says that the power conferred on the High Court is not in derogation of the powers conferred on the Supreme Court. The word 'derogation' must receive its full meaning. It shows that the entirety of the powers possessed by this Court is still intact in spite of the High Court's ability to exercise similar powers in local areas within their jurisdiction. If the powers were co-ordinate why include clause (2) in Art. 226?"*

By strongly favouring the issuance of writs by the Supreme Court to a High Court Justice Hidayatullah made it clear that there should not be any hesitation for issuing such writs on the part of the Supreme Court. At the same time he clarified also that he was not doubting nor underestimating the capacity and strength of the High Court in issuing writs. He again said in para. 121 that,

> *121. "We need not be dismayed that the view I take means a slur on the High Courts or that this Court will be flooded with petitions under Art. 32 of the Constitution. Although the High Courts possess a power to interfere by way of high prerogative writs of certiorari, mandamus and prohibition, such powers have not been invoked against the normal and routine work of subordinate courts and tribunals. The reason is that people understand the difference between an approach to the High Court by way of appeals, etc. and an approach for the purpose of asking for writs under Art. 226....."*

By taking into consideration the example of the Courts of USA, he took strong view that the writs should be issued against a judge of a High Court if a fundamental right is violated by an order of the High Court. In the last line of Para. 122 he observed,

"….. I thinks we should not hesitate to extend our protection to the fundamental rights in our country even if they be breached by the High Courts."

Lastly, in a concluding paragraph he by allowing the writ petition found the case to be fit and appropriate wherein a writ could be issued against a High Court Judge as there was violation of freedom of speech and expression in Art. 19(1)(a) of the Constitution.

The above mentioned observations of Justice Hidayatullah formed minority opinion and hence the Supreme Court did not issue the writ against the High Court. But the opinion of Justice Hidayatullah contains much truth in it. In India, we need not and cannot blindly follow all the principles of British judiciary system. We have to mould, interpret and apply the principles of law according to our need and requirement.

R.J. Mehta v. C.J., Venkata Shrinivas Deshpande[122]

Held, no writ of *mandamus* can be issued against the Chief Justice of a High Court in the matter of assigning cases to the puisne judges.

Avedhesh Maharshi v. State[123]

No writs could be issued against judiciary as the Judicial order cannot violate fundamental rights.

Konkan Railway Corporation Ltd. v. Mehul Construction Co.[124]

In this case the important questions raised before the Supreme Court were:

(i) What is the nature of the order that is passed by the Chief Justice or his nominee in exercise of power under section 11(6) of the Arbitration and Conciliation Act, 1996?
(ii) Even if the said order is held to be administrative in nature, what is the remedy open to the person concerned if his request for appointment of an arbitrator is turned down by the learned Chief Justice or his nominee for some reason or other?

In this case the Chief Justice of a High Court had entered contentious issues and after elaborate consideration it was found that there was no valid arbitration agreement. It was held that the order refusing the appointment of arbitrator could not therefore be subjected to judicial review.

It was held by the Supreme Court that the order of refusal of the Chief Justice of a High Court to appoint arbitrator cannot be challenged under Article 32 of the Constitution of India before the Supreme Court as

122. AIR 1982 Bom. 125, para. 8.
123. AIR 1991 All. 52.
124. AIR 2000 SC 2821.

both the Courts are having concurrent powers. At the same time, such order of the Chief Justice refusing to appoint arbitrator cannot be challenged by way of filing Special Leave Petition before the Supreme Court under Article 136 of the Constitution. It was held that this order refusing to appoint an arbitrator after going into and deciding contentious issues would be an act of non-performance of duty and so the authority which made the order could be directed by a writ of *mandamus* to perform its duty by the High Court itself.

4.6.6 *Mandamus* against Military Courts

In England writ of *mandamus* could not be issued against a decision taken by Army Court or any other judicial authority constituted under the Army Act, 1881.

Rex v. Army Council[125]

In the above case a writ of *mandamus* was sought against the order of the Army Council. An army Officer named Mr. Ravenscroft, whose conduct was brought before a court of inquiry by the order of a general officer in command, complained that the above regulations had not been complied with, and that as the result of evidence given before the court he had been ordered by the Army Council to revert to half-pay. He applied to the Army Council, who refused to reopen the matter. He then obtained rule nisi for a *mandamus* to the Army Council commanding them to cause the court of inquiry to reassemble to hear and determine his case according to law.

It was held that the rule must be discharged and writ of *mandamus* could not be issued against the Army Council. The first strong and convincing reason given by the Court of the King's Bench was that the Court would not intervene in matters relating to military law prescribing rules for the guidance of officers. At the same time other technical reason given by the Court for not interfering with the case by *mandamus* was the presence of another and an equally appropriate remedy, i.e. under section 42 of the Army Act. Further it was observed that the power of the Army Council to assemble a court of Inquiry was a discretionary power, and the Court would not order the authority to exercise discretion in a particular way.

The writ of *mandamus* was not entertained by making the above observations by the Court of King's Bench.

Rex v. Army Council[126]

In this case as well the Court of King's Bench that no writ of *mandamus* could be issued against the Army Council laid down the same ratio. As per the facts of the case, a petition to the Army Council was filed

125. (1917) 2 K.B. 504.
126. (1940) 1 K.B. 719.

to mitigate, remit or commute a sentence of a court martial. This was a criminal cause or matter within the meaning of Sec. 31, Sub-sec. 1(a) of the Supreme Court of Judicature (Consolidation) Act, 1925, and a motion to the Divisional Court to issue a *mandamus* to the Council to perform that duty was filed but the same was not entertained as being a criminal cause or matter. Being aggrieved by the decision of the Divisional Court, an appeal was preferred before the Court of King's Bench. The Court of King's Bench also expressed the same view that appeal against the refusal of that motion was also a criminal cause or matter, and the Court had no jurisdiction to deal with it.

While rejecting the appeal the following observations were made by Goddard, L.J.:

> *"Here we have a charge of felony preferred against the appellant, and that charge was preferred before a court martial, which was a judicial tribunal having jurisdiction to impose punishment. The court martial having convicted and sentenced the appellant, the case came, under Sec. 57 of the Army Act, before the confirming authority, who confirmed it. That sentence having been confirmed, the Army Act, in Sec. 57, Sub-sec. 2, as amended by the Army (Annual) Act, 1909, confers a power on the Army Council to mitigate, or remit, or commute the sentence. When the matter was brought before the Army Council in the manner provided by the King's Resolutions, which for this purpose are analogous to Rules of Court, the Army Council had to consider whether they would mitigate, remit, or commute the sentence, and they came to a decision on that matter. I cannot see, in those circumstances, why the Army Council were not acting just as much as a court as the original court martial. They were both performing duties imposed on them by the Army Act. I think that they were acting as a court, and consequently, that their decision was in a criminal cause or matter within the authorities, so that this Court has no jurisdiction to entertain this appeal, which should be dismissed, with costs."*

In these circumstances the King's Bench did not entertain the appeal and the decision of the Divisional Court of not issuing writ of *mandamus* against the Army Council was confirmed.

Position in India

The same precedent has been followed in India as well regarding the issuance of *mandamus* against the Military Courts. The High Court or Supreme Court generally reluctant to issue writs against the Military Courts.

Ranvir Kumar Sinha, Commander v. Union of India[127]

It is observed by the Bombay High Court in paragraph 9 of the above

127. (1991) Cr. LJ. 1729 Bom.

judgment that *mandamus* can be issued against Court-martials when they exceed their jurisdiction or they commit error of law. But no writ of *mandamus* can be filed on the issues of military disciplines or propriety of its jurisdiction.

Summary

It is well established and clear position in law that lower judiciary is included within the meaning "other authority" and hence "State" under Article 12 of the Constitution and writ against it is maintainable. Writ of *mandamus* is maintainable against the Supreme Court and a High Court on its administrative side but it cannot be issued on the judicial sides of aforesaid court as it is presumed that judicial orders cannot violate fundamental rights of anyone. Majority laid down this ratio in Naresh Mirajkar's case. Subsequently, in the case of *A.R. Antulay* v. *Ram Nayak* the Supreme Court itself observed that the Supreme Court can issue writ even against itself, if the order of the Supreme Court violates fundamental rights.

The view of famous constitutionalist **Shri H.M. Seervai** is different from the aforesaid established law points. He said that writ of *mandamus* should be issued against the judicial order of a High Court or the Supreme Court if such order violates fundamental right of a person. There is no sense in believing that judicial order cannot violate fundamental right. Shri Seervai supported strongly the minority view of Justice Hidaytullah that the writ lies from the Supreme Court under Article 32 against a High Court. He observed,

> *7.116. It is submitted that the dissenting judgment of Hidayatullah, J. is correct on all three questions raised in the petitions. It is to be hoped that the large number of obiter dicta in Mirajkar's case will hereafter be treated as such by the Sup. Ct. and rejected, or will be buried by being "strictly confined to the facts of that case."*[128]

Another established principle, which can be summarized here is that writ of *mandamus* is maintainable against a High Court or the Supreme Court or a Judge/Chief Justice thereof on its administrative side. The interference of the Court by issuance of *mandamus* in the cases of court-martial are very rare and exceptional.

4.7 *MANDAMUS* AGAINST QUASI-JUDICIAL AUTHORITIES—TRIBUNALS

As per Halsbury's Laws of England

As stated by Lord Halsbury regarding issuance of writ of *mandamus* against quasi-judicial authorities, i.e. Tribunals,

128. Constitutional Law of India, para. 7.116, Vol. 1, 4th Edition by H.M. Seervai.

'In cases where application is made for the issue of a writ of mandamus to tribunals of a judicial character, the writ will only be allowed to go commanding such tribunals to hear and decide a particular matter. No writ will be issued dictating to them in what manner they are to decide. Where, accordingly, a county court judge, or a court of quarter sessions, or magistrates, or the Railway and Canal Commissioners, or election commissioners appointed under the Election Commissioners Act, 1852, to inquire as to corrupt practices at parliamentary elections or income tax commissioners, or any other tribunal of a judicial character have in fact, heard and determined any matter within their jurisdiction, no mandamus will issue for the purpose of reviewing their decision. The rule holds good even though such decision is erroneous, not only as to facts, but also in point of law; and although the particular circumstances of the case are such that there is only one way of performing the duty in question. The Court will only interfere when the tribunal has not properly exercised its jurisdiction and has not heard and determined according to law, because it has taken into account extraneous matters and allowed itself to be influenced by them.'[129]

The writ of *mandamus* will issue to tribunals exercising an inferior jurisdiction, commanding them to sit, hear and adjudicate according to their powers in matters which are judicial in their character, in cases of refusal to exercise jurisdiction.

R. v. Mayor of Monmouthy[130]

But the above mentioned powers of the tribunals are subject to the following limitations:

A *mandamus* goes to set a tribunal in motion but not to prescribe the way in which it shall do any particular act, unless it is quite plain that what it has to do is purely ministerial, and not judicial. In other words, a *mandamus* may be issued to command a tribunal to hear and decide a particular matter, but no direction would be given as to the manner in which it is to decide. Thus, an administrative tribunal may be compelled to hear and determine an appeal, within a reasonable time.

Mandamus will issue against an inferior tribunal where an inferior tribunal has refused to carry out the *intra vires* directions of its superior tribunal. In such a case, the High Court cannot refuse to issue *mandamus* on the ground that no manifest injustice has been done by such refusal or that the order of the superior tribunal was erroneous (because the High Court cannot sit in appeal over the superior tribunal in a proceeding for *mandamus* against the inferior tribunal.)

But when a statute vests a discretionary power in a particular authority, that very authority without interference by some other person or

129. Halsbury's Laws of England, Vol. IX, Paras. 1296, 1300.
130. (1870) QB 251 (256).

authority must exercise the discretion. If there is such interference, there is no proper exercise of discretion by the authority in whom the power has been vested by the Legislature and so the Court would quash his order or act.

R. v. Marsham[131]

Where refusal to receive evidence amounts not merely to improper rejection of evidence but to a refusal to exercise jurisdiction over a distinct branch of the enquiry, a *mandamus* to hear and determine is a proper remedy.

Chief Controlling Revenue Authority and Superintendent of Stamps v. Maharashtra Sugar Mills Ltd.[132]

It was held by the Supreme Court (per Kania, C.J.) held that a writ of *mandamus* for the appropriate direction is maintainable against the Revenue Authority and the Bombay High Court was justified in giving directions to the revenue authority to perform its statutory duty.

In an appeal filed by the appellant against the judgment of the Bombay High Court that the Bombay High Court had jurisdiction to order the Revenue Authority to state a case under Section 57(1), Stamp Act. The petitioner challenged the jurisdiction of the Bombay High Court on two grounds viz. (1) that in the revenue matter, the jurisdiction of the High Court is specifically excluded, and (2) that the matter had ceased to be in the stage of assessment but had reached the stage of collection of stamp duty.

The Supreme Court, while answering both the questions held that the jurisdiction of the High Court is not excluded by Section 226, Government of India Act, 1935. The order of the High Court to a Revenue Authority to do his statutory duty would not be the exercise of original jurisdiction in any matter concerning the revenue. It is only asking the Revenue Authority to perform his statutory duty. The fact that the proceedings in the case had passed beyond the stage of assessment and had reached the stage of enforcing payment is again irrelevant because by the relief when granted by the High Court no attempt is made to obstruct the Revenue Authority in the discharge of his duties.

In this way the Supreme Court confirmed writ of *mandamus* issued by the Bombay High Court against the Revenue Authority under section 226 of the Government of India Act.

Parbhani Transport Co-operative Society v. Regional Transport Authority, Aurangabad and others[133]

The petitioner co-operative society preferred a writ petition under

131. (1892) K.B. 371.
132. AIR 1950 SC 218.
133. AIR 1960 SC 801.

Article 32 of the Constitution against the decision of the Regional Transport Authority, Aurangabad, and others, quasi-judicial authorities for the violation of its fundamental rights enshrined under Article 14 and 19(1)(g) of the Constitution. The petitioner was a co-operative society carrying on business of plying motor buses as stage carriages on the public highways in the State of Bombay. Its grievance was that the petitioner society was deprived of its right to carry on this business and has also been subjected to discriminatory treatment in the matter of the grant of permits to run its buses. It was also the contention of the petitioner society that the State of Bombay, the fourth respondent in the petition, who entered the business was given preference and special treatment as compared to the petitioner by the respondent Nos. 1 to 3. Therefore, a writ under Article 32 was filed seeking relief of *mandamus* and other direction or order against the respondents.

The Supreme Court rejected the argument that the petitioner's right under Article 19(1)(g), i.e. freedom to carry on trade, occupation or business is violated by the respondent Nos. 1 to 3. Further it was held that the State (here the State of Bombay) may carry on any business either as a monopoly, complete or partial, or in competition with any citizen and that would not effect of infringing any fundamental rights of such citizen. In fact the favour to the State of Bombay may fall within the reasonable restrictions under Article 19(6) of the Constitution.

As regards the violation of Article 14 of the Constitution, the Supreme Court said that looking to the circumstances of the case, being a co-operative society, the petitioner was entitled to preference over the Government, considered as an individual owner, and had not been given that preference in granting permits to run stage carriages. While talking regarding discriminatory treatment the Supreme Court said in paragraph 17 of its judgment,

> *'....It was contended that thereby the provisions of Article 14 had been infringed. This contention is in our view clearly untenable. The decision of respondent No. 1 may have been right or wrong and as to that we say nothing, but we are unable to see that that decision offending Article 14 or any other fundamental right of the petitioner. The respondent No. 1 was acting as a quasi-judicial body and if it has made any mistake in its decision there are appropriate remedies available to the petitioner for obtaining relief. It cannot complain breach of Article 14.'*

With this observation the Supreme Court refused to grant relief against the respondents in this case. But here the fact remains crystal clear that the writ of *mandamus* can be demanded against the Regional Transport Authority.

Firm Mehtab Majid and Co. v. State of Madras[134]

The Supreme Court issued writ of *mandamus* in this case against the Deputy Commercial Tax Officer in a petition filed by the petitioner firm under Article 32 of the Constitution. The Deputy Commercial Tax Officer levied Sales Tax not by misconstruing certain provisions of a valid Act, but the same was levied by him even though he had no jurisdiction to assess the tax on account of the invalidity of the rules under which the tax was assessed.

In this petition, apart from the merits of the case, the respondents took preliminary objection regarding maintainability of writ petition under Article 32 of the Constitution. But, the Supreme Court negatived the argument with the observation that the writ might not maintainable if the Deputy Commercial Tax Officer levied tax by mis-construing certain provisions of a valid Act. Here it was not a case. In fact the officer had no jurisdiction to assess the tax. Therefore, the writ of *mandamus* was issued to the State of Madras and the Sales Tax Authorities to refrain from enforcing any of the provisions of Rule 16(2) and direct them to refund the tax illegally collected from the petitioner.

Tukaram G. Gaokar v. R.N. Shukla[135]

In the present case five judges' Bench of the Supreme Court held that writ of *mandamus* can be issued against quasi-judicial authority (in this case against Customs Officer) provided there are allegations of *malafide* against him. The Customs Officer has power to stay the criminal prosecution under the Sea Customs Act, (1878). But Custom Officer refused to stay the criminal prosecution in exercise of his discretion. The petitioner leveled no allegations of malafide against the Customs Officer. It was held that no *mandamus* can be issued against him. While rejecting the writ of *mandamus*, **Bachawat, J.** clarified that writ of *mandamus* can be issued against a quasi-judicial authority exercising its discretionary powers only when an allegations of malafide are made against him. He observed in para. (5) of his judgment,

> *'The customs officers have a discretion to stay the proceedings under Ss. 111 to 112 during the pendency of the trial in the criminal Court. In the exercise of their discretion they have refused to stay the proceedings. It is not shown that their action is mala fide or arbitrary. The Court will not issue a mandamus to control this exercise of their discretion.'*

State of Rajasthan v. Karam Chanda and Brothers.[136]

Where a quasi-judicial authority (Sales Tax Officer as well as the State of Rajasthan) has not been acting according to law in dealing with

134. AIR 1963 SC 928, pp. 932-33.
135. AIR 1968 SC 1050.
136. AIR 1969 SC 343.

a matter entrusted to its jurisdiction, *mandamus* may issue to it to proceed according to law.

In this case a writ of *mandamus* was issued directing the State of Rajasthan not to realize sales tax except with regard to the transactions of sale between the period April 1, 1955 and September 6, 1955 both days inclusive. At the same time the Sales Tax Officer was directed by writ of *mandamus* to make appropriate modifications in the order of assessment in the light of the judgment of the Supreme Court.

Durga Prasad v. Chief Controller, Import and Export[137]

It was observed in the above case by the Supreme Court that before granting *mandamus* to direct a tribunal to exercise its jurisdiction, the Court must be satisfied that

(a) the tribunal has jurisdiction to make the order sought;
(b) the order may be enforced if resisted; and
(c) the exercise of the power is obligatory, not discretionary.

With these observations the Supreme Court dismissed the appeal filed by the appellant confirming the order of summary dismissal of the High Court with the following observations made in paragraph 7,

> '7. *The learned counsel for the appellant contends that this matter involved fundamental rights and this Court at least should not refuse to give relief on the ground of delay. But we are exercising our jurisdiction not under Article 32 but under Article 226, and as observed by Gajendragadkar, C.J., in the passage extracted above, even in the case of alleged breach of fundamental rights the matter must be left to the discretion of the High Court.*'

Municipal Corporation of Greater Bombay v. Advance Builders[138]

That three writ petitions were filed originally before the High Court against the Bombay Municipality, in order to implement a scheme for the improvement of the Corporation. The Municipal Corporation for implementing the Scheme for about three years took no actions. Therefore, by way of filing this petition before the High Court, following prayers were demanded:

(a) to issue a writ of *mandamus* or a writ in the nature of *mandamus* against the appellants directing them to construct the roads and drains as indicated in the Town Planning Scheme and to complete the same for use within such time as may be fixed by the Court, and

---

137. AIR 1970 SC 769.
138. AIR 1972 SC 793.

(b) to issue a writ of *mandamus* or any other appropriate writ directing the appellant to remove all the huts, sheds, stables and temporary structures from the 41 plots referred to above.

It was held by the learned Judge of the High Court that under the Town Planning Act and the Scheme, it was the primary responsibility of the Corporation, which was the local authority, to implement the Scheme and, accordingly, the writs as prayed were substantially granted. In appeal, the Appellate Bench of the High Court confirmed the order of the learned Judge with only minor variations. The Corporation, being aggrieved by the order of the Divisional Bench of the High Court, preferred appeal before the Supreme Court.

The Supreme Court in appeal taken a note of the provisions of sections 53, 54 and 55 of the Bombay Town Planning Act, 1955 made it clear that the Corporation is exclusively entrusted with the duty of framing and implementation of the Planning Scheme and, to that end, has been invested with almost plenary powers. Further, the responsibility for removing the huts, sheds, stables and other temporary structures which contravene the scheme is that of the Corporation and not of the owners of plots. It has been long held that,

> *'where a statute imposes a duty the performance or non-performance of which is not a matter of discretion, a mandamus may be granted ordering that to be done which the statute requires to be done.'*[139]

Regarding the issuance of writ of *mandamus* it was contended by the learned Attorney-General that, after all, a writ of *mandamus* was not a writ of course or a writ of right but it is, as a rule, a matter for the discretion of the Court. But when the High Court has exercised its discretion in directing that which is in itself lawful to be done, no other Court can question that discretion in so directing. Therefore, the Supreme Court in an appeal by special leave, will not ordinary question that discretion.

By making above observations, the Supreme Court dismissed the appeal while confirming the judgment and order of the Bombay High Court.

Tara Chand Khatri v. Municipal Corporation of Delhi[140]

It has been observed by the Supreme Court in the above case that a writ of *mandamus* will lie to compel a statutory tribunal to perform its legal duty. Here in the present case it was a duty of the tribunal to record its reasons or findings on material facts, where the relevant statute required it to do so.

In the instant case a dismissal order was challenged by the petitioner, Assistant Teacher in Corporation School appointed by the

139. Halsbury's Laws of England, Third Edition, Vol. II, p. 90.
140. AIR 1977 SC 567.

Commissioner under Section 97 of the Delhi Municipal Corporation Act. The Deputy Commissioner who passed plenary powers in that behalf by virtue of the delegation order passed the dismissal order. Thus there was neither legal bar to the dismissal order nor a breach of the first proviso to Sec. 95(1) of the Act.

During the course of and while deciding a case the disciplinary authority must state reasons supporting the case. The Supreme Court in the present case reiterated this principle. It was observed,

> *'....while it may be necessary for a disciplinary or administrative authority exercising quasi-judicial functions to state the reasons in support of its order if it differs from the conclusions arrived at and the recommendations made by the enquiring officer in view of the scheme of a particular enactment or the rules made thereunder, it would be laying down the proposition a little too broadly to say that even an order of concurrence must be supported by reasons. It cannot also, in our opinion, be laid down as a general rule that an order is a non-speaking order simply because it is brief and not elaborate* '

Thus it was made specifically clear that if the order passed by the quasi-judicial authority is not reasoned order, the same can be challenged by way of writ of *mandamus*.

Union of India v. Kamalakshi Finance Corporation Ltd.[141]

This case was arisen out of the orders passed by the Assistant Collector, Central Excise in contravention of the orders passed by appellate authorities viz. the Collector and Tribunal.

The respondent company was manufacturing electrical insulation tapes. According to the respondent company the goods manufactured by it fall under tariff heading 89.47 of the schedule to the Central Excise Tariff Act, 1985. But the petitioner believed that the goods fall under heading 39.19 of the same schedule. The Assistant Collector, therefore gave show cause notice why the product should not be classified under heading 39.19. The assessee, in reply, pointed out that, in respect of its factory at Borivili, its claim that the goods were classifiable under heading 85.46 and that heading 39.19 had no application had been accepted by the Collector of Appeals. The Assistant Collector, however, did not accepted the assessee's contention. He distinguished the order in respect of the Borivili plant on the ground that there the assessee's claim was for classification under heading 85.46 and not under 85.47. He held, by his order that the products in question fell under heading 39.19.

In an appeal preferred by the assessee, the Collector (Appeals), who set aside the order of the Assistant Collector. He observed that the reason given by the Asstt. Collector, in his order was totally untenable. He set

141. AIR 1992 SC 711.

aside the order appealed against and directed the Asstt. Collector to pass a reasoned and speaking order.

After remanding the issue, matter again went before the Assistant Collector, who passed the same order reiterating the conclusion that had been reached by his predecessor. He gave no reasons as to why the order of the Collector (Appeals) in respect of the Borivili plant was not followed. Moreover, the assessee, in support of his case put the order passed by the Central Excise and Gold Control Appellate Tribunal before the Assistant Collector. But he distinguished it by observing that the said decision had not been agreed to by the Department which had filed an appeal to the Supreme Court therefrom. The second order passed by the Assistant Collector was merely a repetition of the earlier order.

The assessee preferred a writ petition before the Bombay High Court. The High Court quashed the order of the Assistant Collector and directed the department to allocate the matter to a competent officer to pass a proper order.

The Union of India preferred an appeal before the Supreme Court. The learned Additional Solicitor General, appearing for the Union, fairly conceded that on merits he had nothing to say. He was concerned about the passing of severe strictures against the two Assistant Collectors who had dealt with the matter. He tried to explain that both the authorities had no bias or ill-will against the assessee. But here the Supreme Court took the view that the strictures passed by the High Court against both the Assistant Collectors were justified as they by-passed two appellate orders in regard to the same issue which were placed before them, one of them Collector (Appeals) and other of the Tribunal. The High Court had, in the view of the Supreme Court rightly criticized this conduct of the Assistant Collectors and the harassment to the assessee caused by the failure of these officers to give effect to the orders of the authorities higher to them in the appellate hierarchy.

Further the Supreme Court observed regarding the function of the quasi-judicial authority as under:

> *'....It cannot be too vehemently emphasized that it is of utmost importance that, in disposing of the quasi-judicial issues before them, revenue officers are bound by the decisions of the appellate authorities. The order of the Appellate Collector is binding on the Assistant Collectors working within his jurisdiction and the order of the Tribunal is binding upon Assistant Collectors and the Appellate Collectors working within his jurisdiction of the Tribunal. The principles of judicial discipline require that the orders of the higher appellate authorities should be followed unreservedly by the subordinate authorities. The mere fact that the order of the appellate authority is not "acceptable" to the department—in itself an objectionable phrase—and is the subject matter of an appeal can furnish no ground for not following it unless its operation has been suspended by a competent court. If this healthy rule is not followed, the result will only be undue harassment to assessees and chaos in administration of tax laws.'*

With the above mentioned explanation the Supreme Court did not interfere with the strictures passed by the High Court against the Assistant Collectors. While answering that point it was said,

> *'...It is clear that the observations of the High Court, seemingly vehement, and apparently unpalatable to the Revenue, are only intended to curb a tendency in revenue matters which, if allowed to become widespread, could result in considerable harassment to the assessee-public without any benefit to the Revenue. We would like to say that the department should take these observations in the proper spirit. The observations of the High Court should be kept in mind in future and the utmost regard should be paid by the adjudicating authorities and the appellate authorities to the requirements of judicial discipline and the need for giving erect to the orders of the higher appellate authorities which are binding on them.'*

The Supreme Court upholding the decision as well as the observations made by the High Court regarding the functions of quasi-judicial authorities thus rejected the Special Leave Petition filed by the Union of India.

4.8 *MANDAMUS* AGAINST BANKS

4.8.1 *Mandamus* against Reserve Bank of India

All India Reserve Bank Retired Officers Association and others v. Union of India and Others[142]

In the case of *All India Reserve Bank Retired Officers Association and others* v. *Union of India and Others*, a dispute regarding non inclusion of Bank employees who retired prior to 1-1-1986 in the Introduction of Pension Scheme was challenged on the ground that such cut-off date was arbitrary, artificial and whimsical. The benefit of the Pension Scheme should be given to the employees who retired prior to 1-1-1986 as well. The issue was raised before the division bench consisted of Justice A.M. Ahmadi and Justice M.M. Punchi.

The facts of the case are as under:

In exercise of the powers conferred by Sec. 58(2)(j) of the Reserve Bank of India Act, 1934, the Board of the Reserve Bank of India, with the prior approval of the Central Government framed Regulations known as Reserve Bank of India Pension Regulations, 1990. By the said Regulations brought in force with effect from 1-11-1990, a pension scheme was introduced in substitution of the existing Contributory Provident Fund Scheme (CPF). The newly introduced pension scheme was made applicable to all employees entering Bank Service on or after 1-11-1990; for them the CPF scheme did not exist. The in-service employees, i.e. those employees

142. AIR 1992 SC 767.

who were actually in service at the date of introduction of the scheme were given an option to opt out of the pension scheme and continue to be governed by the CPF Scheme. The third category is of those who retired from Bank's service between 1-1-1986 and 1-11-1990. Regulation 3(3), which deals with the applicability of the scheme to said category of retired employees, which is reproduced as under:

3(3) Employees who were in service as on 1st January 1986 (excluding those on leave preparatory to retirement) and had retired before 1st November, 1990, provided they exercise option to be governed by these Regulations and refund, within such period as may be specified, the Bank's contribution to provident fund including interest received by them from the Bank together with simple interest at six percent per annum from the date of withdrawal till the date of repayment. Pension shall be payable to them in accordance with Regulation 31.

It is necessary to study Regulation 31 along with Regulation 3(3) for understanding the pension scheme. Regulation 31 reads as follows:

31. Employees who have retired from the Bank's service on or before 1st January, 1986 and before 1st November, 1990 shall be eligible for pension from 1st November, 1990 or after expiry of leave preparatory to retirement subject to Regulation 22. The payment of pension shall be subject to their refunding Bank's contribution to provident fund including interest at the rate of six percent per annum from the date of withdrawal till the date of repayment. Such employees will be permitted to continue their pension also with effect from 1st November, 1990, after due medical examination.

Thus, by reading Regulation 3(3) together with Regulation 31 it appears that Bank employees who retired from service between 1st January, 1986 and 1st November, 1990 could opt for the benefit of the pension scheme with effect from 1st November, 1990 provided they refunded the Bank's contribution to the provident fund together with interest at the rate of 6 percent per annum from the date of withdrawal till the date of repayment. Bank employees who retired from service before 1st January, 1986 were not eligible to opt for the new introduced pension scheme.

The petitioner No. 1 was an association of retired Bank employees and other petitioners were also amongst the employees who retired before 31st December, 1985. They were not entitled to opt for pension-plan under the aforesaid Regulations. Therefore, the petitioners contended that the cut-off date fixed under the Regulation 3(3) and 31 extracted earlier was wholly artificial and has no relation to the object sought to be achieved by the introduction of the pension-plan in substitution of the extant CPF Scheme. Though the Pension Scheme was a good step taken by the respondents, the employees who retired on or before 31st December, 1985 were deprived from its benefit.

In order to decide the issue, the Supreme Court had to ascertain the legality of Regulations 3(3) and 31. While justifying the judicial review of the aforesaid regulations the Supreme Court reminded that the respondent,

Reserve Bank of India is "State" under Article 12 of the Constitution and observed,

> '.... *There is no doubt that whenever any rule or regulation having statutory flavour is made by an authority which is a state within Article 12 of the Constitution, the choice of the cut-off date which has necessarily to be introduced to differentiate such benefits is open to scrutiny to the court and must be supported on the touchstone of Article 14....*'

While dealing with the issue of the employees of the Bank who retired prior to 31st December, 1985, the Supreme Court also observed the step of the pension scheme introduced by the respondents by appreciating it as follows:

> '*The concept of pension is now well known and has been clarified by this Court time and again. It is not a charity or bounty nor it is gratuitous payment solely dependent on the whim or sweet will of the employer. It is earned for rendering long service and is often described as deferred portion of compensation for past service. Such social security plans are consistent with the socio-economic requirements of the Constitution when the employer is a State within the meaning of Article 12 of the Constitution.*'

Thus, indirectly the Supreme Court took the view that Reserve Bank of India is "State" under Article 12 of the Constitution.

4.8.2 *Mandamus* against Nationalized Banks

State Bank of Bikaner and Jaipur v. Jag Mohan Lal.[143]

The Supreme Court has impliedly accepted the argument in the above case that the appellant bank, being the nationalized bank is covered within the definition of "State" under Article 12 of the Constitution of India. As per the facts of the case it was the case of the retired employees of the bank that the bank was making discrimination among the retired bank employees for giving extension in service. On the other hand, it was argued by the bank that the sole purpose of giving extension of service is, therefore, to promote the interest of the bank and not to confer any benefit on the retiring officers. Incidentally the extension may benefit retired officers. But it is incorrect to state that it is a conferment of benefit of privilege on officers. The officers upon attaining the age of superannuation or putting the required number of years of service do not earn that benefit or privilege. The High Court has completely misunderstood the nature of right and purpose of the proviso providing for extension of service. The Supreme Court, in the above case reversed the decision of the High Court by observing that there was no discrimination in giving extension to the retired employees in

143. AIR 1989 SC 75.

service of the bank in the interest of bank. The observations made by the Supreme Court in para. 12 of the judgment are relevant for the study and they are reproduced herebelow:

> '12. *It was however, argued for the respondent that the Bank falls within the concept of "State" for the purpose of enforcement of fundamental rights. The Bank, therefore, cannot extend the service of some and reject the case of others similarly situated. The concept of Article 14 of the Constitution is relied upon. The argument in our opinion, proceeds on a wrong premise. The Bank has no obligation to extend the service of all officers even if they are found suitable in every respect. ....*'

Thus, while deciding issue of giving extension in service to the retired bank employees, the Supreme Court has indirectly decided the issue that the nationalized banks are covered within the meaning of "State" under Article 12 of the Constitution of India.

Indian Bank

M/s. Hyderabad Commercials v. Indian Bank[144]

In the case of *M/s. Hyderabad Commercials* v. *Indian Bank* a question involved was regarding unauthorized transfer of huge amount (16 lakhs) by the Bank from one account of customer to another. The Bank earlier accepted liability but thereafter raised the plea that transfer was made on party's oral instructions. The customer filed writ petition before the High Court of Andhra Pradesh. But the High Court dismissed the writ petition on the grounds of disputed questions of facts.

In appeal, the Supreme Court took a view that the Bank is an instrumentality of the State and it must function honestly to serve its customers. Where a nationalized Bank transferred huge amount from the account of one of its customers to another unauthorisedly and agreed to rectify the mistake by recrediting the amount to former customer's account but resiled from complying with the same on plea by way of an afterthought that the amount was transferred on oral instructions of the customer, the Bank which is an instrumentality of the "State" was under a legal obligation to pay back the disputed amount to the customer.

The Supreme Court also said that when liability was admitted by the bank, High Court in exercise of its writ jurisdiction could direct it to recredit the amount to the account of the customer and he could not be directed to file suit on the ground that the case involved disputed questions of facts. Such functioning of a Nationalised Bank is detrimental to public interest and if it follows the practice of transferring money of its customers to some other persons account on oral authority, people will loose faith in the credibility of Bank.

144. AIR 1991 SC 247.

After making such observations, the Supreme Court allowed the appeal by reversing the decision of the Andhra Pradesh High Court.

Bank of India

Bank of India v. O.P. Swarnakar[145]

In the case of *Bank of India* v. *O.P. Swarnakar*, preliminary objection of maintainability of writ petition against Bank of India was taken. The Supreme Court without any hesitation held that the writ against the Bank was maintainable as the Bank of India is the nationalized bank. All the nationalized banks are covered within the meaning of "State" under Article 12 of the Constitution. The case law in above case is very well settled and undisputed and therefore, it is not necessary to discuss in detail in the present case.

4.8.3 *Mandamus* against Co-operative Banks

U.P. State Co-operative Land Development Bank Ltd. v. Chandra Bhan Dubey[146]

A question for consideration before the Supreme Court in this case was whether a Co-operative Bank functioning as Society under the Societies Act and constituted under Bank Act of 1964 was amenable to writ jurisdiction or not. The case was little different from other cases decided under Article 12 discussing the scope of writ of *mandamus* in a sense that the Bank was though constituted under the U.P. State Co-operative Land Development Bank Act, 1964, functioning as a society under the U.P. Co-operative Societies Act, 1965. Therefore the Supreme Court entered into the provisions of the Bank Act as well as the Societies Act and the Rules and Regulations framed thereunder.

Like many other cases on this point, the issue arose when the appellant Bank dismissed three of its employees from the service after the departmental inquiry and the delinquent employees challenged the dismissal order on the ground of non-observance of principle of natural justice and other grounds. The appellant Bank took preliminary objection before the High Court that the Bank was not amenable to writ jurisdiction being not an "authority" or "State" within the meaning of Article 12 of the Constitution. On merit the High Court was of the view that relevant Rules regarding holding of inquiry against the delinquent employees were not followed and that the order of dismissal did not contain any reason. The High Court held that the dismissal orders were vitiated by non-compliance with the rules of natural justice and also in violation of the statutory rules as applicable to the employees. However, permission to initiate afresh inquiry from the stage after the receipt of the replies from the employees to the charge-sheets served upon them was granted.

145. AIR 2003 SC 858.
146. AIR 1999 SC 753.

The appellant Bank challenged the judgment of the High Court before the Supreme Court wherein a preliminary objection taken was that the Bank was not an "authority" or "instrumentality of the State" and no writ could be issued against it. In order to ascertain the status of the appellant Bank the Supreme Court went into the relevant Bank Act as well as the Societies Act under which the Bank was formed.

The situation of the Bank can be effectively understood as follows:

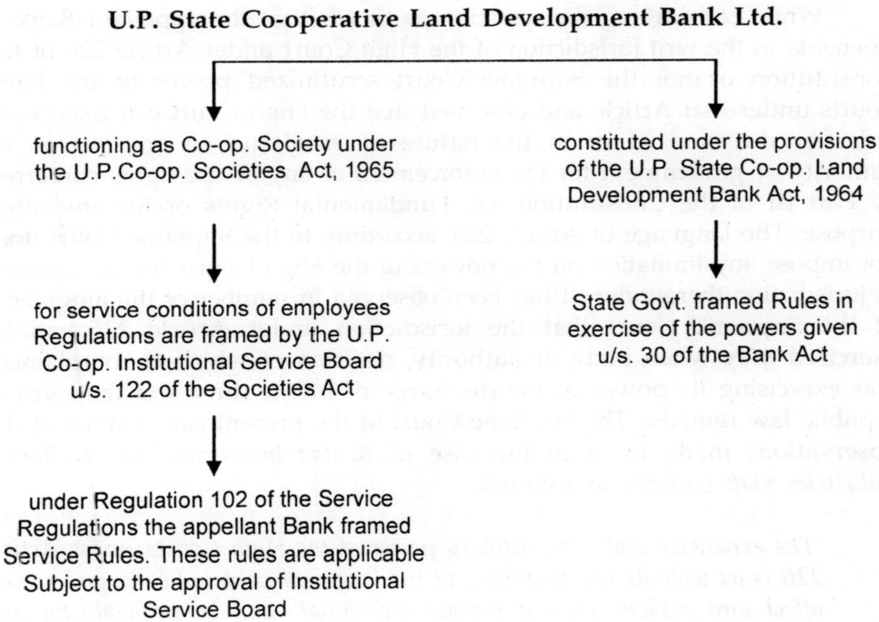

The following points make it crystal clear that the State Government has deep control over the management and other factors:

(1) As per Sec. 3 of the Bank Act, there shall not be more than one State Land Development Bank for the whole of the State of U.P. and that sole Bank is the appellant Bank. It has thus exclusive jurisdiction over the state of U.P. In that sense we can say that it enjoys a monopoly status.

(2) Under Sec. 9 of the Bank Act, the State Government constitutes a Guarantee Fund on such terms and conditions as it deem fit, for the purpose of meeting losses that might arise on account of loan advanced by the Land Development Banks on the security of mortgages not being fully recovered due to such circumstances as may be prescribed. The appellant and the Land Development Banks shall contribute to such fund at such rates as may be prescribed.

(3) Under Rule 6 of the Bank Rules the Guarantee Fund shall be

maintained by the Finance Department of the State Government in the Public Accounts Section the State Accounts.

(4) The Board of Directors of the appellant may from time to time issue debentures of various denominations with the previous sanction of the State Government and the Trustee.

The affairs of the appellant are controlled by the State Government though it functions as a co-operative society.

While considering the question as to whether the appellant Bank is amenable to the writ jurisdiction of the High Court under Article 226 of the Constitution or not the Supreme Court scrutinized power of the High Courts under that Article and observed that the High Court can issue writ, order or direction of or in the nature of *mandamus* to any person or authority or government for the enforcement of any of the rights conferred by Part III of the Constitution, i.e. Fundamental Rights or for any other purpose. The language of Article 226, according to the Supreme Court does not impose any limitation on the powers of the High Courts for the exercise of jurisdiction thereunder. It has been observed in number of the judgments of the Supreme Court that the jurisdiction under Article 226 can be exercised only when body or authority, decision of which is complained, was exercising its power in the discharge of public duty and that writ is a public law remedy. The Supreme Court in the present case reminded the observations made by it in the case of *Rohtas Industries Ltd.* v. *Rohtas Industries Staff Union*[147] as follows:

> *'The expansive and extraordinary power of the High Courts under Article 226 is as wide as the amplitude of the language used indicates and so can affect any person—even a private individual—and be available for any (other) purpose—even one for which another remedy may exist. The amendment to Article 228 in 1963 inserting Article 226(1-A) reiterates the targets of the writ power as inclusive of any person by the expressive reference to "the residence of such person". But it is one thing to affirm the jurisdiction, another to authorise its free exercise like a bull in a china shop. This Court has spelt out wise and clear restraints on the use of this extraordinary remedy and High Courts will not go beyond those wholesome inhibitions except where the monstrosity of the situation or other exceptional circumstances cry for timely judicial interdict or mandate. The mentor of law is justice and a potent drug should be judiciously administered. Speaking in critical retrospect and portentous, prospect, the writ power has, by and large, been the people's sentinel on the qui vive and to cut back on or liquidate that power may cast a peril to human rights. We hold that the award here is not beyond the legal reach of Article 226, although this power must be kept in severely judicious leash.'*

147. AIR 1976 SC 425, p. 429.

The Supreme Court tried to distinguish the powers conferred to itself for issuance of writs under Article 32 and those conferred to the High Courts under Article 226 of the Constitution of India. Quoting number of earlier decided cases as well as the text of Article 226 of the Constitution, the Supreme Court held that the powers of the High Courts for issuing writs are wider than those of the Supreme Court in a sense that High Courts can issue writ, order or directions against any person or authority who is not covered under the definition of "State" as per Article 12 of the Constitution. The Scope and powers of the High Courts are discussed here. While assisting the Supreme Court, learned Attorney General said that it was not necessary for the Supreme Court to enter into any lengthy discussion of the topic nor to rely upon the English cases on the questions of Constitutional Law, Administrative Law and Public Law as the law in India in those branches had traveled ahead of the law in England. Here the Supreme Court reminded the observations made by Justice Subbarao while answering a question as to whether writ of *mandamus* could be issued against the trust, in the case of *Dwarkanath, HUF* v. *I.T.O., Special Circle, Kanpur.*[148]

> *'This article is coached in comprehensive phraseology and it ex facie confers a wide power on the High Courts to reach injustice whenever it is found. The Constitution designedly by used a wide language in describing the nature of the power, the purpose for which and the person or authority against whom it can be exercised. It can issue writs in the nature of prerogative writs as understood in England; but the scope of those writs also is widened by the use of the expression "nature", for the said expression does not equate the writs that can be issued in India with close in England, but only draws an analogy from them. That apart, High Courts can also issue directions, orders or writs other than the prerogative writs. It enables the High Courts to mould the reliefs to meet the peculiar and complicated requirements of this country. Any attempt to equate the scope of the power of the High Court under Article 226 of the Constitution with that of the English Courts to issue prerogative writs is to introduce the unnecessary procedural restrictions grown over the years in a comparatively small country like England with a unitary form of Government into a vast country like India functioning under a federal structure. Such a construction defects the purpose of the article itself.'*

The scope of *mandamus* has also been discussed under the Halsbury's Laws of England regarding its issuance against private person, company or corporations, which says—

> *'It is, however, not necessary that the person or the authority on whom the statutory duty is imposed need be a public official or an official body. A*

148. AIR 1966 SC 81.

mandamus can issue, for instance, to an official of a society to compel him to carry out the terms of the statutes under or by which the society is constituted or governed and also to companies or corporations to carry out duties placed on them by the statutes authorising their undertakings. A mandamus would also lie against a company constituted by a statute for the purpose of fulfiling public responsibilities.'[149]

In support of its view relating to the powers of the High Court of issuance of writ of *mandamus*, the Supreme Court quoted the observations made by it in earlier case of Shri *Anandi Mukta S.M.V.S.S.J.M. Trust* v. *V.R. Rudani*[150]:

'The term "authority" used in Article 226 in the context, must receive a liberal meaning unlike the term in Article 12. Article 12 is relevant only for the purpose of enforcement of fundamental rights under Article 32. Article 226 confers power on the High Court to issue writs for enforcement of fundamental rights as well as non-fundamental rights. The words "any person or authority" used in Article 226 are, therefore, not to be confined only to statutory authorities and instrumentalities of the State. They may cover any other person or body performing public duty. The form of the body concerned is not very much relevant. What is relevant is the nature of the duty imposed on the body. The duty must be judged in the light of positive obligation owned by the person or authority to the affected party. No matter by what means the duty is imposed, if a positive obligation exists mandamus cannot be denied."'

The Supreme Court in the above case tried to expand the scope of issuance of writ of *mandamus* under Article 226 of the Constitution. Writ of *mandamus* can be issued even in the event of violation of constitutional rights other than fundamental rights, statutory rights, common law rights, etc. If the duty imposed upon the body is of public nature, it is sufficient cause for the High Court to issue writ of *mandamus* irrespective of the fact that the respondent is covered under the definition of "State" as per Article 12 of the Constitution or not. Further clarification is made by the apex court that the conditions under Article 12 has nothing to do with the powers of High Court to issue writ of *mandamus*. Supreme Court has lastly added that:

'Here again we may point out that mandamus cannot be denied on the ground that the duty to be enforced is not imposed by the statute. Commenting on the development of this law, Professor De Smith states: "To be enforceable by mandamus a public duty does not necessarily have to be one imposed by statute. It may be sufficient for the duty to have been imposed by charter, common law, custom or even contract." We share this

149. Halsbury's Laws of England, 3rd Edn., Vol. II, p. 52 and onwards.
150. AIR 1989 SC 1607 page 1613.

> *view. The Judicial control over the fast expanding maze of bodies affecting the rights of the people should not be put into watertight compartment. It should remain flexible to meet the requirements of variable circumstances. Mandamus is a very wide remedy, which must be easily available 'to reach injustice wherever it is found'. Technicalities should not come in the way of granting that relief under Article 226. We, therefore, reject the contention urged for the appellants on the maintainability of the writ petition.'*

These observations made by the Supreme Court are very pertinent for the expansion of the scope of the High Court to issue writ of *mandamus*. Here the apex court has specifically observed that the power of the High Court should not be curtailed by taking shelter of technicality. It is clarified by the Supreme Court that though the source of writ jurisdiction is in the British Judiciary System, we should not depend or rely upon the decision or precedent of the British Court as the Indian law has reached far ahead than the law of England. Thus, the ratio laid down by the Supreme Court that the Co-operative Bank, though functioning as Society under the Societies Act is constituted under the Bank Act is "state" under Article 12 of the Constitution. The ratio as well as the observations of the Supreme Court in this judgment regarding issuance of writ by the High Court are very important it has been clarified that for the issuance of writ of *mandamus* by the High Court it is not necessary that the respondent must fall within the definition of "state" under Article 12 of the Constitution. It may be a company, corporation, trust or even a private person discharging work of a public nature are amenable to the writ jurisdiction of the High Court. This is a step ahead from the definition and scope of writ of *mandamus* given under the Halsbury's Laws of England.

4.8.4 *Mandamus* against Regional Rural Banks

M.K. Agarwal v. Gurgaon Gramin Bank[151]

In the case of *M.K. Agarwal* v. *Gurgaon Gramin Bank*, the question involved was with regard to the regularization of an employee. The employee was neither discharged nor confirmed by the Bank. While deciding this issue the Supreme Court had an opportunity to decide as to whether Regional Rural Banks are "other authorities" within the ambit of Article 12 of the Constitution or not.

The bank was constituted under the Regional Rural Banks Act, 1976. There were every reason to designate the aforesaid bank as instrumentality of the "State", as there is direct hold and control of state over the bank activities. The Bank is discharging functions of public importance affecting public at large. Every Regional Rural Banks are working under the supervision and instruction of the Reserve Bank of India.

151. AIR 1988 SC 286.

Regulation (10)(2)(a) of the Gurgaon Gramin Bank (Staff) Services Regulations, 1980 provided exclusive powers of the employer to extend the probation period beyond the prescribed period of 18 months. The Bank neither discharged nor confirmed the employee.

By taking into consideration the constitution and nature of its legal entity and the measure of State control over the Bank, the Supreme Court held that it is an instrumentality of the State and is made of latter's own "flesh and bones" and is, accordingly, "State" within the meaning, and for purposes, of Article 12 of the Constitution. Consequently the Supreme Court declared Regulation (10)(2)(a) as arbitrary and unguided and hence unconstitutional, as it was conferring unlimited powers to the Bank.

From the above referred cases, it can be said that the law regarding issuance of *mandamus* against Nationalised Banks, Reserve Bank of India, Regional Rural Banks, etc. says that *mandamus* against these Banks can be issued. Only co-operative Banks are not covered within the definition of "State" under Article 12. Hence, the Supreme Court of India is not entertaining *mandamus* against Co-operative Banks. But, many High Courts have issued *mandamus* against Co-operative Banks by taking into consideration the fact that the function discharged by them is of analogous to the state machinery and duty cast upon the aforesaid banks are of public nature.

4.9 *MANDAMUS* AGAINST IMPROVEMENT TRUSTS

Port Trusts Constituted under the Major Port Trusts Act

It is made specifically clear by the various decisions of the Supreme Court that the Port Trusts are covered within the definition of "other authority" and hence they are "State" under Article 12 of the Constitution of India. Mumbai Port Trust, Kandla Port Trust, etc. are the Port Trusts covered under the definition of "State".

Mumbai Port Trust

M/s. Dwarkadas Marfatia and Sons v. Board of Trustees of the Port of Bombay[152]

An appeal was filed by the appellant against the judgment of the single judge of the High Court of Bombay in a dispute pertaining to Bombay Rents, Hotel and Lodging House Rates Control Act. The Dispute was pertaining to the exemption given to the Bombay Port Trust from the applicability of the aforesaid Act as provided in section 4 thereof to the public bodies. A writ petition filed by the appellants before the Bombay High Court was rejected taking the contention that the Bombay Rents, Hotel and Lodging House Rates Control Act was not applicable to the respondent Port Trust.

152. (1989)3 SCC 293 = AIR 1989 SC 1642.

The Supreme Court also in appeal observed that the Board of Trustees of the Port of Bombay was a statutory authority. Being a statutory authority, the respondent has been exempted from the operation of the relevant Rent Act. The Supreme Court opined that the respondent was a statutory corporation constituted under the Major Port Trust (Amendment) Act, 1974. (Paragraph 3 of the judgment.) The Supreme Court, with this observation dismissed the appeal of the appellants on merits.

Jamshed Hormusji Wadia v. Board of Trustees, Port of Mumbai[153]

It has been held by the Supreme Court, in Special Leave Application against the decision of the division bench of the High Court that in the field of contracts the State and its instrumentalities ought to so design their activities as would ensure fair competition and non-discrimination.

While answering the question as to what was the status of the Bombay Port Trust as a landlord, the Supreme Court held that the Bombay Port Trust was "instrumentality" and hence "State" under Article 12 of the Constitution of India and amenable to the writ jurisdiction. The Supreme Court also reminded the case of *M/s. Dwarkadas Marfatia and Sons* v. *Board of Trustees, of the Port of Bombay* (discussed above). The Supreme Court also said that the Bombay Port Trust cannot afford to act with arbitrariness or capriciousness as being an instrumentality of the State. Moreover, it was commented that the Trust must act within the four corners of the statute, which has created and governs it and all its action must be for public good.

4.10 *MANDAMUS* AGAINST ELECTION COMMISSION

The Election Commission is a commission constituted through the Constitution of India. In the same way, the posts of the Chief Election Commissioner and other Election Commissioners are Constitutional posts. Constitution of Election Commission and posts of Chief Election Commissioner and Election Commissioners are defined under Article 324 of the Constitution of India. Therefore, it is needless to say that *mandamus* is maintainable against Election Commission and its members. But the power to issue *mandamus* against the Commission and its members is subject to the bar imposed by way of Article 329 of the Constitution of India itself viz. once the process of election is started, the Courts cannot interfere with the election matters. The following case is the example of it.

Kanhiya Lal Omar v. R.K. Trivedi[154]

A writ petition filed by the petitioner under Article 32 of the Constitution of India challenging the constitutional validity of the Election Symbols (Reservation and Allotment) Order, 1968 (hereinafter referred as "Symbols Order") issued by the Election Commission. The principal urged

153. AIR 2004 SC 1815.
154. AIR 1986 SC 111.

by the petitioner in support of his contention was that the Symbols Order which was legislative in character could not have been issued by the Election Commission because the Commission was not entrusted by law the power of superintendence, reservation and allotment of symbols that might be chosen by the candidates at elections in parliamentary and assembly constituencies. It was further urged that Article 324 of the Constitution which vests the power of superintendence, direction and control of all elections to Parliament and to the Legislature of a State in the Commission could not be construed as conferring the power on the Commission to issue the Symbols Order.

The Supreme Court, by taking into consideration the powers of the Election Commission under Article 324 and its powers to issue Symbols Order dismissed the aforesaid writ petition on merits. But from this judgment it can very well be presumed that writ of *mandamus* is maintainable against the Election Commission.

Indrajit Barua and Others v. Election Commission of India and others[155]

In this case the limitations are discussed while filing writ petition against the Election Commission. The petitioners challenged the elections of the State Legislature by way of filing number of different writ petitions under Article 226 of the Constitution before the High Court seeking relief of or in the nature of *mandamus* on the ground of having defective electoral roll. By way of transfer all the petitions were brought before the Supreme Court for the hearing.

The Supreme Court held that writ petition under Article 226 challenging on the ground of defective electoral roll is not an appropriate remedy and hence all the writ petitions filed originally under Article 226 are not maintainable. Such disputes can be challenged only by way of filing election petition in a manner prescribed under the Representation of the People Act, 1950. With this observation the Supreme Court disposed of the matters.

4.11 *MANDAMUS* AGAINST COMMISSIONS OF INQUIRIES

Mandamus can be issued against various Commissions of Inquiry appointed under the Commission of Inquiries Act. This is undisputed facts and supported by number of judgments. The ratio laid down by the Supreme Court in some of the judgments on this point is discussed here below.

Jagannath Rao and others v. State of Orissa and Others[156]

The petitioners challenged by way of *mandamus* the appointment of the Commission of Inquiry under the Commission of Inquiries Act. In this

155. AIR 1986 SC 103.
156. AIR 1969 SC 215.

case though the appointment of the Commission of Inquiry was found to be valid, legal, *intra vires,* but the fact remains that the *mandamus* was issued against the Commission and the reliefs prayed for was not granted and matter was dismissed on merits.

The petitioners herein have challenged the notification issued by the Government of Orissa in exercise of the powers conferred on it by section 3 of the Commission of Inquiry Act, 1952 and prayed to quash and set aside the notification and for appropriate directions before the Orissa High Court. The Schedule of the Notification gave the name of 15 persons against whom inquiry was to be initiated. The Orissa High Court after hearing the petitions dismissed the petitions by delivering a common judgment with the observations that the notification of the State Government appointing the Commission of Inquiry was legal and valid. Against the judgment of the Orissa High Court, the appeals were preferred before the Supreme Court.

By putting forward the arguments on behalf of the appellants, Mr. Ashok Sen raised a question regarding the appointment of the Commission and said that the same was not valid as the notification did not state what was the purpose for which enquiry was to be made. In other words, the notification was not related to any future Government action or legislative policy and hence the notification was bad in law. But this contention was rejected by the Supreme Court. Speaking for the Court S.R. Das, C.J. observed that the object to set-up the Commission of Inquiry in the present case was to take appropriate legislative or administrative measures for maintaining high standards of public conduct and purity of political administration in the State. Hence, the notification of the Orissa Government falls within the ambit of Section 3 of the Act and must be held to be legally valid and *intra vires*. Further, it was observed that it was a valid exercise of power by the State Government in the appointment of the Commission under Section 3. In support of his case Mr. Ashok Sen relied upon the judgment of *Shri Ram Krishna Dalmia* v. *Shri Justice S.R. Tendulkar*[157] in which the appellant challenged the validity of the notification of the Central Government appointing a Commission of Inquiry to inquire into and report in respect of certain companies mentioned in the Schedule attached to the notification and in respect of the nature and extent of the control and interest which certain persons named in the notification exercised over these companies. But the aforesaid judgment was distinguished by S.R. Das, C.J.

That the other question raised on behalf of the appellant was whether the power was exercised by the State Government for the purpose alien to the statute or not. It was contended by Mr. Ashok Sen that there was a bitter political rivalry between the appellants on the one hand and Shri Pabitra Mohan Pradhan, Shri Harekrushna Mahtab, Shri Singh Deo and the other persons who were at that time in charge of the Orissa Administration. Hence, it was argued that the appointment of the Commission was a *mala*

157. AIR 1958 SC 538.

fide exercise of the power and hence the same should be struck down as illegal.

The Supreme Court while disbelieving the arguments of *malafide* observed in the paragraph 8 of the judgment,

'8. It is well settled that if a statutory authority exercises its power for a purpose not authorised by the law the action of the statutory authority is ultra vires and without jurisdiction. In other words, it is a malafide exercise of power in the eye of law, i.e., an exercise of power by a statutory authority for a purpose other than that which the legislature intended. See The King v. Minister of Health, 1929-1 KB 61[9]. But the question arises as to what is the legal position if an administrative authority acts both for an authorised purpose and for an un authorised purpose. In such a case where there is a mixture of authorised and unauthorized purpose, what should be the test to be applied to determine the legal validity of the administrative act? The proper test to be applied in such a case is as to what is the dominant purpose for which the administrative power is exercised. To put it differently, if the administrative authority pursues to two or more purposes of which one is authorised and the other unauthorized, the legality of the administrative act should be determined by reference to the dominant purpose....'

By applying the above test the Supreme Court observed that there was a valid exercise of the power in appointment of the Commission of Inquiry by the Orissa Government in order to promote measures for maintaining purity and integrity of the administration in the political life of the State and not "the character assassination" of Shri Biju Patnaik and Shri Biren Mitra and their groups.

With these observations the appeals were dismissed, but here the point of consideration is that the High Court issued the *mandamus* against the Commission of Inquiry and before the Supreme Court also the power of the High Court to issue the *mandamus* against the Commission was not challenged. Therefore, we can come to the conclusion that the writ of *mandamus* is maintainable against the Commission of Inquiry as well.

4.12 *MANDAMUS* AGAINST STOCK EXCHANGES

K.C. Sharma v. Delhi Stock Exchange and others[158]

A recent judgment pronounced by the Supreme Court, confirming the view of the Division Bench of the Delhi High Court that the Delhi Stock Exchange is "State" within the meaning of Article 12 of the Constitution of India and held the writ petition against the Delhi Stock Exchange maintainable under Article 226 of the Constitution of India.

In this case, the respondent terminated the General Manager, employee of the Delhi Stock Exchange as the actions taken by him against

158. JT 2005 (4) SC 18.

the other members of the Exchange were found to be excessively harsh as well as were outside the official capacity of the General Manager. The Stock Exchange and its members were unhappy with the actions taken by the General Manager. By giving this reason, the General Manager was terminated. The General Manager filed a writ petition before the Delhi High Court. Learned Single Judge of the High Court quashed the said order by holding that the respondent was a "State" under Article 12 of the Constitution and hence there was no question about the maintainability of the writ petition.

In an appeal before the Division Bench of the Delhi High Court, it was held that the writ was maintainable. It was also observed that the appellant, being the permanent employee, his termination from the service was illegal, but as the reinstatement was not advisable in the facts and circumstances of the case, the Division Bench directed the respondent employer to pay Rs. 12 lakhs being the amount of compensation in lieu of reinstatement.

The appellant preferred appeal against the judgment of the Supreme Court, as he was not given reinstatement. The Supreme Court upheld the decision of the Division Bench by holding that the Delhi Stock Exchange was "State" within the meaning of Article 12 of the Constitution of India. The Supreme Court relied upon the guidelines given in the case of *R.D. Shetty* v. *International Airport Authority of India* (discussed earlier). With these observations, the Supreme Court upheld the order of the Division Bench with slight modification regarding payment of amount of compensation in lieu of reinstatement from Rs. 12 lakhs to Rs. 15 lakhs.

5

Mandamus against Private Person

5.1 *MANDAMUS* AGAINST PRIVATE TRUSTS DISCHARGING NON-STATUTORY FUNCTIONS

Shri Anadi Mukta Sadguru S.M.V.S.J.M.S. Trust v. V.R. Rudani[1]

In this case, the scope of writ jurisdiction under Article 226 of the Constitution of India was determined by the Supreme Court and observed that the writ of *mandamus* is maintainable before the High Court even against a private trust.

As per the facts of the case the first appellant was a public trust and the other appellants were the trustees. The trust was running a science college in the city of Ahmedabad. The college was temporary affiliated to the Gujarat University. The revised pay scales of the university teachers and the teachers of the affiliated colleges were recommended by the University Grant Commission. The Vice-Chancellor was given power to implement certain pay scales. The Vice-Chancellor gave his award and directed tc give the revised pay scales and other benefits with retrospective effect. The said award was accepted by the State Government as well as the University. But the appellant, instead of implementing the award served notice of termination upon 11 teachers on the ground that they were surplus and approached the university to remove them. The Vice-Chancellor did not give the permission to remove them. The Management-Trust took a decision to close down the college and the same was done with effect from June 15, 1975. The academic staff was not paid the terminal benefits. Hence, they preferred writ petition under Article 226 of the Constitution in the High Court. The trust appeared as a respondent and resisted the petitions of the academic staff on the various grounds, but the most important ground taken by it was of maintainability of the writ petition. The preliminary

1. AIR 1989 SC 1607.

objection taken by the trust was that it was not a statutory body and is not subject to the writ jurisdiction of the High Court. The High Court disbelieved the argument and allowed the writ petition.

Being aggrieved by the judgment of the High Court, the trust filed appeal before the Supreme Court. On the facts, the appellants had very weak case. The only important question before the Supreme Court for the Consideration was the maintainability of the writ petition for *mandamus* as against the management of the College. The management of the college was a trust registered under the Public Trusts Act and therefore it was not amenable to the writ jurisdiction. This was the argument of the appellant.

The Supreme Court was of the opinion that,

> *'if the rights are purely of a private character, no mandamus can issue. In other words, if the management of the college is purely a private body with no public duty, mandamus will not lie against it. These are two exceptions to Mandamus. But once these are absent and when the party has no other equally convenient remedy, mandamus cannot be denied. It was to be appreciated that the appellants-trust was managing the affiliated college to which public money is paid as Government aid. Public money paid as Government aid plays a major role in the control, maintenance and working of educational institutions. The aided institutions like Government institutions discharge public function by way of imparting education to students. They are subject to the rules and regulations of the affiliating University. Their activities are closely supervised by University authorities. Employment in such institutions, therefore, is not devoid of any public character. .... When the University takes a decision regarding their pay scales, it will be binding on the management....'*

While discussing the scope of writ of *mandamus* under Article 226 of the Constitution, the Supreme Court said that the remedy of the prerogative writs in England started with very limited scope and it had many disadvantages. **Lord Gardiner** requested the Law Commission to take appropriate steps to remove the difficulties. Pursuant to that Law Commission made its report in the year 1976 and the same was implemented by Rules of Court in 1977 and given statutory force in 1981 by section 31 of the Supreme Court Act, 1981. It combined the former remedies into one proceeding called judicial review.

However, the prerogative writ of *mandamus* confined only to public authorities to compel performance of public duty. The "public authority" in England meant at that time, every body which is created by statute and whose powers and duties are defined by statute, e.g. Government Departments, local authorities, police authorities and statutory undertakings and corporations. But, in India, the High Courts under Article 226 of the Constitution have no such limitations for issuing prerogative writs.

The Supreme Court here also reminded that there is a difference of powers of the Supreme Court to issue writs and that of a High Court. Thus the term "authority" used in Article 226 must receive a liberal meaning unlike the term in Article 12. Article 12 is relevant only for the purpose of enforcement of fundamental rights under Article 32. Article 226 confers power on the High Courts to issue writs for the enforcement of the fundamental rights as well as non-fundamental rights. The words "Any person or authority" used in Article 226 are, therefore, not to be confined only to statutory authorities and instrumentalities of the States. They may cover any other person or body performing public duty. While justifying the issuance of writ of *mandamus* against the trust by the High Court, the Supreme Court said in paragraph 19 of the judgment,

> *'The form of the body concerned is not very much relevant. What is relevant is the nature of the duty imposed on the body. The duty must be judged in the light of positive obligation owed by the person or authority to the affected party. No matter by what means the duty is imposed. If a positive obligation exists mandamus cannot be denied.'*

The Supreme Court categorically said that there was no sense in denying the *mandamus* on the ground that the duty to be enforced was not imposed by the statute. It also quoted the statement of **Professor De Smith** from its book Judicial Review of Administrative Act that,

> *'... to be enforceable by mandamus a public duty does not necessarily have to be one imposed by statute. It may be sufficient for the duty to have been imposed by charter, common law, custom or even contract.'*[2]

Justice K. Jagannatha Shetty, while disposing the appeal by confirming the judgment of the High Court finally observed by encouraging the issuance of writs against such private trusts,

> *'.....The judicial control over the fast expanding maze of bodies affecting the rights of the people should not be put into water-tight compartment. It should remain flexible to meet the requirements of variable circumstances. Mandamus is a very wide remedy which must be easily available 'to reach injustice wherever it is found". Technicalities should not come in the way of granting that relief under Article 226. ...'*

This judgment can be considered as very important judgment pertaining to the power of the High Courts to issue writ of *mandamus* in a sense that in this judgment, the Supreme Court has clarified that the writ jurisdiction to issue *mandamus* is wider than that of the Supreme Court. The cases in which the Supreme Court cannot issue *mandamus* under Article 32,

2. Judicial Review of Administrative Act, 4th Edition, p. 540.

the High Court can issue the same under Article 226. The technicalities of Article 12 affect issuance of writ to the Supreme Court but not the High Courts.

Board of Control of Cricket in India (BCCI)

M/s. Zee Telefilms Ltd. and another v. Union of India and Others[3]

A writ petition under Article 32 of the Constitution was filed by the appellant challenging the order of the Board of Control of Cricket in India (BCCI) as being arbitrary and violative of Article 14. The question arose was regarding the maintainability of the writ petition as the BCCI contended that it was a registered society under the Tamil Nadu Societies Registration Act, not covered within the definition of "State" under Article 12 of the Constitution.

The BCCI was having powers to grant telecasting rights of the cricket matches. It granted such rights for a fixed term in favour of appellant in terms of agreement. Another telecasting company (Sony Entertainment) challenged such action by the Board through a writ petition on the ground that the Zee Telefilms was not having experience of Telecasting cricket matches, which was one of the requirements published by the BCCI. Subsequently, Board cancelled the agreement with the appellant Company. The order of cancellation of the Board was challenged by the appellant through this writ petition. A bench of five Judges by majority of 3: 2 held that the BCCI is not "State" and therefore writ under Article 32 of the Constitution is not maintainable before the Supreme Court.

The majority of the Supreme Court (Per **N. Santosh Hegde, B.P. Singh and H.K. Sema, JJ**.) has taken following points for the consideration:

- The Board is a society registered under the Societies Registration Act, not created by a statute.
- It is an autonomous body and no part of the share capital of the Board being held by the Government.
- No financial assistance being given by the Government to the Board
- There was no deep and pervasive State control. However, the Union of India is having certain control over the activities of the Board in regard to organizing cricket matches and travel of the Indian team abroad as also granting of permission to allow the foreign teams to come to India. But this control over the activities of the Board was not found sufficient by the Supreme Court so as to construe it as administrative control.
- The Board enjoys a monopoly status in the field of cricket. Still however, it was not found enough by the Supreme Court to designate the Board as "State" under Article 12.

3. JT 2005 (2) SC 8.

In order to decide the issue as to whether BCCI is "State" or not, the Supreme Court appreciated various judgments upon the term "other authority" and the situation prevailing at the relevant time. It has been observed by it that the intention of the Constitution framers in incorporating the Article 12 was to treat such authority which has been created by law and which has got certain powers to make laws, to make rules and regulations to be included in the term "other authorities".

By taking into consideration the situation prevailing at that time and because of the change in the socio-economic policies of the Government, the Supreme Court considered it necessary by judicial interpretation to give a wider meaning to the term "other authorities" in Article 12 so as to include such bodies which were created by Act of Legislature to be included in the said term "other authorities". Further it was held that the Constitution of the Country is a living organism and it is the duty of Courts to interpret the same to fulfil the needs and aspirations of the people depending on the needs of the time. It is noticed earlier in this judgment that in Article 12 the term "other authorities" was introduced at the time of framing of the Constitution with a limited objective of granting judicial review of actions of such authorities which are created under the Statute and which discharge State functions. However, because of the need of the day the Supreme Court in *Rajasthan Electricity Board and Sukhdev Singh* v. *Bhagatram* noticing the socio-economic policy of the country thought it fit to expand the definition of the term "other authorities" to include bodies other than statutory bodies. This development of law by judicial interpretation culminated the judgment of the 7 judges Bench in the case of Pradeep Kumar Biswas. It is to be noticed that in the meantime, the socio-economic policy of the Government of India has changed and the State is today distancing itself from commercial activities and concentrating on governance rather than on business. Therefore, the situation prevailing at the time of Sukhdev Singh is not in existence at least for the time being, hence there seems to be no need to further expand the scope of "other authorities" in Article 12 by judicial interpretation at least for the time being. By giving further explanation the Supreme Court said that in a democracy there is a dividing line between a State enterprise and a non-State enterprise, which is distinct and the judiciary should not be an instrument to erase the said dividing line unless, of course, the circumstances of the day require it to do so.

The Majority, thereafter, tried to test the present case on the touch stone of the parameters laid down in Pradeep Kumar Biswas's case. For the purpose, it summarized the following important guidelines of Pradeep Kumar Biswas's case:

- Principles laid down in Ajay Hasia are not a rigid set of principles so that if a body falls within any one of them it must exhypothesi, be considered to be a "State" within the meaning of Article 12.

- The Question in each case will have to be considered on the bases of facts available as to whether in the light of the cumulative facts as established, the body is financially, functionally, administratively dominated, by or under the control of the Government.
- Such control must be particular to the body in question and must be pervasive.
- Mere regulatory control whether under statute or otherwise would not serve to make a body a State.

In the present case though the Union of India is exercising certain control over the activities of the Board in regard to organizing cricket matches and travel of the Indian team abroad as also granting of permission to allow the foreign teams to come to India, such control cannot be construed as an administrative control as defined in the tests of Pradeep Kumar Biswas case. There is no financial control of the Government as the Board is not taking any financial assistance from the Government. The Board is an autonomous body. The Government interference in the function of the Board is very limited. Thus, it cannot be said that the Government is having functional control over the Board.

By making above observations the majority held that when a private body exercises its public functions even if it is not a "State", the aggrieved person has a remedy not only under the ordinary law but also under the Constitution, by way of a writ petition under Article 226. Therefore, merely because a non-governmental body exercises some public duty that by itself would not suffice to make such body a "State" for the purpose of Article 12. In the instant case the activities of the Board do not come under the guidelines laid down by the Supreme Court in Pradeep Kumar Biswas case. Hence, the petition filed by the petitioner under Article 32 is not maintainable.

The majority in this case raised an apprehension that if the Board which controls the game of Cricket is declared to be "State" for the purpose of Article 12, there is absolutely no reason why other similarly placed bodies should not be treated as "State". The fact that game of Cricket is very popular in India also cannot be a ground to differentiate these bodies from the Board. Any such differentiation dependent upon popularity, finances and public opinion of the body concerned would definitely violate Article 14 of the Constitution, as any discrimination to be valid must be based on hard facts and not mere surmises. Therefore, also, the Board cannot be singly identified as "other authority" and hence not as "State" for the purpose of Article 12.

Minority View (Per S.B. Sinha and S.N. Variava, JJ.)

The minority opinion was not ready to accept that the BCCI is not "State" under Article 12. After having studied the activities and status of the Board carefully the minority made following observations:

- The Board while enjoying monopoly in cricket exercises enormous power which is neither in doubt nor in dispute. Its action may disable a person from pursuing his vocation and in that process subject a citizen to hostile discrimination or impose embargo. If an action of the Board impinges upon the fundamental [e.g. Article 19(1)(g)] or Constitutional rights of a citizen or if the same is *ultra vires* or by reason thereof an injury or material prejudice is caused to its member or a person connected with cricket, judicial review would lie. Such function of the Board is a public function and would be subject to judicial review.
- Time is not far off when having regard to globalization and privatization the rules of administrative law have to be extended to the private bodies whose functions affect the fundamental rights of a citizen.
- When essential governmental functions were placed or allowed to be performed by the private body; they must be held to have undertaken public duty or public functions. Performance of a public function in the context of the Constitution of India would be to allow an entity to perform the function as an authority within the meaning of Article 12. Further BCCI is considered as a member of ICC and therefore, it is bound to act reasonably. Also the duty to act fairly is inherent in body which exercises enormous power.
- A body which carries on the monopolistic function of selecting team to represent the nation and whose core function is to promote a sport that has become a symbol of national identity and a medium of expression of national pride, must be held to be carrying out governmental functions. The monopoly enjoyed may not be under Article 19 only. It can be a *de facto* monopoly which has overtly or covertly received the blessings of the Union of India. The Board in view of its enormity of powers is bound to follow "the doctrine of fairness and good faith in all its activities".
- Legal meaning attributed to the wordings of the Article 12 would lead to the conclusion that the Board is a "State". It is true that while developing the law operating in the field a strict meaning was not adhered to by this Court but it may not now be possible to put the clock back.
- It is not correct that the Board represents itself in international area. If it represents the country, indisputably it must have the implied sanction of the Government of India to do so. Its activities, thus, far-reaching effect.

It was held by the minority with the application of the above tests to the facts of the case, the Board satisfies the said description. It discharges a public function. It has its duties towards the public. The public at large will look forward to the Board for selection of the best team to represent the country. It must manage its housekeeping in such a manner so as to fulfil the hopes and aspirations of millions. It has thus, duty to act fairly. It cannot act arbitrarily, whimsically or capriciously. Public interest is, thus, a State actor.

Here it appears that the majority view not holding the BCCI as "State" requires further consideration. The reasons given by the majority thereof are not convincing and proper. It seems that the majority has in a hurry to stop the flow of litigations of writ of *mandamus* put restrictions without looking to its future effects. The direction, belief and view appears to be strange and not proper for the following reasons:

- The majority view is quite contrary to the tests suggested by the cases of *Sukhdev* v. *Bhagatram and Ajay Hasia*. By solely relying upon the tests of Pradeep Kumar Biswas's case, the Supreme Court came to the conclusion that BCCI was not "State". Justifying its decision the Supreme Court observes in this judgment that the expansion of the term "State" was necessary because of the change in the socio-economic policies of the Government. A question arises here is that should the approach of the Court be changed with the socio-economic policy of the Government.
- The drastic change in the approach of the government from the year 1979-80 to the year 2004-05 is that the government is withdrawing itself from commercial activities and concentrating itself on governance rather than on business. With this reasoning the Supreme Court found it fit not to expand the scope of "other authorities" by declaring the Board as "State". It is pertinent to note here the fact that the business carried on by the government is always not profit motivated. The factors of providing employment are equally important. Of course, it is none of the function of the Supreme Court to dictate the policy to the Government, but at the same time the Supreme Court should not encourage the privatization of the government businesses by such judicial pronouncements.
- It has been observed here by the majority of the Supreme Court that there is no need to further expand the scope of "other authorities". But as a matter of fact the scope of the term other authorities" has already been expanded by the Supreme Court while pronouncing the ratio of *Sukhdev* v. *Bhagatram* (ignoring the warning given by minority decision of Alagiriswami, J.). In the present case the question was only with regard to the interpretation of the expanded scope. By not declaring BCCI as "State" the Supreme Court is trying to reverse the clock, which is practically impossible.

- The BCCI is enjoying the monopoly status in many aspects such as selection of cricket team of India, giving powers to telecast matches, etc. The cricket team selected by the BCCI represents the country and not BCCI. Therefore, there is implied consent of the Government in the functions of the BCCI. It should be kept in view that the governmental functions are multifacial. There cannot be a single test for defining public functions. Such functions are performed by variety of means.
- There is an administrative control of the Government over certain matters of BCCI such as giving permission to cricketers to go abroad or to permit the foreign teams to play in India. This was also a sufficient ground to declare BCCI as "State".
- If the tests of Pradeep Kumar Biswas case are to be applied in this case, there is an administrative and functional control of the Government over the activities of the BCCI to some extent. Merely because of the fact that the government is not giving any kind of financial assistance to the BCCI, it does not cease to be "State" under Article 12 of the Constitution.
- The approach of the Supreme Court that the writ petition under Article 32 is not maintainable is not just, legal or equitable. Instead of that the Supreme Court concedes that the remedy to approach the High Court in the event of the violation of Article 14 is available. But the approach of the Supreme Court that since the respondent is not covered within the definition of "State" and therefore writ petition under Article 32 is not maintainable appears to be unreasonable and improper.

5.2 *MANDAMUS* AGAINST PRIVATE COMPANIES

Praga Tools Corporation Ltd.
{A Company incorporated under the Companies Act}

Praga Tools Corporation Ltd. v. C.V. Imanual[4]

In the case of *Praga Tools Corporation Ltd.* v. *C.V. Imanual* the point for consideration before the division Bench of the Supreme Court was whether writ of *mandamus* could be issued by the High Court against a Company incorporated under the Companies Act, 1913 or not. Praga Tools Corporation Ltd. was a company incorporated under the Companies Act, 1913 and therefore, a company within the meaning of the Companies Act, 1956. At the material time the union of India held fifty six percent of the shares of the Company and the Government of Andhra Pradesh held thirty-two percent of its shares, the balance of twelve percent shares being held by private individuals. As being the largest shareholder, the Union of India had the power to nominate the company's directors. The Company had

4. AIR 1969 SC 1306.

entered into two settlements with its workmen's union. These settlements were arrived at and recorded in the presence of the Commissioner of Labour. Subsequently, the company entered into another agreement with the union, the effect of which was to enable the company, notwithstanding the earlier two settlements, to retrench ninety-two of its workmen. Some of the affected workmen thereupon filed a writ petition under the Article 226 of the Constitution in the Andhra Pradesh High Court challenging the validity of subsequent agreement. A learned Single Judge of the High Court dismissed the petition on merits. In appeal, a Division Bench of the High Court held that the Company being one registered under the Companies Act and not having any statutory duty or function to perform was not one against which writ could lie. The Division Bench, however, held that though the writ petition was not maintainable, the High Court could grant declaration in favour of the petitioners that the impugned agreement was illegal and void and granted the sad declaration. Being aggrieved by the judgment of the Division Bench of the High Court, the company filed an appeal before the Supreme Court. The Division Bench of Justice Shelat and Justice Bhargava held that the Company being a non-statutory body and one incorporated under the Companies Act there was neither a statutory nor a public duty imposed on it by a statute in respect of which enforcement could be sought by means of a *mandamus*.

In paragraph 6 of the judgment, Justice Shelat has narrated in detail the scope of issuance of writ of *mandamus* under Article 226 of the Constitution, by supporting the view of the Andhra Pradesh High Court as follows:

> *'In our view the High Court was correct in holding that the writ petition filed under Art. 226 claiming against the company mandamus or an order in the nature of mandamus was misconceived and not maintainable. The writ obviously was claimed against the company and not against the conciliation officer in respect of any public or statutory duty imposed on him by the Act as it was not he but the company who sought to implement the impugned agreement. No doubt, Article 226 provides that every High Court shall have power to issue to any person or authority orders and writs including writs in the nature of habeas corpus, mandamus, etc. or any of them for the enforcement of any of the rights conferred by Part III of the Constitution and for any other purpose. But it is well understood that a mandamus lies to secure the performance of a public or statutory duty in the performance of which the one who applies for it has a sufficient legal interest. Thus, an application for mandamus will not lie for an order of restatement to an office which is essentially of a private character nor can such an application be maintained to secure performance of obligations owed by a company towards its workmen or to resolve any private dispute.'*

Justice Shelat here relied more upon the aspect of legal right and corresponding legal duty. According to him, the person claiming the *mandamus* must have a legal right to compel others to do or abstain from doing something. At the same time the respondent must have corresponding statutory duty. He further observed:

> '.......... *Therefore, the condition precedent for the issue of mandamus is that there is in one claiming it a legal right to the performance of a legal duty by one against whom it is sought. An order of mandamus is, in form, a command directed to a person, corporation or an inferior tribunal requiring him or them to do a particular thing therein specified which appertains to his or their office and is in the nature of a public duty. It is, however, not necessary that the person or the authority on whom the statutory duty is imposed need be a public official or an official body. A mandamus can issue, for instance, to an official of a society to compel him to carry out the terms of the statute under or by which the society is constituted or governed and also to companies or corporations to carry out duties placed on them by the statutes authorizing their undertakings. A mandamus would also lie against a company constituted by a statute for the purposes of fulfiling public responsibilities. [Cf. Halsbury's Laws of England (3rd Ed.), Vol. II, p. 52 and onwards].*'

Finally, he observed,

> '*In our view once the writ petition was held to be misconceived on the ground that it could not lie against a company which was neither a statutory company nor one having public duties or responsibilities imposed on it by a statute, no relief by way of a declaration as to invalidity of an impugned agreement between it and its employees could be granted. The High Court in these circumstances ought to have left the workmen to resort to the remedy available to them under the Industrial Disputes Act by raising an industrial dispute thereunder.*'

With great respect to the ratio laid down in the above mentioned case, it is submitted that the concept of instrumentality or agency of the 'state' was not developed at all in the year 1969. Otherwise, the task of the Judges would have become easy and the decision would have been different.

The Union Government was holding 56% of the shares of the appellant company. The State Government was having 32% of the Shares of the Company. Further, the Central Government had power to appoint the directors of the company. This itself was sufficient to prove deep and pervasive state control over the company. Thus, Praga Tools Corporation Ltd. could be considered as an instrumentality of the State.

The judgment of Praga Tools Corporation Ltd. was thereafter, in the year 1986 distinguished by the Supreme Court in the *Case of Central Inland*

Water Transport Corporation Ltd. v. *Brijo Nath*[5] by making following observations:

> *'Though this case (Praga Tools Corporation Ltd.) was strongly relied upon by the Appellants, we fail to see how it is relevant to the submissions advanced by the Appellants. The subsequent agreement enabling the company to retrench some of its workmen was challenged on the ground that it was in breach of the earlier settlements entered into between the company and the workmen's union. No question of violation of any of the Fundamental Rights was at all raised in that case. The only question which fell for determination was whether a writ of mandamus can issue to compel the performance of the earlier settlements or to restrain the enforcement of the impugned subsequent agreement and the dispute, therefore, was one which fell within the scope of the Industrial Disputes Act, 1947.'*

Thus, according to the Supreme Court in this case, it would have been a different judgment in Praga Tools Case, if an issue of violation of fundamental rights of the petitioner was raised. Since the arguments by the petitioners before the High Court and the Supreme Court were on the line of breach of agreement, writ of *mandamus* was denied.

M.C. Mehta v. Union of India (Bhopal Gas Disaster Case)[6]

This is a well known case in which the Supreme Court of India directed a multi-national company—Union Carbide Corporation to pay compensation to the victims or relatives of deceased persons as the tragedy occurred due to leakage of a poisonous gas, i.e. Methyl Isocyanide. Nevertheless, the Supreme Court hesitated to come to any conclusion in this case as to whether UCC is covered within the definition of 'other authorities' and consequently, 'State' under Article 12 or not. It has deliberately kept this question open. In fact, this issue ought to have been decided by the Supreme Court in affirmative. This issue is open even today whether *mandamus* can be issued against multi-national companies like UCC or not. Today by adopting policy of globalization, India has invited so many multi-national companies to carry on their business. If they are exempted from the purview of "State", number of employees will be deprived of the statutory protection available to them under the Constitution of India.

VST Industries Ltd. v. VST Industries Workers' Union[7]

An interesting question regarding issuance of *mandamus* is as to whether it can be issued against a private person or an incorporated company under Article 226 by the High Court or not. It was held in this

5. AIR 1986 SC 1571.
6. AIR 1987 SC 1086.
7. 2000 (8) Scale 95.

case that it was only the circumstances when the authority or the person performs a public function or discharges a public duty. The appellant (before the Supreme Court), was engaged in the manufacture and sale of cigarettes. Manufacture and sale of cigarettes will not involve any public function. Incidental to that activity there is an obligation under section 46 of the Factories Act to set-up a canteen when the establishment has more than 250 workmen. That means, it is a condition of service in relation to a workman providing better facilities to workmen to discharge their duties properly and maintain their own health and welfare. In such cases public duty is owed to the public in general and not specific to any person or group of persons. Further, the damage that would be caused in not observing them is immense. If merely what can be considered a part of the condition of service of a workman is violated there can be no justification to hold that such activity will amount to public duty. A cigarette company merely because it provides canteen facilities to its workmen as required by section 46 of the Factories Act, cannot be said to be amenable to writ jurisdiction and hence writ is not maintainable against the cigarette company, which was merely of a private nature.

Federal Bank Ltd. v. Sagar Thomas[8]

Private company is defined as a company incorporated under Section 3 of the Companies Act, 1956 as distinguished from the Government companies constituted under Section 617 of the same Act.

In the case of *Federal Bank Ltd.* v. *Sagar Thomas,* a question arose was regarding maintainability of a writ petition against a company incorporated under the Companies Act (not being a government company). A disciplinary action was initiated against an employee of a Federal Bank Ltd. and pursuant to it he was terminated from the service. A writ petition under Article 226 of the Constitution of India was filed by the employee challenging his termination order. A preliminary objection to the maintainability of the writ petition was taken by the appellant Bank by saying that it is a private bank and not the State or its agency or instrumentality, within the meaning of Article 12 of the Constitution of India. Hence, a writ petition under Article 226 of the constitution was not maintainable against it.

The learned Single Judge, however, found that Federal Bank performs a public duty, and as such it comes under the definition of "other authorities" within the meaning of Article 12 and as such the writ petition was maintainable. Being aggrieved by the aforesaid judgment of the learned Single Judge, the appellant Bank preferred a writ appeal. The appeal too, was dismissed on merits upholding the decision of the learned Single Judge. Therefore, the Bank approached the Supreme Court by way of fling appeal.

8. (2003) 10 SCC 733.

The six tests given in the case of Ajay Hasia and approved in the later decisions were applied in the present case. The aforesaid tests were confirmed in other cases including the seven Judge Bench decision in the case of Pradeep Kumar Biswas. The application of all the six tests of Ajay Hasia's case to the present case are discussed below:

Application of Ajay Hasia Tests 1 and 2

Share capital of the appellant Bank is not held at all by the Government nor is any financial assistance provided by the State; nothing to say which may meet almost the entire expenditure of the company.

Application of Ajay Hasia Test 3

The third factor is also not answered since the appellant Bank does not enjoy any monopoly status nor can it be said to be an institution having State protection.

Application of Ajay Hasia Test 4

So far as control over the affairs of the appellant Bank is concerned, they are managed by the Board of Directors elected by its shareholders. No governmental agency or officer is connected with the affairs of the appellant Bank nor is any one of them a member of the Board of Directors. In the normal functioning of the private banking company there is no participation or interference of the State or its authorities. The status have been framed regulating the financial and commercial activities so that fiscal equilibrium may be kept maintained and not get disturbed by the malfunctioning of such companies or institutions involved in the business of banking. There are regulatory measures for the purpose of maintaining a healthy economic atmosphere in the country. Such regulatory measures are provided for other companies also as well as industries manufacturing goods of importance. Otherwise these are purely private commercial activities. It would hardly make any difference if such supervisory vigilance is kept by the Central Government in place of Reserve Bank of India.

Application of Ajay Hasia Test 5

Any business or commercial activity, whether it may be banking, manufacturing units or related to any other kind of business generating resources, employment, production and resulting in circulation of money are no doubt, such which do have an impact on the economy of the country in general. But such activities cannot be classified as one falling in the category of discharging duties or functions of a public nature.

Application of Ajay Hasia Test 6

Again, the activity which is carried on by the appellant is not one which may have been earlier carried on by the Government and transferred to the appellant company.

The Supreme Court clarified that even if it may be assumed that one or the other test as provided in the test of Ajay Hasia may be attracted, that by itself would not be sufficient to hold that it is an agency of the State or a company carrying on the functions of public nature. The observations made by the majority view of the seven judges' bench in Para. 40 of the case of Pradeep Kumar Biswas are very important.

> *'40. the picture that ultimately emerges is that the tests formulated in Ajay Hasia are not a rigid set of principles so that if a body falls within any one of them it must, ex hypothesi, be considered to be a State within the meaning of Article 12. The question in each case would be—whether in the light of the cumulative facts as established, the body is financially, functionally and administratively dominated by or under the control of the Government. Such control must be particular to the body in question and must be pervasive. If this is found then the body is a State within Article 12. On the other hand, when the control is merely regulatory whether under statute or otherwise, it would not serve to make the body a State.'*

It was held that merely regulatory provisions, to ensure that business or commercial activity carried on by private bodies' remains within a discipline, do not confer any status upon the company nor put any obligation upon it which may be enforced through issue of a writ under Article 226. After having discussed in detail the relevant judgments based on the point of instrumentality or agency of the government lastly, in para. 30, the Supreme Court held,

> *'...... a private company carrying on banking business as a scheduled bank cannot be termed as an institution or a company carrying on any statutory or public duty. A private body or a person may be amenable to writ jurisdiction only where it may become necessary to compel such body or association to enforce any statutory obligations or such obligations of public nature casting positive obligation upon it. We don't find such conditions are fulfilled in respect of a private company carrying on a commercial activity of banking. Merely regulatory provisions to ensure such activity carried on by private bodies work within a discipline, do not confer any such status upon the company nor put any such obligation upon it which may be enforced through issue of a writ under Article 226 of the Constitution. Present is a case of disciplinary action being taken against its employee by the appellant Bank. The respondent's service with the Bank stands terminated. The action of Bank was challenged by the respondent by filing a writ petition under Article 226 of the Constitution of India. The respondent is not trying to enforce any statutory duty on the part of the Bank....'*

It was further clarified that even though it is a judicially accepted norm that private interest has to give way to the public interest, if private property is acquired in the public interest it does not mean that the party whose property is acquired is performing any function or duty of a public character. Therefore, writ will not be maintainable where there may not be any non-compliance with or violation of any statutory provisions by the private body.

Binny Ltd. v. Sadasivan[9]

This is a case wherein the High Court, in exercise of its writ jurisdiction under Article 226 of the Constitution of India issued *mandamus* against a private limited company. The Company preferred SLP before the Supreme Court challenging the decision of the High Court. Originally the employees of the private company challenged their termination order by way of writ petition seeking the issuance of *mandamus* for their reinstatement in service. The preliminary objection taken by the respondent company was that the High Court had no jurisdiction to issue *mandamus* against the private limited company. Further, it was argued on behalf of the company that it was neither falling under the head of 'public authorities' nor their action involved public law element, for which writ of *mandamus* was available.

The Division Bench of the Madras High Court held that the employees were not entitled to get the relief of reinstatement and back wages and the court granted only a declaratory relief to the effect that the termination order was illegal and the employees had to work out an appropriate remedy before the appropriate forum.

At the time of final hearing of this matter, the Supreme Court had an opportunity to describe the scope of *mandamus* available to a High Court under Article 226 of the Constitution of India. Justice Balakrishnan put reliance upon the issue that the action invoking *mandamus* should be public law element. The following observations made by K.G. Balakrishnan, J. in paragraph 29 of the judgment while discussing about issuance of *mandamus* against private persons:

> '29. *Thus, it can be seen that a writ of mandamus or the remedy under Article 226 is pre-eminently a public law remedy and is not generally available as a remedy against private wrongs. It is used for enforcement of various rights of the public or to compel the public/statutory authorities to discharge their duties and to act within their bounds. It may be used to do justice when there is wrongful exercise of power or a refusal to perform duties. This writ is admirably equipped to serve as a judicial control over administrative actions. This writ could also be issued against any private body or person, specially in view of the words used in Article 226 of the Constitution. However, the scope of mandamus is limited to enforcement of public duty. The scope of mandamus is determined by the nature of the duty*

9. AIR 2005 SC 3203.

to be enforced, rather than the identity of the authority against whom it is sought. If the private body is discharging a public function and the denial of any right is in connection with the public duty imposed on such body, the public law remedy can be enforced. The duty cast on the public body may be either statutory or otherwise and the source of such power is immaterial, but, nevertheless, there must be the public law element in such action. Sometimes, it is difficult to distinguish between public law and private law remedies. According to Halsbury's Laws of England, 3rd ed., Vol. 30, page 682, "a public authority is a body not necessarily a county council, municipal corporation or other local authority which has public statutory duties and carries out its transactions for the benefit of the public and not for private profit." There cannot be any general definition of public authority or public action. The facts of each case decide the point.'

Further, he quoted in paragraph 32 of the judgment,

'32............ writ of mandamus can be issued against a private body which is not a State within the meaning of Article 12 of the Constitution and the High Court under Article 226 of the Constitution can exercise judicial review of the action challenged by a party. But there must be a public law element and it cannot be exercised to enforce purely private contracts entered into between the parties.'

Lastly, it is observed by the Supreme Court that there is no element of public law action in the present case. Therefore, writ of *mandamus* against private company is not maintainable.

5.3 *MANDAMUS* AGAINST CO-OPERATIVE MILLS

General Manager, Kisan Sahkari Chini Mills Ltd. v. Satrughan Nishad[10]

A question arose in the case of *G.M. Kisan Sahkari Chini Mills Ltd.* v. *Satrughan Nishad* that a co-operative sugar mill could be covered within the definition of 'other authorities' as defined in Article 12 of the Constitution of India and whether a writ was maintainable against it or not.

For the purpose of ascertaining the above mentioned fact the Supreme Court straight way sought help of the guidelines provided in the case of *Ajay Hasia* v. *Khalid Mujib*. It was held that the form in which the body is constituted, viz. whether as a society or co-operative society or company is quite irrelevant. The real status of the body with respect to the control of the Government is required to be taken into consideration. There is no hard-and-fast formula for it. In different facts or situations, different factors could be found to be overwhelming and indicative of whether the body is an "other authority" and hence falls within the definition of 'State' under Article 12 or not. After having applied various tests suggested in the case

10. (2003) 8 SCC 639.

of Ajay Hasia and having considered cumulatively, the Supreme Court held that none of the indicia laid down in Ajay Hasia's case exists in the case of the Mill. Hence, the said Mill is neither an instrumentality nor an agency of the Government, it cannot be said as an authority and therefore it is not a 'State' within the meaning of Article 12 of the Constitution.

From the above judgment it can be said that the Co-operative Mill, a private entity, upon which there is no direct or indirect hold of the Government, nor it is receiving any financial assistance of the Government. Hence, it is not covered within the definition of 'State'. The tests laid down in Ajay Hasia's case and International Airport Authority case were simply considered in the present case.

5.4 *MANDAMUS* AGAINST CO-OPERATIVE SOCIETIES, NOT CONTROLLED BY STATE

National Council of Educational Research and Training (NCERT)

Chander Mohan Khanna v. NCERT[11]

In the case of *Chander Mohan Khanna* v. *NCERT* the sole question involved was whether NCERT is "State" as defined under Article 12 of the Constitution? The appellant was terminated from the service by the Secretary of NCERT. He initially challenged the termination by way of filing writ petition under Article 226 of the Constitution before the Delhi High Court. The preliminary objection raised by the respondent NCERT was that it did not come under the definition of "State" as defined under Article 12 and hence writ petition against it was not maintainable. The Delhi High Court rejected the petition of the appellant by upholding the preliminary objection of the NCERT. Being aggrieved by the judgment of the Delhi High Court the appellant approached the Supreme Court by way of filing appeal under Article 136 of the Constitution.

The Supreme Court though considered all the authorities on the issue but came to the conclusion that there are only general principles but not exhaustive test to determine whether a body is an instrumentality or agency of the Government. Further the observations made in general principles that there is no cut and dried formula, which would provide correct division of bodies into those which are instrumentalities or agencies of the Government and those which are not. Which factors should be taken into consideration while declaring any body/authority as 'state' under Article 12? The powers, functions, finances and control of the Government are some of the important factors to answer whether any body/authority is "state" or not.

While deciding the issue Justice K. Jagannatha Shetty observed that the tests for considering any body/authority as "state" under Article 12 should be applied with care and caution. Merely because of the fact that the institution/authority is getting financial assistance from the Government, the same should not be declared as "state" under Article 12.

---

11. (1991) 4 SCC 578.

Over and above the financial assistance, deep and pervasive control of the Government over the institution in policy matters and management is must. He observed in the judgment,

> *'Article 12 should not be stretched so as to bring in every autonomous body which has some nexus with the Government within the sweep of the expression "State". A wide enlargement of the meaning must be tempered by a wise limitation. It must not be lost sight of that in the modern concept of Welfare State, independent institution, corporation and agency are generally subject to State control. The State control does not render such bodies as "State" under Article 12. The State control, however vast and pervasive, is not determinative. The financial contribution by the State is also not conclusive. The unusual degree of control over the management and policies of the body, and rendering of an important public service being the obligatory functions of the State may largely point out that the body is "State". If the Government operates behind a corporate veil, carrying out governmental activity and governmental functions of vital public importance, there may be little difficulty in identifying the body as "State" within the meaning of Article 12 of the Constitution.....'*

While applying the tests in order to ascertain whether NCERT is 'state' or not the work of the Supreme Court became rather easy as the Delhi High Court while rendering its judgment had undergone the exercise. The Supreme Court merely reiterated the work of the Delhi High Court. The summary of the constitution, object, functions and source of financial assistance of NCERT is reproduced herebelow:

(1) That the NCERT is a society registered under the Societies Registration Act, having its Memorandum of Association and the Rules for internal management.

(2) The objects of the Council are as follows:

  (a) to assist and advise the Ministry of Education and Social welfare in the implementation of its policies and major programmes in field of education particularly school education;

  (b) the Council is empowered, for the realisation of above objectives to undertake several kinds of programmes and activities which include co-ordination or research, extension, services and training dissemination of improved education techniques and practices in schools, colleges in educational programmes, distribute ideas and information, preparing and publication of books, materials, periodicals and other literature and allied activities; and

  (c) the Council is free to apply the income and property towards its objectives in of the implementation of programmes and governmental control is confined only to the proper utilisation of grant given by it, which is one of the sources of its funds;

(3) The funds of the Council shall, as per Rule 57 consist of grants made by Government, contribution from other sources, income from the assets of the Council and receipts of the Council from other sources.

After having studied in detail the framework of NCERT the Supreme Court observed that though the main source of the financial assistance of the Council was grant of the Government, the control of the Government was confined only to the proper utilisation of the grant. The Government interference was absent in policy matters. The NCERT was thus largely an autonomous body. The Supreme Court tried to compare this case with the case of *Tekraj* v. *Union of India* (AIR 1988 SC 469), wherein the issue for the consideration was whether the Institute of Constitutional and Parliamentary Studies (ICPS), a registered society under the Societies Registration Act was 'state' under Article 12 of the Constitution of India or not. The facts of both the cases are almost similar in a sense that both the institutions are largely dependent upon the government regarding financial assistance. Both are registered societies. The functions/objects of both the organizations were not controlled by or through the government. The government is not having any interference in the policy or management of the institutions. The Supreme Court has already declared that ICPS is not covered within the definition of 'state' under Article 12.

The counsel appearing for the appellant strongly put reliance upon the ratio laid down by the Supreme Court in the case of *P.K. Ramchandran Iyer* v. *ICAR* (AIR 1984 SC 541), where the Supreme Court held that Indian Council for Agricultural Research (ICAR) was "state" under Article 12. But Division Bench of Justice K. Jagannath Shetty and Justice Yogeshwar Dayal firmly opined that the facts of the present case and that of P.K. Ramchandran Iyer's case were quite different as in the later case ICAR was initially a government department and thereafter it was separated. The same was not case of NCERT. Neither there was any kind of governmental control in policy or internal management of the NCERT. The NCERT was not discharging any functions of government or of public importance. There was no deep and pervasive government control over the NCERT. Hence the Supreme Court said that the ratio laid down in P.K. Ramchandran Iyer was not applicable in this case and thereby held that the NCERT is not covered under the definition of 'state' under Article 12 of the Constitution.

Gayatri De v. Mausumi Co-operative Housing Society Ltd.[12]

Private co-operative societies are not covered within the definition of 'other authorities' under Article 12 of the Constitution of India and therefore, they are not subject to *mandamus*. But the facts of this case are

12. AIR 2004 SC 2271.

little different. A question involved in a writ petition filed under Article 226 of the Constitution of India was regarding allotment of residential house to the legal heirs of the deceased member. The Special officer was appointed by the High Court in the said Co-operative Society to look after the management of the society. The Special Officer re-allotted the house of deceased to the person other than the legal heirs. In a writ petition filed by the legal heirs for the allotment of house, the preliminary objection raised by the Special Officer that the writ of *mandamus* was not maintainable as it was against the Co-operative Society.

The Supreme Court in an appeal said that the same was maintainable as the subject matter of the writ petition was the order passed by the Special Officer in discharging his statutory functions. The Special Officer was appointed under the provisions of the West Bengal Co-operative Societies Act, 1983. Thus, he was considered as the statutory officer and therefore, he should be regarded as public authority as per the view of the Supreme Court, hence subject to the issuance of *mandamus*.

Apart from the fact that the Special Officer was a public authority, the Supreme Court was of the opinion that the writ petition under Article 226 of the Constitution of India was not confined to issuance of writ of *mandamus* only to a public authority, the bar extends also to issue directions to any person (individual). By adding this, the Supreme Court said that the Co-operative Society was under the control of a Special Officer and hence writ of *mandamus* was maintainable.

5.5 *MANDAMUS* AGAINST INTERNATIONAL ORGANISATION SET-UP AS NON-PROFIT RESEARCH AND TRAINING CENTRE

G. Bassi Reddy v. International Crops Research Institute (ICRISAT) and another[13]

International Crops Research Institute is an international organisation and is set-up as a non-profit research and training centre. Its object is to help developing countries in semiarid tropics to alleviate rural poverty and hunger in ways that are environmentally sustainable. The respondent No. 1 ICRISAT terminated the service of the appellant. Hence, he preferred writ petition challenging the action of the respondent before the High Court by way of filing writ petition under Article 226 of the Constitution of India. The High Court of Karnataka dismissed the writ petition with the reason that ICRISAT is neither covered under the definition of 'State' under Article 12 nor the work done by it was of a statutory duty or public function.

Being aggrieved by the judgment and order of the High Court, an appeal was filed by the employee challenging the order before the Supreme Court. Supreme Court (Per Ruma Pal, J.) took into consideration the following main points while deciding as to whether writ petition is

13. AIR 2003 SC 1764.

maintainable against the respondent institute under Article 226 of the Constitution of India or not:

- Object of ICRISAT is to help developing countries in semi-arid tropics to alleviate rural poverty and hunger in ways that are environmentally sustainable.
- It is a non-profit research and training centre by the Consultative Group on International Agricultural Research (CCIAR). The CCIAR is an informal association of about 50 government and non-government bodies and is co-sponsored by the Food and Agriculture Organisation of the United Nations (FAO), the United Nations Development Program (UNDP), the United Nations Environment Program (UNEP) and the World Bank.
- Certain members of the CCIAR agreed to provide funds to support the setting up and continued functioning of ICRISAT. The financing members of CCIAR entered into an agreement in the year 1972 with International Bank for Reconstruction and Development (IBRB) to a special account. The IBRD then entered into an agreement with Ford Foundation undertook to implement the proposal for setting up ICRISAT.
- Immunity from legal process was granted to ICRISAT by the Union of India under section 3 of the United Nations (Privilege and Immunities) Act, 1947.

The Supreme Court applied the tests laid down in the case of Pradeep Kumar Biswas to ascertain whether ICRISAT is 'State' under Article 12 of the Constitution or not. It was held that ICRISAT does not fulfil the test of its being 'State or other authority' under Article 12. It was not set-up by the Government and it gives its services voluntarily to a large number of countries besides India. It is not controlled by nor is it accountable to the Government.

Further it is observed that a writ petition under Article 226 also lies against a 'person' for 'any other purpose'. A writ under Article 226 can lie against a 'person' if it is a statutory body or performs a public function or discharges a public or statutory duty. ICRISAT has not been set-up by a statute nor are its activities statutorily controlled. Although, it is not easy to define what a public function or public duty is, it can reasonably be said that such functions are similar to or closely related to those performable by the State in its sovereign capacity. The ICRISAT has a role which extends beyond the territorial boundaries of India and its activities are designed to benefit people all over the world.

Thus, the Government neither administratively nor financially nor functionally controls ICRISAT and hence writ petition against it is not maintainable under Article 32 before the Supreme Court nor under Article 226 before a High Court.

5.6 *MANDAMUS* AGAINST PRIVATE INDIVIDUAL

Sohan Lal v. Union of India[14]

This matter was arisen out of a writ petition under Article 226 of the Constitution of India directing to restore the possession of the property to a displaced individual. The eviction of a displaced person is in contravention of the express provisions of Section 3 of the Public Premises (Eviction) Act, it can be declared illegal and by issuing writ of *mandamus* or order in the nature thereof can be made against Union of India to restore possession of the property to him from which he has been evicted if the property is in possession of Union of India.

It was further held by the Supreme Court, that if the property is in possession of another displaced person and he is not in collusion with the Union of India or has no knowledge that the eviction was illegal, a writ cannot issue to or an order in the nature of *mandamus* cannot be made against such private individual. There are very few instances wherein the Supreme Court has issued *mandamus* against private individuals.

Analysis and Inferences

The present legal position under the Constitution of India is that a writ of *mandamus* against individual is not maintainable before the Supreme Court and before the High Court. Although Article 226 of the Constitution specifically uses the word 'person' while defining the authorities against whom writ is permissible, yet *mandamus* is not issued against Private Individual in his personal capacity by our courts. It is now high time to reconsider the issue and if the work discharged even by a private individual pertains to discharging of statutory duty or is of a public function, writ of *mandamus* should be issued against him.

14. AIR 1957 SC 529.

6

Conclusions and Suggestions

After having discussed above mentioned cases and studying the past and existing legal position regarding the law relating to the subjects of *mandamus* in India following conclusions can be worked out:

1. So far as the issuance of *mandamus* is concerned against Union of India, State Governments, Parliament and State Legislatures, Public Officials, and Local Authorities, the law is very clear from the commencement of the Constitution till today. *Mandamus* can be issued against all above authorities/bodies. There is no scope of any kind of expansion even in future.
2. The most controversial and important point in the present research is the law relating to the subjects of *mandamus* against "Other authorities" as defined in Article 12 of the Constitution of India. If comparison of the powers to issue *mandamus* of the Supreme Court and those of the High Court is made, the scope of the Supreme Court is very narrow. The Supreme Court can issue *mandamus* only in the event of violation of fundamental rights enshrined in Part III of the Constitution of India. The Supreme Court can issue *mandamus* against the body/person which falls within the definition of "State" as defined under Article 12 of the Constitution; whereas in an appropriate cases the High Court can issue *mandamus* even against a private individual, private trust or any other private body, discharging the work of public importance. The Supreme Court under Article 32 does not exercise these powers.
3. If a survey is made regarding the legal position for issuance of *mandamus* against the body/persons falling within the criteria of "Other authorities" from the commencement of the Constitution of India, it can easily be understood that in the beginning very

narrow and restricted view was adopted by the courts. As the time passed, the Supreme Court found it fit to include more bodies, entities and companies within the parameter of "Other Authorities". Thus, the scope of Article 12 was expanded by the Supreme Court tremendously. At the same time, the Supreme Court expanded the scope of the High Court under Article 226 by approving issuance of *mandamus* even against a private body/person discharging public functions. The guidelines are also given by the Apex Court in the years 1979 and 1981 for the consideration as to whether a body or institution falls within the ambit of "Other Authorities" and hence "State" under Article 12 of the Constitution of India or not. Based upon these guidelines number of cases are decided by the Supreme Court itself.

4. Again, from the year 2002 the view of the Supreme Court has been changed. It appears that now it is trying to curtail the definition of the "State", more particularly definition of "Other Authorities". In the conclusion now summarise in short the view of the Supreme Court at different time in different cases and its adequacy.

A journey from the year 1951 to the year 2005 in issuing *Mandamus:*

The year 1951 was an era where the High Court of Madras did not issue writ of *mandamus* in the case of **University of Madras v. Shantha Bai**[1] even against the University. Thus, University was not found to be subject of *mandamus* in the year 1954. Strict interpretation of the term "Other Authorities" was done by the Madras High Court with the application of the doctrine of *ejusdem generis*. The term "Local and Other Authorities" must be construed *ejusdem generis* with Government and Legislature and hence natural or juristic persons cannot be regarded as instrumentalities of the Government. With this observation, Madras High Court refused to entertain writ of *mandamus* against the University.

Thereafter the Supreme Court impliedly rejected the ratio laid down in Shantha Bai's case by the Madras High Court in the case of **Ujjam Bai v. State of U.P.** by observing that the doctrine of *ejusdem generis* is not applicable while interpreting Article 12 of the Constitution.

Subject of *mandamus* became wider from the case of **Electricity Board, Rajasthan v. Mohan Lal**[2] in the year 1967. The respondent Board was earlier a government department and was subsequently separated from it. It was clarified by the Supreme Court by outrightly rejecting the principle of *ejusdem generis* that the same was wrongly applied by several High Courts. For the application of the principle of *ejusdem generis* there has to be common genesis. Government and legislature cannot be regarded as common genesis. Hence, in absence of the above principle, Rajasthan

1. AIR 1951 Mad. 67
2. AIR 1967 SC 1857.

Electricity Board was considered to be "instrumentality" and "State" under Article 12 of the Constitution. With this observation the Supreme Court held that the Electricity Boards are subject to the application of *mandamus*.

In the year 1975 the Supreme Court in **Sukhdev v. Bhagatram**'s case[3] further widened the scope of subjects of *mandamus* while making statutory corporations like LIC, ONGC and IFC amenable to the writ jurisdiction as falling within the criteria of "State" under Article 12 of the Constitution of India. The majority view expanded the scope of "State" from Rajasthan Electricity Board case. It was observed by the then Chief Justice A.N. Ray while speaking for majority that the body created by or under the statute could be considered as "State" under Article 12. All the corporations had to make rules or regulations for the purpose of internal arrangement. Thus, rules and regulations were subordinate legislations. The corporations had a statutory status. Hence the Corporations were held to be included within the definition of "other authorities" by the majority.

While considering the expansion of the subjects of *mandamus*, one should not forget the contribution given by **Justice Methew** in this case. In his separate confirming opinion, he added the fact that the corporations in question are public corporations and hence they should be included within the definition of "other authorities" as the concept of "State" had undergone drastic changes in the recent years. He was the first judge to observe and narrate that the public corporations were in real sense "**agencies or instrumentalities**" of the State and therefore, could fall within the definition of "State" under Article 12 of the Constitution. Their independent personality did not mean that they were not subject to the control of government or they were not instrumentalities of the government.

The aforesaid judgment is important not because of only general view of the then **Chief Justice A.N. Ray** declaring all the three statutory corporations within the meaning of "Other Authority" and applying the broader concept of 'instrumentality and agency of State' by Justice Methew, but also for the dissenting minority opinion of Justice Alagiriswami. **Justice Alagiriswami** was strictly against the view of declaring the said corporations as part of "Other Authority" and hence "State" under Article 12. Main reason given by him was that the private company employees would then be discriminated and they would be at disadvantageous position as compared to the Corporations or companies created by or under the Statute. He also warned his colleague Judges that by enabling the subject of *mandamus* to the statutory corporations and government companies they were opening flood gate of thousands of writ petitions, which would be dangerous.

This minority view of **Alagiriswami, J.** was not considered even after the judgment of **Sukhdev v. Bhagatram**. In the year 1979, in the case of **R.D. Shetty v. International Airport Authority of India**[4], more reliance was

3. AIR 1975 SC 1331.
4. AIR 1979 SC 1628.

placed upon the majority view while considering the fact as to whether international Airport Authority of India was "State" under Article 12 or not. While giving judgment, **Justice Bhagwati** by appreciating the theory of "instrumentality or agency of the State" developed by Justice Methew in **Sukhdev v. Bhagatram's case**, expanded the definition of "State" and held that the Airport Authority was an instrumentality or agency of the State created by the Central Government and therefore, it was "State" under Article 12 of the Constitution of India. Justice Bhagwati, in his judgment gave certain guidelines to consider any body as "State" or not. By and large the same guidelines/tests were given in the cases of **Ajay Hasia v. Khalid Mujib**[5] and **Som Prakash Rekhi v. Union of India**[6], in the year 1981. The aforesaid guidelines made it very easy to the Supreme Court and the High Courts to ascertain whether a body is an instrumentality or agency of State or not. The aforesaid three judgments opened the flood-gate of thousands of petitions seeking reliefs of *mandamus*. There would be nothing wrong to say that the period after the year 1981 till the year 2002 was just like an express highway. Each and every entity was given status of instrumentality or agency by the Courts if it satisfied any of the six tests given in **Airport Authority case** or **Ajay Hasia**'s case. Statutory Corporations, Government Companies, Registered Societies having control of the Government, Nationalized Banks, Universities and other Educational Institutions getting grant-in-aid, Judicial and quasi-judicial authorities came under the sweep of the term "instrumentalities or agencies" due to one or other guidelines/ tests.

During this period the employees of the aforesaid bodies enjoyed real fruits of democracy as they could easily knock the doors of the Supreme Court or the High Court seeking relief of *mandamus* against the violation of their fundamental rights by the employer. True concept of socialism was said to have been achieved.

As the time passed, the approach and thinking of the Supreme Court started changing. More particularly in the year 2002, when before the bench of Seven Judges the case of **Pradeep Kumar Biswas v. Indian Institute of Chemical Biology**[7] came up for hearing wherein the main issue required to be decided was whether the Council of Scientific and Industrial Research (CSIR) was "State" or not. In other words, the Seven Judges Bench of the Supreme Court reiterated the ratio laid down by the Supreme Court in the year 1975 in the case of Sabhajit Tewary. The Supreme Court, by majority overruled the earlier ratio of not declaring CSIR as "State" under Article 12.

The Supreme Court not only declared CSIR as "State" under Article 12 and permitted issuance of *mandamus* against CSIR, but it gave further guidelines so as to restrict the subject of *mandamus* issued by the Courts. It said that the body or entity could not be declared as "State" even if it

5. AIR 1981 SC 487.
6. AIR 1981 SC 212.
7. (2002)5 SCC 111.

satisfied one or more guidelines laid down in Ajay Hasia's case. Further it added that in order to constitute a body as instrumentality or agency of the State there must be **administrative, financial and functional control** of the State. The important guidelines of Pradeep Kumar Biswas's case are reproduced herebelow:

1. Principles laid down in Ajay Hasia are not a rigid set of principles so that if a body falls within any one of them it must exhypothesi, be considered to be a "State" within the meaning of Article 12.
2. The Question in each case will have to be considered on the bases of facts available as to whether in the light of the cumulative facts as established, the body is financially, functionally, administratively dominated, by or under the control of the Government.
3. Such control must be particular to the body in question and must be pervasive.
4. Mere regulatory control whether under statute or otherwise would not serve to make a body a State.

The above judgment of Pradeep Kumar Biswas case is of seven Judges' Bench and therefore the ratio and the guidelines given in this case is having bind effect. The subsequent case of **Federal Bank Ltd. v. Sagar Thomas**[8], the Supreme Court relied upon the judgment of Pradeep Kumar Biswas case and held that a Company constituted under the Companies Act, 1956, (not a Government Company) is not covered under the definition of 'other authority' and hence not 'State' under Article 12 even though one or two tests of Ajay Hasia's case are attracted, that by itself, would not be sufficient to hold that it is an agency of the State or a company carrying on the functions of public nature.

Lastly, the case of **Zee Tele Films Ltd. v. Union of India**[9], wherein the Supreme Court by solely relying upon Pradeep Kumar Biswas case held that the Board of Control for Cricket in India (BCCI) is not "State" under Article 12 and hence petitioner cannot file writ petition against the action of BCCI under Article 32 before the Supreme Court. The majority view was that the definition of "State" need not be further expanded. State is today distancing itself from commercial activities and concentrating on governance rather than on business. In democracy there is dividing line between State enterprise and non-State enterprise which is distinct. Judiciary should not be an instrument to erase said dividing line unless a circumstance of the day requires it to do so.

It appears from the recent judgments of the Supreme Court regarding the scope of "Other authorities" under Article 12, that a heavy reliance is

8. (2003) 10 SCC 733.
9. AIR 2005 SC 2677.

put upon the present economic policy of the Government, i.e. liberalization. By taking into consideration the fact that the Government is withdrawing itself from the business activities, the Supreme Court found it fit not to expand further the definition of State under Article 12.

In these circumstances, the question regarding issuance of writ of *mandamus* in our country has become very complicated so far as the private persons are concerned. The High Court can issue *mandamus* in a writ petition filed under Article 226 against private persons, if the work done by them is analogous to that of public nature. But the Supreme Court can not issue *mandamus* against private persons as they are not covered under the definition of "State" under Article 12 of the Constitution. In England there was no such difference in issuance of writ of *mandamus* ever existed depending upon the forum of the Court. This difference in India is due to the provisions of Article 12 of the Constitution which specifically excludes petitioner from seeking remedy of *mandamus* from the Supreme Court against private persons.

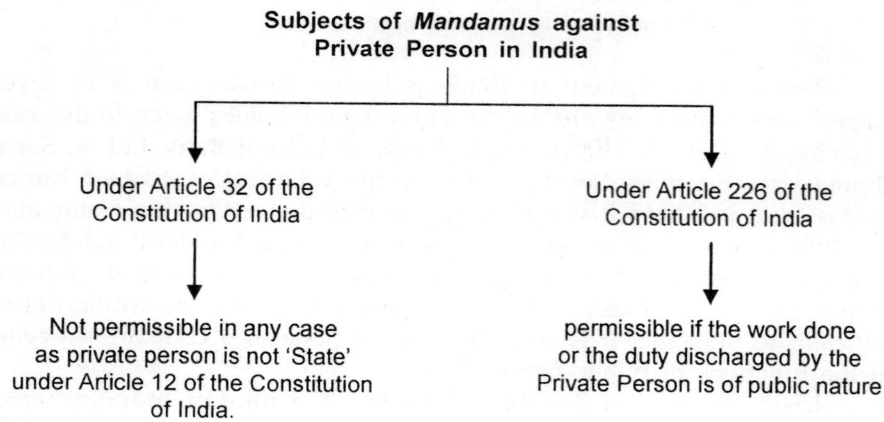

Looking at the definition of *mandamus* given under the Halsbury's Laws of England, it specifically says that *mandamus* is available even against private persons. The law of writs is improved a lot in India and traveled far ahead and now it is high time to think about the issuance of *mandamus* even against private persons by the Supreme Court because of the following reasons:

(a) It is improper to deny the remedy of *mandamus* against private persons by the Supreme Court under Article 32 merely on the ground that they are not covered under the definition of "State". If it is the sole ground, this is a proper time that the private person discharging duty of public nature should be included within the definition of "State".

(b) It is merely an illusion to think that the flow of cases before the Supreme Court can be curtailed by denying issuance of writ of *mandamus* against private persons by the Supreme Court. Most of such writs against private persons decided by the High Court under Article 226 of the Constitution, reaches the Supreme Court by way of an appeal. Hence, the workload before the Supreme Court is not effectively curtailed. On the contrary, it takes much time, expenditure and extra forum to get a case decided. The settled principle of writ jurisdiction says that the High Court and Supreme Court, both are given by and large the same powers and both have concurrent jurisdiction. If it is so, there is no sense in discriminating a private person while issuing writ of *mandamus*.

(c) The law relating to issuance of *mandamus* should be same irrespective of the Court. If the Supreme Court permits issuance of *mandamus* by the High Court against private persons in case duty discharged by him is of public nature, then why not the Supreme Court itself able to issue it. For that, small amendments in Articles 12 and 32 are required to be carried out.

(d) Writ of *Habeas Corpus* is available even against a private person in India then why not *mandamus* be issued against private persons? The writ remedy is a discretionary and extra-ordinary remedy and therefore, it should be left to the discretion of the Court whether to issue writ of *mandamus* against private person or not depending upon the facts of the case.

(e) Today, India is in the era of globalization and privatization. Government is now not keen to start or even to continue with its business activities. On the contrary, it is withdrawing its hands from public ventures and encouraging privatization. India also invites many multi-national companies for the purpose of trading as well as manufacturing of goods. In these circumstances, the employment opportunities in the private sector would increase. At the same time, the opportunities of employment by State or its instrumentalities or agencies will decrease. Private sectors will not give the job protection to its employees as it is given to the Government/neo-Government servants. The employer would terminate its employees at any time, without following principles of natural justice. The protection through writ of *mandamus* would not be available to such employees on the ground of the employer being a private company.

Therefore, it is now a high time to expand the scope of *mandamus* qua the High Court under Article 226 and the Supreme Court under Article 32 of the Constitution of India so as to include even private companies.

SUGGESTIONS

After having traveled in the ocean of the law relating to the subjects of *mandamus* and after summarizing the conclusions the following suggestions can be given:

1. The law relating to subjects of *mandamus* should be expanded so as to issue writ of *mandamus* by the High Court as well as the Supreme Court against private persons viz.

- **(a) private individuals,**
- **(b) private companies,**
- **(c) societies registered under the Societies Registration Act, not controlled by the State, and**
- **(d) multi-national companies.**

This change in the subjects of issuance of *mandamus* is must in the Constitution as India is now entering into the world of globalization and privatization. In the coming years the Government will completely withdraw its hands from the business activities and will promote and encourage the business of the private sectors. Therefore, the job opportunities in the private companies, industries, factories and other sectors will be increased rapidly. But hard reality is that unlike the government servants, the employees of private sectors will not get job protection. They will be at the mercy of the employers of private sectors. This suggestion would help the employees of private sector to obtain job protection by availing remedy of *mandamus*.

Possible Difficulty

This suggested expansion of scope of *mandamus* would open flood-gate of thousands of writ petitions. The courts having writ jurisdiction would be over-burdened with the lakhs of cases. This suggestion, if implemented, would discourage the business of private sectors and no multi-national company would like to come to India and to carry on its business activities. The constitutional protection available to the Government servants in India is unique. Nowhere in the world, such protection is given to the employees against the employer. (here the government). This suggestion will affect the economy of the country as the foreign companies may not start business in India if they are subject to issuance of *mandamus* in the event of violation of fundamental rights of the employees by them.

In India, there are already stringent and rigorous provisions under the existing labour laws protecting the rights of the employees and workmen against their employers. If the scope of *mandamus* as suggested aforesaid is expanded, the employers in India would be discouraged and demotivated to open the industries and offer the employment to the unemployed persons.

Possible Solution

Different Courts over and above High Courts and the Supreme Court can be given powers to issue writ of *mandamus*. By doing this the burden of cases can be distributed and remedy of *mandamus* can be made available to the people even against private persons in a fit and proper case. The Courts other than High Courts and the Supreme Court can be given powers to issue *mandamus* by way of amendment in the Parliament. Article 32(3) of the Constitution of India empowers the Parliament to confer the power to issue *mandamus* to any Court other than High Court and the Supreme Court of India.

Under the fear of oppose by the private sector and foreign companies, it would not be proper to refuse to implement this suggestion. This suggestion to include private companies and foreign companies within the purview of *mandamus* is must as the government is now not keen to enter into the business ventures and withdrawing its hands. To protect the fundamental rights of citizens from the arbitrary actions of the employers of the private sectors and foreign companies, it is necessary to issue *mandamus* against them as well.

2. The definition of "State" under Article 12 of the Constitution of India should be amended so as to include specifically the aforesaid person/entities, i.e. private persons, foreign companies and multinational companies under the preview of "other authorities".

At present, the Supreme Court is not issuing the *mandamus* against private persons. The question as to whether *mandamus* can be issued against multinational companies or not is kept open by the Supreme Court. But, *mandamus* can be issued by High Courts under Article 226 of the Constitution of India against private persons if the work discharged by such private body/persons is of a public nature. The Supreme Court can not issue *mandamus* in the event of violation of fundamental rights against private persons in a writ petition under Article 32 as private persons, i.e. private companies, private trusts not under the control of the Government, co-operative banks, private individuals, etc. since the above mentioned bodies/persons are not included within the definition of "other authorities" and hence they are not "State" under Article 12 of the Constitution.

If High Court under Article 226 can issue *mandamus* against private persons, then why not the Supreme Court under Article 32? Against the decision of a High Court in a writ of *mandamus*, one can file an appeal before the Latters Patent Bench of the same High Court, wherever the jurisdiction is so vested or otherwise an appeal before the Supreme Court. It happens in number of cases where aggrieved persons approach the Supreme Court against the judgment and order of a High Court in a writ of *mandamus*. Thus, there is no reason to prohibit issuance of *mandamus* by the Supreme Court against private persons in the event of violation of fundamental rights by them, a thing which is made indirectly permissible but directly prohibited by the Constitutional scheme. It is a right time to remove this prohibition.

Possible Difficulty

It is difficult to amend the Constitution of India, more particularly, the provisions contained in Part III of the Constitution of India.

Private persons, i.e. private companies, private trusts not controlled by the government, foreign and multinational companies, private individuals, etc. will oppose this possible amendment.

Possible Solution

It may be complicated, but not impossible to make amendments in Article 12 of the Constitution of India. With this amendment, the power of High Courts under Article 226 and that of the Supreme Court under Article 32 to issue writs, order or direction will be increased.

According to the doctrine of the Basic Structure given by thirteen Judges' Constitutional Bench in the case of **Kesavanand Bharati v. State of Kerala**[10], it specifically says that the Parliament has no power to amend the basic structure or essential framework of the Constitution of India so as to take away or abridge or curtail the power of the judicial review of the Court. In the suggested amendment, the powers of High Courts and the Supreme Court will be increased and therefore, it is permissible to amend the Constitution of India as aforesaid.

Mandamus can be issued by a High Court under Article 226 against private persons if the work discharged by such private persons is in the nature of public duty and they violate any of the fundamental rights. By way of this proposed amendment the Supreme Court will be competent to issue *mandamus* against private persons as well. Due to this proposed amendment, aggrieved person will directly knock the doors of the Supreme Court by *mandamus* under Article 32 in the event of violation of his fundamental rights by private persons.

3. This power to issue writ of *mandamus* should be exercised with care and caution against private persons. The Court should use its discretionary powers while issuing writs by perusing facts of each case.

Possible Difficulty

The writ remedy is an extra-ordinary remedy. If writ jurisdiction is expanded so as to include even the aforesaid private person within its ambit then everybody would be tempted to avail writ remedy instead of filing suit in civil courts having original jurisdiction.

Suggested Solution

In the proposed amendment in this research work it is made specifically clear that the issuance of writ of *mandamus* against the private persons should always be subject to the discretionary powers of a judge as well as the general principles of writ jurisdiction. One of the general

10. AIR 1973 SC 1461.

principles of writ remedy says that the petitioner can not file writ if he is having alternative, equally efficacious remedy available at law. Thus, it should be left to the discretion of a Judge whether to entertain writ of *mandamus* against a private person or not. Fear of misuse or improper use of writ of *mandamus* can be avoided by appointing competent and efficient judges.

4. Powers to issue writ of *mandamus* should be given to certain lower courts also e.g. City Civil Court or District Court within local limits of its jurisdiction. By doing so, the excessive flow of writ petitions can be distributed among various courts.

This can be done by the Parliament by enacting a law empowering other courts to exercise writ jurisdiction. Article 32(3) of the Constitution of India permits the Parliament to enact any such law. This power has not yet exercised by the Parliament. If writ jurisdiction is assigned to aforesaid lower courts also, then the people will not rush to the High Courts and the Supreme Court to get speedy remedy.

Possible Difficulty

As said above, the writ remedy is an extra-ordinary remedy. In England only King could issue writs in early days. Such extra-ordinary remedy can not be given to the lower courts. At the same time this would amount to direct interference with the original jurisdiction of the Civil Courts.

Suggested Solution

Law should change with the passage of time and the demand of the people. In England, King delegated his power to issue writs to the Chancellor. Chancery Court started giving justice by issuing writs. Thereafter, the Court of Queen's Bench was given power to issue writs. Subsequently, other courts were also empowered to issue writs.

If delegation of powers of issuance of writs to different courts is justified and made permissible in England, then why the same thing should not be done in this country? At present, High Courts of the States and the Supreme Court are burdened with the excessive pending writ petitions. If City Civil Courts or the District Courts or a newly constituted courts lower than High Court are assigned writ jurisdiction, the flow of writs can effectively be dealt with by such courts. Burden of cases can be decreased in such circumstances as the Lok Adalats or the remedies by way of Arbitration or Conciliation have their own limitations.

By this proposed amendment power to issue *mandamus* will be given to the lower courts only in the event of violation of fundamental rights. Thus, there is no direct or indirect interference with the original jurisdiction of civil courts by way of this proposed amendment.

5. *Mandamus* should be issued by the Courts against the legislature at least in the following cases:

(a) ***Mandamus* should be issued against the Legislature directing it to compel the members of the House to remain compulsorily present at least for certain minimum days when the House is working.**

Member of Parliament or Member of Legislative Assembly is a public servant. He is bound to discharge his duty. One of his essential public duty towards the people of his constituency is that he should remain present in the House and present the problems of his constituency and get it solved. Instead of doing it, he consistently remains absent in the House without any reasons and if no action is taken by the Speaker of the House, he should, by issuance of *mandamus* be compelled to remain present in the House.

(b) **There are number of legislations which are out-dated and not in operation, but yet they are not repealed by the legislature for no reasons. By issuance of *mandamus*, the Courts should direct the legislature to repeal the statutes which are not in operation.**

Possible Difficulty

To issue *mandamus* even in the above cases, would be contrary to the *doctrine of Separation of Powers*. Judiciary cannot direct the legislature in its functioning. This amendment will be difficult to carry out as it will be opposed by the legislatures on the ground that it infringes their absolute privilege.

Possible Solution

Although the *doctrine of Separation of Power* is equally true against the executive, judiciary cannot direct the executive in its functions as per this doctrine. In spite of this position, time and again, the judiciary has directed, by issuance of *mandamus* to the executive, where it has not discharged its functions properly or misused its powers. In the same manner judiciary can even direct the legislature to discharge his functions which are essential in nature. The prime function of the legislature is to enact the laws. It is made specifically clear that no *mandamus* should be permitted against the legislature directing it to enact any law. While maintaining this position, *doctrine of Separation of Power* can be observed without any difficulty.

6. *Mandamus* should be issued for observance of certain fundamental duties enshrined under Part IV-A of the Constitution of India. Strict observance of the following Fundamental duties is must:

(i) **Fundamental duty under Article 51-A(a) to abide by the**

Constitution and respect its ideals and institutions, the National Flag and the National Anthem.

(ii) To uphold and protect the sovereignty, unity and integrity of India under Article 51-A(c).

(iii) To protect and improve the national environment including forests, lakes, rivers and wild life, and to have compassion for living creatures under Article 51-A(g).

(iv) To safeguard public property and to abjure violence under Article 51-A(i).

It must be the prime duty of every citizen of India to honor our National Flag and sing National Anthem. Now after the judgment of the Supreme Court in the case of *Naveen Jindal* v. *Union of India,* every citizen of India can keep National Flag at his residence. If any citizen is given this freedom to keep National Flag with him at his residence then it becomes his duty to see that due and proper respect and honour should be given to the National Flag. Therefore, any citizen dishonours the National Flag or misbehaves or makes insults of it, the same should not be permitted. Thus by issuance of *mandamus* the Supreme Court and High Courts should command the citizens to respect and honor National Flag. In the same manner citizens should be directed by the *mandamus* to sing National Anthem.

To protect and improve the natural environment is also a part and parcel of fundamental duties. The Supreme Court, by expanding the right to life, included right to clean environment of a citizen and issued *mandamus,* directing the Government and even a private person not to pollute the environment. By issuance of *mandamus* this fundamental duty must be strictly observed.

To safeguard the public property and to abjure violence is also a kind of fundamental duty which must be observed strictly. *Mandamus* is the remedy by which citizens can be compelled to observe by command all the above mentioned all fundamental duties.

Possible Difficulty

The people will resist strict observance of the aforesaid fundamental duties. Moreover, these fundamental duties under Article 51-A are not mandatory and therefore, no action can be taken against any citizen in the event of non-observance of any of the fundamental duties by citizens.

Possible Solution

The aforesaid fundamental duties are so important that their strict compliance and observance is must in the national interest. When the Supreme Court is issuing *mandamus* directing the government and private person to comply a fundamental duty by converting it into a fundamental right, there is no need for the Parliament to wait till the further direction by the Supreme Court. (e.g. Right to clean environment is now a fundamental right as declared by the Supreme Court). By way of constitutional amendment, the Supreme Court by way of issuing *mandamus* must observe the above mentioned three fundamental duties.

If the above suggestions are accepted and implemented by the Government, number of problems can be solved and Courts can decide the cases by remaining within the frame-work of Socialism, which is one of the expected goals in the Constitution of India. The Courts can give speedy Justice. The employees of the private sectors will not be at the mercy of their employers, if the suggestions are accepted. Moreover, Members of Legislative Assembly and Members of Parliament will become responsible and conscious towards their duties and they will not remain absent from the house except in unavoidable circumstances. With the implementation of these suggestions, the multinational companies will be careful in establishing its business in India and there will be no more disasters like Bhopal Gas Tragedy. In the direction of advancement of subjects of *mandamus,* India has traveled a lot as compared to other countries, including England. Now it is high time to have further changes in this area with the passage of time, requirement of the people and change in the circumstances.

List of Cases

1. A.C. Mahomed *v.* Corporation of Calcutta (45 C.W.N. 408)
2. A.L. Karla *v.* Project and Equipment Corporation of India (AIR 1984 SC 1361)
3. ABL International Ltd. *v.* Export Credit Guarantee Corporation of India Ltd. [(2004) 3 SCC 553]
4. Action Group Res. In Environment and Educational Development Society *v.* Sakky Bai [(1998) 9 SCC 685]
5. Air India Statutory Corporation *v.* United Labour Union (AIR 1997 SC 645)
6. Air India *v.* B. R. Age (AIR 1996 SC 276)
7. Ajay Hasia *v.* Khalid Mujib (AIR 1981 SC 487)
8. A.R. Antulay *v.* R.S.Nayak (AIR 1988 SC 1531)
9. Ajit Singh *v.* State of Punjab (AIR 1967 SC 856)
10. All India Reserve Bank Retired Officers' Association and others *v.* Union of India and others (AIR 1992 SC 767)
11. All India Sainik School Employees Association *v.* Defence Minister-*cum*-Chairman, Board of Governors, Sainik School Society (AIR 1988 SC 88)
12. Amirabbas Abbasi Sahebzada Saiyed Muhammed *v.* State of M.P. (AIR 1960 SC 768)
13. Avedhesh Maharshi *v.* State (AIR 1991 ALL. 52)
14. B.S. Minhas *v.* Indian Statistical Institute [(1983) 4 SCC 588]
15. Balbir Kaur *v.* Steel Authority of India Ltd. (AIR 2000 SC 1596)
16. Bangalore Medical Trust *v.* B.S. Muddappa (AIR 1991 SC 1902)
17. Bank of India *v.* O.P. Swarnaker (AIR 2003 SC 858)
18. Bhopal Sugar Industries *v.* I.T.O. (AIR 1961 SC 182)
19. Bihar School Examination Board *v.* Subhas Chandra (AIR 1970 SC 1269)
20. Bihar School Examination Board *v.* Subhas Chandra (AIR 1970 SC 1269)
21. Biman Krishna Bose *v.* United India Insurance Company Ltd. [(2001) 6 SCC 477]
22. Binny Ltd. *v.* International Crops Research Institute [ICRISAT] and others (AIR 2003 SC 1764)
23. Board of Examiners *v.* Probhash Chandra Roy (I.L.R. 40 Cal. 588)
24. Bramo Samaj Education Society *v.* State of West Bengal [(2004) 6 SCC 224]

25. British India Corporation Ltd. *v.* Market Committee, Dhariwal (AIR 1983 SC 162)
26. Budhan Choudhary *v.* State of Bihar (AIR 1955 SC 191)
27. Central Inland Water Transport Corporation *v.* Brijo Nath (AIR 1986 SC 1571)
28. Chain Singh *v.* Mata Vaishno Devi Shrine Board [(2004)12 SCC 634]
29. Chairman, Railway Board *v.* Chandrima Das (AIR 2000 SC 988) Chairman/Director, Combined Entrance Examination *v.* Osiris Das [(1992) 3 SCC 543]
30. Chander Mohan Khanna *v.* NCERT [(1991) 4 SCC 578]
31. Chhotelal *v.* State of Utter Pradesh (AIR 1951 All. 228)
32. Chief Controlling Revenue Authority and Superintendent of Stamps *v.* Maharashtra Sugar Mills Ltd. (AIR 1950 SC 218)
33. Chintaman Rao *v.* State of M.O. (AIR 1951 SC 118)
34. Chiranjit Lal Chaudhari *v.* Union of India (AIR 1951 SC 41)
35. Commissioner of Income-Tax, Bombay *v.* Bombay Trust Corporation (AIR 1936 PC 269)
36. Commissioner of Police *v.* Gordhandas (AIR 1952 SC 16)
37. CSIR Scientific Workers' Association *v.* Union of India [(2003) 9 SCC 289]
38. Delhi Transport Corporation *v.* D.T.C. Mazdoor Congress (AIR 1991 SC 101)
39. District Manager, APSRTC, Vijaywada *v.* K. Sivaji and Others (AIR 2001 SC 383)
40. Durga Prasad *v.* Chief Controller, Import and Export (AIR 1970 SC 769)
41. E.A. Co-op. Housing Society *v.* State of Maharashtra (AIR 1966 SC 1449)
42. Electricity Board, Rajasthan *v.* Mohan Lal (AIR 1967 SC 1857)
43. Federal Bank Ltd. *v.* Sagar Thomas [(2003)10 SCC 73]
44. Firm Mehtab Majid and Co. *v.* State of Madras (AIR 1963 SC 928)
45. Ganapathi National Middle School *v.* M. Durai Kannan (AIR 1996 SC 1316)
46. Gayatri De *v.* Mousumi Co-operative Housing Society Ltd. (AIR 2004 SC 2271)
47. General Manager, Kisan Sahkari Chini Mills Ltd. *v.* Satrughan Nishad [(2003) 8 SCC 639]
48. Govind Laxaman *v.* Minicipal Corporation for the City of Bombay [4 DLR (Bom.) 22]
49. Grih Kalyan Kendra Workers' Union *v.* Union of India (AIR 1991 SC 1173)
50. Gujarat State Financial Corporation *v.* Lotus Hotels (P) Ltd. [(1982)3 SCC 379]
51. Gurbachan Singh *v.* State of Bombay (AIR 1952 SC 221)
52. Hamid Hasan *v.* Banwarilal Roy (AIR 1947 SC 90)
53. Harshad J. Shah *v.* L.I.C. of India (AIR 1997 SC 2459)

54. Haryana Housing Board *v.* Haryana Housing Boards Employees Union (AIR 1996 SC 434)
55. Himansu Kumar Bose *v.* Jyoti Prakash (AIR 1964 SC 1636)
56. Hindustan Steel Works Construction Ltd. *v.* State of Kerala (AIR 1997 SC 2275)
57. Hirendra Nath *v.* Calcutta Corporation (AIR 1941 Cal. 386)
58. Indrajit Barua and others *v.* Election Commission of India and others (AIR 1986 SC 103)
59. J.M. Sen Gupta's case (AIR 1925 Cal. 48)
60. Jagannath Rao and others *v.* State of Orissa and others (AIR 1969 SC 215)
61. Jamshed Hormusji Wadia *v.* Board of Trustees, Port of Mumbai (AIR 2004 SC 1815)
62. Jamshed N. Guzdar *v.* State of Maharashtra (AIR 2005 SC 862)
63. Jatindra Mohan Sen Gupta's case (AIR 1925 Cal. 48)
64. K.C. Sharma *v.* Delhi Stock Exchange and others [JT 2005 (4) SC 18]
65. K. Ramdas Shenoy *v.* Udipi Municipality (AIR 1974 SC 2177)
66. K. S. Ramamurthy Raddiar *v.* The Chief Commissioner, Pondicheri (AIR 1963 SC 1461)
67. K.N.Guruswamy *v.* State of Mysore (AIR 1954 SC 592)
68. Kanhiya Lal Omar *v.* R.K. Trivedi (AIR 1986 SC 111)
69. Kapila Hingorani *v.* State of Bihar (AIR 2005 SC 980)
70. Konkan Railway Corporation Ltd. *v.* Mehul Construction Co. (AIR 2000 SC 2821)
71. L.I.C. *v.* Manubhai Shah [(1992)3 SCC 637]
72. Lakshmimoni Dassi (AIR 1941 Cal. 391)
73. LIC of India *v.* Consumer Education and Research Centre [(1995)5 SCC 482]
74. M.C. Mehta *v.* Union of India (AIR 1987 SC 1086)
75. M.K. Agarwal *v.* Gurgaon Gramin Bank (AIR 1988 SC 286)
76. M/s. Dwarkadas Marfatia and Sons *v.* Board of the Port of Bombay (AIR 1989 SC 1642)
77. M/s. Hyderabad Commercials *v.* Indian Bank (AIR 1991 SC 247)
78. M/s. Zee Telefilms Ltd. and another *v.* Union of India and others [JT 2005 (2) SC 8]
79. Mahabir Auto Stores *v.* Indian Oil Corporation (AIR 1990 SC 1031)
80. Maharshi Avadesh *v.* Union of India [(1994) Supp. 1 SCC 713]
81. Mahesh Chandra *v.* Regional Manager, U.P. Financial Corporation (AIR 1993 SC 935)
82. Maila Singh *v.* Bourne (AIR 1931 Range. 326)
83. Managing Committee, Sri Lakshmi N.A. College *v.* Prem Chand [(1999) 9 SCC 262]
84. Maneka Gandhi *v.* Union of India (AIR 1978 SC 597)
85. Manmohan Singh Jaitla *v.* Commissioner, Union Territory, Chandigarh and others (AIR 1985 SC 264)
86. Marbury *v.* Madison (1803 Cranch 137, 2 L.Ed. 60)

87. Mathen *v.* District Magistrate of Trivandrum (AIR 1939 PC 213)
88. Mohammad Yasin *v.* The Town Area Committee, Jalalabad and another (AIR 1952 SC 162)
89. Municipal Corporation of Delhi *v.* Birla Cotton Spinning and Weaving Mills, Delhi (AIR 1968 SC 1232)
90. Municipal Corporation of Greater Bombay *v.* Advance Builders (AIR 1972 SC 793)
91. Mysore Paper Mills Ltd. *v.* Mysore Paper Mills Officers' Association (AIR 2002 SC 609)
92. Naresh S. Mirajkar *v.* State of Maharashtra (AIR 1967 SC 1)
93. Nathmal *v.* Commissioner, Civil Supplies (AIR 1952 Raj. 74)
94. National Human Rights Commission *v.* State of Gujarat and others [(2004) 8 SCC 610]
95. New Manek Chowk Spinning and Weaving Mills *v.* Municipal Corporation of the City of Ahmedabad (AIR 1967 SC 1801)
96. ONGC *v.* Association of NGC Industries of Gujarat (AIR 1990 SC 1851)
97. Olga Tellis *v.* Bombay Municipal Corporation (AIR 1986 SC 180)
98. Om Prakash *v.* State of U.P. (AIR 2004 SC 1896)
99. P.K. Banerjee *v.* L.J. Simonds (AIR 1947 Cal. 307)
100. P.K. Ramchandran Iyer *v.* Union of India (AIR 1984 SC 541)
101. P.S.R. Sadhanatham *v.* Arunachalam (AIR 1980 SC 856)
102. Prabhani Transport Co-operative Society *v.* Regional Transport Authority, Aurangabad and others (AIR 1960 SC 801)
103. Pradeep Kumar Biswas *v.* Indian Institute of Chemical Biology [(2002) 5 SCC 111]
104. Pradyat Kumar Bose *v.* Chief Justice of the High Court of Calcutta (AIR 1956 SC 285)
105. Praga Tools Corporation Ltd. *v.* C.V. Imanual (AIR 1969 SC 1306)
106. Prem Chand Garg *v.* Excise Commissioner (AIR 1963 SC 996)
107. Premji Bhai *v.* Delhi Development Authority (AIR 1980 SC 738)
108. Purno Chundur Dutt (I.L.R. 35 Cal. 915)
109. Queen *v.* Price [(1871) Q.B. 411]
110. Queen *v.* The Judges and Justices of the Central Criminal Court [(1883) Q.B. 479]
111. Queen *v.* The Mayor and Corporation of the Borough of Bangor (1886) Q.B. 349)
112. R. *v.* Devon, J.J. [(1924) 1 K.B. 503]
113. R. *v.* Dunsheath [(1950) 2 All E.R. 741]
114. R. *v.* Kesteven, J.J. [(1844) Q.B. 810]
115. R. *v.* Marsham [(1892) K.B. 371]
116. R. *v.* Mayor of Monmouthy [(1870) QB 251 (256)]
117. R. *v.* Norflok [(1950) 2 K.B. 558]
118. R. *v.* Norflok Quarter Sessions [(1953) 2 All E.R. 3456]
119. R. *v.* Powell [(1841) 1 Q.B. 352]
120. R. *v.* Secretary of State for War [(1891) 2 Q.B. 326]

121. R. *v.* Thomas [(1892) 1 Q.B. 426]
122. R.J. Mehta *v.* C.J., Venkata Shrinivas Deshpande (AIR 1982 Bom. 125)
123. R. *v.* Income Tax Special Purpose Commissioner [(1888) Q.B. 313]
124. Railway Board *v.* M/s. Observer Publications (P) Ltd. (AIR 1972 SC 1792)
125. Rajasthan Adult Education Association *v.* Ashoka Bhatacharya (AIR 1998 SC 336)
126. Ram Chandra Sharma *v.* Modern Food Industries (India) Ltd. [(1998) 8 SCC 719]
127. Ram Gopal Sharma *v.* Sukhdev Raj Rudra [(2001) 9 SCC 201]
128. Ramana D. Shetty *v.* International Airport Authority of India (AIR 1979 SC 1628)
129. Ramprasad *v.* State of Bihar (AIR 1953 SC 215 220)
130. Ranjit Singh *v.* Union Territory of Chandigarh (AIR 1991 SC 2296)
131. Ranvirkumar Sinha, Commander *v.* Union of India [(1991) Cr.L.J. 1729 (Bom.)]
132. Rashid Ahmed *v.* The Municipal Board, Kairana (AIR 1950 SC 163)
133. *re G.A. Satesan* (I.L.R. 40 Mas. 125)
134. Reference case under Article 143 of the Constitution (AIR 1965 SC 745)
135. Reg. *v.* Glamorgan County Council [(1899) 2 Q.B.. 536]
136. Rex *v.* Army Council [(1917) 2 K.B. 504]
137. Rex *v.* Army Council [(1940) 1 K.B. 719]
138. Rex *v.* Barton and Immingham Light Railway Company [(1912) 3 K.B. 72]
139. Rex *v.* Bedwelly Urban District Council [(1934) 1 K.B.333]
140. Rex *v.* Board of Education [(1910)2 K.B. 165]
141. Rex *v.* Commissioners for Special Purposes of Income Tax [(1920) 1 K.B. 26]
142. Rex *v.* Hanley Revising Barrister, Rex *v.* Stake-on-Trent Town Clerk [(1912) 3 K.B. 518]
143. Rex *v.* Hudson [(1915) 1 K.B. 838] [*Mandamus* against the Commissioner]
144. Rex *v.* Poplar Borough Council [(1922) 1 K.B. 72]
145. Rex *v.* Stepney Borough Council [(1933) 2 K.B. 273]
146. Rex *v.* Warran Hastings [(1775) 1 I.D. (OS) 1005]
147. Rex *v.* Wilts and Berks Canal Company [(1912) 3 K.B. 623]
148. Rohtas Industries *v.* Bihar State Electricity Board (AIR 1984 SC 657)
149. Rupa Ashok Hurra *v.* Ashok Hurra [(2002) 4 SCC 388]
150. Ryots of Garabandho *v.* Zamindar of Parlakemidi (AIR 1943 PC 164)
151. S.K. Verma *v.* M.P. High Court and another [(2003) 10 SCC 243]
152. S.N.Sharma *v.* Bipin Kumar (AIR 1970 SC 786)
153. Sabhajit Tewary *v.* Union of India (AIR 1975 SC 1329)
154. Samarth Transport *v.* R.T. Authority (AIR 1961 SC 93)
155. Saurabh Chaudhari *v.* Union of India [(2003) 11 SCC 146]
156. Sheela Barse *v.* Secretary, Children Aid Society (AIR 1987 SC 656)

157. Shri Anadi Mukta Sadguru S.M.V.S.J.M.S. Trust *v.* V.R. Rudani (AIR 1989 SC 1607)
158. Sohan Lal *v.* Union of India (AIR 1957 SC 529)
159. Sohan Lal *v.* Union of India (AIR 1957 SC 532)
160. Som Prakash Rekhi *v.* Union of India (AIR 1981 SC 212)
161. Sree Nivasulu Naidu *v.* Commissioner of I.T. Madras [(1948) 2 Mad. L.J. 386]
162. Star Enterprises *v.* Central and Industrial Development Corporation of Maharashtra Ltd. and Others [(1990) 3 SCC 280]
163. State Bank of Bikaner and Jaipur *v.* Jag Mohan Lal (AIR 1989 SC 75)
164. State of Bihar *v.* Balmukund Sah [(2000) 4 SCC 640]
165. State of J. & K. *v.* A.R. Zakki (AIR 1992 SC 457)
166. State of Mysore *v.* Syed Mahmood (AIR 1968 SC 1113)
167. State of Punjab *v.* Ajaib Singh (AIR 1953 SC 10)
168. State of Punjab *v.* Ajaib Singh (AIR 1953 SC 10)
169. State of Rajasthan *v.* Karam Chanda and Brothers (AIR 1969 SC 343)
170. Steel Authority of India Ltd. *v.* National Union Water Front Workers (AIR 2001 SC 2571)
171. Sukhdev *v.* Bhagatram (AIR 1975 SC 1331)
172. Supreme Court Advocates-on-Records Association *v.* Union of India [(1993) 4 SCC 441]
173. Surajmall *v.* Commissioner of Income Tax (AIR 1930 Pat. 538)
174. Surjit Singh Gandhi *v.* Indian Red Cross Society and others [(1998) 8 SCC 450]
175. Surya Narayan Yadav and others *v.* Bihar State Electricity Board and others (AIR 1985 SC 941)
176. Syed Abdul Mansur Habibullah *v.* the Speaker, W.B. Legislative Assembly (AIR 1996 Cal. 363)
177. Tahir Hussain *v.* District Board (AIR 1954 SC 630)
178. Tara Chand Khatri *v.* Municipal Corporation of Delhi (AIR 1977 SC 567)
179. Tekraj *v.* Union of India (AIR 1988 SC 469)
180. The Kind *v.* Chancellors, Masters and Scholars of the University of Cambridge [92 E.R. 828]
181. The Queen *v.* London and North Western Railway Company [(1894) 2 Q.B. 512]
182. The Queen *v.* Lords Commissioners of Treasury [(1872) Q.B.387]
183. The Queen *v.* The Commissioners of Inland Revenue (re NATHAN) [(1884) Vol. 12 Q.B. 461]
184. The Queen *v.* The Mayor and Assessor of Bolton (1870 Q.B. 251)
185. The Queen *v.* The Mayor and Assessor of Monmouth (1870 Q.B. 251)
186. The Queen *v.* Thomas [(1892) 1 Q.B. 426]
187. Thomson *v.* University of London [(1864) 10 LT 403]
188. Tukaram G. Gaokar *v.* R. N. Shukla (AIR 1968 SC 1050)
189. U.P. Warehousing Corporation *v.* Vijay Narayan (AIR 1980 SC 840)

190. U.P. State Co-operative Land Development Bank Ltd. *v.* Chandra Bhan Dubey (AIR 1999 SC 753)
191. Ujjambai *v.* State of U.P. (AIR 1962 SC 1621)
192. Umarani *v.* Registrar, Co-operative Societies [(2004) 7 SCC 112]
193. Union of India *v.* Elbridge Watson (AIR 1952 SC 601)
194. Union of India *v.* Kamalakshi Finance Corporation Ltd. (AIR 1992 SC 711)
195. Union of India *v.* Krishna Reddy (AIR 2004 SC 1194)
196. Union of India *v.* Naveen Jindal (AIR 2004 SC 1559)
197. Union of India *v.* R.C. Jain (AIR 1981 SC 951)
198. Union of India *v.* S.B. Vora (AIR 2004 SC 1402)
199. United Towns Electric Co. *v.* Attorney General for Newfoundland [(1939) 1 All E.R. 423]
200. University of Madras *v.* Shantha Bai (AIR 1954 Mad. 67)
201. Unni Krishnan, J.P. *v.* State of A.P. (AIR 1993 SC 2178)
202. Vice-Chancellor, Utkal University *v.* S.K. Ghosh (AIR 1954 SC 217)
203. Virendra Kumar Srivastava *v.* U.P. Rajya Karamchari Kalyan Nigam (AIR 2005 SC 411)
204. VST Industries Ltd. *v.* VST Industries Workers' Union [2000 (8) Scale 95]
205. W. B. State Electricity Board *v.* Desh Bandhu Ghosh (AIR 1985 SC 722)
206. Will *v.* United States [(1967) 19 Law Ed 2d 305]
207. Workmen, Food Corporation of India *v.* M/s. Food Corporation of India (AIR 1985 SC 671)

Bibliography

Administrative Law—C.K. Thakkar.

Blackstone's Commentaries, Volume 3.

British Rule in India and After—V.D. Mahajan.

Case Law on the Indian Constitution by N.A. Subramanian.

Commentary on the Constitution of India.

Constituent Assembly Debates.

Constitution of India—V.N. Shukla.

Constitution of India (A.I.R. Commentaries)—Chitley and Rao.

Constitutional Law—Cases and Materials—Paul G. Kauper (U.S.A.).

Introduction to the Study of the law of the Constitution—A.V. Dicey.

Constitutional Law of India—M.P. Jain.

Constitutional Law of India (Volumes 1-3)—H.M. Seervai.

Constitutional Remedies and writs—Durga Das Basu.

Constitutions of the World—M.V. Pylee.

Encyclopedia of Law of Writs—P.M. Baxi.

Fifth Edition Volume III—Durga Das Basu.

Fundamental Rights and Constitutional Remedies -(Volumes 1-4)—Omprakash Aggrawala.

Prakash Aggrawala.

Fundamental Rights and Constitutional Remedies Volumes I and II—V.G. Ramchandran.

Halsbury's Laws of England (Hailsmen's Edition)

History and Constitution of the Courts and Legislative Authorities in India—Cowell.

Judicial Review of Administrative Action in India—Markose.

Law of Writs—V.G. Ramchandran.

Law of Writs (5th Edition)—A.S. Chaudhary.

Law of Writs in India, England and America—Daulat Ram Prem.

Magna Carta (1215).

Outlines of Indian Legal History—M.P. Jain.

Shorter Constitution of India (13th Edition) Durga Das Basu

Specific Relief Act, 1898—Pollock and Mulla.

The Framing of India's Constitution (Volumes I-IV)—B. Shiva Rao.

The General Clauses Act, 1897.
The Government of India Act, 1935.
The Law of Extraordinary Legal Remedies—Ferries and Ferries.
Writ Jurisdiction—B.L. Hansaria.

Dictionaries used

Law Lexicon—by P.K. Ramnatha Iyar.
The Random House Dictionary.
Tomlin's Law Dictionary.
Webster's Dictionary.
Wharton's Law Lexicon, 14th Edition.

Journals used

All England Law Reports.
All India Reports.
Criminal Law Journal.
Indian Law Reports.
Judgments Today.
King's Bench Decisions.
Queen's Bench Decisions.
Scale.
Supreme Court Cases.
Supreme Court Weekly.

Index